LONDON'S UNDERWORLD

LONDON'S UNDERWORLD

THREE CENTURIES OF VICE AND CRIME

FERGUS LINNANE

ROBSON BOOKS

First published in Great Britain in 2003 by Robson Books, 64 Brewery Road, London, N7 9NT

A member of **Chrysalis** Books plc

British Library Cataloguing in Publication Data
A catalogue record for this title is available from the British Library.

ISBN 1 86105 548 X

Typeset by FiSH Books, London WC1
Printed by Creative Print & Design (Wales), Ebbw Vale

Contents

Acknowledgements

Michael Loeffler encouraged me by seeing the larger possiblities in this subject, as did Julian Summers. My sister Norine Riches helped by reading the mansuscript and being discreet about any misgivings she had. My editor, Joanne Brooks, found time while editing 29 other books to answer my footling questions. It is customary to thank the staffs of the various libraries one has used: in my case it is a special pleasure to be able to thank the staffs of the Guildhall and British libraries. Also the staffs of all the other libraries in London and Bromley I have visited. My family have accepted my obsessions with amused tolerance.

Preface

The histrionic gangster funerals of the Kray twins through the crowded streets of east London were just the latest examples of what was called in the nineteenth century the 'popular admiration for great thieves'. Londoners have always taken great thieves to their hearts. The literature of London crime is rich in figures the poor could venerate as heroes of the resistance to authority, and aspiring criminals hope to emulate. It was said that in the eighteenth century Englishmen were no less 'vain in boasting of the success of their highwaymen than of the bravery of their troops'.[1]

This book, which tells the story of organised crime in London from the early eighteenth century to the present day, was written not so much out of admiration for the city's lawless and their leaders but from a feeling that their story is important.

I have tried to show the continuities in time and place of criminal haunts and habits. Also how the almost casual violence of the thieves, footpads and smugglers of the early Georgian years gave way to the more subtle and thoughtful approach of the Victorian criminal. And how at the beginning of the 21st century gangland has become as violent as ever.[2]

Many of the ills touched on in this book are now just footnotes in history. Armies of half-starved young thieves no longer pour out of criminal strongholds each day to plunder honest citizens. Crowds of drunken and raucous whores no longer annoy people in streets, pubs and theatres. Organised crime, however, has become a vibrant if largely unseen strand in our daily lives: anyone who smokes pot, takes ecstasy, lights up a smuggled cigarette, buys a pirated CD, or visits a massage parlour, is probably paying fealty to one of the 39 criminal 'Mr Bigs' identified by Government agencies.

Introduction

The Wild Eighteenth Century

Many voices attest to the violence of London in the eighteenth century. Here is Horace Walpole, the great aesthete and diarist, describing how he was held up by highwaymen in Hyde Park:

> As I was returning from Holland House by moonlight, about ten at night, I was attacked by two highwaymen in Hyde Park, and the pistol of one of them going off accidentally, grazed the skin under my eye, left some marks of shot on my face, and stunned me. The ball went through the top of the chariot, and if I had sat an inch nearer to the left side, must have gone through my head...I was sitting in my own dining room on Sunday night, the clock had not struck eleven, when I heard a loud cry of 'Stop thief!': a highwayman had attacked a post-chaise in Piccadilly, within fifty yards of this house: the fellow was pursued, rode over the watchman, almost killed him, and escaped.

Life was cheap and frequently in peril. It was said that a man could not walk the fifty yards from the Rose Tavern on the corner of Drury Lane to the Piazza in Covent Garden without twice risking his life. Men went out to dinner fully armed, carrying swords and sometimes pistols. The streets were unlit, and no one could be trusted, not even the link boys who carried lanterns to light passers-by safely on their way. It was not unknown for link boys to douse their lights and rob their charges, or lead them into the clutches of dangerous criminals. Policing was hopelessly inadequate, and the decrepit peace officers, mostly ancient and otherwise unemployable, avoided the criminal ghettos if they could. Nobody was safe: gangs of footpads infested the city and because they had to make their getaway on foot were likely to disable their victims, or even kill them. Armed pickpockets were almost as great a menace. They swarmed around Covent Garden, waiting for people to leave the theatres in the area. One of their victims was the Duke of Cumberland, the Butcher of Culloden, who had his sword stolen as he entered a theatre. Smugglers fought pitched battles with the militia. London's parks – and sometimes the fashionable streets of the West End – were plagued by highwaymen. In 1726 the Earl of Harborough was robbed in mid-morning as he was being carried in his sedan chair across Piccadilly. George III lost his watch, cash and shoe buckles to a particularly audacious thief while walking the gardens of Kensington Palace.

In 1718 the City Marshall remarked that it was 'the general complaint of the taverns, the coffee-houses, the shop-keepers and others, that their customers are afraid when it is dark to come to their houses and shops for fear that their hats and wigs should be snitched from their heads or their swords taken from their sides, or that they may be blinded, knocked down, cut or stabbed...'

Gangs flourished in London in the eighteenth century. Criminals found conditions in the expanding city ideal. The rapid rise in the population – from about 575,000 in 1700 to 675,000 in 1750 and 900,000 in 1801 – gradually drove the wealthy to the new suburbs. Behind they left warrens of rickety houses, tangled courts and lanes, and dark alleys which were ill-lit or not lit at all. These gave ideal cover and sanctuary to the thousands of criminals who thronged the capital.

In 1751 in his *Inquiry into the Causes of the late Increase of Robbers*, the novelist and reforming magistrate Henry Fielding wrote:

Whoever indeed considers the Cities of London and Westminster, with the late vast Addition of their Suburbs, the great Irregularity of their Buildings, the immense Number of Lanes, Alleys, Courts and Bye-places; must think, that, had they been intended for the very Purpose of Concealment, they could scarce have been better contrived. Upon such a View, the whole appears as a vast Wood or Forest, in which a Thief may harbour with as great Security, as wild Beasts do in the deserts of Africa or Arabia...It is a melancholy Truth that, at this very Day, a Rogue no sooner gives the Alarm, within certain Purlieus, than twenty or thirty armed Villains are found ready to come to his Assistance.

It has been reckoned that by 1720 there were at least 10,000 criminals in the capital. Charles Hitchen, the Under City-Marshal who gave the notorious racketeer Jonathan Wild his first big opportunity, claimed he knew personally 2,000 people in London who lived by theft. The influential magistrate and pioneer criminologist Patrick Colquhoun claimed in his *Treatise on the Police of the Metropolis* that '115,000 persons in London were regularly engaged in criminal pursuits'.

Most of these criminals were desperately poor opportunist thieves who emerged from the squalor of the criminal ghettoes known as Alsatias to try their luck in the city's bustling streets. There was also a much smaller elite of successful highwaymen, robbers and smugglers, a handful of whom lived in some style. They were serviced by an army of 'fences' or receivers, who sometimes provided the capital for large-scale operations. This was particularly so in the plunder of ships' cargoes on the River Thames, which with smuggling was the most capital-intensive and profitable area of eighteenth-century crime. Among other services, the receivers provided the large sums of cash needed to bribe customs officers to look the other way.

The criminal elite flourished amid a more informal culture of crime. They had their own code, their own customs and even their own private language, the 'canting' vocabulary.[1] They had safe houses, known as 'flash houses', in such notorious streets as Chick Lane, Cock Lane near Smithfield and Black Boy Alley near the present Farringdon Road, where they could repair to share out the loot or, if hard-pressed by pursuers, sit out the hue and cry. But with bounty hunters like Jonathan Wild, who sent most of the major gangs to the gallows, constantly scouring the city for new victims they were never really safe.

The law had its successes, and was usually merciless. Between 1688 and 1820, as the legal system was weighted ever more heavily in favour of the propertied classes, the number of capital offences rose from about eighty to more than three hundred. This was known as the Bloody Code. 'Hanging crimes ranged from murder, rape, sodomy, arson and forgery through burglary, house-breaking, maiming cattle and shooting at a revenue officer to cutting down trees in an avenue, concealing the death of a bastard child, destroying turnpikes and sending threatening letters.'[2] Some of the capital offences were bizarre: being disguised within the Mint, maliciously cutting hop-binds growing on poles, being a soldier or seaman and wandering about without a pass, consorting with gypsies, stealing a fish out of a river or pond, impersonating the out-pensioners at Greenwich Hospital. The reason for this excess of penal legislation was a general reluctance to countenance an efficient police force: one result of this, as we shall see, was mass executions.

Violence was endemic. Sailors were lashed, children were thrashed, blood sports were common and justified as trials of skill and strength. The multiple hangings at Tyburn – now Marble Arch – and other places of execution, the not uncommon sight of people flogged through the streets or battered to death in the pillory, bloody battles between smugglers and excisemen and shoot-outs with highwaymen throw a harsh light on men and manners.

A seven-year-old girl was hanged at Norwich for stealing a petticoat. As late as the1830s a nine-year-old boy was sentenced to death for stealing two-pennyworth of paint, although he was not executed. Fifteen-year-old Joseph Harris, who had stolen two sovereigns and some silver, rode to his execution at Tyburn with his head in his weeping father's lap. In 1767 an eighty-year-old man was executed for taking a small quantity of cotton and a piece of rope from a wreck. A boy of eleven was hanged for setting fire to his mother's house; in 1785 a girl of seventeen was hanged with her brother; in 1763 a girl of sixteen 'who was probably an idiot' was hanged for murder. In 1814 a fourteen-year-old boy was hanged for stealing, and two years later a sixteen-year-old drummer was hanged for having been sodomised by an ensign. A child of seven was held to be responsible for his or her actions in law. Five children, one aged only eight, were sentenced to death at the Old Bailey on one day in 1814. In the 1780s a quarter of the fifteen and sixteen-year-olds who were sentenced to death were executed.[3]

The last woman sentenced to be burned alive at the stake was Prudence Lee, who was executed in 1652 for murdering her husband. After that the practice was to strangle the condemned woman on a low gibbet before covering her with faggots and setting them alight. But in 1726 the executioner bungled the killing of Katherine Hayes at Tyburn. Instead of first garotting Hayes, who had incited two men to murder and dismember her husband, he lit the faggots and was driven off by the flames before he could put her out of her agony. Two other women whose bodies were burned at the stake for murder were Isabella Condon in 1779 and Margaret Sullivan in 1788. Both had been the victims of 'brutal sadists'. Burning at the stake ended in 1789.

Eight times a year London's muffled church bells were rung to signify a public holiday for a 'hanging match'. Commenting on the eager expectation with which these were greeted, a visitor observed: 'You would, perhaps, think that they look upon these executions as so many public shews due to the people, and that a stock of thieves must be kept and improved to that end.'

Hangings were public spectacles. James Boswell confessed that he never missed a public execution. At Tyburn, wooden grandstands were erected, known as Mother Proctor's Pews after their owner. When Earl Ferrers was hanged in 1760, Mother Proctor collected the enormous sum of £500. As a peer Ferrers, who had murdered his steward, went to his death in his wedding suit embroidered with silver. He asked to be hanged with a rope of silk.

Many condemned men felt obliged to put on a show of courage. The mob entered into the spirit of things. They shouted encouragement to the doomed felons, and chanted anti-government slogans. A seventeenth-century ballad said: 'His heart's not big that fears a little rope.' Isaac Atkinson, an Oxford-educated murderer who stabbed the chaplain accompanying him to the gallows, cried out to the audience: 'There's nothing like a merry life and a short one.'[4] In 1717 a condemned man, addressing the crowd waiting to see him executed, said: 'Men, women and children, I come hither to hang like a pendulum to a watch, for endeavouring to be rich too soon.' Hanging days were known as Sheriff's Balls or Hanging Fairs. Hawkers sold food and drink, taverns took drinks out to customers in the streets and ballad sellers peddled cheap copies of the condemned man's last words, real or imaginary. Pickpockets moved through the excited crowds, practising their art. Many in the crowd would be drunk, and the hangman himself was not always sober. 'In 1738 the hangman was intoxicated with liquor, and supposing there were three for execution was going to put one of the ropes around the parson's neck as he stood in the cart and was with much difficulty prevented by the gaoler from so doing'.[5]

A Swiss visitor to the capital, César de Saussure, described a multiple hanging at Tyburn in his book *A Foreign View of England in the Reigns of George I and George II*:

Some time after my arrival in London...I saw thirteen criminals all hanged at the same time. The day before the execution those who desire it may receive the sacrament, provided the chaplain thinks that they have sincerely repented and are worthy of it. On the day of execution the condemned prisoners, wearing a sort of white linen shirt over their clothes and a cap on their heads, are tied two together and placed on carts with their backs to the horses' tails. These carts are guarded and surrounded by constables and other police officers on horseback, each armed with a sort of pike. In this way part of the town is crossed and Tyburn, which is a good half-mile from the last suburb, is reached, and here stands the gibbet. One often sees criminals going to their death perfectly unconcerned, others so impenitent that they fill themselves full of liquor and mock at those who are repentant.

When all the prisoners arrive at their destination they are

made to mount on a very wide cart made expressly for the purpose, a cord is passed round their necks and the end fastened to the gibbet, which is not very high. The chaplain who accompanies the condemned men is also on the cart; he makes them pray and sing a few verses of the Psalms. The relatives are permitted to mount the cart and take farewell. When the time is up – that is to say about a quarter of an hour – the chaplain and the relations get off the cart, which slips from under the condemned men's feet, and in this way they all remain hanging together. You often see friends and relations tugging at the hanging men's feet so that they should die quicker and not suffer.

The bodies and clothes of the dead belong to the executioner; relatives must, if they wish for them, buy them from him, and unclaimed bodies are sold to the surgeons to be dissected. You see most amusing scenes between people who do not like the bodies to be cut up and the messengers the surgeons have sent for the bodies; blows are given and returned before they can be got away, and sometimes in the turmoil the bodies are quickly removed and buried...These scenes are most diverting, the noise and confusion is unbelievable, and can be witnessed from a sort of amphitheatre erected for spectators near the gibbet.

Justice could be even rougher than this. In 1742, the year his father Robert's corrupt career as Britain's first Prime Minister came to an end, Horace Walpole described a truly horrifying incident involving some parish constables:

A parcel of drunken constables took it into their heads to put the laws in execution against disorderly persons, and so took up every woman they met, till they had collected five or six-and-twenty, all of whom they thrust into St Martin's Roundhouse, where they kept them all night, with the doors and windows closed. The poor creatures, who could not stir or breathe, screamed as long as they had any breath left, begging at least for water: one poor wretch said she was worth eighteen pence, and would gladly give it for a draught of water, but in vain! So well did they keep them there, that in the morning four were found stifled to death, two died soon after and a dozen more are in a shocking way. In short, it is horrid to think what the poor creatures suffered: several of them were beggars, who, from having no lodging, were necessarily found in the street, and others honest labouring women. One of the dead was a poor washerwoman, big with child, who was returning home late from washing.

This was bad enough, but it transpired that some of the women had been arrested in a raid on a Covent Garden brothel, ordered by the hated magistrate Sir Thomas de Veil, notorious both for his harshness on the bench and his wanton private life.[6] During the raid three young aristocrats, including the brother of the Duke of Marlborough, were caught but then released. As a further proof of the double standards of the authorities in dealing with rich and poor, no one was hanged for the murders of the women. As Hogarth's biographer Jenny Uglow puts it, Londoners had good reason to hate their harsh and hypocritical magistrates.

Covent Garden, where some of the women were arrested, was the centre of the city's vice and gambling industries, much as Soho was in the twentieth century. The square had been created by the architect Inigo Jones for Francis Russell, Duke of Bedford, in the seventeenth century. The result was a residential area described by the Duke as 'fit for the habitations of gentlemen and men of ability'. Later the area was colonised by establishments devoted to vice in all its forms. A visitor to London noted:

A tavern-keeper in Drury Lane prints every year an account of the women of the town entitled Harris's *List of Covent Garden Ladies*. In it the most exact description is given of their names, their lodgings, their faces, their manners, their talents and even their tricks. It must of course happen that there will be sometimes a little degree of partiality in these details; however, notwithstanding this, 8,000 copies are sold annually.[7]

The taverns where these women took their clients were awash with a cheap new drink, gin. The city was in the grip of gin mania. The liquor had been introduced by the Dutch who arrived with William III, and its sale was encouraged by the government because it produced vast profits for the distillers and the landowners who had a glut of grain. It was potent and cheap and, as we shall see in a later chapter, its effects were hideous. Among the poor, almost everyone drank it – men, women and children.

To its critics the clattering, stinking, overcrowded city was a 'wen' or wart, Babylon, Sodom, a nursery of every vice. Writers and artists such as Fielding and Hogarth exposed its vanities and deceits, moral and physical decay.[8] A visitor, Georg Christoph Lichtenberg, paints an almost surreal word-picture of the clamorous, barging street life:

> In the road itself chaise after chaise, coach after coach, cart after cart. Through all of this din and clamour, and the noise of thousands of tongues and feet, you hear the bells from the church-steeples, postmen's bells, the street-organs, fiddles and tambourines of itinerant musicians and the cries of the vendors of hot and cold food at the street corners. A rocket blazes up stories high among a yelling crowd of beggars, sailors and urchins. Someone shouts 'Stop, thief,' his handkerchief is gone. Everyone runs and presses forward, some less concerned to catch the thief than to steal a watch or a purse for themselves. Before you are aware of it a young, well-dressed girl has seized your hand. 'Come, my lord, come along, let us drink a glass together,' or 'I'll go with you, if you please.' An accident happens not forty paces away. 'God bless me,' calls one. 'Poor fellow', cries another. A stoppage ensues and you look to your pockets. Everyone is intent on helping the victim. There is laughter again: someone has fallen into the gutter. 'Look there, damn me,' cries a third, and the crowd passes on. Next comes a yell from a hundred throats as if a fire had broken out, or a house were falling, or a patriot had looked out of a window. In Gottingen you can go anywhere and get within forty paces to see what is happening. Here, that is at night and in the City, you

are lucky to escape with a whole skin down a side alley until the tumult is over. Even in the wider streets all the world rushes headlong, as if summoned to the bedside of the dying. That is Cheapside and Fleet Street on a December evening. [9]

Riots too were endemic. The American statesman Benjamin Franklin wrote in 1769 in his autobiography of a visit to Britain: 'I have seen, within a year, riots in the country about corn; riots about elections; riots about workhouses; riots of colliers, riots of weavers, riots of coal-heavers; riots of sawyers; riots of Wilkesites; riots of government chairmen; riots of smugglers, in which customs house officers and excisemen have been murdered, the king's armed vessels and troops fired at.'

Adding to the terrors of the streets were gangs of young upper-class toughs called Mohocks. The writer L O Pike described the antics of 'the roisterers who made night hideous in the eighteenth century. The "Mohocks", the "Nickers", the "Tumblers", the "Dancing Masters" and the various bully-captains . . . If they met an unprotected woman, they showed they had no sense of decency; if they met a man who was unarmed or weaker than themselves they assaulted and, perhaps, killed him'.[10] The Sweaters would surround a victim and prick his buttocks with swords as he tried to flee. The Bold Bucks specialized in rape. If they could not find victims in the streets they would enter houses and drag out screaming women.

Some have suggested that the Mohocks and their kindred spirits were not much more than a media event, and it is probable that their activities have been exaggerated. But the historian Christopher Hibbert has written that they forced prostitutes and old women to stand on their heads while they pricked their legs with their swords, bored out the eyes of their victims and waylaid and slashed servants, all in a state of drunken delirium.[11]

The Original Godfather

A vast crowd had been waiting for hours outside Newgate Prison to see the cart with the condemned men start its journey to the gallows at Tyburn. When it finally appeared the drunken, raucous mob pressed forward and a hail of missiles and abuse was directed at the slumped figure of one man at the back of the cart. Dead cats and dogs, stones, rotten fruit, vegetables and eggs bounced around him. A large stone struck his head and blood poured down his face, but he scarcely responded. He had taken an overdose of laudanum the night before and was now only half-conscious.

The scene was repeated as the cart made its way along Holborn and Oxford Street. Many thousands of people lined the route: 'Never was seen so prodigious a concourse of people before, not even upon the most popular occasions of that nature,' wrote Daniel Defoe, an eyewitness. 'In all that innumerable crowd, there was not one pitying eye to be seen, not one compassionate word to be heard; but on the contrary, wherever he came, there was nothing but hollowing and huzzas, as if it had been upon a triumph.'[1] The year was 1725 and Jonathan Wild, public enemy number one, was on his way to his execution.

The crowd was bitterly hostile to the man who betrayed many of his own gang and even gloated at their executions. He was particularly hated because one of his victims, the young cockney burglar Jack Sheppard, was a popular hero.

Wild was in a sense London's police chief and at the same time a gangster, the most ferocious and successful Britain has known.

1

He was a receiver and fence, and worst of all, a thief-taker or bounty hunter who styled himself Thief-Taker General of Great Britain and Ireland. Under the guise of public benefactor he consigned more than 120 men to the gallows – many of them his own gang members.

Anyone who refused to cooperate was in danger of being framed and delivered up to the hangman. He brought a ruthless new business efficiency to the world of crime. He would instruct his men to steal, then return the goods to their owners for a fee. He had warehouses where some of the goods were altered for sale here or abroad, and even a ship to take the loot to the continent.

Wild's reign of terror imposed a kind of order on the underworld. For the government he was an important tool of social control, wiping out London's other established gangs and in his own career maintaining a precarious balance between law-enforcing and law-breaking, making a great show of his wealth and aspiring to at least middle-class respectability. At a time when there was no police force the state relied upon thief-takers to cope with the growing crime wave. Wild was paid £40 for each wretch that he sent to the gallows.

In the second decade of the century mail robberies were costing the government more than £10,000 a year. Wild was consulted by the Privy Council about the increase in highway robberies. He recommended increasing the bounty, which was first raised temporarily to £100 a head and later to £140. So Wild, who was already amassing a fortune from his rackets, had in effect voted himself a large pay rise. In mid-1724 he rounded up the largely-Irish Carrick gang, earning himself £900 in reward money – the annual income of a prosperous knight at the time. Wild was rich, successful, apparently secure.

Wild's methods were surprisingly modern. Through his vast network of spies he would get word of a crime and where the criminals were hiding. Accompanied by members of his gang he would corner and arrest them. The prisoners would then be questioned separately, and each told that the others had confessed and implicated him. This way they would be persuaded to betray each other. Sometimes he offered reduced sentences as an inducement to inform. Thus he would add another recruit to his so-called 'Corporation of Thieves', a man who owed him his life.

Wild invented the double cross. He kept detailed notes about criminals and their crimes. When he had enough evidence to convict a man he would put an X against his name. And when he decided to betray him, he would add a second X – the double cross.

Perhaps the worst of all his ferocious crimes was to lure destitute children into a life of thieving, only to betray them for the £40 reward. Defoe, who interviewed Wild and wrote his biography, and had a sneaking regard for his enterprise and rough courage, was moved to a fit of moral outrage: 'First to tempt and then accuse, which is the very nature of the devil; first to make poor desolate vagabond boys thieves, and then betray them to the gallows! What can one think of such a thing without a just abhorrence? Who can think it to be less than the worst sort of murder?'[2]

Wild was born in Wolverhampton and baptised on 6 May 1683 – his date of birth is not known. His parents were poor but regarded as respectable and honest. He served an apprenticeship as a buckle-maker. However, as Defoe said, his thoughts were 'above his trade'. He went on: 'Jonathan wanted application, which is generally observed to be the fault of men with brisk parts; work and him were too much at variance for him to thrive by his trade; he seemed to follow it only at a distance, often playing the loose, wandering from one alehouse to another, with the very worst, though the merriest, company in the place; and he was very fond of the strolling actors that now and then frequented the county.'[3]

He moved to London, and one story speaks of him as a debt collector – shades of things to come. At first he didn't prosper. He is next found as an inmate of a debtors' prison, the Wood Street Compter. Wild by his own account spent four years there, leaving in September 1712. They were the years of his second apprenticeship, this time in crime. He ingratiated himself with his jailers and the other prisoners, absorbing much inside knowledge about the underworld.

His last months there were enlivened by the company of Mary Milliner, a prostitute later regarded as his wife. She had a thorough knowledge of the underworld and its inhabitants, which was invaluable to Wild. Defoe writes:

He improved his time during his acquaintance with this Mary Milliner to a very great degree, for she brought him acquainted with several gangs and societies of the sharping and thieving world. In so much, that in a little time he knew all their several employments and the several parts they acted, their haunts and their walks, how they performed, how they managed their effects when they had met with success. And as he seemed to set up for a director to them, under the government of that dexterous lady his first instructor.[4]

When he left the debtors' prison they set up home together. Mary was a buttock-and-file, that is a prostitute (buttock) who was also a pickpocket (file). She would rob clients while they were having sex with her. Wild would lurk in the background to see that clients did not cause too much trouble if they discovered the theft.[5] He also ran a brothel.

His big breakthrough came when he was invited to become a thief-taker by the Under-Marshal Charles Hitchen shortly after he was released from Wood Street. Hitchen was himself a vicious criminal, and had been suspended from office but retained the title while the government sought a replacement. So Wild began to accompany Hitchen on his rounds as he sought out thieves, prostitutes and even innocent passers-by who could be bullied or blackmailed into parting with money.

Hitchen's methods were a revelation to Wild, who was to refine them greatly. Hitchen would force prostitutes to give him the pocket-books they stole from clients. One night he came across a man whose wallet had been stolen while he stood enjoying the suffering of a poor wretch in the pillory at Charing Cross. The wallet contained lottery tickets and bills worth several hundred pounds. He offered Hitchen a reward of £30.

Hitchen, with his widespread knowledge of the underworld, soon found the pickpocket. In exchange for the wallet he gave him a stolen gold watch he got from a whore and claimed the £30 reward.

Another night Hitchen took Wild to a male brothel. The clients, many in female dress, addressed Hitchen as 'madam' and 'your ladyship'. He was clearly very much at home.This secret was to prove his undoing later when he and Wild fell out.[6]

The following year Hitchen was reinstated as Under-Marshal and Wild went into business on his own. With a mixture of ruthlessness and efficiency he now raised receiving almost to an art. He brought to it the subtlety that Hitchen lacked.

Wild's system was better for the thieves but worse for the original owners of the stolen property. By paying the thieves more than they could get from a fence he ensured that they brought their spoils to him. Then of course he had to charge the owners more to cover his costs. He improved on Hitchen's technique, and avoided transgressing the Receiving Acts by making sure that he never took possession of the stolen goods. Once he knew where the goods were he would call at the owners' houses and say that he had heard underworld rumours of a theft, and that he knew where the goods were – perhaps at a pawnbroker's.[7]

Wild would arrange for the owner to meet one of his henchmen, who would hand over the goods. The beauty of the system was that Wild never handled them, or apparently even saw them.

He set up office in the Blue Boar tavern in Little Old Bailey which he called the 'Office for the Recovery of Lost and Stolen Property'. Soon it was widely known that whenever anything was stolen Jonathan Wild was the man to get it back. Luxury goods were uncommon and valuable, and if an item had sentimental value the owner would be all the more anxious to recover it.[8]

Defoe describes the procedure when someone went to Wild's office to ask him to recover something. Jonathan would come out from behind his desk, shake hands warmly and offer his client a seat in the strong Staffordshire accent he never lost. After accepting a guinea finding fee – more than twice the average weekly wage of a labourer; his fee was only five shillings. when he first opened his office in the Old Bailey – and writing his client's name and details down in his ledger, he would take extensive notes about the place and time of the theft, what exactly was taken, and then promise to do his best to recover it.[9]

With his network of spies, convicts who had returned illegally from transportation, his bodyguards and his able lieutenants Quilt

Arnold and Abraham Mendez, Wild gradually took control of the London underworld. To do this he had to destroy the capital's other main gangs.

In 1716 he launched a ferocious onslaught on the underworld, smashing gangs and capturing highwaymen, including the notorious James Goodman. He destroyed a gang of footpads who had murdered a Mrs Knapp. This crime was a cause célèbre, and the publicity did much to enhance Wild's reputation as a 'thief-taker'.[10]

Worse was to come for the organised section of the underworld. Between 1720 and 1723 Wild waged an all-out war to bring the underworld under his total control, or wipe out those who stood in his way. First in the firing line were the Spiggot gang of footpads, who were rounded up in 1721. Spiggot refused to plead, and was subjected to the judicial torture known as *peine forte et dure*, in which increasingly heavy weights were placed on a prisoner's chest. A prisoner who refused to plead could not be tried. The author of *The New State of England* described the torture, which took place in 'some low dark room'...

> ...all naked but his privy members; his back upon the bare ground, his arms and legs stretched with cords, fastened to the several quarters of the room, and as much irons and stones laid upon his body as he can well bear. The next day he is allowed but three morsels of barley bread, without drink; and the day after as much...water, and that without any bread. And this is to be his diet, till he die.

If a prisoner kept silent he could not be found guilty, and so his estate could not be taken from his family by the state.

After being pressed by an iron weight of 400 pounds Spiggot agreed to plead. He and his men went to the gallows. Next it was the turn of the Hawkins gang. Apart from the bounty Wild had a particular reason for destroying it – they had defied his overlordship by refusing to deal with him and by sending their loot to be sold in Holland instead.

The Hawkins gang, who numbered only about six, were particularly audacious. One of its members, Ralph Wilson, described some of its escapades: 'One morning we robbed the Cirencester, the Worcester, the Gloucester, the Oxford and the Bristol stagecoaches, all together; the next morning, the Ipswich and Colchester, and a third morning perhaps the Portsmouth coach. The Bury coach has been our constant customer; I think we touched that coach ten times.'

During the South Sea Bubble crisis of 1720 the gang plagued the area around Exchange Alley, preying on the coaches and sedan chairs of the speculators. When the gang murdered a Dr Philip Potts some of the members were alarmed, and Wild used bribery and threats to 'turn' them. As his gang dwindled Hawkins joined forces with the followers of the reckless highwayman James Shaw. Shaw was a killer whose men were unsettled by his brutality, and already Wild was picking them off. Soon only Shaw himself remained free.[11]

Hawkins formed a new gang, and in 1722 he began a series of highway robberies and attacks on the mail. On three successive nights they held up the Worcester, Bristol, Gloucester, Cirencester, Oxford, Ipswich and Portsmouth stages.

In 1722 Shaw was captured and executed. Hawkins and his team were trapped in a London tavern after robbing the Bristol mail. They were executed and their bodies hung in chains on Hounslow Heath.

That left only the formidable Carrick gang to deny Wild total control of the underworld. The gang, mostly immigrant Irishmen, was 32 strong. 1722 was the year of one of the Jacobite plots and the Carricks, as Irishmen, were suspected of Jacobite inclinations. Carrick was arrested and executed on charges of Jacobitism, and the rest of the gang were no match for Wild. Between 23 July and 4 August 1722 he caught 22 members of the Carricks.[12]

Wild was king of the underworld. His receiving business alone was bringing in at least £200–300 a year, and he had moved to a bigger, more imposing office near the old one. Defoe wrote: 'He acquired a strange and indeed unusual reputation for being a mighty honest man, till his success hardened him to put on a face of public service in it, and for that purpose to profess an open and brave correspondence among the gangs of thieves, by which his house became an office of intelligence for inquiries of that kind, as if all stolen goods had been deposited with him in order to be restored.'[13]

But there were rumours that while Wild was receiving his respectable clients in this office another house nearby was being used for his real business. In 1844 the site of the Red Lion tavern in West Street, Clerkenwell, and the shop next door were excavated. Human remains and instruments of torture were found, and a knife engraved J Wild. The buildings were a maze of passages and hiding places. There was an underground opening into the Fleet Ditch, which flowed into the Thames.

Wild began flaunting his wealth. Defoe says that he 'now became very eminent in his profession of thief-catching, and made a considerable figure in the world, having a silver-mounted sword and a footman at his heels, and scarce an assize passed but Jonathan slew his man.'[14]

The statesman Lord Chesterfield, one of Wild's clients, describes his receptions thus: 'His levee was crowded with persons of the first rank, who never regretted any expense or imposition that gave them the opportunity of paying court to so illustrious a man. Jonathan was a merry facetious fellow, had a very dexterous volubility of speech, yet received them rather with an awkward familiarity than with that submission and civility which he owed to his superiors.' Obviously gangster chic is nothing new.

Defoe says Wild had a country house in Dulwich 'and in company affected an air of grandeur'.[15] Clearly he still had ideas above his station. In 1723 he had the effrontery to apply for the Freedom of the City of London. He cited his 'great trouble and charge in apprehending and convicting divers felons'. His application was refused, a sure sign of the ambiguity of the official attitude to him.

Wild had a gift for self-advertisement. This report in the *Weekly Journal* of 13 June 1719 presents a picture of him as the fearless law-enforcer:

Jonathan Wild, the British Thief-Taker, going down last week into Oxfordshire with a Warrant from the Lord Chief Justice to apprehend two notorious Highwaymen, who infested that country, met them within a few miles of Oxford on the road. But they hearing of his design met him, and one of them fired a pistol at him: but Jonathan having on the old Proverb for Armour, received no hurt, and then he discharged a Pistol at them, which wounded one of them so terribly that his life is in great danger: the other was pursued and taken and committed to Oxford jail, and Jonathan has given Security to appear the next Assizes to justify his Conduct.'

With the help of Arnold and Mendez, Wild 'divided the city and even the surrounding country into so many districts and appointed gangs to each. He encouraged the thieves under his protection to specialise, appointing one set to steal in churches during divine service, another to pick pockets at fairs and so on.'[16]

One branch of his gang were known as the Spruce Prigs. They were personable young men, who had worked in great houses as valets and footmen, were trained by a dancing master, and so were able to pass themselves off as upper class. Wild taught them to steal and they were always ready to go to Court on 'Birth nights, to Balls, Operas, Plays and Assemblies, for which Purpose they were furnished with lac'd Coats, brocade Waistcoats, fine Perriwigs, and sometimes equipp'd with handsome Equipages, such as Chariots, with Footmen in Liveries, and also *Valets-de-Chambres*, the Servants all being Thieves like the Master.' Furthermore, 'Wild had a list of *seven thousand* Newgate birds now in service in this City and parts adjacent, all with intent to rob the Houses they are in.'[17]

Wild demanded total loyalty. When a young cheesemaker who had become a highwayman with Wild's help disappeared with the horse and pistols Wild had given him, rather than go on handing over more than half his earnings, Wild had to act. He set off 'stuck round with pistols as thick as an orange with cloves' and tracked him down. The young man pleaded for his life but Wild shot him dead.

Another young criminal, a small-time burglar named Jack Sheppard, was to be Wild's nemesis. Sheppard was the very embodiment of the wild spirit of the eighteenth century. His daring exploits – in particular a series of prison escapes – seized the popular imagination partly because he successfully defied a justice system that was corrupt and unfair, and also because he defied the hated Jonathan Wild. Sheppard refused to cooperate with Wild or to use his receiving network, something Wild could neither overlook nor forgive.

Sheppard was born in White's Row, Spitalfields, in 1702. His ancestors as far back as his great-grandfather had been carpenters. His mother, widowed while still young, had to go into service, so she put Jack into the newly opened Bishopsgate workhouse, where he stayed for a year and a half. He was later apprenticed to a carpenter, broke his indentures and became that bogeyman figure, an idle apprentice and then a thief. But during the period he had worked as a carpenter, however brief, he showed great skill and ingenuity, particularly as a locksmith. Although slightly built and only about five feet four inches tall, he was also surprisingly strong, with large sensitive hands. While he was living with his master, a man called Woods, he would be locked out at night if he was late, but he 'made a mere Jest of the Locks and Bolts and enter'd in and out at Pleasure'.

In April 1724, after a run of good luck, Sheppard was betrayed by a friend and imprisoned in St Giles Roundhouse. Within hours he had broken out through the roof. After cutting through the ceiling and removing some tiles he used a sheet and a blanket as a rope to lower himself to the ground, then mingled with the crowd attracted by the sound of falling tiles.[18]

In May he was again arrested and sent to the New Prison. With him was his mistress Elizabeth Lyon, also known as Edgeworth Bess, a buxom good-time girl. They were held in the most secure part of the prison, and Jack was burdened with two weights of 14lb each.

Friends smuggled tools into the prison and in what to connoisseurs of the time was his greatest escape, Jack sawed off the weights, and with 'unheard of Diligence and Dexterity' cut through an iron bar. He then drilled through an oak bar nine inches thick. He and Edgeworth Bess lowered themselves 25 feet to the ground below using a rope made of sheets, gowns and petticoats.

Once there they realized that they had escaped from one prison into another: the wall of the New Prison adjoined Clerkenwell Bridewell. Undaunted, Jack drove spikes into the wall and he and

Edgeworth Bess climbed to freedom. His astounded jailers kept the chains and bars 'to Testifie and preserve the Memory of this extraordinary Event and Villain.'[19]

For the next three months Jack was busy. He robbed coaches and broke into shops. He stole cash, bonds, cloth, silver spoons, a wig, a hat, a handkerchief and a penknife. One of his victims was a former employer, a Mr Kneebone. Jack had secretly cut the bars of the cellar window before the break-in. Inside the house he picked the locks of door and cupboards while his accomplice, Joseph 'Blueskin' Blake, held a candle to give him light. Kneebone informed Wild of the theft, in the hope of getting his property back. Wild had been following the career of the young burglar, and although Jack never showed any tendency to violence, feared that he would become the leader of a revived Carrick gang, with whose members he had begun robbing. Worse, Sheppard had bypassed his receiving operation with his loot. Wild tracked down Edgeworth Bess, got her drunk and found out where Sheppard was staying. He sent Quilt Arnold to arrest him, and after an exchange of gunfire Sheppard was taken to Newgate. He was tried and although 'he begged earnestly for Transportation to the most extream Foot of his Majesty's Dominions', on Wild's testimony he was found guilty and returned to the condemned hold under sentence of death by hanging for robbing a shopkeeper.[20]

Newgate, which dated from the fifteenth century, was a filthy deathtrap. In 1719 Captain Alexander Smith wrote: 'Newgate is a dismal prison...a place of calamity...a habitation of misery, a confused chaos ... a bottomless pit of violence, a Tower of Babel where all are speakers and no hearers.' Jail fever was rife, and about thirty of the inmates died each year. Because of this physicians refused to enter the jail. Pedestrians stayed clear of the walls because prisoners urinated from the upper windows, and the area was permeated by a ghastly stench. Yet for those with hard cash – known as rhino – almost anything might be bought, including sex. Drink brewed inside the prison was freely available. It was mainly gin, and was known among other names as Kill-Grief, Comfort, Poverty and Meat and Drink.[21] The King's Bench

Prison had 30 gin shops which sold 120 gallons of the fiery liquid a week. The gin was given various names, including Mexico, Skyblue and Crank. Prisoners without money were starved. Young girls traded their bodies for a crust. Older women gave sex free, in the hope of getting pregnant and being able to 'plead their bellies' – pregnant women would not be hanged. Fielding called Newgate 'a prototype of hell'.

On 30 August, the night before he was due to be executed, Sheppard broke out again. Edgeworth Bess and another woman criminal had smuggled a woman's costume into his cell. He slipped into it while the warders were distracted. He had earlier loosened one of the rods in the window of his cell, and the women pulled him out through it. 'Then like a Freeman [he] took his Rambles through the City and came to Spitalfields and there lay with Edgware Bess.'

By now his exploits had all London in an uproar. He was news, and the new popular press made the most of him. His quips, such as 'a file is worth all the bibles in the world', were on everybody's lips.

Sheppard's short career had three more months to run. The *Quaker* wrote: 'Woe to England, for Sheppard is escaped; Woe to the Shopkeepers, and woe to the Dealers in Ware, for the roaring Lion is Abroad, and their Goods will not lie on their Hands.' The shopkeepers fortified their houses and hired guards.

Jack went on the run with William Page, a butcher's apprentice, first to Chipping Warden in Northamptonshire. Page had relatives there, but they could not afford to keep the two fugitives, who returned to London after only three days. Jack was recognised by a cobbler in Bishopsgate and a milkman in Islington, and the news spread. The two fugitives robbed a watchmaker's shop in Fleet Street, pawned one of the watches, went out drinking, and then sought out the milkman and upset his pans and pipkins, covering him with cream.

They knew they had been recognised, and they set out for Finchley. A team of Wild's men found them on Finchley Common. Sheppard was held in the strongest room in Newgate, the Stone Castle at the top of the prison. He was chained to the floor with iron staples, and special leg irons and handcuffs were made for him. He was under constant observation by the turnkeys.

His new celebrity status brought a stream of visitors to see him. They included James Figgs, the boxing champion. Sheppard promised to stop on his way to execution at Tyburn and drink a glass with him.

Sheppard's cockney wit and sarcasm seemed unaffected by his present straits. When several divines took him to task he called them 'Ginger-Bread Fellows' who wanted to 'form Papers and Ballads out of his Behaviour.' He deplored Wild's profession of thief-taker, saying he deserved the gallows just as much as thieves did. 'They hang by proxy, while we do it fairly in person.' When in the prison chapel one Sunday a man asked one of the turnkeys to point out Sheppard, Jack replied: 'Yes, sir, I am the Sheppard, and all the jailers in the town are my flock, and I cannot stir into the country but they are all at my heels.'

Friends once again brought him tools. A warder who went into his cell unexpectedly was astounded to find Jack walking around unfettered. 'Twas troublesome to be always in one posture', Jack explained. He was loaded down with even heavier chains, his wrists clamped in enormous handcuffs.

The stage was set for Sheppard's greatest escape. At some stage during the evening a stream of officials, including the Keeper of Clerkenwell Bridewell, the Clerk of the Westminster Gatehouse and Captain Geary, Keeper of the New Prison, inspected Jack's handcuffs and leg irons. Then a turnkey asked Jack if he needed anything else, as he would not be back to check on him before morning. After he left, Jack got to work in total darkness. First, using a nail he had found on the floor and hidden, he picked the locks of his handcuffs.

Then with 'main strength' he twisted asunder a small link in the chain binding his legs. Using the broken link as a tool he removed an iron bar from the chimney. With this he removed some of the chimney masonry, and climbed to the room above. There he found a large nail and with it broke through the wall, dislodged the door bolt and entered the chapel. There Jack broke off a spike from one of the railings, and with this he wrenched off the bolt-box of the next door. This and the next two doors were all bolted on the other side but none could stop him. Now he came to the last door. Once through it he had access to the lower leads of the roof. The sleeping city spread out below him. He knew that 'the smallest Accident would still spoil the whole Workmanship', so rather than risk leaping on to one of the adjoining houses, which was quite possible, he made his way back into the Stone Castle and found his blanket. He then climbed back on to the roof, drove the chapel spike into the wall, attached the blanket to it and lowered himself on to a neighbouring roof. He stole softly down two flights of stairs. 'I was once more, contrary to my Expectation, and that of all Mankind, a Freeman.'

Daniel Defoe interviewed the stunned turnkeys, who showed him Sheppard's chains and padlocks and the doors he had escaped through.

For the Walpole government, deeply unpopular and corrupt, Sheppard's escapes were embarrassing. The effect of Sheppard's flouting of authority on popular opinion was all too evident. For Wild the latest escape was a disaster. His hold on the underworld depended on him being seen as all-powerful. Now this maverick thief was on the loose again. Worse, Sheppard's achievements had attracted other underworld figures, most notably Joseph 'Blueskin' Blake, a former member of Wild's Corporation of Thieves. Blueskin, who had joined the Carrick gang of footpads, was one of those arrested when Wild broke up that gang, but he was released. Wild, as usual obsessed that no-one should escape his 'justice', continued to pursue him. On 9 October 1724 Blueskin was arrested by Wild, Mendez and Arnold. On Wild's evidence he was tried and condemned to death.

In the condemned cell, where Wild had gone to gloat, Blueskin asked him to put in a good word for him. When Wild told him: 'You are certainly a dead man, and will be tuck'd up [hanged] very speedily,' Blueskin, as the *British Journal* reported, 'seized Wild by the Neck and with a little Clasp Knife cut his Throat in a very dangerous Manner'. Wild was lucky to survive, but his reputation for invincibility did not.

Blueskin told the judge he was sorry he had not succeeded, 'for never did such a rogue as Wild live, and go unpunished so long'.

Meanwhile Sheppard's latest escape was front-page news. The *London Journal* wrote: 'Nothing contributes so much to the talk of the town at present as the frolicksome and desperate adventures of the famous house-breaker and jail-breaker John Sheppard.'

After going on the run Sheppard tore his clothes to make himself look like a beggar, and went round the taverns to hear what people were saying about him. His behaviour was reckless. His mother begged him to flee the country, but Sheppard behaved as though he was invulnerable. He went about the town in various disguises. He joined in alehouse discussions about his own exploits, listened in the streets to ballad sellers singing the same tales. He said afterwards: 'The Company was very merry about the matter.'

On 29 October, the last free day of his short life, he robbed a pawnshop in Drury Lane – one of the streets where the shopkeepers had been most in fear of his activities – and stole a black suit, a silver sword, diamonds, watches, some cash and 'other pretty little Toys'. With a sweetheart on his arm he set out by coach on a pub crawl. He even drove through Newgate itself. In his finery he paraded through the gin-shops and taverns of Clare Market. That evening he was recaptured, almost insensible from drink.

This time the authorities were determined there would be no escape. Sheppard was loaded down with 300 pounds of iron and locked into the strongest room at Newgate. The turnkeys charged the hundreds of people who came to gape at the great escapologist 1s.6d. a time, and the artist Sir James Thornhill painted his portrait.

On 10 November an enormous crowd gathered to see Sheppard taken before the Court of King's Bench. He told the judge that he had never had 'Opportunity to obtain his Bread in an honest Way'. He offered to demonstrate to the court his skills as an escaper: he challenged them to put handcuffs on him, saying that he would remove them on the spot. There was no demonstration, and no escape. The Earl of Macclesfield, Lord Chancellor and a greater crook by far than Jack, had a private interview with him. Then he was taken back to Newgate.

On the morning of Monday 16 November 1724 the open cart taking Jack Sheppard to the gallows at Tyburn began the two-hour journey, its progress at times being halted by the dense throng of spectators. Many were weeping women. Girls pressed forward to give Jack flowers, men to shake his hand.

The theory of public executions was that the awful spectacle would deter others from following the same disastrous path, but the novelist and magistrate Henry Fielding pointed out that there were so many executions they had lost their power to shock, and were instead a form of entertainment. The mob was also moved to admiration for the condemned. 'The day appointed by the law for the thief's shame is the day of glory in his own opinion. His procession to Tyburn and his last moments there are all triumphant; attended with the compassion of the weak and tender-hearted, and with the applause, admiration and envy of all the bold and hardened.'

Another novelist, Samuel Richardson, was shaken by the spectacle; the clergyman was an object of ridicule, 'the psalm was sung amidst the curses and quarrelling of the most abandoned and profligate of mankind'; and 'unhappy wretches' preparation for death produced barbarous mirth not humane sympathy'.

Although the mob were on Sheppard's side, they did not usually intervene to stop executions, although they would sometimes prevent a prisoner being rehanged if the rope broke. In 1717, however, the mob was responsible for three condemned men being reprieved. As they were being taken to Tyburn a writ was served on the hangman, William Marvell, and in the confusion he was knocked unconscious. The procession continued without him to Tyburn where a bricklayer offered to deputise for the absent hangman. He was beaten by the crowd and despite the offer of a large fee there were no further volunteers. The condemned men were eventually reprieved.

On the day Jack Sheppard was hanged, the cart stopped at a tavern on what is now Oxford Street and he drank a pint of wine with the boxer James Figgs, as he had promised. When he reached Tyburn Jack produced a pamphlet called *A Narrative of All the Robberies, Escapes, Etc of John Sheppard* and asked that it should be published as his confession.

Then the noose was fastened round his neck and the cart moved away, leaving him dangling. Because of his slight build he did not weigh enough to choke quickly as he dropped off the cart. Some of the spectators, hoping to end his agony, pulled at his legs to break his neck.

The *Newgate Calendar* describes Jack's demise thus: 'He behaved with great decency at the place of execution, and confessed having committed two robberies for which he had been tried and acquitted. He suffered in the twenty-third year of his age. He died with difficulty and was much pitied by the surrounding multitude.'

After fifteen minutes a hearse ordered by Daniel Defoe to take Jack's body away so that attempts could be made to revive him approached the gallows. This was to thwart the surgeons, who had the right to use criminals' bodies for dissection, a practice the working class were vehemently against. They felt there was always a faint hope that the condemned man could be revived. They also objected to medical experiments on their dead heroes. The driver was attacked by the crowd, who feared that the body was being taken away for just that purpose.

Jack's battered corpse was taken to the Barley Mow tavern. Another riot broke out when his friends tried to take it away for burial, but eventually, at about midnight, it was buried in St Martin-in-the-Fields churchyard at the bottom of Drury Lane, scene of some of the more dramatic episodes in Jack's life.

Jack lived on in the popular imagination and particularly in the theatre: just two weeks after his death *The Harlequin Sheppard*, a popular opera, opened at a Drury Lane theatre. It was the first of many dramatisations of his life, of which John Gay's *The Beggar's Opera* became the most popular opera of the eighteenth century. The two central characters, Macheath and Peachum, are clearly based on Sheppard and Wild. The play is also a coded attack on the Prime Minister, Sir Robert Walpole, and his corrupt administration.

Attention now turned to Jonathan Wild, Jack's tormentor. Jack's exploits and cheek had brightened the lives of his cockney class, and what remained of respect for the Thief-Taker General evaporated.

Wild was still recovering from his wound and had missed Jack's execution. He now faced a new crisis. One of his men, Roger Johnson, captain of a ship which carried stolen goods to Flanders for resale, was arrested and one of the gang's warehouses raided. After a series of scrapes including a fight between Wild's men and the constables Johnson was released.

Wild's veneer of respectability was in shreds, and he went into hiding. When he emerged there were further signs that he was losing his grip. On 6 February he was called to Leicester House, the residence of the Prince of Wales, to help retrieve a stolen watch. This should have been a marvellous propaganda coup for Wild. It was certainly a chance to restore his credibility with the upper classes. Strangely, he replied that the watch was 'past all hopes of recovery'. Perhaps he was still suffering from the effects of his wound, perhaps distracted by the backlash of popular opinion after Sheppard's death. Ten days later he was arrested.

Wild was held in Newgate, where to begin with he did not seem to realise how serious things had become. He continued to advertise for business, believing that his usefulness as a thief-taker would make the government reluctant to move against him. And indeed there were those who would have shown leniency if Wild's gang had not been so greedy when stealing jewellery during the instalment ceremony for the Knights of the Garter at Windsor the previous August.[22]

A Warrant of Detainder was issued, listing Wild's crimes. He was charged with 'forming a kind of Corporation of Thieves of which he was the head or director'. Whoever drew up the warrant clearly knew a great deal about Wild's activities, so much in fact that it seems odd that he wasn't arrested sooner. It described how he organised robberies, forced transported criminals who had returned to this country illegally to carry out crimes under threat of the gallows, how he received, sold and smuggled stolen goods and sold the lives of his own henchmen.

Wild fought back, producing at the Old Bailey on 15 May 1725 a list of the criminals he had captured. It included 35 highway robbers, 22 house-breakers and ten criminals who had returned from transportation illegally. Far from convincing the court of his services to the cause of justice it proved his callous inhumanity.

In the end, Wild was not tried for any of the crimes he was accused of in the warrant. Instead, probably to his shame at being brought down by so trivial a matter, he was accused of stealing and receiving a quantity of lace from a shop in Holborn. Wild had incited two criminals to steal the lace, then sold it back to the owner.

His accomplices gave evidence against him. He was found guilty of receiving, and sentenced to death.

Wild petitioned the King, citing his services to society.

I have been a most wicked and notorious offender, but was never guilty or inclined to treasonable practises, or murder, both of which I hold in the utmost detestation and abhorrence, which affords me great comfort in the midst of my calamity and affliction. I have a sickly wife, loaded and oppressed with grief who must inevitably go to the grave with me if I suffer; or lead at least a most miserable life, she being already *non compos mentis*.

... If I receive your Majesty's royal favour of a reprieve, I do firmly resolve to relinquish my ways and to detect (as far as in me lays) such as shall persevere therein, as a testimony of which I have a list ready to show to such whom your Majesty shall appoint to see it, which is all that can be offered by your Majesty's most dutiful, loyal and obedient petitioner.

The list was never called for; there was no reprieve. Wild's last hours were haunted by fears of death. He who had faced death many times and bore the scars of these encounters was now subject to religious terrors. On the night before he died he asked the chaplain the meaning of the phrase 'cursed is everyone that hangeth upon a tree'. They discussed suicide.

Early in the morning Wild took an overdose of laudanum. Efforts by fellow prisoners to rouse him made him vomit violently and probably, for the moment, saved his life.[23]

The criminal mastermind's last night was miserable, if dulled by the drug. At midnight he heard the bell of St Sepulchre's, which was tolled the night before an execution, and the sexton of that church then rang a smaller bell outside his cell and intoned a verse beginning:

> All you that in the Condemned Hold do lie;
> Prepare you for tomorrow you shall die...

Wild's last night was untypical. Some condemned men entertained the chaplain to dinner on the night before their execution, but drinking and gambling were more normal ways of spending the night. The highwayman Jack Rann spent his last evening with seven girls and some cronies.

In the morning Wild was taken to the prison chapel to hear the final service; then he began the journey to Tyburn sitting between two chaplains on an open cart, although he had earlier requested a closed carriage.

> The rudeness of the mob to him, both at his first going into the cart and all the way from thence to the place of execution, is not to be expressed, and shows how notorious his life had been, and what impression his known villainies had made on the minds of the people. Contrary to the general behaviour of the streets in such cases, instead of compassionate expressions and a general cast of pity which ordinarily sits on the countenances of the people when they see miserable objects of justice go to their execution; here was nothing to be heard but cursings and execrations. Abhorring the crimes and the very name of the man, throwing stones and dirt at him all the way, even at the place of execution.

Thus wrote Defoe in his biography. Wild was only semi-conscious. He arrived at the gallows with three other condemned men, two highwaymen and a forger. The highwaymen were hanged first, then the forger. The crowd became restive.

> The hangman giving him [Wild] leave to take his own time, and he continuing setting down in the cart, the mob impatient, and fearing a reprieve, though they had no occasion for it, called furiously upon the hangman to dispatch him, and at last threatened to tear him to pieces, if he did not tie him up immediately.
>
> In short there was a kind of universal rage against him, which nothing but his death could satisfy, or put an end to, and if a reprieve had come, it would have, twas thought, been

difficult for the officer to have brought him back again without him receiving some mischief, if not his death's wound from the rabble. So detestable had he made himself by his notorious crimes, and to such a height had his wicked practices come.[24]

Wild, dressed in a nightshirt and wig, was so drugged that he did not suffer as the hangman 'turned him off' and left him dangling. He had the scars of seventeen sword and pistol wounds on his body: his skull was mortised together with silver plates where it had been fractured.

A few days after his execution Wild's grave was secretly opened and the body stolen. On 15 June the *Daily Journal* reported:

Last Sunday morning there was found upon Whitehall Shore, in St Margaret's Parish, the skin, flesh and entrails (without any bones) of a human body: the coroner and jury that sat upon it, ordered it to be buried, which was done on Tuesday last, in the Burial Ground for the Poor, and the surgeon who attended, gave it as his opinion, that it could be none other than the remains of the dissected body. It was observed, that the skin of the breast was hairy, from whence people conjecture it to be part of the renowned Jonathan Wild.

Upper-class ambivalence to Wild continued after his death. There was no one to take his role as a thief-taker, and nowhere to recover stolen goods. The working class felt that one of their greatest oppressors was gone, but Lord Chesterfield wrote thoughtfully: 'At one great period of his life Jonathan Wild seemed rather born to a riband about his shoulder than a rope about his neck...He was certainly a man of parts, and had he set out in the world in an honest, instead of a dishonest road, we might have seen him reckoned a patriot, instead of a pickpocket.' Lord Chesterfield added: 'And it must be confessed that, in his whole conduct, he showed a steadiness, that wanted nothing but better principles to support it – one almost regrets that such a man should be lost in such a cause.'

There was something demonic about Wild, in his relentless pursuit of his victims and his fiendish exultation over their fate. In

1786 Captain A Smith wrote in his *True and Genuine Account of the Life and Actions of Jonathan Wild*:

> I shall here take notice that every execution day, Jonathan being mounted on horseback, he would in great triumph ride a little way before the criminals that were going to die, and at some taverns in the way call for a half-pint of wine, telling the people about him, with the greatest exultation and joy imaginable, that some of his children were coming, they were just behind: so when he went deservedly to be hanged, several thieves went a little way before the cart, telling people their father was coming, he's just behind.

Wild was the first modern criminal. He elevated crime to a new level, turning it into a business. Before him most criminals eked out short and miserable lives. He would have understood the extortion rackets and the long-firm frauds of such twentieth-century London gangs as the Krays and Richardsons. He would not have flinched at drug dealing or the ruthless violence needed to stay at the top in gangland today.

Let Defoe have the last word as he summed up the remarkable life:

> Thus ended the tragedy, and thus was a life of horrid and inimitable wickedness finished at the gallows, the very same place where, according to some, above 120 miserable creatures had been hanged whose blood in great measure may be said to lie at his door, either in their first being brought into the thieving trade, or led on in it by his encouragement and assistance; and many of them at last betrayed and brought to justice by his means, upon which worst sort of murder he valued himself, and would have it passed for merit, even with the government itself.

Thief-taking did not end with the death of Jonathan Wild. For a time the authorities continued their dangerous complicity with criminals simply because the idea of a proper police force was abhorrent and they could think of nothing else.

Soon the thief-takers were framing innocent people or inducing hapless young criminals to commit crimes and then denouncing them. They would stage robberies in which the 'victim' was one of the gang. An innocent member of the public, seeing the robbery take place, would intervene, only to be accused of the crime.

In 1756 a particularly vicious example of this crime brought matters to a head. A gang of thief-takers led by Stephen MacDaniel arrested two men, Peter Kelly and John Ellis, accusing them of robbing a breeches-maker named James Salmon. Two witnesses, John Berry and James Egan, swore that Kelly and Ellis were the robbers. But the High Constable of Blackheath, Joseph Cox, was tipped off that it was a plot to destroy innocent men.

Cox found a fence, a man called Blee, who acted as a receiver for the MacDaniel gang. Blee agreed to turn king's evidence in return for immunity. Cox arrested the four main conspirators and confidently expected their conviction.

Because of a legal technicality the men were found not guilty. A worse fate awaited them. They were tried for falsely obtaining rewards, and sentenced to the pillory. In their case it amounted to a death sentence. The mob were baying for the blood of these men who had sworn away innocent lives.

The first to go into the pillory were MacDaniel and Berry. At the end of an hour they emerged bloody and battered from the missiles hurled by the mob. Egan and Salmon then followed, and the fury of the mob was if anything more intense. The barrage of stones and dead animals was so fierce the constables tried in vain to protect the two men. When they were finally released Egan was dead and Salmon was little better. He died soon afterwards in Newgate from his injuries, as did MacDaniel and Berry.[25]

The Great Wen[1]

Wild's fall led to widespread rejoicing among London's poor, who had little enough to rejoice about. Many of them arrived healthy from the countryside only to die of hunger and disease, unable to find work or charity. The city was seen as sucking in the healthy and devouring them. London was pestilential, but there was another cause of the shocking mortality: the orgy of spirit drinking known as gin mania.

This degraded a whole generation of the London poor. The reason for the epidemic was government encouragement of distilling: farmers were producing a glut of grain, and Parliament, where gentlemen farmers were the most powerful group, was happy to create a market for it and so reduced taxes on gin. The duty was only 2d a gallon, sellers didn't need a retail licence and soon the drink was being sold in thousands of premises of varying degrees of respectability – in 1725 there were 6,187 in the capital excluding the City and Southwark. By contrast, the vastly bigger London of 1945 had only 4,000 pubs.

Gin was cheap – 'Drunk for a Penny, Dead Drunk for two pence, Clean Straw for Nothing' was the boast of the gin shops. Most of the distilling of gin took place in London, and most of the drinking. Among the poor, almost everyone drank it – men, women and children, even infants. It was used as an anaesthetic to silence starving children. It was a food substitute for their starving parents. The drink's vile taste and lethal potency – it was sold at the strength it came from the still, much stronger than the gin sold today – were disguised by heavy sweetening with sugar and flavouring with cordials.

The results were appalling. Judith Defour fetched her two-year-old child from a workhouse where it had been given new clothes. She strangled it, sold the clothes for 1s 4d, left the naked body in a ditch at Bethnal Green, split the money with the woman who had suggested the crime and spent the rest on gin.

People reeled about the streets or collapsed in gutters at all hours of the day and night. In the middle of the day men, women and children lay stupefied in the streets in slum areas such as St Giles and Whetstone Park. Inside the gin shops unconscious customers were propped up against the walls until they came round and could start again. The liquor was ubiquitous: the outlets included street stalls, back rooms in private houses and cellars as well as the regular gin shops. In 1743 eight million gallons of the fiery spirit were consumed, according to official estimates, but some thought the figure was as high as nineteen million gallons. And by far the greatest part of it went down the throats of the poor of London.

Hogarth's famous print *Gin Lane* is set in St Giles, where every fourth house was a gin shop. There were also 82 'twopenny houses' – lodging houses which were also brothels. In 1750 one house in fifteen in the City was a gin shop, and Holborn, where there were notorious slums, had 1,350 retailers, almost one house in five. As many as thirty thousand people were employed in the trade. In the words of Dorothy George: 'It would hardly be possible to exaggerate the cumulatively disastrous effect of the orgy of spirit-drinking between 1720 and 1751.'[2]

There was widespread contemporary concern. Henry Fielding, in *An Inquiry in the Causes of the late Increase of Robbers*, wrote:

A new kind of drunkenness, unknown to our ancestors, is lately sprung up amongst us, and which, if not put a stop to, will infallibly destroy a great part of the inferior people. The drunkenness I here intend is that acquired by the strongest intoxicating liquors, and particularly by that poison called Gin; which I have great reason to think is the principal sustenance (if it may be so called) of more than a hundred thousand people in this metropolis. Many of these wretches there are who swallow pints of this poison within the twenty-four hours; the dreadful effects of which I have the misfortune every day to see, and to smell too. But I have no need to insist on my own credit, or on that of my informers; the great revenue arising from the tax on this liquor, (the consumption of which is almost wholly confined to the lowest order of people) will prove the quantity consumed better than any other evidence.

Particularly disturbing was the extent to which women were 'habituated' to gin. 'We find the contagion has spread among [women] to a degree hardly possible to be conceived,' reported a committee of the Middlesex magistrates in 1736. 'Unhappy mothers habituate themselves to these distilled liquors, whose children are born weak and sickly, and often look old and shrivelled as though they had numbered many years; others, again, give [gin] daily to their children, whilst young, and learn them, even before they can go [walk] to taste and approve of this great and certain destroyer.'

The government, alarmed too late, tried to curb the gin mania it had created. In 1729, following a campaign for restriction led by the Middlesex magistrates, a licence fee of £20 for retailing spirits was imposed, and the spirit duty was raised from 2d to 5s a gallon. These measures were found to be unworkable and repealed in 1733, a move which was followed by another wave of drunkenness and disorder. This in turn led to the more draconian 'Gin Act' of 1736 requiring a £50 licence for retailing.

There was rioting, an explosion in Westminster Hall and threats to the life of the Master of the Rolls, Joseph Jekyll, seen as the chief initiator of the Act. Five informers under the Gin Act were stoned to death, one of them in New Palace Yard. A particular hate figure was the magistrate Sir Thomas de Veil, loathed among other things for his attempts to implement the Gin Act. In William Hogarth's print *Night* a figure which would have been clearly recognisable to contemporaries as Sir Thomas has the contents of a chamber pot poured over his head. This refers to a story that Sir Thomas was one day sampling gin, only to find that an ill-wisher had replaced it with piss. In January 1738 a mob besieged his house in Frith Street, threatening to burn it and kill his informers.

Popular violence effectively killed the law, and in seven years only three of the expensive licences were paid for. The law spawned a horde of informers: in a period of less than two years there were 12,000 cases, and nearly 5,000 convictions. The public took its revenge by hunting down the informers, a number of whom were murdered.

A side effect of the gin mania was high infant mortality caused by drunken nurses. An expert on population wrote in 1757:

> In and about London a prodigious number of children are cruelly murdered by those infernals called nurses. These infernal monsters throw a spoonful of gin, spirits of wine or Hungary water down a child's throat, which instantly strangles the babe. When the searchers come to inspect the body, and inquire what distemper caused the death, it is answered, 'convulsions'. This occasions the articles of convulsions in the Bills [Bills of mortality] so much to exceed all others.[3]

Hogarth's *Gin Lane* shows all the disorder and misery the craving for the drink was causing. It rises far above his usual moralising journalism, the chaos orchestrated to a kind of frozen music. A beggar and a dog compete for a bone. Ragged citizens, desperate for gin, sell all their worldly goods for the price of a drink. A woman is dropped naked into her coffin, her child weeping on the ground. A mother tips a glass of gin into her child's mouth, a riot breaks out and other children toast each other with drams. The central figure, a young but diseased mother, is so drunk she does not realise her infant child is plunging into an abyss. Glowering over the scene are the slums of St Giles and the steeple of St George's Bloomsbury.

In the background a house is collapsing, as some of the houses hastily thrown up after the Great Fire of 1666 did in fact collapse. Recalling the city of his youth, Dr Johnson wrote 'falling houses thunder on your head'[4] and to the citizens the moral ambivalence of the times must have suggested that the sky was falling. In May 1725, the same month that Wild was tried and hanged, another trial took place – that of Thomas Parker, Earl of Macclesfield.

Lord Chancellor in Walpole's administration and a close friend of King George I, Macclesfield was accused of accepting bribes, selling offices and embezzling more than £100,000 of Chancery funds. He was fined £30,000 – his friend the King promised to make good his loss out of the Privy Purse in £1,000 instalments, but died after only one payment – and the press and the government's opponents made much of the parallels between the cases, and between the methods of the great criminal, Wild, and the great statesman, Walpole.

Another cause for much moral confusion were the hordes of prostitutes who thronged the city and many of whom were, incidentally, victims of the gin craze. It was customary in liberal circles to pity fallen women and rail against the men who were responsible for their plight. Dr Johnson wrote in the *Rambler*:

> These forlorn creatures, the women of the town, were once, if not virtuous, at least innocent; and might still have continued blameless and easy, but for the arts and insinuations of those whose rank, fortune or education furnished them with the means to corrupt or to delude them. Let the libertine reflect a moment on the situation of that woman, who, being forsaken by her betrayer, is reduced to the necessity of turning prostitute for bread, and judge of the enormity of his guilt by the evils it produces.

Yet for some young women prostitution brought riches and fame otherwise beyond their reach. These included the famous wit and beauty Sally Salisbury, born in poverty in St Giles in 1692, who numbered the future George II among her conquests, and the working class actress-whores Harriet Lamb and Liz Farren, who both married into the peerage.[5]

Adding to the atmosphere of corruption and moral queasiness was the coverage of politics in the daily papers. Literacy was surprisingly high – probably about 70 per cent of men could read in 1750, with a slightly lower rate for women. The Swiss visitor César de Saussure commented: 'All Englishmen are great newsmongers. I have often seen shoeblacks and other persons of that class club together to purchase a farthing paper.'

The new coffee houses were where many men went to read the news. By 1700 there were about 500 in the city. A visitor to the city wrote: 'You have all manner of news there: you have a good fire, which you may sit by as long as you please; you have a dish of coffee; you meet all your friends for the transaction of business, and all for a penny.'[6] The author Ned Ward described these bustling, cheerful, gossipy places: 'Some going, some coming, some scribbling, some talking, some drinking, some jangling, and the whole room stinking of tobacco like a Dutch barge or a boatswain's cabin.'[7]

What their newspapers told the customers around the year 1720 was a tale of corruption in high places. The most obvious symptom was the South Sea Bubble, a rampant and crooked speculation which made some rich but ruined many more.

The South Sea Bill was introduced in the Commons in April 1720. It was proposed that the South Sea Company should take over a large part of the national debt in exchange for annual interest of 5 per cent and a monopoly of trade with the Pacific Islands and the West Indies. The dealing in stock was crooked from the beginning. Large amounts were given 'on credit' to MPs, ministers and members of the royal family. Promoters relentlessly boosted the stock, and everyone who could lay hands on money gambled on it going ever higher. By the time the Bill became law in May the price had quadrupled. But the whole of the £2 million raised in subscriptions had been handed over as bribes to politicians and brokers. There were no trading profits to provide dividends and by August the value of the stock was slipping inexorably.

The Bubble had burst, leaving chaos and ruin in its wake. The main swindle spawned lesser swindles. Financial backing was sought for dealing in woad or importing broomsticks from Germany. One advertisement conveys the atmosphere of fevered credulity: 'this day, the 8th instant, at Sam's coffee house, behind the Royal Exchange, at three in the afternoon, a book will be opened for entering into a co-partnership for carrying a *thing* that will turn to the advantage of all concerned'. Backers were even sought for 'A Company for carrying on an Undertaking of Great Advantage, but Nobody to know what It is.' The promoter took £2,000 in deposits on the first day and vanished.

Among the speculators was the mathematician Sir Isaac Newton; he sold £7,000 of stock in April and made a profit of 100 per cent. He went back into the stock and lost £20,000. 'I can calculate the motions of the heavenly bodies,' he is quoted as saying, 'but not the madness of people.' The London bookseller Sir Thomas Guy had for a long time been helping poor sailors by buying the more or less worthless promissory notes the government gave them in lieu of wages. When the South Sea Company took over the national debt the notes were converted into stock. Guy sold his huge holding in stages as the market rose and ended up with £234,000, said to be the largest fortune made out of the Bubble. He built Guy's Hospital with part of it.

Few were so lucky. Ballad-sellers sang, to the tune of *Over the Hills and Far Away*:

> A bubble is blown up in air,
> In which fine prospects do appear;
> The Bubble breaks, the prospect's lost,
> Yet must some Bubble pay the cost.
> Hubble Bubble; all is smoke,
> Hubble Bubble; all is broke,
> Farewell your Houses, Lands and Flocks,
> For all you have is now in Stocks.

Robert Walpole now saw his opportunity. His own inept speculations in the Bubble stock had brought him to the edge of ruin, yet he decided to shield the Court and other guilty parties as far as possible from what he called 'odious inquiries'. Penalties were mostly light: one director of the company, Sir John Blount, had crossed Walpole by providing Parliament with evidence of the swindle. He forfeited most of his money. A clerk who absconded with £4,000 was hanged. Others paid fines and some were also expelled from the Commons. By and large, Walpole screened most of the the South Sea directors, the politicians and the Court from public scrutiny and punishment so successfully that he became known as 'Skreen-Master General'. It worked, confidence was restored, and the following year Walpole had his reward when he

became First Lord of the Treasury and Chancellor of the Exchequer
– in effect, the first prime minister. His time in office would be
marked by bribery, nepotism, extravagance, adultery and a flagrant
disregard of the rule of law. The wine he and his guests drank in
huge quantities at Houghton, the great Palladian house he built in
Norfolk, was often smuggled. The apple-chomping Norfolk
magnate pulled down the local village and removed it from the
park, rebuilding it elsewhere. He bought the office of Ranger of
Richmond Park for his son and installed his own mistress, Maria
Skerrett, in the hunting lodge there.

Walpole opposed all parliamentary inquiries for fear that one day
his own affairs would be scrutinised. He had made a huge fortune
from office, and he needed it. He and his wife were recklessly
extravagant. On resuming office in 1720 he said he was 'lean and
needed to get some fat on his bones'. He succeeded in every sense:
because of his great bulk George II called him '*le gros homme*',

Sir Robert's eldest son was given a post worth £7,000 a year and
a peerage, aged 22; his second son one worth £3,000 a year plus
other perks; his third son, Horace, was made Controller of the Pipe
and Clerk of the Estreat when still at school and Usher of the
Exchequer before he was 21. The rest of the family similarly
prospered.

Despite his bluff front Walpole was hypersensitive to attacks by
satirists and caricaturists. He tried to buy them off and if that failed,
to arrest them. The most telling attack on him was John Gay's
Beggar's Opera, ostensibly the story of Jack Sheppard and Jonathan
Wild but really a thinly veiled satire on Walpole. Gay met Wild at
Windsor races in 1719, and Wild 'discoursed with great freedom on
his profession, and set it in such a light, that the poet imagined he
might work up the incidents of it for the stage'.

The first performance was given at Lincoln's Inn Fields in 1728.
The play ran for 62 nights, a record for the time, and the theatre
owner, John Rich, packed the audiences in, even having nearly a
hundred seated on the stage itself. It was said the play made Gay
rich, and Rich gay.[8]

The political innuendoes of the plot were not lost on the audience.
Although the two central characters, Macheath and Peachum, are

based on Sheppard and Wild, Gay had left room for other interpretations. It was possible to see Walpole as the highwayman Macheath, or as the gang leader Peachum, or even as Lockit, the Newgate jailer.

Walpole is said to have sat through a performance with his teeth gritted, and even called for an encore, an act of some political astuteness. Yet it rankled: he had the play's successor, *Polly*, banned, and Gay's patrons, the Duke and Duchess of Queensberry, banished from Court. In the end, the attacks became too much for Walpole. Swift, who had encouraged Gay to write *The Beggar's Opera*, again drew the parallel of robbers high and low:

> A public or a private robber;
> A statesman or a South Sea jobber.
> A prelate who no God believes;
> A Parliament or den of thieves.

And Fielding's attacks on Walpole in his plays led to the government introducing a Licensing Act which effectively drove political satire off the stage.

The worlds of Wild and Walpole had first collided in 1723 when the Waltham Black Act was passed. It decreed that any man in disguise or with his face blackened was guilty of a felony. It was a savage piece of legislation, ostensibly aimed at deer stealing and poaching but so worded it could be used to create a wide range of capital offences.

This 'Bloody Code', by no means always enforced, was intended among other purposes to show the value the establishment placed on its own property. A poacher or robber, sentenced to death and then shown 'mercy' by a property-owning magistrate, had been given a very powerful demonstration of the power of property.

Footpads and Pickpockets

The poet William Shenstone wrote: 'London is really dangerous at this time. The pickpockets, formerly contented with mere filching, make no scruple to knock people down with bludgeons in Fleet Street and the Strand, and that at no later hour than eight o'clock.'

Footpads were the most feared criminals of all. They operated as armed gangs, and because they were on foot and could not make a quick getaway, they had no compunction about killing their victims. By doing so they were eliminating the witnesses to their crime and buying time to escape.

Some footpads competed with highwaymen in attacking coaches, and they were far more feared than their mounted counterparts. One ploy was to attack a coach when it was forced to slow down, because of a steep hill or because the road narrowed. In June 1772 a coach carrying a Mr Fry and six young ladies was held up as it slowed down to cross Richmond Bridge. To stop it the footpads fired through the coach window, grazing a woman's ear and blowing away her earring. The gang, who got away with four guineas on that occasion, had held up two post-chaises from Richmond two days earlier.

The gang of footpads led by Obadiah Lemon used fishing rods to hook hats and wigs out of passing coaches. Coach owners then fitted a kind of grille to the windows. So the Lemons took to jumping on to the back of coaches, cutting a hole in the roof and stealing the valuables through it.

Pickpockets were another menace. Their favourite venues included fairs, race meetings and public hangings. Women were sometimes pickpockets. Often they were also prostitutes, like Jonathan Wild's Mary Milliner. The most famous and skilled of the women pickpockets was Jenny Diver, heroine of both Gay's and Brecht's *Beggar's Opera*. An Irishwoman, her real name was Mary Young. She was taught how to pick pockets by her countrywoman Anne Murphy in a 'kind of club' near St Giles. This was a school for pickpockets. Knapp and Baldwin's *Newgate Calendar* says:

> She now regularly applied two hours every day in qualifying herself for an expert thief, by attending to the instruction of experienced practitioners; and, in a short time, she was distinguished as the most ingenious and successful adventurer of the whole gang.

One of the crimes that established her reputation was stealing a ring from a gentleman outside a church in Old Jewry as people queued to listen to a popular preacher. Jenny spotted the ring, and held out her hand, which the gentleman took to assist her up the steps. Later he noticed that his ring was missing, but Jenny had slipped away.

She had been taught to read and write and do needlework by her parents, and what was called her 'superior address' was an asset in her new career. She had a costume which made her look pregnant, and she designed false arms and hands which folded across her bulging belly. Sitting in church, looking demure, she could plunder the people on either side by slipping her hands out unseen under her dress. One Sunday evening she seated herself between two elderly ladies in the church in Old Jewry and stole both their gold watches, which she passed to an accomplice. The devotions being ended, the congregation was preparing to depart, when the ladies discovered their loss and a violent clamour ensued. One of the injured parties exclaimed that her watch must have been taken either by the devil or the pregnant woman, on which the other said she could vindicate the pregnant lady, whose hands she was sure had not been removed from her lap during the whole time of her being in the pew. Afterwards Jenny went to a nearby public house, changed her clothes, returned to the church for a later sermon and stole a gentleman's gold watch.

With an accomplice posing as a footman, she robbed the gentry in church, at Exchange Alley, in the theatres, at fairs and tea-gardens. She fleeced a rich young Yorkshireman who fell for her when he saw her at the theatre: Jenny took him to an inn, and as they were about to get into bed, Anne Murphy, in the guise of her lady's maid, knocked on the door and said that Jenny's husband had suddenly returned from the country. Jenny told the young man to hide under the bedclothes, then she and her accomplices took his clothes, gold-hilted sword and the rest of his belongings. Her share of the spoils amounted to seventy pounds.

Inevitably, despite her sleight of hand, wit and charm she hanged in 1740. As befitted a famous felon, she was allowed to drive to Tyburn in a private coach with her own clergyman at her side, a privilege denied to the great Jonathan Wild. She died repentant.

Other notable women thieves included Moll Raby, a specialist in the crime or 'lay' of 'buttock and twang'. She would pick up a sozzled 'cull, cully or spark' in an alehouse and take him to a dark alley ostensibly for sex. While 'the decayed fool is groping her with his breeches down, she picks his fob or pocket of his watch or money. And giving a sort of "Hem!" as a signal that she has succeeded in her design, then the fellow with whom she keeps company, blundering up in the dark, he knocks down the gallant and carries off the prize.' A variant of this lay was still being practised late in the nineteenth century.

Nan Holland was an expert in the simple 'service lay', which entailed hiring herself out as a servant and then stealing from her master. It was said she could 'wheedle most cunningly, lie confoundedly, swear desperately, pick a pocket dexterously, dissemble undiscernibly, drink and smoke everlastingly, whore insatiably and brazen out all her actions impudently'.

Usually picking pockets was a male preserve, the traditional way for a young man to begin his criminal career. 'Most of those apprehended were between twelve and fourteen years old. Usually these lads worked in gangs under the direction of an adult (much as Fagin's gang did in *Oliver Twist*). A pickpocketing combination of sixteen very young boys was reported in 1764.[1]

Light and Heavy Horsemen

There are fashions in crime. At the beginning of the twenty-first century smuggling is very much *à la mode*: smuggling drugs, people, weapons, stolen works of art, alcohol, cigarettes. In the 1960s and 1970s bank and payroll robberies were all the rage. Security was so lax that there was no need for elaborate planning: some robbers would simply drive round looking for banks or payroll vans that seemed particularly vulnerable.

The problem of security in the London docks in the eighteenth century was even worse. The port had become the largest and richest in the world, with 620,000 tons of foreign shipping visiting it annually. The docks and the ships themselves were the focus of an epidemic of crime. Everything that Londoners needed was there: food, liquor, clothes, silks, tobacco, sugar, spices. It was a vast floating emporium, and a mighty force of thieves, both amateur and professional, assembled to exploit it.

A vast traffic jam built up as ships waited to be unloaded. They were still moored in midstream and their cargoes were taken off in open lighters which transferred the goods to the quays where supervision was lax. Goods might lie about untended in the open for weeks on end. There were few protected warehouses. Apart from outright robbery there was pilfering on a massive scale. About a third of the workers were either thieves or receivers. The most formidable of this army of criminals were known as 'heavy horsemen' and 'light horsemen'. The 'heavy horsemen' were the lumpers, what we would now call dockers, who loaded and unloaded ships. Dishonest lumpers dressed in specially adapted clothes, as Patrick Colquhoun, the man who eventually brought some law and order to the river, wrote:

Many of them were provided with an under-dress, denominated a 'Jemmy', with pockets before and behind; also with long narrow bags or pouches which, when filled, were lashed to their legs and thighs, and concealed under wide trousers... By these means they were enabled to carry off sugars, coffee, cocoa, ginger, pimento, and every other article which could be obtained by pillage.[1]

Ships that were easy targets were known by the cant expression 'game ships'. Some lumpers would work for nothing, so profitable was it to work on a game ship.

Coopers, so indispensable for sealing and unsealing cargoes, were another problem. Many goods were shipped in barrels of various sizes, from the 500 pound hogshead to the small half-anker of spirit. One of the cooper's tasks was to open the barrels so the goods could be quality tested. In some cases – sugar was one – he was allowed to draw off and keep three-quarter pound samples, but he would also fill a bladder with pilfered liquor and take it ashore secretly in his tool bag. The barrels might also be as much as 20 pounds underweight because the cooper had caused excessive 'spillage'. This spillage was the sugar or other commodity left on the barrel when the cooper had taken the sample. It would be swept up and sold for the benefit of the warehouse workers. The coopers' perks were so valuable that when the West India merchants set up their own police force in 1798 the coopers demanded more money to cover their loss of earnings.

The daytime thieves or 'heavy horsemen' had their night-time counterparts, the 'light horsemen'. They were organised gangs of robbers who would steal whatever they could sell, but their main targets were the cargoes of sugar. It has been estimated that towards the end of the eighteenth century £70,000 worth of sugar was being stolen every year.

This plunder was the most organised form of eighteenth-century crime. It required a network of receivers, who handled the goods and provided the considerable funds needed to bribe the revenue officers. They waited by the riverside as convoys of small boats took the goods ashore. Meanwhile 'mudlarks' waited in the mud at the river's edge to catch or retrieve things the lumpers threw overboard. Between them they could strip a lighter of its cargo in a night. Sometimes they would cut a boat adrift and let it ride down on the tide to a quiet spot where it could be emptied.

Against this highly organised and efficient system of plunder the authorities had as yet no answer. The customs service had its hands full trying to control smuggling: they turned a blind eye to other crimes, as Colquhoun claimed. Sometimes they were well paid to do so. Ship owners did employ night watchmen. They were usually from the same pool of broken-down unemployables as the parish watch, and found it wise to sleep through a robbery or even join in. When privately hired watchmen or vigilantes tried to intervene large fires were started in warehouses by the Pool of London (the area beneath Tower Bridge, lined with quays and crowded with ships).

About £500,000 was being lost each year. Of this the West India Company was losing £150,000. The company approached Patrick Colquhoun, a merchant and magistrate who had written a *Treatise on the Police of the Metropolis*. He set up a force of 200 armed men, called the Marine Police Institute, in 1798 and soon they were fighting bloody battles with the robbers.

The effect of the new police was startling. Colquhoun had notices entitled *Caution against Pillage and Plunder* nailed to the masts of ships which were about to be unloaded, and a marine police officer would read out the new regulations for unloading. As we have seen, the coopers demanded more money for their lost perks, and the lumpers sometimes left the ships immediately if they realised there would be no more plunder. Colquhoun claimed that losses from the West India ships in the first year of the new regime were cut to *one fiftieth* of the previous rate.

As the success of the new force became obvious, other ships' owners and merchants sought to get its protection extended. Gradually the Thames River Police came into being, but not without resistance.

One night in October 1799 two coal heavers and a waterman's boy were arrested for stealing coal. They were taken to the Marine Police offices at Wapping New Stairs where a magistrate found them guilty and fined them forty shillings each.

A mob gathered outside and after the three were sentenced it began hurling cobbles at the Marine Police office. Its members shouted that they would kill those inside.

All the windows in the building had by now been shattered. One of the police officers fired a pistol from a window, and killed one of the rioters. The magistrates from the office went out to read the Riot Act but were driven back. A shot said to have been fired by the rioters killed a man helping the police, one Gabriel Franks. After order was restored one of the mob, James Eyres, was arrested and charged with murder. The authorities were by no means sure of their case. The indictment reads: ' ... not that any evidence can be offered to you that he discharged the pistol by which Franks was killed, but that he was an active man in the riot, encouraging and inciting it.'

Eyres said the rioters were unarmed, and the shots came from inside the police office, but he was convicted and sentenced to death. The judge said to him: 'Prisoner, may the Lord have mercy on your soul.' Eyres replied: 'Amen, I hope he will.'

Lawlessness on the river had passed its peak by then, but the problems of protection for cargoes were not finally solved until the building of enclosed docks at the beginning of the nineteenth century. This heroic project lined the river eastwards from Wapping to Blackwall with fine warehouses.

Highwaymen and Smugglers: Gentlemen and Ruffians

Highwaymen, the so-called 'gentlemen of the road', were in most cases a cut above the common criminals who became footpads or burglars. Some took to the roads because of bankruptcy or gambling debts, or because they were from that stratum of society bred to polite living without the means to sustain it: thus many were the sons of parsons.

Others were tradesmen dissatisfied with the returns from honest work: many of those executed for highway robbery in the eighteenth century were butchers.

A disproportionate number of butchers were hanged at Tyburn. Some had been forced out of business by large-scale wholesalers and retailers who took over the official markets. These rogue butchers used their knowledge of the trade and the routes drovers and smallholders used to take their stock to market to ambush them. From this it was a small step to combining in gangs for highway robbery.

The most notorious of the highwaymen was Dick Turpin, who was born in 1706, the son of an Essex farmer. Turpin was immortalised in Harrison Ainsworth's *Rookwood*, which paints a romanticised and inaccurate picture both of the man and the way of life. Turpin was in fact a vicious and ruthless criminal.

His first venture into crime was cattle stealing, for which his apprenticeship as a butcher fitted him, and when a warrant was issued for his arrest he joined a gang of deer stealers and smugglers in Epping Forest in Essex.

Turpin soon took to holding up stagecoaches, but he was adaptable, and had other criminal enterprises. He managed an inn, the Bull-Beggars' Hole at Clayhill in Essex, and used to rob his customers as they slept. He was associated with Gregory's Gang, a large band of housebreakers who used a clearing in Epping Forest as their base. Together they robbed the graziers coming to market and the houses of London merchants.

In 1753 Turpin teamed up with the highwayman Tom King, whom he had tried to rob. King is famously reported to have said: 'What, dog eat dog? Come come, brother Turpin, if you don't know me I know you, and shall be glad of your company.'

The two formed a successful partnership, so successful that they caught the attention of bounty hunters attracted by the reward of £100 offered for the duo, dead or alive. When two bounty hunters tracked Turpin to the cave in Epping Forest that he and King used as a hideout, Turpin pretended to surrender, then proceeded to shoot one of the bountyhunters dead. The other fled. Turpin later killed King while shooting at a constable. This is the reality behind which the legend of Dick Turpin, the highwayman with a burning sense of social justice, was built.

Turpin was so successful that he had to go north because things were getting too hot for him around London. He used the alias John Palmer and operated as a horse thief. When he shot a cockerel and had to give sureties for his good behaviour there were inquiries into his background. Turpin wrote to his brother in Essex for help in getting character references but did not pay sufficient postage. His brother refused to pay the postage and the letter was returned to the Essex postmaster's office, where the handwriting was recognised by Turpin's old schoolmaster.

When he was caught, the government had his trial moved from York to the Old Bailey 'where it might serve a larger exemplary purpose'. Turpin's courage at his hanging in York in 1739 was grist to the mill of the myth-makers. He showed no sign of fear except that his leg trembled, and he attempted to stop it by repeatedly stamping it on the scaffold. As often happened, the mob surged towards the corpse to rescue it from the hovering surgeons. His grave was also unusually deep, to thwart body snatchers, but early the following morning it was dug up. Jackson's *Newgate Calendar* says '...the populace having an intimation whither it was conveyed, found it in a garden belonging to one of the surgeons of the city. Hereupon they took the body, laid it on a board, and having carried it through the streets in a kind of triumphal manner, they then filled the coffin with unslaked lime, and buried it in the grave where it had been before deposited.'

Turpin's life and legend contributed to the image of the noble rebel, refusing to be shackled by convention, fighting a corrupt establishment on behalf of the wretched of the earth. A ballad called 'Turpin's Appeal to the Judge' sums it up nicely:

> He said, the Scriptures I fulfilled
> Though this life did I lead
> For when the naked I beheld
> I clothed them with speed:
> Sometimes in cloth and winter-frieze,
> Sometimes in russet-grey;
> The poor I fed, the rich likewise
> I empty sent away.

Another London butcher turned successful highwayman was Cocky Wager. Rather than trust to random hold-ups he courted people who could provide information: innkeepers, ostlers, wagoners, turnpike-keepers. After he was captured outside London the arresting officer described the ride back to the City:

Twas as much as we could do to get Wager home, though I made a man ride behind him, for he was very unruly, pulling the horse about, making Motions with his Hands at every Body that came near him, as if he was firing a Pistol, crying Phoo! Cocky was very uneasy and curs'd and swore bitterly on the Road, and when we got to Town the Mob was so great that I could not carry him direct to the Justices for fear of a Rescue, so I got him with much Difficulty to New Prison.[1]

Highwaymen would arm themselves to the teeth: some carried as many as seven pistols, though it has to be remembered that in a shoot-out it was unlikely that the raider would have had time to reload his one-shot weapons. Some wore black masks over their eyes and silk handkerchiefs over their faces.

The highwayman's reputation for courtesy and gallantry was sometimes justified, sometimes not. They might beg to be excused for being forced by necessity to rob, and some showed chivalry towards women, refusing to search them or returning objects of sentimental value.

Claude Duval, a seventeenth-century highwayman, took gallantry to extremes. Once his victims were a man and his beautiful young wife. Duval asked for permission to dance with the wife, then helped her out of the coach and danced a minuet with her by the roadside. After he was hanged his torch-lit funeral was attended by hundreds of weeping women. His epitaph at St Paul's Covent Garden read:

> Here lies Du Vall, Reader, if male thou art,
> Look to thy purse, if female, to thy heart.
> Much Havock he has made of both; for all
> Men he made stand, and women he made fall.
> The second Conqueror of the Norman race
> Knights to his Arms did yield, and ladies to his face.
> Old Tyburn's Glory, England's illustrious thief,
> Du Vall, the ladies' Joy, Du Vall the ladies' Grief.

The *Weekly Journal* of August 1723 tells of a highwayman who took a man's watch, then agreed to return it to him for two guineas. The victim suggested they ride to his home, where he would get the money. They rode to the man's home, the money was handed over and 'after the drinking of a bottle of wine, with mutual civilities they took leave of each other'. On Wimbledon Common a highwayman demanded that a young married woman hand over a ring. When she said she would 'sooner part with life' he replied: 'Since you value the ring so much, madam, allow me the honour of saluting the fair hand which wears it, and I shall deem it a full equivalent.' The lady stretched forth her hand through the coach window, the highwayman kissed it and departed.

Most highwaymen, however, were merciless thugs. Sir John Verney wrote to a friend:

Six forraigners goeing for France were robb'd in the Dover stage coach at Shooters Hill, & lost about 300 pounds, & one of them kill'd by the rogues who gott off with the prize...On Sat. on Hounslow Heath 3 highwaymen robbed three chariots and servants as they returned from the Wells at Richmond. The D. of North umberland rob'd. Lord Osultstone was on his coachbox, his man in the coach snapt a blunderbuss but it went not off, soe the rogues kill'd one of my lord's horses and rob'd him too...

Condemned highwaymen knew they had a role to play as heroes. Dick Turpin at his execution did not wait for the hangman to move the cart away from under him, but flung himself off. Another highwayman, the celebrated James Macleane, kicked off his shoes and jumped into the air with the noose around his neck, holding his knees to his chest to increase the force of the 'drop' and hasten his death.

It was Macleane who shot at Horace Walpole in Hyde Park in 1752: his pistol went off accidentally, and the bullet grazed the great aesthete's head. Macleane, a country parson's son, lived in 'splendour', according to the account of his career in the 1764 *Select Trials*. His apartment in the fashionable area of St James's where he lived with his mistress was maintained on the proceeds of nightly hold-ups. Well known in society, he was believed to finance his life-style with the income from a (nonexistent) estate in Ireland.

Macleane had been a grocer, but he took to the road after his wife died. His partner was William Plunkett, a journeyman apothecary. Plunkett too lived in style, with an apartment in Jermyn Street.

The partnership was successful, their victims including Lord Eglinton and Sir Thomas Robinson. When Macleane was finally taken high society flocked to his cell in Newgate. Among the visitors were members of White's Club, and highborn ladies who included Lady Caroline Petersham. Horace Walpole, to whom Macleane apologised for the accidental shooting, wrote:

The first Sunday after his condemnation 3,000 people went to see him. He fainted away twice with the heat in his cell. You can't conceive the ridiculous rage there is of going to Newgate, and the prints that are published of the malefactors and the memoirs of their lives and deaths set forth with as much parade as – as Marshall Turenne's – as we have no generals worth making a parallel.[2]

Walpole told the recipient of the above letter, Sir Horace Mann, that he wished Macleane could have been saved but that it was not possible without setting a bad example. Macleane contributed to the highwayman's reputation for gallantry by sending apologies to a victim he had wounded accidentally. He offered to give him back his valuables if he would meet him at Tyburn gate at midnight.

John Rann, known as 'Sixteen-string Jack' because of the silk strings he attached to the knees of his breeches, also put on a show for the mob when he was executed in 1774. Rann was a dandy, and made his final appearance in a new pea-green suit, a ruffled shirt and a hat surrounded with silver rings. In his buttonhole he wore a huge nosegay.

One of the most successful of all highwaymen was William Page. A meticulous planner, ingenious, fearless and lucky, he committed more than 300 robberies with his partner Darwell in the years 1755–8.

Page made maps of the areas where he intended to strike. He would dress in gentleman's finery, drive out in a phaeton and pair and having hidden the coach in a wood change into highwayman's attire. After the robbery he would return to the carriage and change back into his finery.

One of his victims was Lord Ferrers, one day to hang almost like a common criminal. Ferrers drew a pistol but Page disarmed him.

Page's luck and audacity got him out of many scrapes. When stopped, as he often was as he drove away after his crimes, he would warn those who questioned him that a highwayman was stalking the road. He sometimes claimed that he too was a victim of the highwayman.

He had a close call at Putney when he was pursued by armed men after a robbery. As he was making his getaway some haymakers found his coach and his change of clothes. The haymakers were honest and handed the goods over to the authorities, who advertised for the owner. Page feared it could be a trap, but he claimed the coach and clothes anyway. His story was that he had been the victim of a highwayman, who had stripped him naked. He got his property back.

Inevitably he was finally arrested, and Lord Ferrers was one of the witnesses against him. In perhaps his greatest stroke of audacity Page put forward an ingenious defence. He did some research into Ferrers's past and found out that the year before he had been excommunicated for contempt of the Bishop of London's consistory court after his wife had petitioned there for divorce on the grounds of cruelty. Page claimed Ferrers could not give evidence against him because of his excommunication, and the court had to accept his defence.

His respite was short. The following month he was arrested for a highway robbery at Blackheath and hanged at Maidstone in March 1758.

Thomas Butler, who was executed in 1720, was one of the highwaymen with a Jacobite background. The Jacobites maintained that the Stuarts had been illegally supplanted by the Hanoverians, and that all Hanoverian property was therefore the result of theft. Butler fought for the Pretender, and was employed as a spy during the Duke of Ormonde's rising in 1715. He fled to the continent, but ran out of money. He returned to England and took up highway robbery. For some time he and his servant lived in style in London, and were received in polite society.

With such a large section of the disaffected populace so sympathetic to their cause, highwaymen found London an ideal place to work and hide. They needed safe houses to operate from – taverns, inns and stables. They also needed fences or receivers and here men like Wild were vital, although as we have seen, anyone dealing with Wild was taking his life in his hands.

Among the safe houses were the Blue Lion in Gray's Inn Lane and the Bull and Pen in Spa Fields. St George's Fields between Southwark and Lambeth had many havens, including the notorious

Dog and Duck, the Shepherd and Shepherdess, Apollo Gardens and the Temple of Flora. Young boys used to go to the Dog and Duck to watch the highwaymen mount up and say goodbye to their 'flashy women' before setting off to prey on travellers on the highways.

Jonathan Wild, the self-styled Thief-Taker General, broke up the major gangs of highwaymen in London; he also pursued some of the more famous solo operators. One of these was Benjamin Child, a womaniser and gambler who truly lived up to the romantic image of his profession. He made a fortune from his crimes, and was said to have left over £10,000 in his will. One of his exploits was to use part of his loot to free all the debtors in Salisbury jail.

There is no direct evidence that Wild caught Child, but John Hawkins, a highwayman who was one of his victims, swore that he would be avenged on the man who had impeached Child, and it was widely believed that he was referring to Wild.

Wild proved his courage and ruthlessness many times, none more so than when he arrested James Wright, a member of the Hawkins gang. Wright had held up the Earl of Burlington and Lord Bruce in Richmond, taking a sapphire ring from the former and a gold watch from the latter. Lord Bruce offered Wild a huge reward for the return of the stolen items, and Wild was furious that he could not oblige – presumably the goods had already been sold. In 1720 he captured Wright by 'holding him fast by the chin with his teeth, till he dropped his firearms, surrendered and was brought to Newgate'.[3] Wright was acquitted and went back to his old trade of hairdressing.

Although the highwayman Tom King asked Dick Turpin, 'Shall dog eat dog?' terminating Turpin's wish to rob him, as we shall see, thieves frequently did fall out. The twentieth-century phenomenon of the supergrass was foreshadowed long ago.

Two eighteenth-century highwaymen, John James and Nathaniel Hawes, had eighteen successful hold-ups to their credit in their first two weeks of operating together. When Hawes returned a ring to one of their victims James threatened to shoot him in the head. They quarrelled again when James refused Hawes's request to return a whip to its woman owner, and there were disagreements about the division of the spoils. Hawes became convinced that James was going to betray him to the authorities and went himself to Jonathan Wild. The Thief-Taker General had an added motive for going after James: the highwayman operated outside his Corporation of Thieves, and it was imperative for Wild to destroy him before others saw how a robber could prosper without being part of his network.

Wild paused only to get a warrant and then burst into James's lodgings in Monmouth Street where the outlaw was in bed with one of his mistresses. James, a successful robber who was able to keep his wife, three children and two mistresses in comfort, was hanged. Hawes got a prison sentence, escaped, and was recaptured by a man he tried to hold up on Finchley Common.

When the judge at his trial refused to let him have the clothes he was arrested in and in which he wished to be hanged, Hawes refused to plead. The judge ordered that he be subjected to *peine forte et dure*. Although Hawes had boasted '...as I have lived with the character of the boldest fellow in my profession I am resolved to die with it and leave my memory to be admired by all the gentlemen of the road of succeeding ages,' he could bear the pressure of a weight of 250 pounds for only a few minutes before giving in. He didn't get his clothes. The torture was abolished in 1772.

The numbers of highwaymen usually increased sharply with the ending of military campaigns, as soldiers and sailors, many of whom had been pressed into service, were disbanded. But towards the end of the eighteenth century their numbers went into sharp decline. An important factor was the growing expertise of the Bow Street Runners, the police force founded by the Fielding brothers.

In one of their successful manhunts the Runners had been on the trail of the famous highwayman Richard Ferguson, and had arrested him several times but had to release him for lack of evidence. They caught up with him again after he had robbed a coach at Aylesbury in 1800.

The following year two of the Runners picked up the trail of a gang of four young highwaymen who had just carried out a robbery at Shooters Hill in south London. They tracked them to a wood, then called on the military at the nearby Woolwich barracks for help. The troops found the gang, and the four men were later hanged.

Highway robbery reached epidemic levels at times in the

eighteenth century. There was a distinct lull while Jonathan Wild held sway, but the numbers increased afterwards, particularly after the end of the American War of Independence. Battle-hardened soldiers unable to find work returned to plague the capital, joining the many criminals who had taken to the roads after being freed from London prisons by the mob during the Gordon Riots of 1780. Horace Walpole, who was himself held up three times, wrote in a letter to Sir Horace Mann: 'When highway robberies are arrived at that pitch to be committed at noon-day, in a public road, in the sight of several passengers, who is safe from their depredations? Sunshine is now no security.'

The last mounted highway robbery took place in 1831. Frank McLynn, in *Crime and Punishment in Eighteenth-century England*, gives several reasons for the decline of the highwayman. He quotes George Borrow's *Romany Rye* where an ostler declared that the authorities' refusal to license public houses like the Dog and Duck, known haunts of the criminals, was a factor. Another, said the ostler, was the enclosure system that destroyed many of the wild heaths the highwaymen favoured for their hold-ups. Third was the coming of the Bow Street Runners and the permanent mounted patrol operating out of London. To these McLynn adds the spreading suburbs and improvement in roads. And finally the role of money: bigger rewards and the growth of the banking system, which ensured people did not have to carry large amounts about with them when they travelled, meant the highwaymen had had their day.

Although highwaymen formed gangs, their hold-ups were often carried out by just one or two men. Smuggling was much more highly organised, and sometimes involved gangs of up to fifty men. It was also very violent, with pitched battles between the smugglers and the forces of law. Even when up against trained troops the smugglers did not always lose.

Out of a population of eight million, it is estimated that as many as 20,000 people were full-time smugglers. Tea was for a time the mainstay of the smugglers: it has been reckoned that 21 million pounds of tea were smuggled into Britain annually in the eighteenth century. Wine, brandy, gin, tobacco, coffee, silks and linen were also imported illegally. Robert Walpole, the country's first 'prime minister', used the Admiralty barge to smuggle in wine, lace and other goods. Lady Holdernesse, whose husband was Warden of the Cinque Ports and a former Secretary of State, used Walmer Castle to run a business selling smuggled French gowns and furniture. She had previously been caught in possession of 114 Parisian silk gowns.

London was naturally the hub of all this activity. Along the great roads leading into the city the smugglers had caches. One was in the Fleet prison, but try as they might the excisemen could not find it. They were either driven off with stones or the warden and his turnkeys helped the inmates hide the contraband.

The public condoned smuggling, but not the brutality of the smugglers. Among the most violent were the Hawkhurst gang in Kent. A parliamentary inquiry in 1745 was told that the gang could muster 500 men in an hour, and from their base in the village of Hawkhurst near Hastings they kept five counties in an uproar.

Much of their activity took place in Sussex, and there were local gangs involved too. Sussex, although a short distance from London, was *ultima Thule* as far as Horace Walpole was concerned when he wrote in 1749: 'If you love good roads, conveniences, good inns, plenty of postilions and horses, be so kind as never to go to Sussex. We thought ourselves in the northest part of England; the whole country had a Saxon air, the inhabitants are savage, as if King George the second was the first monarch of the East Angles. Coaches grow there no more than balm and spices...'

The Hawkhurst gang's reign of terror was challenged by the people of the nearby village of Goudhurst, who formed a militia. Its leader, John Sturt, had been a sergeant in the army, and soon he was training the villagers for defence.

The leader of the Hawkhurst gang, Thomas Kingsmill, who had already with the help of 92 men and a pack of vicious dogs routed the people of Folkestone, led his men in an attack on Goudhurst. They captured one of the Goudhurst villagers, took him back to Hawkhurst and tortured him until he revealed details of the village's defences. The man was then sent back to Goudhurst with a warning that the smugglers would return on 20 April 1747 and burn the village to the ground, slaughtering every man, woman and child.

The smugglers duly arrived and attacked. They were met by a volley from the defenders, and in the ensuing firefight Kingsmill's brother George was shot dead with another of the smugglers, and many more were wounded. The Goudhurst men chased the smugglers back to Hawkhurst.

Later that year the Hawkhurst gang carried out their most audacious exploit: they raided the custom's house at Poole Harbour under the guns of a Royal Navy ship and made off with a huge cargo of tea.

The tea had been seized on the smugglers' ship *The Three Brothers* by customs and impounded. Some of the smugglers escaped and made their way back to Hawkhurst. Kingsmill rounded up sixty of his men and set out for Poole, crossing from Kent into Sussex and Hampshire and finally Dorset on horseback. When they arrived they found that the Navy ship was moored at the quay with its guns trained on the door of the customs house. But the tide was ebbing and Kingsmill knew that with it the ship would sink below the top of the quay and its guns would be useless. At low tide he and his men broke into the customs house and retrieved the tea.

A shoemaker named Daniel Chater, who had seen the smugglers as they returned in triumph through Fordingbridge, turned informer, and an elderly customs man, William Galley, was told to escort him to a Sussex magistrate.

When they stopped to eat at the White Hart at Rowland's Castle the landlady, who was sympathetic to the smugglers, contacted the local branch of the Hawkhursts. Soon some of the smugglers arrived at the inn and after getting them drunk, took Chater and Galley prisoner. After beating them they tied them to their horses and took them to a park, whipping them all the way. By 2 a.m. Galley was almost dead. The smugglers cut off his nose and testicles, and buried him, possibly while he was still alive.

Chater's ordeal was still not over. For three days he was kept chained up in a shed, then he was half-choked with a rope and thrown down a well. Boulders were thrown down on him.

The widespread revulsion at the crimes was one reason the Duke of Richmond now got involved: he was also a fanatical anti-

Jacobite, and there were thought to be connections between smugglers and the Jacobites. The Duke now launched a ferocious campaign against the Hawkhurst gang. He established a special commission so that reliable judges could be brought from London, rather than trust the local justices to try the killers of Chater and Galley. Then he offered large rewards for information.

One of the killers was eventually arrested for another crime, and turned informer. Soon seven of the gang were arrested and executed. Then Kingsmill and four more of the gang were caught. Their trial at the Old Bailey was told that the Poole raid was 'the most unheard of act of villainy and impudence ever known'. After their execution their bodies were exhibited on gibbets.

Richmond's two-year campaign broke the gang. He died in 1750, having had 35 Hawkhurst men executed: another ten escaped the noose by dying in prison. What remained of the gang made a last stand in 1751. In a pitched battle with the army the gang's last leader was taken.

Still the war between the smugglers and the authorities went on. In 1775 a large body of armed smugglers forced two witnesses who were to give evidence against one of their colleagues at Winchester Assizes to turn back to Southampton. There were battles between smugglers and the authorities at Orford and Southwold, and at Cranbourne Chase a party of dragoons who ambushed fifty smugglers were defeated, having to give up their arms and horses.

What had started as small-scale crime changed with the rocketing prices after the Seven Years War (1756–63). When Edmund Burke took office in 1783 he called for a report on smuggling. The report, compiled by the Board of Trade, informed him that the illegal imports had trebled since 1780, and estimated that a staggering 21,132,000 pounds of tea were being smuggled in annually. The accountant of the East India Company believed that only one-third of the tea consumed in Britain was legally imported.

The next government, headed by William Pitt, struck a major blow against the smugglers by reducing the tax on tea from 119 per cent to 12 per cent. The results were startling. In 1784 4,962,000 pounds of tea passed through customs: the following year, the first year of reduced duties, the total was 16,307,000 pounds.

But the war against the smugglers was by no means over. Liquor smuggling had been big-time crime since the reign of William and Mary. The reason again was high taxation: the tax on French wines, rum and brandy in 1735 was £1 a gallon. Consumption of liquor was high: early in the century, 11.2 million gallons of spirits were being drunk every year in London. That is about seven gallons per adult. There were 207 inns, 447 taverns, 5,875 ale-houses and 8,659 brandy shops.

It was a hard-drinking society. Samuel Johnson recalled that when he was young, 'all the decent people of Lichfield got drunk every night, and were not thought the worse of'. And the Sussex shopkeeper Thomas Turner described the rustic revels of the 1750s in his diary. 'We continued drinking like horses, as the vulgar phrase is, and singing till many of us were very drunk, and then we went to dancing, and pulling wigs, caps and hats; and thus we continued in this frantic manner, behaving more like mad people than they that profess the name of Christians.'

The destitute drank gin: the better off drank wine and spirits. In 1774 at the Lord Mayor's dinner at the Mansion House the guests drank 626 dozen bottles of wine. Robert Walpole got his wine cheap when it was smuggled: nevertheless, his annual bills were prodigious. In 1733 his household consumed 1,200 bottles of White Lisbon alone.[4] Two years earlier Lord Hervey wrote to Frederick, Prince of Wales: 'Our company at Houghton [Walpole's new house, of which he was justly proud] swelled at last into so numerous a body that we used to sit down to dinner with a snug little party of thirty odd, up to the chin in beef, venison, geese, turkeys, etc; and generally over the chin in claret, strong beer and punch.' In 1733 Walpole spent the enormous sum of £1,118 12s 10d with the wine merchant James Bennett, and £48 2s 0d with Schaart & Co.[5]

Cutting the duty on tea had been a striking success. In 1784 Pitt also struck at the alcohol smugglers. The duty on all French wines was slashed from £90 3s 10d a tun to £43 1s 0d. Then he introduced the Hovering Act which enabled the excise to confiscate all ships under sixty tons carrying wine, tea or coffee within three miles of the English coast. Other restrictions on shipping tightened the screw on the smugglers. Shooting at naval or revenue officers was now punishable by hanging.

This left the very lucrative smuggling of tobacco. It has been estimated that about seven and a half million tons were smuggled in annually. The rewards were high. Tobacco could be bought on the continent for three pence a pound. With added expenses of five and a half pence to cover the costs of importing it, they were still able to make almost a shilling a pound when they sold it in England.

Pitt ignored advice to deal with the problem by slashing the duty on tobacco as he had done with tea and alcohol. Instead he proposed a system of warehouses for tobacco, and decreed that only London, Bristol, Liverpool, Glasgow and another seven ports could import it. These measures worked up to a point, but the war with France in the 1790s forced up duties and by 1806 the tax on tea had risen again to 96 per cent. The smugglers were back in business.

One of Pitt's more effective measures was burning the smugglers' boats. The town of Deal in Kent was a thorn in the authorities' side. Pepys wrote in 1660: 'What a pitiful town Deal is.' William Cobbett was more damning. 'Deal is a most villainous place. It is full of filthy looking people. Great desolation of abomination has been going on here.' The town's mayor and citizens took the side of the smugglers against the authorities. In 1785 Pitt learned that heavy gales in the Channel had forced the smugglers to pull their boats high up on to the beach, and he asked the War Office to send troops to cordon off the area and destroy the boats. The Secretary for War replied that this would be illegal. Pitt went ahead anyway.

A whole regiment, a particularly intimidating force, was sent to the town. The inhabitants took down the signs of inns and taverns and pretended that there was no room for the soldiers in the town. The commanding officer rented a barn on a two-year lease, then took his men to the beach and burned the boats.[6]

Citadels of Vice and Crime

The underworld today is almost an abstraction. Vastly profitable and ubiquitous, it is nevertheless elusive. Most of us will never meet a gangster, and would not know where to look for one.

For more than two hundred years it was very different. London's various underworld strongholds, known in the nineteenth century as rookeries, were an ever-present threat: they were located mainly near the wealthier areas of the city and in the worst the police were either permanently absent or entered only in force. Honest citizens went in fear of the denizens of Alsatia south of Fleet Street, St Giles near Oxford Street, and the Mint in Southwark. Walk the revitalised streets round Centre Point in New Oxford Street today and you will find few clues to the vanished criminal ghetto of St Giles, yet for two hundred years this teeming slum was one of the most feared places in the capital.

In the eighteenth and nineteenth centuries rich and poor lived almost cheek by jowl: if you strayed a few yards from one of the most fashionable thoroughfares – say, Fleet Street – you would find yourself surrounded by prostitutes and thieves, among gin-shops and tenements so broken down and squalid they 'oozed filth', and you would be lucky to escape without being robbed or even attacked. In the eighteenth century the denizens of these urban jungles might sally forth en masse to attack their richer neighbours. In the nineteenth, their spirits still untamed by pauperism, squalor and overcrowding, hordes of ragamuffins, beggars, prostitutes and criminals poured out of them each day to plunder the city in their various ways. Their congested alleys and courts were penetrated from time to time by coroners' officers, doctors, missionaries, police and the occasional journalist, who brought word to the outside world. In some cases the mansions of the rich overlooked these slums.

Some of these criminal strongholds persisted over centuries. In 1717, for instance, John Gay warned visitors to the Drury Lane area east of Covent Garden in central London:

> O may thy virtue guard thee throw' the roads
> Of Drury's mazy courts and dark abodes!
> The harlot's guileful paths who nightly stand
> Where Catherine Street descends into the Strand.

In 1730 things were obviously worse: Local shopkeepers and traders appealed to the Westminster Sessions:

> Several people of the most notorious character and infamously wicked lives and conversation have of late...years taken up their abode in the parish...There are several streets and courts such as Russell Street, Drury Lane, Crown Court and divers places within the said parish and more particularly in the neighbourhood of Drury Lane infested with these vile people...there are frequent outcries in the night, fighting, robberies and all sort of debaucheries committed by them all night long to the great inquietude of his majesty's subjects.

At the end of the nineteenth century the social topographer Charles Booth would still refer to the area as the 'dark side' of central London. 'From Seven Dials going east the tone gets lower and lower till we reach that black patch consisting of Macklin Street, Shelton Street and Parker Street.'

Henry Mayhew, the pioneering Victorian social commentator, suggested that the 'rookeries' had grown up around the far older 'sanctuaries' and the old hospitals of the capital. These rookeries swept east in a line very roughly from Westminster along the Strand and Fleet Street, then north and east in a great arc around the City, ending south of the Thames with the ancient and infamous Mint in Southwark. The

City was for many years virtually under siege from this great concentration of criminals, for reasons we shall see later.

We begin in the west, with Westminster. Although this was a wealthy district in the reign of Elizabeth I it had no industries, unlike the areas east of the City and south of the Thames. Already the poor were clustered around the Abbey of Westminster, 'for the most part without trade or mystery... many of them wholly given to vice and idleness'. In Victorian times there was an area to the south and west of the Abbey inhabited by cracksmen, prostitute thieves and the male thieves who lived with them. One court was so notorious because of the young thieves who lived there that police would not allow goods to be taken in or out without searching them. The boys overcame the problem by fencing (dealing) their stolen goods before going home.[1] The area around Pye Street was known as Devil's Acre, and Charles Dickens drew attention to it in *Household Words* in 1850. After Victoria Street was driven through the worst part of Westminster John Hollingshead wrote of the overcrowding thus created, and described seventy streets and their courts either side of it. He singled out Orchard Street and Pye Street, the 'openly acknowledged high street of thieves and prostitutes'.[2] According to the writer Thomas Beames, the inhabitants used force or obstruction to defeat forays by the police.[3]

Next we travel east along the Strand. To the north lies Covent Garden, long the centre of the capital's vice and entertainment industries. In the eighteenth century there were public houses in the area where a kind of striptease was performed by 'posture molls'. They 'stripped naked and mounted upon the table to show their beauties' and also offered flagellation. The Rose Tavern was called 'that black school of SODOM' by the writer Thomas Brown, who said it was a place where men 'who by proficiency in the Science of Debauchery [are] called *Flogging Cullies*... pay an excellent Price for being scourged on their posteriors by *Posture Molls*'. The entertainments were not for the squeamish: women would wrestle with each other, stripped to the waist while the customers, who included homosexuals and transvestites, cheered and took bets. At the Shakespeare's Head there was a 'Whores' Club' which met every Sunday, presided over by a 'Pimpmaster General'.

There were also 'Mollie houses' and clubs for homosexuals, among them the Bull and Butcher, the Spiller's Head, the Fountain, the Sun and the Bull's Head. Respectable City businessmen would go there to pick up young homosexuals. The writer Ned Ward complained in the *London Spy* in 1700 about the antics of male prostitutes at the Fountain, a tavern in Russell Square. Dressed as women, they would enact mock childbirths using a doll, which would be 'Christened and the Holy Sacrament of Baptism impudently Prophan'd'.

Covent Garden swarmed with criminals of all kinds; pickpockets, footpads – violent robbers – fraudsters, even on occasion highwaymen. There were brothels and low drinking dens and hordes of prostitutes. Many of the nearby courts and alleys were home to thieves and prostitutes, and the rich pickings also attracted criminals from outside the area.

Further north, perhaps travelling along Drury Lane, we come to the hideous slum of St Giles, or the 'Holy Land', the most feared and deplorable of all the rookeries, described eloquently by Dickens and Henry Mayhew. It was said to have had for Dickens 'a profound attraction of repulsion'. Early in the nineteenth century a parish beadle [officer] had defined the core of the area as: 'One part of the High Street, back of Great Russell Street, and what we call the back settlement, down the right side of George Street [otherwise Dyott Street] including Buckeridge Street, Church Street, Church Lane, Bainbridge Street, Carrier Street and Lawrence Street'. It is easier to grasp its boundaries today if we think of it as extending from Great Russell Street south to Long Acre, with Drury Lane and Charing Cross Road as its eastern and western boundaries. It was not the most extensive or dangerous of the capital's rookeries. What made it so feared was its location. It was easily accessible from Leicester Square, the Haymarket and Regent Street, the haunts of masses of thieves and prostitutes. They could slip down dark alleys and courts and reach the asylum of St Giles in minutes.

The evil reputation of the area was not new. As far back as 1751 over a quarter of its 2,000 houses were gin shops, and it had 82 lodging houses which harboured prostitutes and receivers. It was the setting for some of Hogarth's liveliest engravings, including *Gin*

Lane. Its impenetrability and the fact that it had a large Irish population made it seem even more alien. By 1851 it had 54,000 inhabitants, about one fifth of them Irish, living on average about twelve to a house.

Mayhew quotes a description by Inspector Hunt of the Metropolitan Police of St Giles in the 1840s, before parts of it were pulled down to make way for New Oxford Street. Many of the decayed and verminous buildings had been built in the seventeenth and eighteenth centuries. The streets were so narrow that in places a man had to turn sideways to get between the buildings. On the corner of Church Street and Lawrence Street was an infamous brothel where the rooms were rented by prostitutes. As Inspector Hunt explained, robbery rather than sex was the business that went on there. The prostitutes would pick up drunken men in the streets round nearby Drury Lane or even as far west as Regent Street and take them back to the brothel. 'When they had plundered the poor dupe he was ejected without ceremony by the others who resided in the room; often without a coat or hat, sometimes without his trousers, and occasionally left on the staircase as naked as he was born.' The girls might be as drunk as their customers. Inspector Hunt said: 'In this house the grossest scenes of profligacy were transacted.' When the house was pulled down it was found to be connected by a series of secret escape routes to other houses in the rookery.

These escape routes were a feature of the houses in St Giles. They linked the houses in one street 'by roof, yard and cellar' to those in another, and made it almost impossible for the police to arrest a fugitive there. In some traps had been set for the police. One cellar held a large cesspool, so camouflaged that a pursuing officer might stumble in and disappear into the sewage. Some cellars had holes two feet square low down in their walls. These effectively stopped pursuit, for no police officer would risk crawling through the holes on his hands and knees in the dark.

Behind the lanes that traversed the area were the 'back settlements', a network of yards and passages that were dangerous even for parties of armed police. When a group of armed plain-clothes officers raided a coiner's or counterfeiter's in Carrier Street in November 1840 the desperate spirit of the neighbourhood was roused. According to *The Times*, the police seized and handcuffed three coiners and started to withdraw. A crowd had gathered and when they saw the handcuffed criminals there were shouts of 'Rescue! Rescue!'. Stones were flung and some of the officers were hurt. Reinforcements of police arrived and the whole party began to force their way north towards the nearest open space, Bloomsbury Square. When they reached it the mob made a final charge. Their leader, who was armed with a knife, was tackled and disarmed, and the mob subsided.

At the heart of the rookery was Rats' Castle, a 'large, dirty building' which stood on the foundations of an eleventh-century leper hospital. Dickens visited it in the company of two police officers.

> Saint Giles's Church strikes half past ten. We stoop low, and creep down a precipitous flight of steps into a dark close cellar. There is a fire. There is a long deal table. There are benches. The cellar is full of company, chiefly very young men in various conditions of dirt and raggedness. Some are eat ing supper. There are no girls or women present. Welcome to Rats' Castle, gentlemen, and to this company of noted thieves![4]

On other occasions he would persuade people to accompany him as he prowled the alleys and courts. 'Good Heaven!' he would exclaim, 'what wild visions of prodigies of wickedness, want and beggary arose in my mind out of that place!'

> Wretched houses with broken windows patched with rags and paper; every room let out to a different family, and in many instances to two or even three – fruit and 'sweetstuff' manufacturers in the cellars, barbers and red-herring vendors in the front parlours, cobblers in the back; a bird-fancier in the first floor, three families on the second, starvation in the attics, Irishmen in the passage, a 'musician' in the front kitchen, a charwoman and five hungry children in the back one – filth everywhere – a gutter before the houses, and a drain behind – clothes drying, and slops emptying from the windows; ... men

and women, in every variety of scanty and dirty apparel, lounging, scolding, drinking, smoking, squabbling, fighting and swearing.

W A Miles, collecting information for an official inquiry in the 1830s, wrote of 'rooms and small tenements, crowded with a population existing in all the filth attendant upon improvidence, crime and profligacy, as if the inhabitants by common consent deem themselves only "tenants at will", until the gallows or the hulks [prison ships] should require them...There is, moreover, an open communication at the backs of all the houses, so that directly a panic is created, men, women and boys may be seen scrambling in all directions through the back yards and over the party walls, to effect an escape...'[5]

As we have seen, another area with a bad reputation lay to the south of High Street St Giles – Seven Dials, where the gangster Billy Hill was born in 1911, and the streets around it, Drury Lane and its adjacent streets and alleys and Covent Garden nearby. For much of the nineteenth century these were known as places where thieves and prostitutes lodged. One reason was the theatres nearby. This should not suggest a strong interest in the theatre among these women. Theatregoers were among their best customers.

Retracing our footsteps to the south we come to Alsatia, the district which gave its name to all the criminal sanctuaries in the eighteenth century. This was located between Fleet Street and the Thames, on the site of the former Whitefriars Monastery. After the monasteries were dissolved by Henry VIII the inhabitants claimed they were exempt from the jurisdiction of the City. Their claim was upheld first by Queen Elizabeth, and then by James I in 1608. Criminals flooded in and the area was like a wide-open town in the American Wild West. It was called Alsatia after the disputed territory of Alsace on the borders of France and Germany.

When William Hogarth showed his Idle Apprentice being arrested, having been betrayed by his whore, he located the event in a cellar in Alsatia. The historian Macauley wrote that 'at any attempt to extradite a criminal, bullies with swords and cudgels, termagant hags with spits and broomsticks poured forth by the hundred and the intruder was lucky if he escaped back to Fleet Street, hustled, stripped and jumped upon.' The Chief Justice needed the backing of a company of musketeers to serve a warrant there.

The privileges were withdrawn in 1623 but here, as in the other sanctuaries around the capital, it was many years before law and order was restored.

We travel north and east again, perhaps along Fetter Lane, to Saffron Hill, between Clerkenwell Green and Smithfield. Saffron Hill, which spawned the Darby Sabini gang of Italians in the twentieth century, was already notorious for its brothels in the reign of James I. Smithfield itself had many dangerous streets: they included Shoe Lane and Field Lane, and the courts and alleys around them. The worst of these streets was Field Lane, which in 1816 was a well-known haunt of receivers and young thieves. In the 1830s Dickens made the area the scene of the activities of the Jewish gang leader and fence (dealer in stolen property) Fagin.

The notoriety of the area increased still further in the 1840s during the demolitions for the building of Farringdon Road. Two houses in West Street, which dated from the mid-seventeenth century, were found to contain 'dark closets, trap doors, sliding panels and means of escape'. The houses were opened to the public so they could see these clues to the area's long criminal history, and they attracted large crowds who presumably didn't know that they were in an area infested with real criminals. Thomas Beames regarded Saffron Hill as second only to St Giles as a criminal stronghold.[6]

The demolitions forced out many of the criminals: some of the 'lower class' went west to the courts around Gray's Inn Road and Baldwin's Gardens, but most went east to Clerkenwell, an area already infamous and later the power base of the Sabini gang. The Select Committee on Police in 1817 was told that part of St Luke's in Clerkenwell – Whitecross Street, Golden Lane, Bunhill Row and Grub Street – was 'the known resort of thieves and prostitutes'. 'If the magistrates were to refuse licences to all those houses against which they have had complaints, they would suppress at least half of those in Whitecross Street, Golden Lane, and the alleys leading out of them,' the committee heard.

The Whitecross Street area was particularly important to the underworld because it had been reinforced by refugees from the demolitions in St Giles and the Field Lane area, and had taken on the latter's role as a haunt of fences. By the beginning of the 1860s there were said to be forty 'leaving shops' (petty pawnbrokers and fences) in the two streets.

The rise in the value of the land from the 1860s drove the criminals northwards across Old Street. On Charles Booth's 1889 map of criminal areas the part of Clerkenwell with the most extensive black area – indicating the highest concentration of criminals – was that around Old Street and Goswell Road, but the shift to less valuable districts continued, at any rate as far as the poorer members of the criminal class were concerned. G A Duckworth was told in 1898 that the Old Street-Clerkenwell area was still a great receivers' centre – 'the melting pot of London', where practically all stolen silver and jewellery were fenced – and it still had black spots where pickpockets and housebreakers resided, but, the police told him, only the skilled criminals remained and the 'rough working class' had moved out. The rough working class and the lesser criminals who were indistinguishable from them had gone to Hoxton.

Hoxton was one of those places where the wild spirit of the eighteenth century seemed to survive longest. The Select Committee on Mendicity was told in 1814: 'The village of Haggerstone [part of Hoxton] is inhabited chiefly by brick-makers of the lowest class of society, and perhaps some of them of the very worst character; so much so, that no man or woman towards dark will walk across that way towards Hackney, though it might be somewhat nearer; and so bad, that if a thief was pursued and ran to Haggerstone, no constable or Runner would go beyond a certain line; it has been called the City of Refuge.'

In 1902 Charles Booth wrote: 'Hoxton is the leading criminal quarter of London, and indeed of all England[7].' By then it was used as the standard of comparison by police officers, much as St Giles had been earlier. In the early twentieth century the Hoxton Mob was one of the capital's more formidable gangs. The district, notorious also for the Nile Mob, a gang of pickpockets ['whizzers or dips'] will be mentioned again and again in this book.

Next we travel further east to the districts of Whitechapel and Spitalfields, for long known as criminal 'hot spots' on the map of the capital. The eighteenth-century burglar Jack Sheppard, hero of Gay's *The Beggars' Opera*, was born in Spitalfields, and the area had a long tradition of riotous dissent, particularly among the silk weavers of the eighteenth century. This area, with Hoxton, had criminal traditions that lasted well into the last century.

Nearby was the Nichol, the district called the Jago in Arthur Morrison's novel *A Child of the Jago*, which was published in 1896. It was bounded by High Street Shoreditch and Hackney Road on the north and Spitalfields to the south. Arthur Harding, a noted gangster of the early twentieth century, was born there in 1886.

In the mid-nineteenth century, before the rise of gangsters like Harding, the Nichol was known more for its crushing poverty and the rebellious spirit of its young than for crime. Thomas Archer, who wrote about the area in *The Pauper, the Thief and the Convict* in 1865, noticed the young men promenading in Club Row one Sunday afternoon, and pondered on their future. 'Shambling, tight-trousered, sleek-haired, artful but yet hulking youths of seventeen or eighteen,' their faces framed with side-whiskers known as 'Newgate Knockers', they sound like just the kind of cocky young men who give their elders anxiety in every generation. Archer thought that many of them, if not professional criminals, belonged to 'that dangerous class which is found occupying a position between pauper and convict' and were likely to prove a great social nuisance in the future. He felt they lacked the 'moral restraint' to starve or half-starve when there was no work. Some of them had experienced the workings of the Poor Law and tasted workhouse gruel, and were determined to have nothing more to do with it. As one of these untamed young men told Archer, they knew 'a trick worth two of that'.

This area shared with others the advantage of being just outside the City, with easy access to its plunder. Before 1829 thieves could slip over the border away from the City and escape the attentions of its better organised and more vigorous police. After the establishment of the Metropolitan Police in 1829 the process worked in reverse: thieves could slip into the City, where the police were not reformed until 1838–9, to escape the attentions of the new force.

Young thieves would be taught from childhood the quickest escape routes from the City to the safety of the nearest rookery.

It was this borderland just beyond the City limits, an arc from Bishopsgate round to Aldgate and beyond, which contained the most prominent criminal areas. Perhaps the most famous street in the area was Petticoat Lane, known to be the best place for disposing of stolen goods. 'If the King's crown were to come within half-a-mile of Petticoat Lane,' a thief boasted in 1835, 'money would be found in an hour for its purchase.' Ikey Solomons, the 'Prince of Fences', had a house in Bell Lane.[8]

Other streets noted for criminal activity were Brick Lane and Church Lane. Wentworth Street had the distinction in 1836 of having six consecutive houses, Nos. 102–107, which were all brothels. Mayhew said it ranked with St Giles as the worst places, 'both as regards filth and immorality'. Other notorious streets in the area were Essex Street, Church Street, Fashion Street, Flower and Dean Street, Thrawl Street, Lower Keate Street and George Yard.

In Wapping there was an area known as the Mint which was another Alsatia. In the mid-1720s law officers attempted to expel criminals who used it as a stronghold, but were driven off. One of them was ducked in a cesspit, and another frog-marched away with a turd in his mouth.

Our journey takes us south of the River Thames, to the Old Mint in Southwark, alongside the Borough High Street, notorious since Elizabethan times as an area exempt from City authority. Clearly the Act of 1623 and another in 1696 did not succeed in rooting out the criminals who mingled with the debtors who took refuge there, for another Act of 1722 declared that 'many evil-disposed and wicked Persons have ... unlawfully assembled and associated themselves in and about a certain place in the Parish of St George in the County of Surrey, commonly called or known by the name of Suffolk-Place, or the Mint, and have assured to themselves ... pretended Privileges altogether scandalous and unwarrantable, and have committed great Frauds and Abuses upon many of his Majesty's good Subjects, and by Force and Violence protected themselves, and their wicked Accomplices, against Law and Justice.'

The new Act laid down that debtors owing less than £50 could not

be arrested. Henry Mayhew and his colleague John Binney
described what happened when the Act came into force:

> The exodus of the refugee-felons and debtors, in July, 1723 . . .
> is described as having been like one of the Jewish tribes going
> out of Egypt, for the train of 'Minters' is said to have included
> some thousands in its ranks, and the road towards Guildford
> (whither they were journeying to be cleared at the Quarter
> Sessions of their debts and penalties) to have been positively
> covered with the cavalcades of caravans, carts, horsemen, and
> foot-travellers.[9]

Instead of going to Guildford some of the denizens of the Mint
went to Wapping and Stepney, where they soon became a problem.
Two years after the exodus from the Mint a further Act denounced
the 'evil-disposed and wicked Persons' who had gathered in the
'Hamlet of Wapping-Stepney, and Places adjacent in the County of
Middlesex' and who had committed 'great Violences and
Outrages'. It was made an offence, punishable by transportation to
the colonies, for any three people to assemble for protection against
the collection of debt.

Apart from the Mint there were the gin shops in Tooley Street, the
resorts of seamen and used for planning the spoliation of the port,
for many years the biggest criminal undertaking in the capital. An
inspiration to aspiring gangsters was the pub in Red Cross Street in
the Mint where the most ferocious and successful of all London's
gangsters, Jonathan Wild, had kept his horses and drank with his
cronies before he was hanged in 1725. Like football fans, young
thieves still drank there to his memory.

The persistence of criminality in the Mint long after the amnesty
of 1722 is an example of the difficulty of erasing these areas, other
than by demolition. In 1861 Hollingshead wrote that 'no speculator
has been bold enough to grapple with the back streets – the human
warrens – on the south side of the metropolis; to start from
Bermondsey, on the borders of Deptford, and wriggle through the
existing miles of dirt, vice and crime as far as the Lambeth
Marshes.' He said scores of streets were 'filled with nothing but

thieves, brown, unwholesome tramps' lodging houses and smoky receptacles for stolen goods'.

Things had not improved when Booth wrote in *Life and Labour of the People in London* about the area in 1891, finding nests of courts and alleys around St George's Church 'still harbouring an appalling amount of destitution not unmixed with crime' even though the Marshalsea Road had been cut through the Mint. He said the Mint still contained 'a very large amount of poverty and lawlessness, particularly in the many common lodging-houses'. Ten years later, visiting the area again, Booth 'brought away the same black picture, the same depression of soul'.

Bermondsey was the location of Jacob's Island, a riverside district east of St Saviour's Dock. It was here that the burglar Bill Sikes died in *Oliver Twist*, and Dickens described it as 'the filthiest, the strangest, the most extraordinary of the many localities that are hidden in London, wholly unknown, even by name, to the great mass of its inhabitants'. An official report of 1843 on the death of a woman in Bermondsey conveys the full horror of conditions in the rookeries. She lived with her husband and son in a room without furniture, not even a bed:

> She lay dead beside her son upon a heap of feathers which were scattered over her almost naked body, there being neither sheet nor coverlet. The feathers stuck so fast over the whole body that the physician could not examine the corpse until it was cleansed, and then found it starved and scarred from the bites of vermin. Part of the floor of the room was torn up, and the hole used by the family as a privy.

Finally worth mentioning in this survey of the major criminal haunts of the capital is the Lisson Grove area of Marylebone, a late-comer to the list. A policeman told W A Miles in the 1830s: 'Lisson Grove is the haunt of thieves ... The worst and of all sorts, were about Lisson Grove; but they spread themselves over London by day, in order to work (i.e. thieve). The neighbourhood is swarming with youth of both sexes, from eight to twenty years of age – all thieves. He thinks they fence the property in the Grove.'

There were many lesser criminal strongholds. The map of criminal haunts in the eighteenth century would show, besides the major sanctuaries, trouble spots in Holborn including Shoe and Fetter Lanes, and parts of Barbican and Bankside. The law-abiding would avoid Chick Lane in Clerkenwell, Thieving Lane near Westminster Abbey and Petty France in Westminster. 'The riverside area from St Catherine's to Limehouse was widely considered a "no-go" area.'

The map of the underworld changes with the destruction of the old rookeries. Those of St Giles and Clerkenwell, 'ancient citadels of vice and crime', were partly obliterated in the 1840s and 1850s with the building of New Oxford Street, Queen Victoria Street and Farringdon Road. Victoria Street penetrated the Pye Street rookery in the shadow of Westminster Abbey in the 1850s, and Commercial Street was cut through Whitechapel and Spitalfields. The ruthless destruction gathered pace later in the century with Shaftesbury Avenue, Charing Cross Road, Clerkenwell Road and Holborn Viaduct being driven through working-class areas. Between 1830 and 1880 an estimated 100,000 people were evicted by the new roads. The Nichol went in the late nineteenth-century slum clearances. In the 1890s it was replaced by the Boundary Street Estate, the first of the London County Council developments.

In Holborn and the Strand about 6,000 tenants from thirty filthy courts and alleys between Bell Yard and Clement's Lane were evicted in the late 1860s to make way for the Law Courts, and thousands more were cleared out for the construction of Holborn Viaduct. Where did the poor who lived in these areas go? Superintendent G W Cornish of Scotland Yard believed the crimes associated with these areas were dispersed across London, but mostly the poor crowded into neighbouring areas such as Spitalfields, making conditions there even worse. Church Lane, one of the streets that survived the building of New Oxford Street through northern St Giles in 1844–7, was invaded by refugees from the demolished slums. The 28 houses in Church Lane had a population of 655 in 1841: by 1847 it had risen to 1,095. These ousted Holy Landers were soon reinforced by a flood of Irish refugees fleeing famine in their homeland.

Slum clearance was inevitable, given the urgent need for new roads, railways and docks, but it was also seen as a cheap and easy method of getting rid of 'congregations of vice and misery'. It suited the authorities, and it suited the developers, who found slum land relatively cheap and slum dwellers easy to get rid of.

Schools of Vice

Dickens's description of Fagin's school for young thieves in *Oliver Twist* touched a nerve. There had long been fears that similar 'schools of vice' really existed, and the startling increase in the number of juvenile criminals, starting in the Regency period and continuing into the Victorian, seemed to bear this out. In 1816, 514 prisoners under the age of twenty were committed to Newgate, of whom 284 were under seventeen and 51 under fourteen. One was nine years old. The figures from the prison hulks were even more depressing. The Superintendent of the Hulks [dilapidated warships used as prisons] reported in 1828 that of the 300 boys in the *Euryalis* – they were all aged sixteen or less and had been sentenced to transportation or had a sentence of death commuted to transportation – two were eight years old, five were nine years old and 171 were under the age of fourteen.

Henry Grey Bennet, MP, chairman of the 1816 select committee on the police, who reported the Newgate figures quoted above, said there were 'above 6,000 boys and girls living solely on the town by thieving, or as the companions and associates of thieves'. He pointed out that he had heard much higher figures quoted. Most of these children were hardened criminals, and although many were almost certain to be hanged or transported for life the camaraderie of the streets and the rough glamour of their calling kept them at it. Dying on the scaffold might crown a life of hardship, especially if one's friends were there to see one die in stolen finery, defiant to the end.

The camaraderie of the oppressed was something that Oliver Twist experienced when he was taken to Fagin's house in the Field Lane rookery. Instead of the cruelty and hostility of the workhouse, he found, for the first time, ample food and cheerful companions. Fagin taught the boys to pick pockets, and was on the whole a genial master. In real life the trainers of young thieves were seldom so amiable. In the winter of 1850–1 a constable who watched through a window of a lodging house as a man taught children to steal handkerchiefs from a coat saw two of them 'knocked down and kicked for not having exhibited the requisite amount of tact and ingenuity'.

S P Day wrote in 1858 of 'several establishments throughout the metropolis ... herein the novice is initiated into his future art, and practised daily in sleight-of-hand exercises ... '[1]

In a sense a boy would be lucky to get into one of these schools, as there were far more young criminals than the market could absorb. The brighter and more skilful ones would be chosen, and if they became expert they would be valuable assets, so much so that their adult mentors would lavish money on them for food and drink and a woman.

If they were lucky and particularly skilful they might become members of the Swell Mob, the elite of street pickpockets. In *Oliver Twist* Fagin believed the Artful Dodger had the qualities to become such a 'great man', perhaps even to aspire to furnished rooms in Camden Town 'with a smart dolly to share them'.

The swell mobsman dressed well and could steal as much as twenty or thirty pounds in a good afternoon. Not for him the filthy flash house in some slum court, full of those who had failed to make it on the streets.

Boys were sometimes members of the gangs which carried out the more aggressive forms of pickpocketing. In 1839 the Committee on the Constabulary Force heard of the methods of the Swell Mob when they had chosen a victim:

Two go before their man, the others close up behind; their victim is hemmed in, a push takes place, he is jostled and hustled about, the thieves cry out to those behind not to press so, the press is increased; the victim being surrounded, his pockets are presently turned inside out. No time is lost; if he does not readily raise his hands, but keeps them in his pockets, or at his side, to guard his property, his hat gets a tip behind, perhaps it is knocked over his eyes. To right his hat he raises his arms, nor does he get them down again till eased of everything in his possession. His fob and vest pockets are emptied by the thief standing beside him...the trouser pockets and coat-pockets are emptied by those behind.

The pickpockets divided the capital into areas which were allocated to particular gangs. A witness told of the youngsters forming groups to work these areas, one group by day and the other by night. The whole group would meet to divide the spoils, and one boy claimed that on one occasion these amounted to £400.

Mayhew described a lodging house in Whitechapel's Cat-and-Wheel Alley (later Commercial Street) run by a one-legged Welshman known as Taff. He was the organiser of a gang of child thieves. 'Taff was a notorious receiver of stolen goods,' said one of his lodgers. 'I knew two little boys who brought home six pairs of new Wellington boots, which this miscreant bought at 1s. a pair; and, when they had no luck, he would take the strap off his wooden leg, and beat them through the nakedness of their rags.'[2]

Most experts agreed that 'flash houses' were responsible for much juvenile crime. They were low lodging-houses or brothels, perhaps associated with public houses, where boys mixed with mature thieves and prostitutes, and girls of their own age, who were often their mistresses. A nine-year-old boy named Burnet, who had a long criminal record and had been sentenced to hang but reprieved, had a mistress aged thirteen. Some of the flash houses were exclusively for the young. In one of them, in St Giles, according to the reformer William Crawford '...four hundred beds are made up every night; a boy who was in the habit of visiting this house confessed that he had slept there upwards of thirty times with girls of his own age, and he particularly named five: this boy was fourteen years of age, the girls were to be met with at the flash houses to which he resorted.'[3]

Older criminals would be on the look-out for promising recruits. Thomas Vance, a magistrate whose district included Bermondsey, Brixton, Tooting and Vauxhall, told the select parliamentary committee on the police that in his district...

> There are a number of designing thieves constantly on the look-out for children, who are naturally more inclined to be idle than to work, and who commence with petty thefts at the wharfs, and other places where property is exposed; these the confirmed thieves seize hold of, and make them the catspaw in doing those things which they otherwise would do themselves, and for which they would probably suffer detection and punishment, hoping that, in consideration of their youth, commiseration may be excited in the breasts of the Magistrates, and that they [the children] may be dismissed.

Another witness said that children were often 'trained up' to steal by 'relatives and connexions'. Other children got their first lessons in crime in prison, where they were not segregated from older prisoners, who made it their business to systematically corrupt them, no matter how young. Philip Holdsworth, the Marshall of London, who was responsible for the policing of the City, told the committee that there was no doubt that children were 'trained by thieves who are adepts'. Many of them were as young as six.

The promiscuity of the young criminals was shocking. A former Newgate prisoner, Gibbon Wakefield, wrote that most boys there who were over twelve years old, and some even younger, had mistresses who visited them in prison by pretending to be their sisters.[4] In 1836 the Prison Inspectors for the Home District said that some of the girls were only twelve or thirteen years old. Sixteen years later the select committee on juvenile offenders heard that many young criminals lived with prostitutes, and that they had been known to have venereal diseases at the age of twelve. This sexual precocity was noted by Henry Mayhew, who remarked of the street children 'their most remarkable characteristic...is their extraordinary licentiousness'. This led him to think that the onset of puberty came much earlier than was commonly believed. Couples as young as thirteen could live openly together in respectable working-class districts and have children.

The 1816 committee was told of brothels especially for children. The prostitutes were mainly under fourteen, and some only eleven or twelve. The customers were also youngsters. Another witness named a girl then aged sixteen who had been working as a prostitute in her father's brothel for the past five or six years. In 1852 a London judge told a Select Committee about girls aged fourteen or fifteen who could not remember when they first had intercourse.

The promiscuity of the lodging houses was shocking to the Victorians, with their pronounced attitudes to female modesty. The beds were verminous and inmates of both sexes often lay on them entirely naked. A girl recalled: 'There were very wicked carryings on. The boys, if any difference, was the worst. We lay packed on a full night, a dozen boys and girls squeedged into one bed...I can't go into all the particulars, but whatever could take place in words or acts between boys and girls did take place, and in the midst of the others ... Some boys and girls slept without any clothes, and would dance about the room in that way. I have seen them and, wicked as I was, I felt ashamed...'[5]

The 1816 committee heard remarkable stories of the careers of young criminals, too often cut short by the gallows or by transportation. Grey Bennet told of a young Irish boy named Leary, a gang leader described by the chaplain of Newgate as 'an extraordinary boy'. Grey Bennet was obviously struck by the boy's manner. He was about thirteen years old, 'good-looking, sharp and intelligent, and possessing a manner which seemed to indicate a character very different from what he really professed'. Bennet saw him in Newgate when he was under sentence of death for stealing a watch, chain and seals.

He had been five years in the practice of delinquency, progressing from stealing an apple off a stall to housebreaking and highway robbery. He belonged to the Moorfields Catholic School, and there became acquainted with one Ryan in that school, by whom he was first instructed in the various arts and practices of delinquency; his first attempts were at tarts, apples etc., then at loaves in bakers' baskets, then at parcels of halfpence on shop counters, and money-tills in shops; then to breaking shop windows and drawing out valuable articles through the aperture; picking pockets, housebreaking etc. etc.; and Leary has often gone to school the next day with several pounds in his pockets as his share of the produce of the previous day's robberies; he soon became captain of a gang, generally known since as Leary's gang, with five boys, and some times more, furnished with pistols, taking a horse and cart with them; and if they had an opportunity in their road, they cut off the trunks from gentlemen's carriages... He has been concerned in various robberies in London and its vicinity; and has had property at one time amounting to £350; but when he had money he either got robbed of it by elder thieves who knew he had so much about him, or lost it by gambling at flash houses, or spent it among loose characters of both sexes. After committing innumerable depredations, he was detected at Mr Derrimore's at Kentish Town, stealing some plate from that gentleman's dining-room, when several other similar robberies coming against him in that neighbourhood, he was, in compassion to his youth, placed in the Philanthropic [a home run by the Philanthropic Institution]; but being now charged with Mr Princep's robbery, he was taken out therefrom, tried, convicted and sentenced to death, but was afterwards respited and returned to the Philanthropic. He is little and well-looking; has robbed to the amount of £3,000 during his five years career.

Leary had been in and out of every prison in London, including Newgate two or three times. Finally he was transported for life. While he was in Newgate he refused to attend the school set up by the chaplain, preferring the company of the older criminals.

Grey Bennet insisted that something had to be done to suppress the flash houses. Although some police officers had denied that they even existed, and others said that they should not be closed down because they were useful sources of information, Bennet responded:

I say then, that there are above two hundred regular flash houses in the metropolis, all known to the police officers, which they frequent, many of them open all night; that the landlords in numerous instances receive stolen goods, and are what are technically called fences; that this fact is known also to the officers, who, for obvious reasons, connive at the existence of these houses; that many of the houses are frequented by boys and girls of the ages of ten to fourteen and fifteen, who are exclusively admitted, who pass the night in gambling and debauchery, and who there sell and divide the plunder of the day, or who sally forth from these houses to rob in the streets.

Bennet went on to accuse the police of taking bribes for keeping the activities of the flash houses secret from the magistrates, and to name some of the more notorious houses. There was the Black Horse in Tottenham Court Road, frequented by thieves such as Huffey White and Conkey Beau. The landlord, Blackman, 'has been considered a thief for fifteen years...there is not a regular flash house in London that is not known to the officers of the police, from the Rose in Rose Street, Long Acre, kept by Kelly, which he kept long with impunity, to the Bear, opposite to Bow-Street office, the infamous character of which is notorious, and which unites the trades of brothel and public-house.'

The flash houses were central to the whole criminal enterprise. Criminals used them to eat and sleep, to plan robberies, to exchange information, to recruit new gang members, and to dispose of or acquire stolen goods. These lodging houses abounded all over the country, but were particularly numerous and scandalous in London. In 1851 the Common Lodging House Act was passed in an attempt to control them. Police were given powers to inspect and close them if they failed to reach an elementary standard of decency and cleanliness. Hundreds were closed, and in the remainder put their prices up to meet the costs of the new standards. Some of the poor were thus made homeless because they could not afford to pay.

The connection between public houses and crime, particularly prostitution, was obvious, and some morals campaigners fought a

Gallows humour: broadsheets like this were sold at Jonathan Wild's execution. Wild had gloated at the executions of many of his victims, some of them his own gang members.

Jack Sheppard in his specially designed handcuffs and leg-irons. His daring escapes gave heart to the oppressed and made him a hero of the underclass for many years after his death.

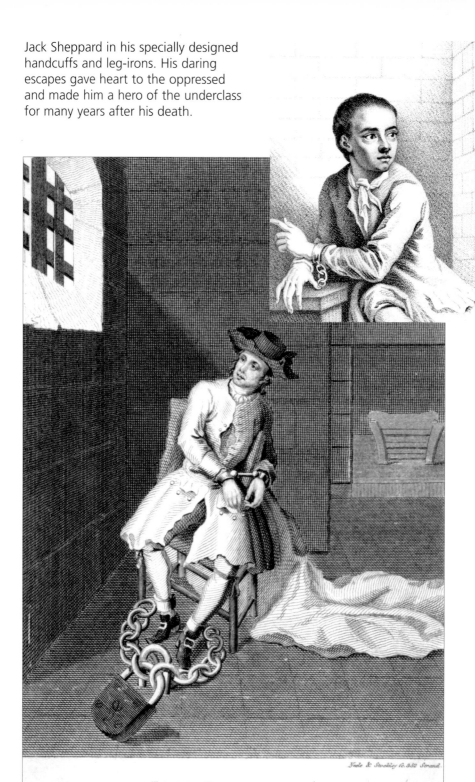

Neele & Stockley 6. 352 Strand.

JACK SHEPPARD.

in Special Irons.

Above: The decrepit men of the Marylebone Watch House get ready to go out on patrol. They were known as 'Charleys' and were the butt of much crude humour.

Below: The confused hurly-burly as prisoners are examined by magistrates at Bow Street. The famous Bow Street Runners, the police force founded by the Fieldings, were based here.

Above: Condemned prisoners pray round a coffin in the chapel of Newgate Prison. Some prisoners were likely to be drunk or defiant. The preacher is the hated ordinary, or chaplain.

Right: Hard labour in the Water Engine Court at Coldbath Fields Prison. Two cringing men prepare to take the place of two who have finished their task. Much prison labour was meant to be meaningless.

Above: The pillory at Charing Cross. The fate of the prisoners was in the hands of the crowd. Some were pelted with stones and died: Daniel Defoe was showered with flowers.

Below: The mob get in the mood for an execution outside Newgate in 1848. The behaviour of the crowd shocked Dickens, and such scenes led to executions being carried out inside prisons.

Poverty and escape: the apathetic slum
dwellers of Orange Court, Drury Lane (*left*),
take the air in an airless alley while addicts
(*above*) smoke opium in a den in Bluegate
Fields, Shadwell. This may have been the
den visited by Dickens and mentioned in
Edwin Drood.

Opposite page: Darkest England,
as seen by Gustave Doré. Dudley
Street, Seven Dials, was an area
notorious from the seventeenth
century onwards for strident vice,
poverty and overcrowding.

Young thieves and their girls gambling in a 'flash house'. The girls are probably prostitutes – the promiscuity of young boys and girls shocked Victorian commentators, including Henry Mayhew.

determined but losing battle to close down the worst examples. They were up against powerful vested interests, particularly the brewers, who were making a fortune from the most disreputable of the public houses.

The parish of Shadwell in Stepney was the scene of a lengthy struggle between the parish trustees and corrupt officials, particularly a crooked brothel keeper and local government grandee named Joseph Merceron. In 1819 the *First Report from the Committee on the State of the Police of The Metropolis* told how the area had become plagued by prostitutes who used 'the superabundance of public houses' in the area. The report stated:

> ... some of them for a long time past have been the constant resort of the most abandoned and profligate women; and being in a situation affording a peculiar convenience for their evil practices, and purposely fitted for their accommodation, they have occasioned the increase of the worst kind of houses of ill-fame, the inhabitants whereof bid defiance to all decency and restraint. The prostitutes and procuresses filled the streets both night and day; and the parishioners have been thereby deprived of the trade; for those public houses, being situated in the High Street, it was impossible for respectable persons to approach the shops without having their eyes and ears offended by scenes and language the most awful and disgusting ... the parish appeared as if it were doomed to be the receptacle of all the profligates of the neighbourhood.

The exasperated residents complained to the parish trustees and the magistrates. They claimed their servants and sons were constantly exposed to seduction, 'and too often became a prey to the wretched beings with whom they were continually surrounded'. Constables and the Watch were bribed to look the other way. The parish trustees set up their own patrols and found a deplorable state of affairs. Dance halls attached to the public houses were being used by prostitutes to pick up clients and take them to nearby brothels, in some cases also owned by the pub landlords.

The trustees applied to the licensing magistrates to have the

licences of the pubs suspended. Their petition was accepted with
great reluctance, but the licences were suspended pending an appeal
by the publicans. The Committee on the State of the Police reveals
the network of corruption which the parish trustees were up against:
'The most notorious of these houses was the Duke of York, kept by
— Hennekey, but supplied with porter by Messrs Meux and Co.
who had lent a large sum of money upon the house, and which was
producing an immense return, the draught of beer and spirits being
enormous.' In the interval before the hearing Meux and Co. did
everything they could to get the petition thrown out. In the forefront
of this campaign was the corrupt local magnate, Merceron, himself
one of the licensing magistrates. The result, says the report on the
police, was that the local publicans, particularly Hennekey of the
Duke of York, 'not only continued their indecent practices, but with
the greatest impudence...defied and threatened the parish officers,
insulting them in the public streets and daring them to do their
worst'.

The magistrates' panel which heard the appeal was made up of
the chairman, Sir Daniel William, Merceron, two clergymen, Messrs
Robson and Thirlwall, and others. The leader of the parochial
trustees was Joseph Fletcher, a local shipowner and churchwarden.
Fletcher told how he and the parish officers had gone to the Paviors
Arms, and found it filled with 'the lowest class of prostitutes and
lascars...drinking, half-naked, and both men and women sitting in
indecent and improper postures, and using very dreadful
language...' While he gave evidence he was heckled by Merceron
and the clergyman Robson. He went on to describe the situation in
the Duke of York and the White Hart, which were full of prostitutes
and sailors dancing. Robson interrupted to say that dancing among
sailors and girls 'could not be considered as an evil', and Fletcher
felt obliged to go into more detail. He said he 'did not hesitate to say
what was awfully true, that from one to three hundred women of the
town were constantly assembled in these rooms, which were the
high exchange of prostitution, where every indecency and obscenity
were carried to the greatest pitch; that the procuresses and their girls
walked the streets in open day, to the annoyance and terror of the
inhabitants, that they decoyed men and boys into these houses,

where they were plied with liquor, and assailed with women and music, and the floor was constantly occupied with their dancing in the most libidinous manner; that amongst these scenes of riot and debauchery, the bargain was made with the procuresses, and the price of prostitution paid, while the immediate communication with the brothel afforded an easy transition to complete the ruin of those who had been so unfortunately betrayed . . . '

Despite the powerful advocacy of Merceron and his friends the licences of the three public houses were withdrawn for the coming year. The brewers then began a campaign to get the licences back. They pointed out that they had lent Hennekey a large sum, and now stood to lose it. They asked for a certificate of approval from the parish officers – a prerequisite for getting a licence from a magistrate. This was refused. A director of the brewers, a Mr Lucas, then approached the parish churchwardens and said that justice had been done and there was no reason for his company to lose its money. When the churchwardens pointed out 'the extreme indecency of his request' Mr Lucas indignantly asserted that 'such houses were necessary in all seaports, and were always winked at by the magistrates'. Eventually the brewers produced another publican, apparently a man of good character named Birks, who promised to clean up the place, and he was granted a licence for the King's Arms. Within a short while the King's Arms was even worse than the Duke of York, with prostitutes flaunting themselves there.

So the struggle went on. At one time the parish consulted the Attorney-General to see whether they could bring a criminal action against the magistrates. He ruled that there was nothing to suggest that they had acted corruptly, although they might have acted against the public interest. Yet there undoubtedly was corruption in the granting of licences. It is interesting that the clergyman Robson put forward the same justification for the brothel-pubs as the police did for keeping the flash houses: prostitution and crime were inevitable, and it was better to have them where they could be controlled than spread across the streets of the capital.

Garotters and Dragsmen

Picking pockets was for many the first step to a life of crime. Young men quickly graduated to other forms of thieving, partly because they soon lost the dexterity and speed required to be a successful pickpocket. Even the members of the Swell Mob could not expect their skills to last into middle age. There were many other forms of street stealing, however, most of which required little skill. One of them, almost exclusive to women, was stealing from children, the despised 'kinchin lay'. Here is Fagin explaining it in *Oliver Twist*:

> The kinchins, my dear, is the young children that's sent on errands by their mothers, with sixpences and shillings; and the lay is just to take their money away – they've always got it ready in their hands – then knock them into the kennel [gutter] and walk off very slow as if there's nothing else the matter but a child fallen down and hurt itself.

There were many variants. Some thieves specialised in stealing packets from little shop messengers – milliners' apprentices with parcels of expensive silk were a favourite target. Then there was 'skinning', luring children to some quiet spot where they could be stripped of their clothes and shoes. This 'lay' produced its best results in the winter, when the children would be wearing extra clothes.

The *Household Narrative* reported that about Christmas 1850 a woman named Susan Nunn of St George's-in-the-East, 'a showily dressed young woman of thirty', was arrested for working the skinning lay. 'A swarm of little boys and girls, estimated by the gaoler to be nearly fifty in number', turned up with their parents and identified her as the woman who had taken their clothes. She was sent to the Old Bailey for trial.

Opportunistic thieves might go in for what Mayhew's collaborator Binney called 'area diving', also called area-sneaking. This involved sneaking down into basement areas or up to back doors in the suburbs, trying the door handles and snatching anything of value before fleeing.

Apart from the kinchin lay, one of the few forms of thieving that suited women was shoplifting. The voluminous clothes fashionable in the Victorian era were ideal for concealing many stolen goods. The full, heavily petticoated bell-shaped skirts reaching to the ankles could conceal a large pouch, extending all round the body.

Round large railway stations and the roads leading from them lurked the 'dragsmen', thieves who specialised in stealing luggage from cabs. The dragsmen would follow the cab in a light cart and slash the ropes and straps holding the luggage, which would fall into the road and be spirited away.

Although by Victorian times violent robbery was dying out there were still criminals who found it easier to knock a man down and rob him than learn a more skilful lay. These thugs, the Victorian equivalent of the old footpads, were called 'rampsmen'. Their crime was known as 'propping' or 'swinging the stick'. A variation was called 'bearing up'. A woman would pick up a victim, preferably tipsy, in a pub or in the street and take him to a dark alley. Her accomplice would then confront him in the role of an outraged husband. The confused and frightened dupe would usually be more than glad to buy him off.

A more dramatic form of street robbery caught the public imagination in the early 1860s, particularly among a newspaper readership which had recently been reading about thuggee crimes in India. This was the outbreak of garotting, all the more terrifying because of the swiftness and silence of the robbers. It had probably started more or less unnoticed in east London and after being perfected there was used in the west, where it became news.

Speed and silence were the essence of the crime. This lay was worked by teams of at least three – two to rob the victim and a third, perhaps a woman, to act as look-out. The garotter would attack the victim from behind using a rope, cloth, stick or just his powerful arm around the throat to half-strangle him and pull his head back. His accomplice then used a cosh to batter him into submission and rob him. It was all over in seconds.

In July 1862 an MP named Pilkington was garotted and robbed as he walked from Parliament to his club in Pall Mall. There were five policemen on their beats nearby but the silent and savage garotting raised no alarm. That same night Edward Hawkins, a distinguished antiquary who was in his eighties, was attacked between St James's and Bond Street.

Winter was approaching with its long foggy nights and alarm grew. Soon the attacks claimed their first fatalities. In November a woman described as 'respectable-looking' stopped a jeweller in the street, and her hidden companions then garotted him. His throat was crushed, and he died several days later. In another attack the victim, a gunsmith, had his hand so badly mangled it had to be amputated and he too died.

Anti-garotting societies were set up and soon no suspicious-looking character wearing a loose scarf was safe from being dragged to a police station and denounced. The press as usual played its part in fanning the flames. Finally, early in December 1862, the *Weekly Dispatch*, which had not been blameless, wrote: 'The manner in which anti-garotters proceed along the streets at night, clanking their sword canes and ready to draw at a moment's notice, is calculated to strike terror into the breasts of others as well as those of the great enemy.'

More people were hanged in 1863 than in any year since the end of the Bloody Code. In July 1863 legislation known as the 'garotting Act' was passed. Offenders could be flogged, with the punishment inflicted in instalments to allow the men to recover between floggings, which made it more terrifying. Men were known to collapse in the dock when the sentence was passed. The attacks died out as suddenly and mysteriously as they had begun.

The Greatest Train Robbery

If the Great Train Robbery of 1963 seemed to set new standards for organisation and ingenuity in the twentieth century, another sensational train robbery just over a century before was, if anything, even more professional and audacious. It also drew together a wildly improbable cast of characters, including a successful barrister who was a secret criminal mastermind, a burglar of rare resource who was also a businessman, and there was even a bit part – although he was on the side of the angels – for one of the entrepreneurs of the age.

In 1855 thieves stole a quarter of a ton of gold bullion from the London to Folkestone express. What was known as The Great Bullion Robbery or The Great Train Robbery was an intriguing mystery which thrilled the readers of mid-century newspapers: how had the thieves opened the safe containing the gold without damaging it? How had they spirited the gold away, leaving the safe weighing exactly as much as when it was full of bullion? How had they vanished without trace?[1]

Edward Agar was ostensibly a successful businessman in 1853 when he returned to England after ten years in Australia and America. Apart from other investments he had £3,000 in consols (government securities). He lived with a young mistress in Cambridge Villas, Shepherd's Bush, indistinguishable from the other successful professional men in this fashionable area. He had indeed a profession, and he was successful. Agar was a burglar, and he was about to embark on the crime of the century. To help he recruited Jem Saward, a successful Queen's Bench defence counsel known to his clients as 'Barrister Saward'. Secretly he was also a desperate gambler who had been a professional criminal for nearly forty years.

Saward, who was in his late fifties, was the notorious forger Jem the Penman, who used his contacts in the underworld to acquire stolen cheques and then forge them for large sums. He would be the fence for the stolen gold.

Another of the gang was William Pierce, who had been employed by the South-eastern Railway until his superiors learned that he was a gambler. After his dismissal he worked as a clerk in a betting office in Covent Garden. It was through their shared interest in gambling that he and Saward met.

Through his contacts in the railway industry Pierce heard of gold shipments to Paris by London bullion dealers. It was suggested that shipments of gold, weighing perhaps several hundredweight at a time, were being sent to the Bank of France.

Pierce alerted Agar, and over a long period they painstakingly built up a picture of the shipments: the coins and gold ingots were packed into metal-bound bullion merchants' chests, sealed with the merchants' wax stamps, and packed into one of the latest Chubb safes, which was then locked. There were two locks on the safe, and the two keys were held by two different officials. The safes were then loaded on to the guard's van of the South-eastern's Folkestone express. At Folkestone there were also two keys, one held by the railways superintendent, the other locked in a cupboard in an office on the harbour pier. When the train reached Folkestone the safe would be taken out and opened, and the bullion chests weighed to check that the weight was exactly the same as when they left London.

The bullion chests were then loaded on to a paddle steamer bound for Boulogne. When they arrived they were again weighed, and taken by train to Paris.

At first Agar felt that the robbery was beyond them. 'I said I believed it would be impossible to do,' he said. The safes could not be broken into, and he could see no way to get hold of the two keys so that he could make copies.

It was his young mistress, Fanny Kay, who proved the catalyst. She had been a barmaid at Tonbridge station in Kent, and knew various employees of the South-eastern. Among them was James Burgess, a guard on trains from London to Folkestone, who despite his respectability and caution would be drawn into the conspiracy by Pierce.

The last of the conspirators was William Tester, a well-educated young man with a monocle who seemed destined for higher things. He was assistant to the superintendent in the traffic department at London Bridge. It is not clear why he joined the plot, but he became a vital member.

Against this team was the South-eastern under its new secretary Samuel Smiles, who would one day write those bibles of the Victorian work ethic *Self-Help* and *Duty*. He had a degree in medicine and had been a radical journalist. With him at the helm the company seemed a formidable opponent.

Agar, who had come round to the idea that the robbery was not impossible after all, now set about getting hold of the two safe keys so that he could make wax impressions of them. In the spring of 1854 he went to Folkestone to study the procedure for opening the safe when it arrived on the express. He discovered that sometimes the safe contained not bullion but packets of other goods for delivery locally in Folkestone. On these occasions the safe might be locked with only one key: the other, held by the superintendent of the railway, would not be needed.

But for all their patient intelligence-gathering the gang were no nearer their goal of getting their hands on the keys. Then they had an extraordinary piece of luck. One of the keys at Folkestone was lost, and the safes were sent back to Chubbs to have new locks and new keys. William Tester was given the job of liaising with Chubbs.

When the safes and keys were ready Chubbs notified Tester. Agar hired a room at a public house in Tooley Street, near London Bridge station, and Tester brought him the keys. Agar pressed them into tins of wax and returned them. The whole thing had taken a matter of minutes.

The keys were returned to London Bridge station and handed over to the two officials whose job it was to guard them. Only then did Agar realise that Tester, instead of bringing him two different keys had brought him two copies of the same one.

They were almost back where they had started, but Agar refused to give up. Once more he turned his attention to Folkestone. He took a room at the Royal Pavilion Hotel overlooking the pier where he knew a copy of the second key was kept in a locked cupboard in the railway office. He already knew from his previous observations that although staff were supposed to man the office at all times, they sometimes left it locked but empty for about ten minutes while they met the ferry.

Agar waited until the staff were out and made an impression of the lock on the main office door. With this he made a key. Next he sent himself a parcel by the South-Eastern Railway to be collected at Folkestone. When it arrived, he went to the office on the pier to collect it.

John Chapman, the railway official in charge of the office, opened a wall cupboard with a key he kept in his pocket. From the cupboard he took the all-important safe key, and went out to open the safe, leaving the cupboard key in the lock. While he was away, Agar took an impression of the cupboard key.

Agar returned to London, made a copy of the cupboard key and contacted Pierce. Some weeks later they went to Folkestone. This time Pierce, dressed in a railway uniform, entered the railway office while the staff were out meeting the ferry and got the safe key from the cupboard and took it to the waiting Agar, who made impressions from it. By the time the staff returned the key was back in the locked cupboard.

Agar knew that keys made from wax impressions would not be precise enough to open the Chubb locks. He needed to be alone with the safes so that he could try them out and gradually refine them until they fitted. To do this he travelled in the guard's van when the safe was empty and Burgess was the guard.

In May 1855 the gang were ready. On the 15th, while Agar watched, Burgess walked on to the forecourt of London Bridge station and gave a prearranged signal: it meant that the train was carrying bullion that night.

Agar and Pierce bought tickets for Dover, and Pierce got into a first-class carriage. While their luggage was being loaded into the guard's van Agar strolled along the platform. Burgess walked along the length of the train, ringing a handbell. At the last moment, as the train was about to depart, Agar joined him in the guard's van.

When the train pulled out of London Bridge heading for its first stop, Redhill in Surrey, Agar opened his luggage, which consisted of leather courier bags and carpet bags loaded with lead shot, a set of scales, and tools to open the bullion boxes. He used his keys to open the safe, removed the first of three bullion boxes and replaced the gold ingots with an equal weight of lead shot. Finally he replaced the bullion merchants' wax seals with seals he had made up himself, reasoning correctly that they would pass muster in the dark on the quay at Folkestone.

When the train pulled into Redhill, Tester was waiting. A bag full of gold bars was passed to him, and he vanished into the night. Pierce left the first-class carriage and joined Agar and Burgess in the guard's van. The first stage of the robbery had gone without a hitch.

The train pulled out of the station, heading for Tonbridge in Kent, and Agar opened the other two bullion chests. One contained hundreds of American gold coins called Eagles, which could easily be exchanged for cash. The third chest contained yet more gold ingots.

The robbers had a problem. They hadn't reckoned on finding so much gold, and hadn't brought enough lead shot. Pierce wanted to take all the gold, but Agar told him that the boxes would be weighed at Folkestone before they had time to make a getaway. So reluctantly they left what gold they could not replace with lead shot.

At Folkestone Agar and Pierce left the guard's van and sat in a first-class carriage. When the train reached Dover they alighted and went back to the guard's van to collect their luggage. Weighed down by almost a hundredweight of gold each, they went to the Dover Castle Hotel and had supper. Then they caught the train to London.

The following day they cashed some of the Eagles. Pierce got just over £200 for two hundred of the gold coins. Some idea of the value of the haul can be gained from the fact that this was enough to buy a suburban villa.

When the bullion boxes arrived in Boulogne some officials noticed that one of them was damaged, but after being weighed they were sent on their way to Paris. There they were opened at last and the lead shot discovered.

The bullion merchants now demanded compensation. The South-eastern refused, claiming the robbery had taken place in France. The French company *Chemins de Fer du Nord* denied this. The redoubtable Samuel Smiles and the other directors of the South-eastern would not budge and there, for a year, the matter rested. Scotland Yard's detectives had no leads to go on.

Agar and Pierce melted down the gold bullion in a furnace they built into a bedroom fireplace in Agar's house at Cambridge Villas. They were courting disaster because of the very high temperatures involved. Once a mould broke as Agar was lifting it and the molten gold set fire to the floorboards, leaving a charred area in front of the fire. Meanwhile Agar was selling the gold through Saward and splitting it equally with the others. Pierce leased a betting office, claiming that he could afford it because he had won a large sum on a horse.

Burgess, who liked to speculate in bonds, bought Turkish bonds because the Crimean war between England and France on one side and Russia on the other seemed to be going well for the allies. Tester and Pierce also bought bonds, and the latter also went into property.

Agar's mistress Fanny, later said in the Central Criminal Court to have 'fallen from the position a virtuous woman always occupies in this country' had become an embarrassment. She was brought home drunk in a wheelbarrow, and soon the couple parted despite having a child, Agar moving out of Cambridge Villas. He met a nineteen-year-old named Emily Campbell, one of the girls run by a pimp named William Humphreys. Agar had been introduced to Humphreys by Pierce. Humphreys took the girl's defection badly, and succeeded in framing Agar for a cheque fraud. He was sentenced to transportation to Australia.

While still in prison awaiting transportation Agar asked Pierce to give Fanny some of the money he had left with him for safe keeping. Pierce foolishly cheated Fanny, even turning her out of her home. Although she knew nothing of the gold, Fanny was aware that there had been a plot of some kind to defraud the South-eastern, and she went to see the governor of Newgate Jail. What should have been a perfect crime now unravelled because of human frailty. After eighteen months of fruitless inquiries the authorities were about to be handed the solution to the mystery.

When the trial of the conspirators opened at the Central Criminal Court in January 1857 Agar gave Queen's evidence. Burgess and Tester got fourteen years' transportation. Pierce, who played a bigger role than either, got only two years because of a technicality – he was not an employee of the South-eastern.

Edward Agar got no reduction in his life sentence, although the judge, Sir Samuel Martin, expressed a grudging admiration for him.

> The man Agar is a man who is as bad, I dare say, as bad can be. But that he is a man of most extraordinary ability no person who has heard him examined can for a moment deny ... he gave to this, and perhaps to many other robberies, an amount of care and perseverance one tenth of which devoted to honest pursuits must have raised him to a respectable station in life, and considering the commercial activity in this country in the last twenty years, would probably have enabled him to realise a large fortune.

There was a final delicious twist to the affair. Because Agar had turned Queen's evidence he had not been charged with the theft. So Samuel Smiles and the South-eastern could not claim back the proceeds. Instead the judge directed that all the money should go to Fanny Kay. *The Times* wrote: 'By this decision, Agar's wish will be realised and the woman Fanny Kay will become possessed of a sum which will enable her to lead an easy, and, if so inclined, a reputable life.'

Saward had not been named by Agar and was free to carry on both with his successful legal practice and his forgeries. As he later revealed: 'I had made several thousand pounds a year by various sorts of crime.'

Saward's work as a defence barrister brought him many useful contacts in the underworld, men he could recruit as accomplices. His main criminal activity was forging cheques. Safebreakers were useful for breaking into commercial premises, opening safes and removing blank cheques. Company officers carrying blank cheques would have their pockets picked.

When two of his henchmen were caught and sentenced to transportation for life, Saward went into hiding. He was arrested in a coffee-shop in Oxford Street after a tip-off. At the Central Criminal Court he and an accomplice were also transported for life.

Charlies, Peelers and the Met

At the beginning of the eighteenth century the British were strongly opposed to the idea of a professional police force. The French had a widely admired force, but the British feared for their ancient liberties, and pointed to the despotism of the Bourbons and their use of informers and secret police. The social analyst Le Blanc thought the British had a greater tolerance for footpads and highwaymen than for ministerial prying into their private lives.[1]

When two families, seven people in all, were murdered in their homes on the Ratcliffe Highway in 1811 John William Ward, a future Foreign Secretary, said : 'I had rather half a dozen people's throats should be cut in Ratcliffe Highway every three or four years than be the subject of domiciliary visits, spies, and all the rest of Fouche's [Napoleon's police chief] contrivances.'

Thief-taking was a cheap alternative to policing, but it was an experiment that failed: it was too open to exploitation by crooks like Wild. The MacDaniel case also showed the dangers of relying on criminals to catch other criminals.

As the eighteenth century wore on there were fears that the authorities were losing their grip, and that a crime wave was about to engulf society. Horace Walpole wrote in 1782: 'We are in a state of war...I mean from the enormous profusion of housebreakers, highwaymen and footpads; and what is worse, from the savage barbarities of the latter, who commit the most wanton cruelties...one dare not stir out after dinner but well-armed.' Walpole, who had been shot at by a highwayman in Hyde

Park, also wrote: 'One is forced to travel, even at noon, as if one was going to battle.'

London was policed by about 3,000 unarmed men – constables, beadles and the parish watch and ward, overseen by justices of the peace and magistrates. Constables were unpaid and were elected annually from rotas of citizens. The job was unpopular and citizens would pay deputies to do it on their behalf.

This force had been inadequate even before the expansion of London after the Great Fire. The watch, supervised by the beadle, operated from the watch house, and the officers, poorly paid, usually old and decrepit and probably unable to get other employment, issued forth in the evenings with their lanterns and cudgels to patrol the streets. Thomas Rowlandson painted a picture of one of these pathetic creatures, an object of scorn to criminals and of embarrassment to those who wanted to improve policing in the capital.

Officers of the watch had sentry boxes from which they were supposed to venture on the hour to patrol the streets, but the temptations to stay in the box, especially on cold winter nights, must have been great.

Because the responsibilities of the watch ended at the parish boundaries, and there was little cooperation between parishes, criminals knew that they were unlikely to be caught: they could steal in one parish and lie low in another. Although some of the magistrates were honest and hard working, many were corrupt, and would take bribes from criminals. They were known as 'trading justices' and took cash, liquor or sex in return for not guilty verdicts. They brought the whole system of justice into disrepute.

One of these venal magistrates was the despised Thomas De Veil, who nevertheless brought a new efficiency to law enforcement. De Veil turned part of his house in Bow Street into a kind of court, where cases were heard openly and the public were encouraged to take part as witnesses or observers. His successors were the novelist and leading magistrate Henry Fielding, who wrote the satirical *Life of Jonathan Wild the Great* which was published in 1743, and his blind half-brother John. They took the first steps towards founding a police force by making the Bow Street court a police office, which sifted evidence and brought some order to the process of the law by weeding out malicious and trivial complaints. They also brought a human face to the practice of justice. The *Covent Garden Journal* reported:

> ... several wretches being apprehended the night before by Mr Welch, were brought before Mr Fielding and Mr Errigton: when one who was in a dreadful condition from the itch was recommended to the overseers; another, who appeared to be guilty of no crime but poverty, had money given to her to enable her to follow her trade in the market.

The Fieldings created a team of constables, known as the Bow Street Runners because of their supposed fleetness of foot, paid one guinea a week and a share in the rewards from successful prosecutions. This was later to lead to accusations of corruption: some officers were said to encourage young criminals until they had built up a record and became worth arresting.[2]

The Treaty of Paris in 1763, which ended the Seven Years' War, 'unleashed a horde of veterans on to the streets and lanes of England and the crime rate soared', and Sir John Fielding, who took up the crusade for policing after his half brother died in 1754, was given an experimental mounted patrol of eight men for six months.

In 1772 Fielding proposed a General Preventative Plan for an embryo national police force. But when he suggested that high constables should become full-time criminal investigators he upset the county authorities: his proposals seemed to raise once again the spectre of a professional police force. He died in 1780 with his dream of an efficient police force unfulfilled, but with the Bow Street Runners, the forerunner of such a force, well established. Moreover, his successful bulletin the *Weekly Pursuit*, which gave magistrates all over the country details of stolen goods and suspects, became the *Police Gazette* after 1829.

The Gordon Riots of 1780, when watchmen melted into the night as anti-Catholic mobs wrecked the newly-rebuilt Newgate Prison and burned and looted for days, were a further spur to the setting up of a regular police force. But opposition was still intense and in 1785 proposals to set up a London force were rejected. The year before the City got a force of blue-coated Day Constables. Seven more offices modelled on Bow Street were set up in 1792 by Act of Parliament. Each had three salaried magistrates and up to six paid police officers.

While the footpad and the highwayman were the greatest threat to the public, the greatest incitements to crime in the capital were the shipping and the cargoes on the Thames. In 1798 the Thames Police Force was founded by Patrick Colquhoun and John Harriott. This was the first fully organised police force in the country.

Giving impetus to the calls for a police force was the continuing scandal of the watchmen. In 1821 a mock advertisement appeared which laid bare all their weaknesses:

> Wanted, a hundred thousand men for London watchmen. None need apply for this lucrative situation without being the age of sixty, seventy, eighty or ninety years; blind with one eye and seeing very little with the other; crippled in one or both legs; deaf as a post; with an asthmatical cough that tears them to pieces; whose speed will keep pace with a snail, and the strength of whose arm would not be able to arrest an old washerwoman of fourscore returning from a hard day's fag at the washtub...

The Bow Street Horse Patrol was successfully revived in 1805. It consisted of about sixty carefully chosen men, many of whom had served in cavalry regiments, and its job was to protect travellers on the principal roads around London.

Between 1812 and 1827 five parliamentary select committees rejected the idea of full-scale professional policing for the capital. The realisation that things could not go on this way came gradually, with a shift in both public and political opinion. There was a growing belief that London was a den of crime and vice. The demobilisation of thousands of soldiers and sailors at the end of the Napoleonic wars in 1815 brought fears of a new crime wave. Political disorders too kept the propertied classes in a constant state of anxiety. Riots over the Corn Laws, the Cato Street plot, mob support for Queen Caroline, which produced some of the biggest rallies that London had ever seen, perhaps all played their part in softening up public opinion, but when the Home Secretary, Sir Robert Peel, campaigned for a police force in the 1820s it was crime he focused on, writing to the Duke of Wellington, who was then Prime Minister, in 1829: 'I want to teach people that liberty does not consist in having your house robbed by organised gangs of thieves, and in leaving the principal streets of London in the nightly possession of drunken women and vagabonds.'

Peel moved to get a new select committee in February 1828 and used the criminal committal figures, which showed that crime was indeed growing, to make his point. A succession of witnesses, magistrates, high constables, clerks of the peace and parish officers told of the various forms of crime spawned in rookeries and carried out by an army of criminals, many of them children.

In the end, the Metropolitan Police Bill had an easy passage through Parliament in 1829, and in May 1830, when the force was fully operational, the 'New Police' comprised 3,200 men. Peel was strongly aware of the corruption of the Bow Street Runners, so he emphasised the preventive rather than the detective role of the new force. The police were to establish a visible presence on the streets – the 'bobby on the beat' – and lower ranks were forbidden to mix with criminals and informers in public houses. Constables wore blue swallow-tailcoats and top hats, they were armed with truncheons and, on dangerous beats, cutlasses. A small detective force was formed in 1842.

The City, which had strongly opposed the new force, retained its old inefficient watch system until 1839, when the City of London Police was formed.

The new force faced bitter hostility, principally, but not only, among the poor. They were vilified, spat upon, stoned, blinded, mutilated, spiked on railings and generally molested. In 1831 an unarmed constable was stabbed to death at riots in Clerkenwell. A coroner's jury brought in a verdict of 'justifiable homicide'. An annual banquet was held to commemorate the event for many years afterwards.

Working-class fear and suspicion of the police has deep roots. The Kray twins believed 'coppers is dirt' and the costers (selling fruit etc. from stalls) of the Victorian East End would have agreed. Mayhew wrote:

To thwart the police in any measure the costermongers readily aid one another. One very common procedure, if a policeman has seized a barrow, is to whip off a wheel while the officers have gone for assistance; for a large and loaded barrow requires two men to convey it to the greenyard [a pound]. This is done with great dexterity, and the next step is to dispose of the stock to any passing costers, or to any 'standing' in the neighbourhood, and it is honestly accounted for. The policemen, on their return, find an empty and unwheelable barrow, which they must carry off by main strength, amid the jeers of the populace.

Coster vengeance against the police was a point of pride. 'To serve out a policeman is the bravest act by which a costermonger can distinguish himself,' wrote Mayhew. They would have a whip-round for those who attacked the police. A coster with a grudge against a particular policeman might track him for months waiting for an opportunity to strike. One of Mayhew's informants nursed his resentment for six months before he saw his chance. One day when the policeman became involved in breaking up a street brawl outside a public house the young coster pushed his way into the crowd and kicked the officer savagely, shouting 'Now you bastard, I've got you at last.'

When the boy heard that his persecutor was injured for life, his joy was very great and he declared that the twelve months' imprisonment he was sentenced to for the offence would be 'dirt cheap'. The whole of the court where the lad resided sympathised with the boy, and vowed to a man that had he escaped, they would have subscribed a pad or two of dried herrings, to send him into the country until the affair had blown over, for he had shown himself a 'plucky one'.

The law was surprisingly lenient with those who attacked the police, as long as there was no threat to property. A costermonger who attacked a policeman from behind and disabled him for life was imprisoned for a year. 'This was at a time when the penalty for stealing a few pounds' worth of goods might well be ten years' transportation'. Some costers were jailed a dozen times for assaulting officers.

At first low pay and drunkenness led to a huge turnover of police staff. In the first two years of its existence the new force lost almost 2,000 men who were dismissed for drunkenness. Another 1,000 resigned, unwilling to accept the conditions, poor pay and danger.

By no means everyone shared the costermongers' hatred of the police: the new force quickly won the confidence of ratepayers and property owners, those who had most to gain from efficient policing. Commentators like Dickens, who was a great admirer of the police – partly because they were such good copy – helped enhance their reputation. James Grant wrote in *Sketches in London* in 1838: 'Person and property are now incomparably safer than they were under the old system. The new police are now the objects of universal approbation, and deservedly so... Almost all the extensive federations which then existed for the purpose of carrying on a regularly organised system of robbery... have been broken up and scattered in all directions... with respect to crimes against the person, they are now comparatively rare.'

What struck commentators particularly forcibly was the psychological dominance the police had established over the lower echelons of the underworld. John Murray's *World of London*, published in 1843, while critical of the police, pointed out that a lone policeman could disperse a brawling mob, such was the authority of the police uniform. W O'Brien wrote in the *Edinburgh Review* in July 1852: 'The habitual state of mind towards the police of those who live by crime is not so much dislike, as unmitigated, slavish terror... a ruffian will drop his usual tone of bullying audacity, and follow every look of the police officer like a beaten hound creeping to lick its master's feet.'

The old Watch had been known as 'Charleys', and the Bow Street Runners as 'Robin Redbreasts' or 'Raw Lobsters' because of their red vests. Among their clients the new force were known first as 'Peelers' and 'Bobbies', obvious references to Sir Robert Peel. Then they were known as 'Coppers' from cop for arrest, and 'Crushers', perhaps from the size of their boots. More recently there have been 'Bluebottles', 'Rozzers', 'Fuzz', 'Filth' and of course Old Bill.

The underworld the new force faced was very different. London threw up no new crime overlords in the nineteenth century. There were a handful of highly successful robbers and fraudsters: there were the Fagins with their teams of pickpockets, and brothel keepers and ponces and an innumerable horde of prostitutes and desperately poor petty criminals. The lawbreakers described in Mayhew's *London Labour and the London Poor* (1861–2) are mostly losers, destined to die young or in the workhouse.

On the whole during the rest of the nineteenth century, crime rates fell. While the papers gave the impression that the streets were still unsafe, major crime was rare: in the 1830s and 1840s there were on average only ten convictions for murder or manslaughter in London, and only 130 for burglary, shopbreaking, housebreaking and robbery. On the other hand, there were 2–3,000 arrests each year in the 1840s for assaulting police officers, and around 300 for attempting to rescue a prisoner from police custody.

Working-class hostility to the police continued, indeed has never quite died away. In Notting Dale police were sometimes besieged inside their stations, and in 1906 a local magistrate spoke of how the police 'were kicked and battered about, and many and many a time a man has gone home wounded and injured, and has had to leave the Force, because of the injuries received in that district...' After Harry Roberts and an accomplice shot dead three policemen in 1966, football crowds taunted officers with cries of 'Harry Roberts, he's our man, he kills coppers, bang, bang, bang'. Roberts later said: 'The police aren't real people to us...They're the enemy.'

Press outrage and panic about armed burglars in the 1880s led to Metropolitan Police officers being issued with revolvers on their beats. It was not until the last decades of the twentieth century, however, that armed police regularly appeared on the streets of the capital.

The reputation of the police had been improving steadily throughout the twentieth century, and major gang trials made some of the senior detectives household names, the Krays' nemesis Leonard 'Nipper' Read in particular. Until the fifties, when full employment and the post-war crime wave forced change, the police had been badly paid. Pay improved, as did the public perception of the police, but there were setbacks. A series of trials showed that there was systematic corruption in the London force, especially among those officers who had contact with the porn and vice industries of Soho. And relations with black Londoners led to serious social unrest.

A New Kind of Criminal

In June 1832 *Fraser's Magazine* warned its readers of the existence of a new class of criminals, highly organised, confident, a kind of criminal 'club' that thought itself almost invulnerable. These men were not part of the large Victorian underclass of the rookeries. Successful Victorian criminals were more likely to live in the prosperous suburbs, taking on the camouflage of their surroundings. Russell Square and the New Kent Road were likely addresses for successful burglars and safe-breakers, rather than the slums of the East End.

But when the public thought of a professional underworld they thought of the rookeries and their hordes of criminals. In 1851 a serious underestimate suggested there were 13,120 criminals and 6,849 prostitutes in London. In the 1830s there were believed to be 80,000 prostitutes, although this was just a guess.

Mayhew takes us on a tour of the fashionable parts of London, pointing out the various criminals strolling in the streets on the lookout for victims. The criminals who haunted the West End were now more subtle and less violent than their Georgian counterparts. There were magsmen – confidence tricksters and card sharps – well-dressed pickpockets like the two 'tall gentlemanly men' in suits of 'superfine black cloth, cut in fashionable style' and the two natty young men bedecked with glittering watch-chains and gold rings. What was not immediately apparent was that their fingertips had been skinned so that they could identify playing cards by a number of tiny pinpricks in each card.

Mayhew begins in Oxford Street, which he describes as 'one of the first commercial streets in London, and one of the finest in the world'.

> On the opposite side of the street we observed a jolly, comfortable-looking, elderly man, like a farmer in appearance, not at all like a London sharper...He was a magsman...We saw a fashionably-dressed man coming towards us, arm-in-arm with his companion...they were in the prime of life and had a respectable, and even opulent appearance ... the two magsmen strutted off, like fine gentlemen, along the street on the outlook for their victims. Then we saw another young man, a burglar, pass by. He had an engaging appearance, and was very tasteful in his dress, very unlike the rough burglars we met at Whitechapel, the Borough and Lambeth.

Mayhew then leads us along Holborn to Chancery Lane and into Fleet Street, 'one of the main arteries of the metropolis, reminding us of London in the old feudal times, when the streets were crowded together in dense masses, flanked with innumerable dingy alleys, courts and by-streets, like a great rabbit warren.'

> Elbowing our way through the throng of people, we passed through one of the gloomy arches of Temple Bar, as issued into the Strand, where we saw two pick pockets, tall, young gentlemanly men, cross the street from St Clement's Church and enter a restaurant...They entered an elegant dining room, and probably sat down to costly viands and wines.
>
> Leaving the Strand we went up St Martin's Lane, a narrow street leading from the Strand to Seven Dials. We saw here a young man, an expert burglar, of about twenty-four years of age and dark complexion, standing at the corner of the street. He was well-dressed, in a dark cloth suit with a billicock hat. One of his comrades was taken from his side about three weeks ago on a charge of burglary.
>
> Entering a beer-shop in the neighbourhood of St Giles, close by the Seven Dials, we saw a band of coiners and ringers of

changes. One of them, a genteel-looking slim youth, is a notorious coiner, and has been convicted...One of them is a moulder; another was sentenced to ten years' penal servitude for coining and selling base coin. A modest-looking young man, one of the gang, was seated by the bar, also respectably dressed...looking out, while they are coining, that no officers of justice come near, and carrying the bag of base money for them when they go out to sell it to base wretches in small quantities at low prices. Five shillings of base money is generally sold for tenpence...

We returned to Bow Street, and saw three young pickpockets proceeding along in company, like well-dressed costermongers in dark cloth frock-coats and caps.

The reason for this plague of criminals was the prosperity of the main streets nearby and the people who did business there. Mayhew observes of the young prostitutes round Seven Dials: 'Most of the low girls in this locality do not go out till late in the evening, and chiefly devote their attention to drunken men. They frequent the principal thoroughfares in the vicinity of Oxford Street, Holborn, Farringdon Street and other bustling streets.' In periods of acute distress these streets could also be a magnet to the poor. The winter of 1886 was the coldest for thirty years and unemployment was high. On 8 February a vast mob of unemployed dockers and building workers, perhaps 20,000 strong, who had been attending a rally in Trafalgar Square, went on the rampage through Mayfair and St James's, robbing the rich and plundering the shops of Piccadilly and Oxford Street. For two days there was panic as rumours spread that mobs were gathering all over London to sack the West End again.

Burglars were the aristocrats of the Victorian underworld, as highwaymen had been in the Georgian. Their skill and daring, the meticulous planning of their crimes, the risks they took in scaling tall buildings, raised them in the public imagination far above the ranks of the innumerable petty criminals. Mayhew's collaborator John Binney described them as having the look of 'sharp businessmen'. They were successful burglars of country mansions and shops and warehouses, and 'generally contrive to get safely away with their booty'. He called them 'these crack burglars', and said they generally lived in streets adjoining the New Kent Road and Newington Causeway... 'groups of them are to be seen at the taverns beside the Elephant and Castle, where they regale themselves luxuriously on the choicest wines, and are lavish of their gold. From their superior manner and dress few would detect their real character. One might pass them daily in the street and not be able to recognise them.'

Some of these burglars, known as 'attic thieves' or 'garret thieves', targeted houses in the fashionable West End. They would seek out houses which were empty or temporarily unoccupied, make their way to the roof and by clambering along roofs and parapets reach the house they were to burgle. They generally struck between seven and eight o'clock in the evening, when the family were at dinner on the first floor. They would break in through the garret windows, descend to the bedrooms on the second floor and ransack them for jewellery.

At the other end of the scale were the practitioners of the 'kinchin lay' – the despised robbers of children. Binney described the practice of 'child stripping' which he said was carried out by 'old debauched drunken hags who watch their opportunity to accost children in the streets, tidily dressed with good boots and clothes'. With promises to buy the children sweets the women would lure them away to a low neighbourhood and take their clothes, telling them to wait there until they returned. 'This is done most frequently in mews in the West End, and at Clerkenwell, Westminster, the Borough, and other similar localities. These heartless debased women sometimes commit these felonies in the disreputable neighbourhoods where they live, but more frequently in distant places, where they are not known and cannot easily be traced.'

Despite the teeming rookeries, violence was on the wane. Although street robberies in London increased sharply in the early 1820s, and one writer in 1829 spoke of gangs being ready to 'hustle, rob or knock down' people for their valuables, he also pointed out that 'there have been few instances lately of forcing houses in the old-fashioned way, at the front, and taking possession by *coup de main.*' In November 1832 a writer in *Fraser's Magazine* declared that the character and feelings of the thief had changed over the past thirty years. 'Formerly the heroes of their party were fellows conspicuous and famed for open and daring acts of plunder, in which the whole body had a pride, and whom they all felt ambitious to imitate; failing only to do so for lack of the same quantum of courage ... All this kind of heroism has subsided; their leaders are now men rendered famous for scheming, subtlety and astuteness.'

Some saw the growing efficiency and acceptance of the police as the main reasons for the decline of violent crime, others the establishment of reformatory schools. Particularly marked was the decline in juvenile crime. The hordes of desperate, starving young criminals so familiar to Mayhew may have been almost the last of their kind.

The East End

Towards the end of the nineteenth century the first organised criminal gangs appeared in the East End. Immigration from eastern Europe had brought in waves of people who had all the characteristics of future gangsters: fear and hatred of the police, learned under czarist political and racial persecution, an instinct for combining together against their enemies and expertise with firearms. These proto-gangsters started protection rackets, levying cash from coffee stalls, controlling prostitutes and running 'spielers' – illegal gambling dens.

Chief Inspector 'Nutty' Sharpe wrote in his memoirs: 'Flocks of aliens, mostly Russians, were arriving at Irongate Wharf at the foot of Tower Bridge and were being housed in the Docks area. Russians in top-boots and leather leggings and little round fur hats, wild-looking people from the most outlandish parts of that great uncivilised land, a lot were desperadoes and went in for crime straight away.'[1]

The most formidable of the new gangs were the Bessarabians, from the predominantly Russian-Jewish Whitechapel area, and the Odessians. Detective Sergeant B Leeson, who joined the police in 1895, called the Bessarabians the 'Stop at Nothing' gang. 'They were the greatest menace ever known in London,' he wrote, and claimed that in the early years of the century they made the capital 'almost as dangerous a place to live in as Chicago is today [1930s]... In fact there is every good reason to believe that a good many members of the Bessarabian gang which we broke up in the

East End thirty years ago are still to be found in the ranks of the gunmen plying their gentle trade in that American city.'[2]

Leeson said the gang was made up of 'a mixture of Russians, Poles, Roumanians, Greeks, Jews, Tartars and a sprinkling of gipsies.'

Both gangs, which hunted in packs of up to forty men, were essentially protection racketeers. The methods of the Bessarabians now seem quaint. Leeson says one of their scams was to approach wealthy families whose daughters were about to be married and threaten to spread defamatory rumours about the brides. Apparently they were usually paid off.

Most of their victims were fellow immigrants, shopkeepers or the proprietors of coffee stalls. Like the gangsters these men had suffered under the czarist police, and could be relied on to keep their mouths shut. The Bessarabians met any resistance or protest with guns, bottles, knives and fists.

Frederick Wensley, one of Scotland Yard's most famous commanders, wrote in his autobiography *Detective Days* in 1931: 'In the main...the victims were persons who for some reason or another were a little shy of bringing their troubles to the notice of the police. Keepers of shady restaurants, runners of gambling dens, landlords of houses of resort, street bookmakers and other people on the fringes of the underworld were among those peculiarly open to trouble.'

The Bessarabians came to grief when they tried to collect protection money from a giant Jew named Weinstein, who ran a restaurant called the Odessa. Weinstein fought back with an iron bar and put five of the Bessarabians in hospital. Admirers of this exploit founded the Odessians. The gang warfare between the two groups came to a head at a pub and music hall called the York Minster in Philpot Street, off the Commercial Road. The proprietor heard the Bessarabians planned to show up during a display of Russian dancing, and he turned to the Odessians for help.

The Bessarabians turned up and a fight broke out in the hall. A man named Kaufman was surrounded by Odessians and stabbed to death. A successful Jewish boxer, Kid McCoy, was arrested. He told the police: 'If they are going to top me [hang me] I will give you the name of the actual murderer. Otherwise I will keep my mouth shut.'

He got ten years' penal servitude and kept his promise of silence. But others in the East End, shocked by the scale of the violence, talked, and the area became too hot for the two gangs, some of whose members went to America. 'Many of them are leaders of Chicago gunmen to this day, while others have met the usual end of members of this fraternity, and have been 'bumped off' or 'taken for a ride' by more successful rivals, wrote Leeson.'[3]

Wensley was a young constable in Whitechapel, and wrote of the problems presented by the presence of 'the off-scourings of the criminal population of Europe – Russians, Poles, Germans, Austrians and Frenchmen.' The immigrants preyed on each other. 'There was an enormous amount of personal robbery with violence. The maze of narrow, ill-lit alleys offered easy ways of escape after a man had been knocked down and his watch and money stolen.'

Wensley believed murder was far more common then than official statistics would suggest. Bodies with obvious wounds were frequently found near 'disreputable' houses but coroners would return open verdicts because of lack of precise evidence about how the victims came to die.

Wensley investigated many of the crimes involving alien and Jewish gangs, including the Houndsditch Murders of 1910. A gang of anarchist burglars, led by a Latvian named George Gardstein, rented rooms in Exchange Buildings, which backed on to a jeweller's shop at 119 Houndsditch. On the evening of 16 December they attempted to smash their way through the wall into the shop, and neighbours, alarmed by the noise, called the police.

Two sergeants, Bentley and Bryant, knocked at the door and were allowed in. Shots were fired, Bentley fell dead and Bryant, badly wounded, staggered from the house. A Sergeant Tucker was then shot dead and a constable shot in the thigh. Another constable, Choate, grappled with Gardstein. He was shot repeatedly and pulled Gardstein with him as he fell to the floor. Choate, who had been shot eight times, was also kicked in the face. In the confusion, Gardstein was shot in the back by one of his own gang.

The gang fled, dragging Gardstein with them. They took him to their base at 55 Grove Street off Commercial Road. There Gardstein was left with two women, Sara Trassjonsky, and Luba Milstein, while the gang escaped. The horrified women watched as Gardstein died in agony, refusing to be taken to a hospital.

Wensley, then a detective inspector, was called in. Press and public pressure for results was great. *The Times* wrote that 'officers disguised as shoeblacks, as Jewish pedlars and as street hawkers have been in the streets from early morning until late at night.'

The sense of public outrage was all the greater because of another 'anarchist' crime. Early in 1909 two Latvian revolutionaries had held up a wages car outside a factory in Tottenham High Road. They were chased by a large crowd, and a policeman and a small boy were shot dead. Trapped, they shot themselves. During the chase they were said to have fired 400 bullets with their pistols, and wounded another 27 people. Just carrying so much ammunition would have been a considerable feat.

An ugly outbreak of press attacks on 'anarchists', as all the extreme left-wing groups were called, and eastern European immigrants in general ensued. The *East London Observer* wrote: 'It is doubtful if there is more than a score of English families living within a radius of 500 yards of Sidney Street. Certainly there is not a single English tradesman there; the public houses are tenanted by Jews and foreigners, and foreign drinks are almost solely consumed.'

The Times added to the flames. In a feature headed 'The Alien Immigrant' the paper stated that 'the average immigrant is unsavoury in his habits; he is personally unclean.' A leading article in the same paper said: 'Now the British criminal never does a thing like that. Burglars very rarely use firearms at all . . . a savage delight in the taking of life is a mark of the modern Anarchist criminal. We have our own ruffians, but we do not breed that type here and we do not want them.'

On 22 December the City of London police offered a £500 reward for information, and an informer gave away two of the gang, Jacob Peters and Osip Federov. Peters was acquitted at the Old Bailey and was later to become deputy head of Lenin's infamous *Cheka*, the precursor of the KGB, and so was responsible for countless deaths before he too was liquidated in Stalin's purges of the 1930s.[4]

After a tip-off other members of the gang were trapped in a house in Sidney Street, between Mile End Road and Commercial Road. Armed police surrounded the house and the anarchists opened fire. Troops were brought in and the Home Secretary, Winston Churchill, arrived. He proposed that artillery should be brought in to blast open the front of the house. By the time it arrived the house was on fire in a kind of Wagnerian climax to the whole affair. The flames forced the men inside to retreat and one of them, Jacob Vogel, was shot. His accomplice, Fritz Svaars, died in the flames. During the assault on the house by police and troops Sergeant Leeson was shot in the chest. He said to Frederick Wensley: 'Mr Wensley, I am dying. They have shot me through the heart. Give my love to the children. Bury me at Putney.' He lived. Some spectators were injured by gunfire, and one of the firemen died later. The government was criticised, particularly for calling in the troops. Only one person was convicted at subsequent trials, and that verdict was overturned.

Guns and Gangsters

In 1882 Thomas Galliers and James Casey with about twenty other members of the Green Gate Gang confronted Frederick Williams and Arthur Thompson of the Dover Roaders and 'thrashed them with square brass buckled belts'. Williams later died of his injuries, and after the ensuing trial C Vincent of Scotland Yard wrote to the Clerk of Arraigns at the Old Bailey;

> I have to request that you will have the goodness to furnish me with copies of Mr Justice Hawkins' observations as to the prevalency of organised bands of roughs in the metropolis, as expressed by him at the trial of Galliers and Casey for manslaughter at the Central Criminal Court on the 4th inst and Kennedy and others for riot at Hackney.
>
> The Commander of the Metropolitan Police is particularly desirous of having that portion of the learned judge's remarks relating to the existence of 'gangs' on the streets and of the alleged general lawlessness of the roughs. He would also like to have a copy of the evidence adduced in support of the statement that such bands do exist, and that on a certain occasion through the absence of police some roughs scoured the neighbourhood of Hoxton for three hours stabbing people as they went.

Such a state of ignorance on the part of the Commander of the Metropolitan Police is astonishing. Law and order was breaking down in the East End, and less than thirty years later gunmen were fighting it out in the streets.

One morning in September 1911 a defendant who appeared at Old Street Court after an underworld battle told the magistrate that armed gangsters were waiting outside to murder him. The magistrate called in the police inspector in the case and told him to telephone Scotland Yard for a large force of armed policemen. The Yard officers arrived and after some shooting arrested five armed men, led by Arthur Harding, who had indeed been waiting to murder two defendants. Today, even with the high incidence of armed crime and murder in the capital, it is almost inconceivable that gangsters would surround a courthouse and prepare to assassinate men in police custody.

Harding was a leading East End hard man and later an invaluable chronicler of those times. His lifetime spans the era of the razor gangs, the racecourse wars, and finally the Krays and the Richardsons, from the hard times of the late Victorian era to the world of the modern TV *EastEnders*.

Harding was born in 1886 in the Nichol, the district called the Jago in Arthur Morrison's novel *The Child of the Jago*, which was published in 1896. As Harding later told the author Raphael Samuel, whose *East End Underworld* is based on Harding's dictated memoirs: 'The Nichol was something of a ghetto. A stranger wouldn't chance his arm there... The whole district bore an evil reputation, and was regarded by the working-class people of Bethnal Green as so disreputable that they avoided contact with the people who lived in the Nichol.'

Harding grew up to be a familiar figure in the East End underworld, leader of a gang of young armed tearaways. In the evolution of organised crime such groups were one stage on from the old street-fighting gangs, but not yet the professional outfits such as the Sabinis and the Krays. Harding was also at different times a cabinet maker and street trader, even a wardrobe dealer – a door-to-door buyer of secondhand clothes – and tried to make an honest living. In the end he went straight. 'Graduating from pickpocketing and "shoot-flying" – grabbing wallets or gold watches – in his early days to armed hold-ups and protection, he was a well-known local "terror", "looking after" the market stallholders and the street bookies, and taking some part in racecourse wars and struggles for territorial supremacy.'[1]

Carrying a gun was not illegal at the time, and many gangsters armed themselves as a matter of course. Guns played a big part in the Vendetta Case, as the siege of Old Street Magistrates Court was called. It was a feud between Harding, also known by the police as Tresidern, and another local gang leader, a Jew named Isaac Bogard, who was dark-skinned and known as Darky the Coon.

Darky had an impressive criminal record which included a sentence of flogging for living off prostitutes. He had also been jailed for punching a policeman and then climbing to a rooftop and bombarding the pursuing police officers with tiles.

The two gang leaders first clashed when a former ally of Harding's, George King, joined up with Darky and another gangster, Philip Shonck, who was planning to kill Harding. Instead Shonck was shot and wounded by one of Harding's men. This led to a series of shoot-outs in the East End. However, it was prostitutes and their earnings which led to the final showdown with Harding's gang. Harding told Raphael Samuel that the Coons were all foreigners and 'shundicknicks' or ponces.

> Darky was a big man and a fighter – he'd think nothing of giving someone a rip, and he could be very vicious... He was the gaffer over all the Jewish chaps up Whitechapel and Aldgate... He was very flamboyant. He dressed like a cowboy... He used to wear a big open shirt, like a woman's blouse, and a flash belt with something stuck in a case... It wasn't illegal to carry a gun at that time; he had a big weapon stuck down his belt; a big panama hat on – he was quite a character in his way.

One of Harding's men, Tommy Taylor, had been seeing one of Darky's prostitutes, and Darky attacked him. At about half past eight in the evening of 10 September 1911, Harding and his men attacked Darky and his gang in a pub called the Blue Coat Boy in Bishopsgate. Seven of Harding's men carried guns – he had an Irish Constabulary revolver, a favourite weapon of the time.

When they first entered the bar, Darky, who spoke with an American accent, asked Arthur if he would like a drink. Arthur accepted a drink and threw it over Darky, then smashed a glass and slashed his face; 'The Coon had a face like a map of England.' His men meanwhile beat up Darky's followers. No guns were used.

Darky was taken to hospital and after his face was stitched, discharged himself. But the following Sunday he was attacked again by Harding and his gang. This time Darky and another man were arrested for disorderly conduct, and ordered to appear at Old Street Magistrates' Court on the following Monday. Darky decided to ask for police protection, a move that infuriated the Harding gang.

The magistrate, Sir Chartres Biron, later wrote:

One morning two men were charged before me with disorderly conduct. One of them applied for police protection on the grounds there was an armed body of men waiting outside the court to murder them.

I sent for the Inspector of Police and saw him in my private room.

'Is this true?' I asked. 'Yes,' he said, 'it is ...'

'Telephone at once to Scotland Yard,' I said, 'mention my name and state the facts, Tell them ... to send down an overwhelming force of armed police as soon as possible to deal with the situation ...' This was done and Scotland Yard adopted my suggestion ... Just after five o'clock ... the police force arrived.

Leading from Old Street Court there were two roads. These the police had blocked with two hooded vans, filled with a force armed with revolvers. 'Now,' I said, 'let the two men out. ' In a second firing began and the police surrounded the gang. There were five, all armed, and they were five of the most desperate characters in Hoxton, led by their chief, Tresidern. In a few minutes they were arrested and that day's work was the beginning of the end of what is hardly an exaggeration to call a reign of terror ...[2]

Harding's account of the siege, dictated many years later, differs in detail but is if anything even more insouciant. In it he refers to

Scotland Yard Commander Frederick Wensley, an old foe who was one of the most successful of the capital's organised crime fighters. He blames Wensley for the Coon getting police protection.

Harding and his fellow gangsters were tried at the Old Bailey in December 1911. Darky was still so fearful that he had to be summoned to give evidence. Wensley did Harding no favours when he outlined his criminal career to the court. He said that when he was fourteen he was bound over for disorderly conduct and possessing a revolver. 'At the age of seventeen he became a terror to Bethnal Green, and captained a gang of desperadoes.' He claimed Harding had become a cunning and dangerous criminal who now, at the age of 25, had fourteen criminal convictions.[3]

Harding was sentenced to 21 months' hard labour, with another three years' penal servitude to follow. Recalling the trial and its aftermath, Harding said Darky joined the army during the First World War and was decorated with the Military Medal for courage. After the war he became a protection racketeer, 'looking after' the stalls at the back of Petticoat Lane and Golston Street. Arthur was freed from prison after five years and met Darky, who still had the scars of their last encounter on his face, in the street near Aldgate.

...he said, 'Come and have a drink' and, do you know, it was genuine; he meant it. He didn't have any evil in him. He said 'Hello Arthur,' and put his hand out. He never talked about what we had done to him. I've never seen him since.

Harding had graduated from One-eyed Charlie's gang, a loose association of very petty criminals, to form his own team. They were, he says, 'a collection of small-time thieves ripe for any mischief'. That included snide-dropping, counterfeiting, van-thieving and shoot-flying – snatching gold chains. 'We were ready to steal anything. Sometimes we went in couples, sometimes alone – it was only when there was a big fight on that we went as a gang.'

Guns were common. Harding's Constabulary revolver cost him half a crown [12$\frac{1}{2}$p], and he used it when he and his gang held up gambling dens, or spielers. He recalled firing it in a fight with a man called Sawyer, 'a good fighting man but we were at loggerheads'.

Although he was just feet away he missed. He said it was a good thing he'd never hit anyone as the bullets the gun used were the biggest he had ever seen.

He recalled a shooting incident in Brick Lane, an area he said had become very dangerous because of the number of people carrying guns. One night he was standing outside an Italian ice-cream shop with some members of his gang when a policeman passed. One of his men, called Long Hymie, drew a pistol and fired it towards the policeman. The bullet missed narrowly, lodging in a shutter. The policeman, who knew Arthur well, said 'That was a wicked thing to do, Arthur,' but amazingly left it at that. Arthur knew what a narrow escape they'd all had, and expelled Long Hymie from his gang. 'He only wanted to start banging away, and we thought him too dangerous.'

After another spell in prison Harding admitted that he became more vicious, and even the police avoided him. He terrorised the other local gangsters. 'If we'd wanted money we could have made a fortune – everybody in Brick Lane was scared of us. But money wasn't a great influence on me. If my mother and sister was all right, that was enough for me.'

There were other gangs, career criminals, on whom money was a considerable 'influence', and inevitably Harding and his men would soon clash with them.

Career Gangsters

One of the gangs Arthur Harding clashed with were the Titanics, so called, it seems, because they dressed well – like the well-heeled customers on the famous liner. The two gangs fought over the protection of a coffee-stall in Brick Lane, but Harding's gang came off worst. As soon as the fight began the police arrived, and Arthur realised it was a trap. 'I always had it in for them afterwards. I thought, "You twisters – you have the bogies on your side".'[1]

These gangs belonged to the past. They were what Harding called hooligans. Of another well-known and long-lived gang, the Hoxton Mob, he said: 'They weren't such good-class thieves as the Titanics... They all finished on the poor law, or cadging. Their leader died a pauper, whereas the leader of the Titanics ended up owning a dog track.'[2]

In an altogether different league were the Italian Darby Sabini gang. They dominated the London underworld from the early years of the nineteenth century for two decades from their base in Clerkenwell. Although there were many strands to their rackets they were essentially protection racketeers, whether on the racetracks or in the clubs of Soho. They brought a new level of control and professionalism to gangland, and with it a greater degree of lawlessness. Their dominance did not go unchallenged, and there were shootings, stabbings and slashings in pubs, cafés and streets, particularly around their heartlands of Clerkenwell and Holborn, and in the West End.

Darby was born in 1889 in Saffron Hill, in the area known as

Little Italy. In the nineteenth century it vied with St Giles in notoriety. An Italian colony developed there in the 1840s.

Darby showed early promise as a boxer but preferred the easier life of a street tough before graduating to big-time gang crime. At the time, that meant gambling in one form or another. Gangsters offered protection to spielers. Street gambling was illegal so racecourse betting was big business. It has been estimated that illegal gambling had an annual turnover of between £350 million and £450 million a year, making it bigger than any other industry except the building trade.[3]

With his brothers Harry-boy, Joseph, Fred and George, who were important members of his gang, Sabini worked the racetracks and in effect extorted money from bookies under the guise of protection. As Harding recalls, 'The racecourse business was a profitable one. When a gang went to a racecourse like Brighton they could clear £4,000 or £5,000 easy. At Epsom, on Derby Day, it could be £15,000 or £20,000.'[4]

Such easy pickings naturally attracted rival gangsters, and the gang warfare that followed throughout the 1920s and 1930s prefigured later rivalries. The criminals were known as razor gangs, but in fact they used a wide range of weapons, including guns. Detective Chief Superintendent Edward Greeno of the Flying Squad said: 'Darby Sabini and his thugs used to stand sideways to let the bookmakers see the hammers in their pockets.'

A police officer who remembered the racecourse wars wrote:

The safety razor embedded in the peak of the pull-down cloth cap, which would gouge out a man's cheek with one swipe, originated in Glasgow. The same kind of blades, preferably rusty to set up infection, stuck into a big potato with only a quarter of an inch of metal showing, came from the Midlands. In the eyes of the owners this possessed the merit of leaving warning weals once the wounds had healed, without risking a murder charge.

The flick knife was unknown at the time and even recently I have heard this backwardness on the part of the manufacturers deplored in certain circles. Coshes came in infinite variety,

many weighted with lead to give the gangster the right 'feel' –
like a golfer with his set of clubs. Then there were bayonets
with serrated blades, the metal shavings from workshop lathes
enclosed in old cotton stockings, carefully chosen lead piping
which would go down a trouser leg, tyre levers with non-slip
rubber grips, the hair-splitting stilettos of the Sabini gang from
Clerkenwell, bottles of vitriol and other acids.[5]

The bookmakers, or bookies, were the targets of the gangs, who
would extort money for the track-side pitches on which the bookies
set up their chalk boards. The Sabinis would drive bookies off the
best pitches and then hire them out to other bookies. The gangs also
charged the bookies for various 'services'. They had to pay for the
chalk with which they wrote the odds on their boards, and even for
sponging down the boards. The stools on which they stood also had
to be hired from the gangs.

The gangs also sold the sheets of runners, which cost less than a
penny to produce, to the bookies for half a crown. Every so often
there would be a collection for the wife or family of a gangster who
had been jailed, and the bookies were expected to make a generous
donation.

If the bookies didn't cooperate they might be beaten unconscious,
but there were means other than crude violence to bring them into
line. Gang members would surround their pitches so that the punters
could not get through to place a bet. Or their boards would be wiped
clean of the runners and odds before betting had finished.

One criminal who got off to a bad start in life on the racetracks
was Mad Frankie Fraser, later a member of the Billy Hill and
Richardson gangs, who as an eight-year-old helped with scrubbing
the bookies' boards. 'They could have done it for themselves quite
easily,' he recalled, 'but it was part of the ritual that they had to pay
for this wonderful benefit.'

Harding and his gang had brushed up against the Sabinis from time
to time. The Sabinis had made a collection for them when they were
tried at the Old Bailey for the Vendetta affair. Later bookmakers who
were paying protection money to the Sabinis turned to Harding for
help. One of them, Hymie Davis, asked Arthur Harding for protection

at the Kempton Park racecourse after the Sabinis threatened to 'do him'. Sixty of Harding's men travelled to the course and were drinking at a booth when they were surrounded and attacked by the police. Harding watched the battle from afar. Hymie Davis later gave him a gold watch and chain as a reward. 'By that time Darby Sabini lived in Brighton, and had the local police all tied up.'

Harding says the Sabinis, who formed an alliance with Jewish gangsters, would import recruits from Sicily, and Darby was said to have Mafia links. The Sabinis fought a long war with a Birmingham gang called the Brummagen Boys, led by a bookmaker named Billy Kimber. But Sabini had connections with the police. 'Directly there was any fighting it was always the Birmingham mob who got pinched. They was always getting time, five-year sentences and that.'

Kimber could not compete with the combination of the Sabinis and the police, and confined his activities to Midlands and northern racetracks. But the war didn't end there. Among other incidents, Darby Sabini was cornered at Greenford trotting track on 25 March 1921 and escaped a beating by the Birmingham mob by shooting his way out of trouble. He was arrested but acquitted when he pleaded self-defence.

That same year Kimber joined forces with a mob from Leeds to eliminate the Sabinis. An all-out attack was planned for the last day of the Derby meeting at Epsom. But in the confusion the Kimber gang ambushed the Leeds men by mistake, and a pitched battle followed, which ended only when one of the Leeds men shouted: 'You have made a bloomer. We are Leeds men.'

Twenty-three men were later convicted and the Home Secretary, Sir William Joynson-Hicks, vowed to wipe out the gangs. 'It may be difficult to get rid of these gangs all at once, but give me time,' he said.

There were periods of truce, and during one of them Kimber went to Darby Sabini's home at King's Cross. He was later found in the street shot in the side. The Jewish bookmaker Alfie Solomon gave himself up to the police. Solomon said Kimber had threatened him with a revolver, and he had taken it from him. Then, claimed Solomon, who was acquitted at a subsequent trial, the gun had gone off accidentally. Arthur Harding later said that the Sabinis were too cunning for the Birmingham mob, who were all 'rough house, they weren't as clever as the Darby Sabini lot.'

Another gang the Sabinis clashed with early on were the Titanics from Hoxton, one of the long-lived mobs who crop up over the years. There had been a fight in a West End gambling club and the Sabinis were driven out. Darby decided to take the battle to the Titanics' heartland. According to gangland legend, a convoy of cars drove from one of the pubs the Sabinis used as their headquarters, the Griffin in Clerkenwell, and travelled eastwards towards Hoxton. Their destination was a pub called the Albion, known as the 'Blood Tub', which was one of the Titanics' haunts. In the cars were about twenty men with at least ten guns and a hamper of ammunition.

The Titanics had been warned, and when the convoy drove into Nile Street on its way to the Albion they were armed and waiting. One of their leaders, Jimmy Bond, a war hero, was in command. He positioned ten gunmen behind upturned market stalls along a fifty-yard length of Nile Street. Other gunmen were placed in the Albion, which commanded a view west along Nile Street.

The colourful gangland version of the tale has Darby sending an outflanking car through the back streets. 'Suddenly the door of the Blood Tub burst open and an Italian tearaway known as [Paul] Boffa emptied two chambers of a revolver into the polished bar front, a foot or so from where Bond was standing.'[6]

The rest of Darby's men took cover behind fruit barrows on the other side of the street and opened a lively fire on the pub. Two of the Titanics were wounded, and Boffa was knocked unconscious with a length of lead pipe. He was stripped by the Titanics' women who gave him a vicious beating. Bond intervened to save him.

Then suddenly it was all over. As police car bells rang out, the wounded were hustled away and the guns were hidden. The police found Boffa lying unconscious behind an upturned stall, but witnesses claimed he was an innocent bystander who had been caught up in the affray.

One reason the casualties were low in proportion to the firepower deployed by both sides was that no one wanted a killing. The death penalty was still in force, and Darby had given strict instructions that no one was to shoot to kill.

A low-intensity war rumbled on between the Sabinis and their rivals all over London and at racetracks. One challenge came from within their own ranks, from the Cortesi brothers – Augustus, George, Paul and Enrico, known collectively as the Frenchies. Initially they claimed a bigger slice of the cake, and the Sabinis agreed. Then another challenge came from some of the Jewish members of the confederation, known as the Yiddishers. Concessions were made to them, too, but soon the Frenchies and the Yiddishers united. In an audacious move the new combination hijacked the Sabini protection money from the bookmakers at Kempton Park in the autumn of 1922. After the inevitable reprisals Harry Sabini was convicted of assaulting George Cortesi, and five other gang members were jailed for attempting to murder a member of the Cortesi coalition.

Another defining episode of the power struggle was the battle in the Fratellanza Club in Great Bath Street, Clerkenwell, on 19 November 1922. Darby and Harry Sabini were set upon by the Cortesis. They had been ambushed on enemy territory – the Cortesis lived only a few doors away from the club. Harry was shot and wounded, and Darby was punched and beaten with bottles. Darby later told a magistrates' court that his false teeth were broken in the affray. He added; 'I am a quiet peaceable man. I never begin a fight. I do a little bit of work as a commission agent, sometimes for myself and sometimes for someone else. I live by my brains.'

During the trial the Cortesis' lawyer, who had been told that Darby always carried a revolver, asked him if he was armed. When Darby replied that he wasn't, the lawyer insisted on him being searched. Nothing was found. As Darby left the court at the end of the day one of his team handed him back his gun.

The Old Bailey judge, Mr Justice Darling, who prided himself on being a bit of a linguist, addressed Darby in Italian. Darby, who had never spoken anything but English, was baffled. Later the judge told the jury that the name Sabini meant the family were descended from the Sabines, an ancient Italian tribe whose women were raped and carried off by the Romans. Despite this rough treatment, he said, the women seemed to have fared rather well in the years that followed.

What the jury made of all this is not recorded, but two of the Cortesis were later each sentenced to three years' penal servitude. Judge Darling turned down the jury's suggestion that the brothers should be deported and commented:

I look upon this as part of a faction fight which has raged between you and other Italians in consequence of some difference which the police do not entirely understand.

You appear to be two lawless bands – the Sabinis and the Cortesis. Sometimes you are employed against the Birmingham people, and sometimes you are employed against each other. I have the power to recommend an order for your deportation. I am not going to do it. I can see no reason to suppose that you two men are worse than others who have been convicted in these feuds and have not been recommended for deportation. But the whole of the Italian colony should know of the Grand Jury's recommendation, and I wish to say to you all, if this kind of lawless conduct goes on, those who get convicted in future will be turned out of this country with their wives and children.

That was the end of the Cortesi challenge. The Sabinis were free to extend their empire into the West End, taking shares in gambling and drinking clubs and installing one-armed bandits. They also preyed on other criminals, demanding a cut of their loot. As the gangster Billy Hill, who felt that he and robbers like him were not being given the respect they deserved, was later to recall:

Burglars and thieves had no chance. If they wandered up West they had to go mob-handed. And they had to be prepared to pay out if they were met by any of the Sabinis. If they went into a club it was drinks all round. The prices were usually especially doubled for their benefit. If they did go into a spieler they never won. They knew better than to try to leave while they were showing even a margin of profit. If one word was spoken out of place it was all off. The Sabinis, who could rustle up twenty or thirty tearaways at a moment's notice anywhere up West, stood for no liberties, although they were always taking them.

Night after night some thief or other was cut, or had his head bashed in. Merely because he was a thief, and not only a tearaway. Probably because he did not have enough loot on him to pay the Sabinis when they put the bite on him. That was the West End in the 1920s, when I was a kid.[7]

The Sabinis had rivals. The most important were the White family from Islington, led by Big Alf White, who had been a lieutenant of Darby's. Lesser gangs were led by Hill, one day to become the self-styled Boss of the Underworld, whose team were burglars and smash-and-grab raiders, and his later rival Jack 'Spot' Comer, a racecourse thug.

The racecourse wars were almost over. After a running battle at Lewes racecourse on 8 June 1936, when Hoxton and Islington allies of the Whites set out to attack the Sabinis, sixteen men were arrested and sentences totalling 53½ years were handed down.

It was time for a truce. In the settlement that followed, the Sabinis would have the West End, the Whites the King's Cross area. 'The latter became known as the King's Cross Gang and Alf White would hold court in the Bell public house or Hennekeys in the Pentonville Road, exercising strict discipline among his followers. "No bad language was allowed," says John Vaughan, a police officer from King's Cross. "First time you were warned. The next time – out." It was the same with Darby Sabini: women were to be treated properly: Italian youths could not drink before they were twenty. It was a reasonably benevolent dictatorship.'[8]

The long Sabini era was coming to an end. Darby, who after years avoiding the limelight was named in a Sunday paper as the king of the underworld, sued for libel and lost. He denied being the 'king of the Sabini gang' and also denied making 'twenty to thirty thousand pounds a year' – an immense sum at the time. He was unable or unwilling to pay the £775 costs. Somehow he had managed to fritter away his huge earnings.

Darby had another problem. One of the strengths of his gang was that it was a coalition of Italians and Jews. The Jews provided both muscle and brains, and some of the up-and-coming Jewish bookies were allies. But the rise of the Fascists in Italy had infected the Italian community in London to some extent, and Darby found that the Jewish and anti-Semitic elements were becoming polarised.[9]

Darby moved to Brighton, where he had a penthouse in the Grand Hotel. He is the gangster Colleoni in Graham Greene's novel *Brighton Rock*. His power was on the wane and when, at the beginning of the Second World War, the brothers were interned as enemy aliens, their West End empire was carved up between various rivals. Jack Spot was one of the claimants, as were the Whites.

Darby went to prison for receiving – having been framed by some of his old gang, according to one account – and while he was inside his son was killed in action with the Royal Air Force. Darby never recovered, and he died in 1950. He apparently left little money, despite gangland legend that he was a very wealthy man. Oddly enough, one of his henchmen was stopped as he prepared to leave the country for Italy with £36,000. Darby's funeral was a quiet affair, attended by few of his old comrades. His old foe Jack 'Charlie Artful' Capstick, a legendary Scotland Yard commander and founder of the Ghost Squad of gangbusters, was there and placed a red rose from his buttonhole on the coffin.

There is a much-published photograph of the Sabini gang. Darby is seen in his normal attire of dark suit, muffler and cloth cap. Unlike the flamboyant characters around him, he does not look like a gangster, much less like the leader of the most feared and powerful gang of his time.

Capstick was asked by Sabini's biographer, Edward T Hart, how he rated Darby. According to Hart, the detective compared him very favourably to other gang leaders.

> The majority of them have been mindless thugs who understood only how to terrorise...But Darby...had the charisma needed to build a huge gangster army. He was strong enough to control these men of violence without ever needing to raise his voice. And above all he was intelligent enough to out-think and out-manoeuvre his enemies over and over again.[10]

Allowing for the tendency to inflate the virtues of one's vanquished foes, Capstick's portrait of a master criminal sheds some light on Darby Sabini's enigmatic character.

Like Arthur Harding, the Sabinis were a link between the old-style gangs of 'terrors' and a later era. Ronnie Kray, writing in Broadmoor, said that one member of the family, Johnny Sabini, 'though now an older man, comes to see me'.[11]

Changing the Map
of the Underworld

The arrival of waves of immigrants from eastern Europe changed the geography of the underworld. Some East End criminals moved south of the river. They included elite criminals such as safe-breakers and the more ambitious thieves, but also forgers, pickpockets and fraudsters.[1]

This criminal diaspora spawned new gangs, who in the 1920s and 1930s clashed with gangs from north of the river, including the Sabinis. The south London teams included Monkey Benneyworth's Elephant Gang. It is said that a fight with Benneyworth led to Darby Sabini's rise to power. The south London gangster had attacked a barmaid in Sabini's favourite pub, the Griffin in Clerkenwell, tearing off her dress. Although Benneyworth was a much bigger man Darby Sabini thrashed him, knocking him out and breaking his jaw and cheekbone. Benneyworth later returned with his Elephant Gang but was driven out by Sabini and a crowd of young Italians who were to form the nucleus of his gang.

The bombing of the East End and other areas with strong criminal traditions in World War Two dispersed some of the criminal families. Robert Muphy says in *Smash and Grab* that until they were destroyed in the Blitz some London streets were virtually no-go areas for the police. He names Campbell Road near Finsbury Park, Edward Square and Bemerton Street in Islington, Wilmer Gardens and Essex Street in Hoxton, and parts of Notting Dale.[2]

Campbell Road, a terraced street of a hundred houses built in the 1860s and known as 'the Bunk', was described by the local sanitary inspector in 1909 as 'the king of all roads'. Here crime was petty, a kind of cottage industry, but the poverty was of the type Mayhew would have recognised. The residents included prostitutes and criminals, and even beggars. Those with jobs were costermongers, street sellers, entertainers, charwomen and casual labourers.[3] The sanitary inspector's report said:

> I have been in practically all the slums in London: Notting Hill, Chelsea, Battersea, Fulham, Nine Elms, and also the East End, but there is nothing so lively as this road. Thieves, Prostitutes, cripples, Blind People, Hawkers of all sorts of wares from boot-laces to watches and chains are to be found in this road, Pugilists, Card Sharpers, Counter Jumpers, Purse Snatchers, street singers and Gamblers of all kinds, and things they call men who live on the earnings of women ... Of course, there are a few who perhaps get an honest living, but they want a lot of picking out.

In the 1920s the road was still conspicuous for poverty and crime. The police entered the street with caution, and the traditional crime of rescuing arrested men still prevailed in Campbell Road.[4]

Bombs, the rebuilding of the post-war years and waves of new immigrants from the Commonwealth changed the face of gangland. Until the war there were remnants of Victorian London across the capital, reminders of the 'padding kens' or low lodging houses if not the flash houses. 'Darkest England' as William Booth of the Salvation Army saw it, had gone for ever.

Our knowledge of underworld geography and its tribes in the immediate aftermath of the war is enlarged by the Billy Hill. Describing how he formed a coalition to take over the West End from Alf White's Islington mob he gives a valuable list of the major gangs:

> I saw a chance to clean up the West End. So the Elephant mob came my way, and over the bridge from South London with them came the teams from Brixton and Camberwell and Southwark and Rotherhithe. From Shepherd's Bush and Notting Hill the burglars came, and the King's Cross gang and

the Holloway team joined in. The Paddington and Kilburn lot fell in behind as well.

Then the other mobs from down East said they wanted to join us. Timber Jim and Wooden George from Ilford came along with their team. Bugsy Reilly brought the Upton Park mob along. A handy gang from Dagenham turned up. Then Fido the Gipsy from Essex joined in. If necessary Fido could have brought along 1,000 gipsies with him to settle this argument.[5]

Pushing back the boundaries during and just after the war were the spivs, who were seldom professional criminals but acted as go-betweens for the underworld and a public which was willing to pay for what the underworld could provide. The public were ordinary decent people who had grown tired of shortages and official exhortations to 'export or die'. More and more of them took advantage of the booming black market, and in 1945–6 the racketeers used the expertise gained in wartime to consolidate their empires.[6] One of the most notorious of the spivs was Stanley Setty. David Hughes, in his compelling article on spivs in *The Age of Austerity*, writes about him:

Nobody knew how Stanley Setty had spent the war. He entered it without assets, as unprepared as England, and in the late Forties he popped up miraculously rich, like Germany. In pre-war days he had always lived on his wits, gambling at the fringes of a basically honest society and mostly losing. But in 1949, four years after the war, when that same society had learned that only a touch of dishonesty gave any spark to life at all, Setty was reckoned to have a capital of fifty thousand behind him and always paid for his triple-price double whiskies from a roll of two hundred fivers.

Most days he stood on the corner of Warren Street, that cracked axle of the used-car trade, where he waited for business to come his way. He worked alone, his bank in his pocket, his brain furnished as slickly as an office. His only premises, a garage in a dead-end mews off Albany Street, were concealed close at hand, and he lived evasively in that flashy, decrepit half world of sloppy pubs and steamed-up caffs, linked by bomb-sites (for violence) and railway stations (for quick thefts), which described a crooked circle from Aldgate round the Euston Road to Hammersmith and on round to the Elephant. This was an area where crime, or the half-operatic post-war version of it, was hard to disentangle from decent enterprise.

The black market, and the opportunities the blackout and the depleted police force offered, spurred the underworld to new levels of ingenuity. By the end of the war a crime wave broke over the capital and the police feared they were losing the battle. Lorry hijackings and warehouse raids had reached unprecedented levels. Mark Penney wrote in December 1945:

The crime wave for which the police have been preparing ever since the end of hostilities is breaking over us. Armed robberies of the most violent and vicious kind feature daily in the newspapers. Even the pettiest crimes are, it seems, conducted with a loaded revolver in hand. And well-planned robberies, reminiscent of the heyday of Chicago gangsterdom, have relieved Londoners of £60,000 worth of jewellery in the past week alone. Hold-ups of cinemas, post office and railway booking offices have become so commonplace that the newspapers scarcely bother to report them. To deal with the situation the police are being forced to adopt methods more akin to riot-breaking than crime detection.[7]

A London CID officer wrote that in 1945 'the soaring black lines on the crime graphs in the map room at New Scotland Yard showed unmistakably that the police were losing the struggle'.[8] That December, 2,000 policemen poured into Soho and checked the papers of people in places of entertainment, including the gambling clubs. Billy Hill wrote: 'They checked thousands upon thousands of service passes and identification cards... Identity cards? They were as pieces of paper we could get any day we liked. Army passes? We

could print them if you wanted them... which all goes to show how
organised we were, and how handicapped were the law in trying to
fix us.'

After the war the map of the underworld was further redrawn as the
racecourse wars died out and the White family from Islington and a
coalition of gangs led by Jack Spot and Billy Hill vied for control of
the West End.

Hill wrote of the Whites, whom he refers to in his book as the
Blacks: 'When the last war broke out in 1939 the Sabinis, being
Italians, were interned. Overnight the Blacks took over. They were
a gang of hoodlums run by five brothers named Black... They
looked at the Sabinis and came to the conclusion that there was
room for two at that game... The war was a godsend to them. It
automatically destroyed the vast empire that had been built up by
the Sabinis, and left the huge gap to be filled in by the first-comers.'

The Spot–Hill combination eventually won and imposed a peace
on the underworld which lasted for about ten years, breaking down
spectacularly when they fell out. Perhaps it was surprising that the
cold, reserved Hill and the flamboyant Spot had managed to coexist
for so long. Hill felt that Spot had become jealous, Spot that Hill
was overbearing and uncooperative. The alliance ended in a welter
of slashings and bone-breakings – but no shootings.

Billy Hill had been against the use of firearms. 'We were in
business to live and enjoy life, not to shoot the town apart like a
bunch of film-star "gangsters".' Darby Sabini carried a gun but
never shot to kill, and his fellow gangsters of the racecourse-wars
era favoured razors, knives and coshes. But by 1955 a young gang
of East Enders were a growing force in the underworld and their
leader, Ronnie Kray, was a psychopath who dreamed of shooting,
slashing and blasting his way to the top.

The Battle for the West End

Gang crime in London in the immediate post-war years was dominated by the battle for control of the West End, an area of overlapping gang territories and aspirations. The main claimants were Hill, Jack Spot and the Whites. Spot was born in 1912 in Whitechapel, the son of Polish immigrants. He started out as a petty crook and hustler, a protection racketeer and housebreaker.

In spite of all this he achieved hero status for his part in defending the local Jewish community against Oswald Mosley's Blackshirts before the Second World War. Spot later claimed he took on Mosley's top bodyguard, an all-in wrestler known as Roughneck, and knocked him unconscious with a chair leg filled with lead when the Blackshirts marched down Cable Street in 1936. This is unlikely, as the Cable Street confrontation was between the anti-Fascists and the police, the Blackshirts having moved off elsewhere. In 1937 he was given six months' jail for attacking another Blackshirt. Spot probably did help protect the Jewish shopkeepers from the fascists but for a price: it was an old-fashioned protection racket.

Early in the war there was a clampdown on spielers and other gambling clubs, and Spot and his cohorts were rounded up and drafted into the army. He didn't like the discipline and got into a fight with an anti-Semitic corporal. After that he made a nuisance of himself, and in 1943 the Marine regiment he was serving in discharged him on grounds of mental instability. He returned to a blitzed East End, and after a fight in a club in the Edgware Road where he hit an anti-Semitic gangster over the head with a teapot, he fled to Leeds, the black-market capital of the north.

Spot prospered, taking control of the local racecourse gangs and reaching an accommodation with the Polish gangsters who had dominated the Leeds underworld. According to Robert Murphy in *Smash and Grab*, the Poles agreed to restrict their activities to taxis and petrol rationing.[1]

Spot brought order to the clubs and racecourses, dispensing rough justice. He recalled how his gang clashed with 'Fred, leader of a big mob in Newcastle... Newcastle Fred was not only a gangster but a racecourse operator as well. He thought he had the say-so on flogging out bookmakers' pitches, but he made a mistake when he tried to get nasty with me and a few of my pals at Pontefract races.' In the ensuing battle Newcastle Fred was left battered and bloodied in the mud.[2]

At the end of the war Spot returned to London and opened an illegal spieler called the Botolph Club in Aldgate. By now a big, flamboyant, bombastic man with a large cigar, he used a bogus company called the Aldgate Fruit Exchange as cover. He described the staff of the bogus company thus: 'All these geezers with respectable ties and tea-shop manners who acted as clerks and were on my payroll.' The club was a success, with Spot claiming he took £3,000 a week from the *chemin de fer*, faro and rummy. He said of his clients: 'We had a rum mixture. There were big businessmen. There were bookmakers with pockets full of sucker money. There were spivs and screwsmen from the underworld getting rid of the cash they had picked up for the gear they had stolen. And of course the biggest players of all were the black-market boys.'

Gambling was flourishing in the immediate post-war period. The easy money made by spivs and black-market racketeers, and restrictions on travelling, which kept the rich at home rather than at their old continental playgrounds, meant that gambling clubs boomed. Arthur Helliwell wrote in the *People*:

> I watched gin rummy being played for £1 a point. I saw a Slippery Sam school where the kitty averaged between £200 and £250 a hand. I drank a glass of champagne with a suave, silver-haired,

slickly tailored character who takes a rake-off on a £15,000 to £20,000 turnover every time he runs a chemmy party.

I visited a poker game where you couldn't see the green baize for fivers, and I rounded off my tour watching a Negro dice game that shifts its rendezvous and changes its entrance password every night. 'I'm driving a Ford V8' was the open sesame the night I called. There were three other white men in the dingy smoke-filled room. The rest were zoot-suited, sombrero-hatted, jazzily-necktied coloured boys. A chocolate-coloured dandy in a long black overcoat with an astrakhan collar had the dice.

Spot also established himself as a kind of godfather to Jewish communities around the country, if you accept his usually unreliable accounts. He was frequently quoted by the daily newspapers and took the opportunity to give a highly coloured version of events.

I didn't have to buy nothing. Every Jewish businessman in London made me clothes, gave me money, food, drink, everything. Because I was a legend. I was what they call a legend to the Jews. Anywhere they had anti-Semitic trouble – I was sent for: Manchester, Glasgow, anywhere. Some crook go into a Jewish shop, says gimme clothes and a few quid, the local rabbi says Go down London and find Jack Spot. Jack, he'll know what to do. So they did and I'd go up and chin a few bastards. The Robin Hood of the East End, a couple of taxi drivers told me once. 'You helped everyone,' they said.[3]

Soon Spot was climbing the ladder towards leadership of the underworld and ready to challenge the White gang from King's Cross for control of the racetracks. In July 1946, with the help of Arthur Skurry, leader of the ferocious Upton Park gipsies, he wrested control of Ascot from Jimmy Wooder and the Islington gang. Next he had to deal with the Whites.[4]

The Whites had seized much of the Sabini empire in Soho and the West End when the Italians were interned at the start of the war.

Billy Hill, wrote in his book *Boss of Britain's Underworld*:

> They took over the horserace-tracks and the dog-track concessions. They continued the blackmail of club-owners, café proprietors and publicans. They even ran some of the brasses [prostitutes] on the streets and got them to steer the mugs into their spielers and drinking clubs... All through the war years they had it all their own way. No one could open a drinking club or spieler in the West End without the Blacks' [whites'] permission. And their permission usually meant the payment of a dollar in the pound [25 per cent] out of takings.
>
> At that time I had my own manor [territory]. I was guv'nor of Camden Town, that part of London that is bordered by Regent's Park, Hampstead Road and King's Cross. The Blacks came out of Islington, which is next to King's Cross. So you can see they did not have much love for me. Most of London was split up into various dominions. The Elephant mob from over the water had south London running their way. That included Brixton, Camberwell and New Cross. Over at Notting Hill and Shepherd's Bush another mob was in command. Down in the East End Benny-the-Kid [Jack Spot] had become king.

Although Hill gives himself the central role in the war against the Whites, Jack Spot seems to have played a more important part. Spot was moving in on the racecourses. The mayhem that followed was on a much less intense level than the racecourse wars of the thirties, but it could be painful for those involved.

In January 1947 Johnnie Warren, a cousin of the Whites, provoked Spot by making a derisive comment about his teetotalism. Spot beat him up in a pub toilet. The showdown came shortly afterwards in the Stork Club in Sackville Street off Piccadilly, where the Whites had tracked Spot down. Both sides later gave widely different accounts of what happened. Here's what Sidney Williams of the *Daily Herald* wrote after interviewing Harry White, Alf's son:

His fear of Spot began in January 1947 in a club in Sackville Street, off Piccadilly. He was drinking with racehorse trainer Tim O'Sullivan and a third man. Spot walked in with ten thugs, went straight up to Harry and said: 'You're Yiddified' – meaning he was anti-Jewish. White denied it. He said: 'I have Jewish people among my best friends.' Spot wouldn't listen, and hit him with a bottle.

As White collapsed in a pool of blood, the rest of Spot's men attacked O'Sullivan and the third man, who was employed by White. O'Sullivan was beaten unconscious and pushed into a fire in the corner of the club. The other man was slashed with razors and stabbed in the stomach.

Spot gave his version to the *Daily Sketch* eight years after the event:

The biggest, toughest and most ruthless mob was the King's Cross gang, led by a bookmaker called Harry who had taken over the racecourse protection racket from the Sabini boys. Their word was law not only on the racecourses but in the clubs and pubs – even the fashionable nightclubs of the West End... We finally ran them down at a place in Sackville Street off Piccadilly. Harry had several of his toughest boys with him when I led my pals into the room. There wasn't any politeness this time. They knew what I'd come for and I sailed right in. At the first smack I took at them Harry scarpered. You couldn't see the seat of his trousers for dust.

One of the White mob, 'Big Bill' Goller, had been wounded so badly that there were fears he might die. Spot was persuaded by his wealthy Jewish backers to lie low, and he went to Southend in Essex. He was seen there by Arthur Helliwell of the *People*, who wrote that he had seen 'the notorious missing gang boss who ducked out of London a week or two ago when the heat was on'. Goller lived, and soon Spot was back in circulation. He took control of the racetracks, raising the £2 fee for a pitch to £7. The Whites failed to answer the Hill–Spot summons to a final showdown.

For many years Heathrow Airport was notorious as a focus for crime. In 1948, however, when Jack Spot's gang planned an ambitious robbery there, the airport was still being built.

Sammy Josephs, a Jewish thief who was associated with the Spot gang, learned that valuable cargoes were kept overnight in warehouses at the airport. He told Spot, and soon plans were being made to steal nearly one million pounds worth of bullion and other valuables.

The planning was meticulous. Members of the robbery team went on guided tours of the airport, parcels were sent from Ireland and Josephs and another member of the team, Franny Daniels, were able to check out the customs shed as they collected them. On the night of 24 July the team were in place and the raid began.

The raiders had drugged the tea of the regular (BOAC) staff but police, who had been tipped off, had taken the place of the BOAC men. When the ten raiders, armed with coshes and iron bars, entered the warehouse they saw men in BOAC uniform apparently drugged, and tied them up. They began to open the safe.

Suddenly officers from the Flying Squad who had been waiting in the shadows were swarming around them. In what became known as the Battle of Heathrow the Spot mob came off worst. Eight of the robbers, bloody and battered, were arrested. Two others got away. Teddy Machin, fabled knife man, fell into a ditch as he fled, and was knocked unconscious by his fall. He woke after the police had left and staggered away to safety. Franny Daniels hid under one of the Black Marias that were taking his comrades off to police stations. When it drove away he clung to the chassis. The Black Maria was driven to Harlesden police station, and like Machin, Daniels was able to escape into the night.[5]

On 30 July 1948 the *Daily Herald* reported: 'Eight bloodstained men, alleged to have been arrested at a London Airport warehouse said to contain £6 million worth of diamonds and £3 million in gold, appeared in court today. The men, several of whom wore bandages and slings, were guarded by nine policemen grouped around the dock. As the men filed in, a blonde woman pushed her way into court, cried out and had to be helped out again.'

The eight Spot men got from five to twelve years' penal

servitude, long sentences for the time. The judge, Sir Gerald Dodson, told them: 'You were, of course, playing for high stakes. You made sure of your position by being ready for any situation with weapons of all kinds. This is the gravity of the offence. A raid on this scale profoundly shocks society. You went prepared for violence and you got it. You got the worst of it, and you can hardly complain.'

Spot, who had taken care to distance himself from the operation, was in the clear, even though he sheltered Daniels and Machin. But his operations came under intense pressure from the police, and the Aldgate club, which had been such a money-spinner, was forced to close. But by now Spot was ready to take over the underworld.

Harry White's father 'Big Alf' White was on the way out as a major force. His alliance with the more anti-Semitic of the Italians never achieved more than local control, and in 1939 he was beaten up at Harringay Greyhound Stadium by a gang of young toughs from Stoke Newington. For the moment the future belonged to Jack Spot.

Spot had style, and understood the importance of playing a role – in his case, that of a successful criminal and gang leader. Leonard 'Nipper' Read, the senior detective who became the scourge of organised crime, recalled the stylish and charming Spot of his heydays in the forties and fifties. Spot, he said, dressed in well-cut suits and would spend the mornings in the Bear Garden at the Cumberland Hotel being consulted and giving advice like Don Corleone in the film *The Godfather*.[6]

The crime reporter Michael Jacobson thought Spot was little more than a thug. 'He had no initiative of his own. He was never a gang leader. Hill was.'

Spot's great rival, Billy Hill, was born in Seven Dials near Leicester Square in 1911. The area was one of the traditional crime rookeries of London, and the extended Hill family – Billy was one of 21 children – was a sort of crime wave in itself. His father had served time for assaulting the police, and his mother was a receiver. His brother Jimmy was a pickpocket, a brother-in-law a notorious villain. But the star of the show was his sister Maggie, known as

Baby Face and the Queen of the Forty Elephants, who was a major-league shoplifter. One theory was that she got the nickname because she hid the shoplifted goods under her clothes, but Stanley Firmin, a *Daily Telegraph* crime reporter, said it came about partly because of her association with the Elephant and Castle and partly because her team of women shoplifters included some hefty six-footers who could beat up young tearaways.

Hill is variously described as looking like Humphrey Bogart, or in the words of Nipper Read, 'short, slim and with his hair greased and pasted back ... he looked every inch a spiv of the 1950s.' He was above all a planner and organiser, but he understood the value of clinical and extreme violence, and even torture, in the world of the protection racketeer.

Hill says in his autobiography that he did his first stabbing at the age of fourteen. 'Suddenly he took a liberty with me. Without the slightest qualm I got hold of a pair of scissors and drove them into his back. And it came quite natural to me. It was as easy as that.'[7]

He worked as a delivery boy for a grocer, and improved the occasion by making notes of likely burglary targets for his brother-in-law. By the beginning of the Second World War he was a gang leader, well-placed to take advantage of the opportunities wartime disruption offered. His gang of smash-and-grab raiders were so successful that he claimed many young villains wanted to work with him and he had to put them on a rota. The blackout and the fact that the youngest and fittest policemen had gone into the armed services meant that a new line, breaking into post offices around London and cracking their safes, was ridiculously easy. Hill says that he was taking an average of £3,000 a week from these raids. 'Money? It was coming to us like pieces of dirty paper. I rarely went out without a monkey [£500] or a grand in my pocket. That was spending stuff. Emergency funds in case I got nicked, or in case the bite [request for money] was put on me. That was apart from the remainder of a steady fortune I had piling up.'[8]

Hill and numerous other criminals also exploited the black market. As the black market blurred the distinctions between criminals and ordinary honest citizens they were joined in this by a wide range of people who might otherwise have led blameless lives:

businessmen who diverted part of their production to take advantage of the higher prices on the black market, farmers who did the same with their produce, and of course the resentful citizens who bought the goods.

Market towns around London – Romford was the centre of the black market – saw a huge rise in business as traders from London arrived to swop their goods for agricultural produce. There was also a brisk trade in stolen clothing coupons and ration books.[9]

Another source of supply for the black market was bomb-damaged shops and businesses. Criminals raided warehouses and hijacked lorries. Deserters and spivs swelled the ranks of those involved in this commodity crime. Spivs were essentially contact men, fixers, who acted as an interface between the public and the real criminals.

Wherever the spiv met up with his mates – down Old Compton Street, outside the forum in Kentish Town, anywhere – there was always a caff round the corner, less sinister than it looked, where deals were struck. Rings flashed on middle fingers, hats were crushed rakishly down on duck-arse haircuts, and the mood, as if sustained from the war, was one of tough casual humour in the face of grave hardships: such as how to dispose at high speed of a hot lorry-load of socks, twelve and a tanner in the stores, four bob to you. Luckily for the spiv a surprisingly large number of people were soon wearing the socks (or drinking the Scotch or luxuriating in the sheets) and keeping mum about it.[10]

Hill prospered. With his organising ability and his wide network of criminals he had an edge on the mainly amateur spivs. As his black-market business grew he acquired an eighteenth-century manor house at the village of Bovington in Hertfordshire. There is a photograph of a sharp-suited Hill at the manor house, soft hat on head, every inch the gangster. What did the neighbours in this quiet country village make of such exotic metropolitan fauna as Hill and his men? We do not know, but neither they nor the police ever asked any questions. Hill wrote:

Our Bovington run-in was packed tight with bent gear, and I now had a relay of my own cars bringing it up to London as the demand needed it. All I had to do was take a stroll around the West End and I was literally besieged by people wanting to buy almost anything from a pair of nylon stockings to a fresh salmon or a shoulder of good smoked bacon. There were many times when that barn was filled chock-a-block with nicked gear – sheets, towels, furniture, shoes, textiles, rolls of silk, tea, even rare spices which fetched a fortune from the Soho cafe proprietors who needed that sort of thing.[11]

Hill explains how easy it was to get his supplies. Mostly he simply stole them, for example from a Services bedding store in the West Country. His team also emptied a warehouse full of fur coats. 'Then there was whisky. Most of the trivial villains were making bombs out of manufacturing their own brands, and sticking the vile rubbish in proprietary brand bottles. I liked to think that if I was crooked, at least I was bent in an honest way. I sold only real whisky. Good stuff at that...I sold each barrel of whisky for £500 a time.'

By the fourth year of the war the black market was booming. Hill and his fellow gangsters and thieves were making fortunes both by supplying the black market and by running gambling clubs which also flourished. He wrote:

All thieves were so prosperous that they adopted a sort of competitive spirit to display their wealth by dressing up their wives and girlfriends in as expensive jewellery and clothes as they could buy – from the black market, of course. By common consent, Monday was regarded as a truce day...usually we all had bombs to spend, and we congregated in a club in Archer Street. What with all the villains in their Savile Row suits and their wives and girlfriends wearing straight furs and clothes by the best West End dressmakers, that club looked like the Ascot of the Underworld.[12]

There were moments of sickening brutality. At this stage of his career Hill always carried a knife – 'my closest friend, a well-sharpened knife with a five-inch blade never left me' – and often used it. He liked to carve a V sign in his victims' cheeks.

> One afternoon I was in one of these Soho clubs having a drink and thinking about tomorrow when I went to the toilet. When I opened the door I saw two young tearaways from over the water belting the life out of my old friend Dodger Mullins with an iron bar. In his time Dodger had been a twenty-four carat villain. He was well into his sixties now... We all liked Dodger ...Now two young tearaways were reaching for the crown of glory in being able to say they had beaten the life out of Dodger ...I got out my chiv [knife] and gave one tearaway my favourite stroke, a V for Victory sign on his cheek. Then I cut the other monkey to ribbons...
>
> Then there was the night when another fight broke out in a boozer, all over nothing. I was minding my own business as it was. That is, until someone broke a glass and pushed the jagged end into my face. It stuck there like a dart in a dartboard. I pulled the glass out of my face with one hand and my chiv out of my pocket with the other. Then I got to work doing a bit of hacking and carving. I don't know how many blokes I cut that night. I didn't care. When you get a jagged glass shoved into your face you don't bother about counting the blokes you chiv. You just hack away until your knife gets blunt or the others swallow it [surrender or retreat].

In 1947 Hill was arrested for warehouse-breaking, a crime he claimed he didn't commit, and after being granted bail, decided to leave the country rather than spend more time in prison. 'It would mean turning my back on London for good and all. It would mean goodbye to the Big Smoke, farewell to Odd Legs, Tosh, Franny, Horrible Harry, Taters Mutton and all the boys. I wondered if I could stand the severance of not being with Strong Arms again, or Wide Gaiters Alf, or Long Stan or Big Jock.'[13]

He went to South Africa, and in Johannesburg teamed up with British former boxer and villain Bobby Ramsey. They opened a gambling club, and found themselves in conflict with the local gang leader Arnold Neville, a seventeen-stone wrestler. When Neville and his team arrived to smash up the club they encountered some London-style retaliation. Neville needed nearly a hundred stitches.

The local paper, the *Rand Daily Mail*, reported: 'His assailants slashed his head and buttocks with razors and his condition is serious. It is alleged that shots were fired during the attack.'

Hill was arrested but went on the run again and made his way back to Britain. After lying low for a while and carrying out a £9,000 robbery with two of Spot's associates he gave himself up and was sentenced to three years in Wandsworth.

When he left prison in 1949 Jack Spot was waiting at the prison gates to welcome him as a partner. Hill was now nearly forty. Spot described him as being 'as thin as a pickled herring'. Compared to the suave and well-dressed Spot, now the most powerful crime boss in the country, he cut a sorry figure. But Spot was glad to have him as a lieutenant. Hill was vastly experienced and respected.

There were also considerable advantages in the alliance for Hill. With his record of convictions he faced a long sentence if he was convicted again. It was time for him to take a back seat, and the role Spot was offering, looking after the spielers, was ideal.

Spielers, the small-time gambling clubs Arthur Harding had made a speciality of holding up early in the century, had come a long way since the war. Now they attracted the profits of the booming black market, and of course all the underworld characters involved in it. It wasn't a question of just raking off protection money – there was a real job of protection to be done.

Some of the fights that broke out in spielers were legendary. Jackie Reynolds of the Upton Park gipsies ran a successful club in Southend. He fell out with Teddy Machin, one of Spot's team of robbers and a virtuoso with a chiv or razor. The bloody fight which followed showed just how much the spielers needed control.[14]

Nobody was going to take liberties like that with Hill. Like Spot he was a teetotaller, and with his icy manner and cold eyes ('it was like looking into black glass') he had a natural authority.

Hill said of the spielers: 'They do not have names and committees and all that stuff. They just start, usually in a cellar or any suitable premises that can be found, and word gets round that there's a game on. Then the customers come in. They range from regular villains and tearaways to every kind of person from titled aristocrats down to cab-drivers and waiters. We never did allow any steamers [steam tugs = mugs] in. Our game was not to trim mugs who wanted to play for some sort of thrill. There was no need for that.'

In July 1947 the Spot and Hill gang drove the Whites off the scene for good. Both Spot and Hill later told how they had massed their men, armed to the teeth, for a final confrontation with the Whites which never came. Hill, who calls Spot Benny-the-Kid in his autobiography, wrote: '"It's all right", I said to Benny the Kid, "we won't need shooters in this town any more. Get 'em off the boys and get rid of them." They collected the shooters and the bombs and the machine gun and destroyed them. They were actually thrown down a manhole.'[15]

In Spot's version he is giving the orders. He said he was warned by the police that they would not tolerate gang warfare in London. 'When I got back to Aldgate I called the heavy mob together at once. "We've got to pack it up," I said. "Get rid of the ironmongery." So we collected all the Stens, the grenades, revolvers, pistols and ammunition, loaded them into a lorry and dumped the whole lot into the Thames.'[16]

The police officer involved, Chief Superintendent Peter Beveridge, has yet another version, saying that the gangs

> ...were planning to resume their fight at Harringay Arena on the night of the Baksi v. Woodcock fight. So I went along to see the leader. I had never met him before but he had a tough reputation and I expected a battle, at least of words. Instead he was very meek and mild and accepted my hint that I would view any trouble at Harringay in a very personal way. He made only one point – that I tell the other gang the same thing.[17]

The result was an unprecedented period of peace in the underworld. Hill called the years 1950 and 1951 'peaceful and profitable...The truth was we had cleared all the cheap racketeers out.'

Spot and Hill both became involved with women who were to

play a part in the evolution of their partnership. Spot met Rita, a beautiful Irish woman who was to become his wife, at Haydock races in June 1951. She later told a newspaper: 'I looked round for the nicest-looking bookmaker, someone I could trust. Then I saw him. Broad-shouldered, expensively dressed – master of all around him. I went across. I looked appealingly into his eyes. He met my gaze. "Could I have ten shillings each way?" I asked him. I had FALLEN IN LOVE WITH JACK SPOT.'

Jack turned on the charm, even following Rita back to Dublin. After they were married Rita said: 'He was good to Mum, so I married him.'[18]

Hill's woman was Gypsy Riley, a hot-tempered good-time girl. She had been involved with a Belgian Jewish refugee called 'Belgian Johnny' who was a pimp. Gypsy told Hill that Belgian Johnny was trying to get her to become a prostitute again. Hill retaliated by attacking Belgian Johnny in a West End restaurant, slashing his face and neck.

This reckless attack was just the kind of behaviour that could put Hill away for a long time, and he implored Spot to visit Belgian Johnny in Charing Cross Hospital. Spot paid the Belgian enough to make it worth his while to go back to Belgium.

Spot then took Rita, Hill and Gypsy for a holiday to the south of France. When they all returned, Spot announced his retirement. Arthur Helliwell wrote in the *People* on 13 October 1951, without naming Spot, that he had been visited by 'Britain's Al Capone, the self-confessed Czar of Gangland'.

Helliwell went on to say: 'After nearly twenty-five years as a mobster, he has finally reached the conclusion that crime does not pay! He walked into my office with two bodyguards and announced his intention of quitting the shady side of the street and going into what he calls "legit business". No one knows who the next Big Shot will be – but I don't need a crystal ball to predict that in the months following his retirement the streets of Soho, the racetracks and gambling dens will be decidedly unhealthy spots.'

Spot didn't retire, but he probably foresaw the end of the good times. He had divided his empire with Hill, keeping control of the racetracks and turning the spielers over to his partner. Both of these sources of income were now coming under pressure from groups who wanted to clean up gambling. Hill's spielers were less visible and so less vulnerable. With the Jockey Club and the big corporate bookmakers pressing for the legalisation of betting shops, and the racing authorities increasingly taking control on the courses, Spot was being squeezed.

While his role diminished, his partner was looking for new opportunities, and the spielers, which were an efficient information exchange for the underworld, were the ideal place to find them. He decided to pull off a couple of major jobs before he retired.[19]

The £287,000 mailbag robbery in Eastcastle Street in May 1952 was his pension fund (See page 201). Although he never admitted it, he said in *Boss of Britain's Underworld*:

> Walk along Old Compton Street or down Wardour Street, or over the heath at Newmarket on any racing day, or along the promenade at Brighton any week, and ask anyone who thinks they know. Ask them who planned the Big Mailbag Job. The one when £287,000 in freely negotiable currency notes, in hard cash, was nicked, in May 1952, and they'll all tell you, 'We don't know who did it, but we've got a good idea. In any case, we know that Billy Hill planned it. Only he could have done that.'

The mailbag robbery brought unprecedented pressure from the police. Questions had been asked in the House of Commons and Sir Winston Churchill himself weighed in, saying the robbers must be caught. Hill wrote: 'All my friends were turned over. My spielers were raided and closed down. Friends of mine going abroad on holidays were turned over by the Customs people. One of my lads even had his car taken to pieces, yet he did not have a criminal conviction. All my telephones were tapped for years afterwards. My mail going through the post was steamed open and read.'

Just when they needed to calm things down, Hill's lover Gypsy provoked another gangland fight. She encouraged Slip Sullivan, a croupier who worked for Hill, to attack a Maltese vice operator named George Caruana. The incident had something to do with her past as a prostitute.

Unfortunately Caruana was being guarded by Tommy Smithson, a fearless ex-boxer and tearaway from Hackney who ran a protection racket preying on small-time Maltese gambling clubs. He beat Sullivan badly and slashed his throat. Retribution was inevitable after Gypsy urged Hill to avenge 'poor Slip'.

Smithson was invited to a 'peace conference' at the Black Cat cigarette factory in Camden Town. An old ally of his, Jim Barnett, later told what happened next: 'There was Moisha Blueball, Billy Hill, Jackie Spot and they said, "Look, you know you're carrying a gun, give us the gun". He gave them the gun and Billy Hill hit him over the head with it.' Then a furniture van arrived and between eight and ten men jumped out, including Sullivan's brother Sonny. Smithson was slashed across the face, arms, legs and chest. He was then thrown over a wall and left to die, but survived to fight another day. Forty-seven stitches were put in the V-shaped cuts on his face. Because he refused to talk to the police Jack Spot gave him £500 and promised to open a night club for him.

With the opposition dispersed or grown old and soft, Hill and Spot enjoyed the rich criminal pickings of the West End more or less unchallenged for more than ten years. There were other gangs – the Messinas, Maltese whoremasters, in particular. Hill and Spot, secure in their monopoly, were content to reach an accommodation with them. There was enough for everybody: nightclubs, drinking clubs, spielers and protection rackets were making them wealthy.

They weren't criminal masterminds – they didn't need to be. They were sensible enough to stay on good terms with the police, and as far as possible they banned the use of firearms. The fact that murder carried the death penalty may have had something to do with it. Knives and razors were still the weapons usually used when gangs clashed, and Hill claims he was a reluctant knifeman. 'I never chivved anyone unless I had to. There's no point in cutting up people if it's not necessary. And I would stand for plenty of liberties before eventually I did use the knife.' (He himself contradicts this).

Then it all fell apart. From his comfortable retirement in a large villa in Spain, Hill later recalled: 'Jack was becoming insecure and a bit jealous of me. He was an older man, you see, and once he got this persecution complex he was impossible to work with any more.'

Spot wrote: 'Billy Hill was a friend of mine. But he had his own way of working. His own personal ambitions and his own ideas and plans; ambitions and ideas can sometimes clash.'

Elsewhere he wrote: 'I made Billy Hill. He wrote to me when he was in jail, wanted me to help him. Then he got to be top over me. If it wasn't for me he would never have got there. I should've shot Billy Hill. I really should.'

On 21 September 1954 robbers stole £45,000 in gold bullion from a KLM lorry in Jockey's Fields, a narrow street off Theobalds Road in Clerkenwell. Hill had an alibi: at the time of the robbery he was at the *People*, dictating the concluding part of his autobiography to the journalist Duncan Webb. It included details of how the KLM robbery had been organised.

In April 1955 Hill and Gypsy sailed for Australia. The Boss of the Underworld was rich enough to retire, and he planned to emigrate for good. But the Australian authorities would not let him enter and in June he sailed back to Britain.

While he was away Spot had come under renewed pressure. The take from the racecourses was falling away, and some of the Italian bookmakers, led by Albert Dimes, no longer recognised his rule.

Spot had taken Hill's claim to be the Boss of the Underworld badly, and he hit back at the man he blamed for putting Hill up to it, Duncan Webb. The journalist was lured to the Horseshoe pub in Tottenham Court Road, where Spot broke his arm with a knuckleduster. After Webb complained to the police Spot was tried and fined £50.

This clumsy act of revenge bore out what some had been saying: Spot was losing control. In *Jack Spot: Man of a Thousand Cuts* Hank Janson wrote: 'Jack Spot, who was the Boss of the Underworld, was now living a Jekyll and Hyde existence. He was a happy, contentedly married man in his home, and a scheming, planning master-mind at his club.'

Another important player in the drama was Albert Dimes, a popular Italian criminal well known in Soho, at least in part for his sense of humour. He gave Ronnie Scott, the jazz club owner, a magnum of champagne to be opened when the club started making money. Years later, the unopened magnum was still there.[20]

Dimes grew up in Little Italy and was allied to the Sabinis. In May 1941 he had been charged with the murder of Harry 'Little Hubby' Distleman, the doorman of the West End Bridge and Billiards Club in Wardour Street, who had been stabbed to death. There had been a fight and Antonio 'Baby Face' Mancini, who managed the club downstairs, said he went to investigate. He claimed he heard someone shout, 'There's Babe! Let's get him.' and had stabbed Distleman in self-defence. Mancini was hanged for the murder. Dimes and another man were convicted of unlawful wounding.

Spot was now estranged from Hill, and he had also fallen out with Dimes. His own team were getting too old and comfortable for rough stuff. Hill's mob, on the other hand, were becoming more formidable. 'Mad' Frankie Fraser, a young tearaway who would stop at nothing, had gone over to Hill, as had Billy Blythe, another hard man, who had a conviction for cutting a Flying Squad officer in the face. Another friend of Hill's was the former boxer George Walker, who later founded the Brent Walker business empire.

At the 1955 spring Epsom race meeting Hill turned up with Dimes and other Italian hard men. Spot needed allies, and in desperation he turned to the Kray twins, Ronnie and Reggie, young East End thugs who were starting to make a reputation. He wanted them to protect his pitches, and he made them the surprise offer of their own pitch. Spot was taking a real risk, as indeed were the twins. They had a local reputation in the East End for violence, but here they were up against the elite of the underworld.[21]

Their job was to 'mind' one of Spot's bookmakers, and keep an eye on Hill. He had his own pitch, and with him, apart from Dimes and the Italians, were Fraser and Blythe. Hardened veterans of the racecourse wars waited for the first blow to be struck, convinced that the twins were about to be cut to pieces. The only people who seemed unaffected by the tension were the twins, who laughed and joked with their friends.[22]

Finally they collected their money and drove off without even bothering to thank Spot. Fraser and Blythe seem to have issued a challenge to the twins for a showdown in a pub in Islington. This was just what Ronnie Kray wanted – gang warfare. There had been speculation for some time that things were changing at the top in the underworld, and Ronnie had dreamed of blasting and cutting his way to the top. He and Reggie had been planning for just such a battle, and they had the guns and the team ready. They drove to the pub and waited in vain for the Hill mob to show up. Billy Hill had heard of Fraser's challenge and called the showdown off. Gang warfare was the last thing he wanted. The Krays drove away, their dreams of gangland glory on hold.

Things went from bad to worse for Spot. Hill discovered that Spot had given evidence against three men in an assault case back in 1937. He got the depositions of the case and had copies pasted up in underworld pubs.

Mad Frankie Fraser thinks that what happened next was an attempt by Spot to regain his status. Spot was in a Soho drinking club, the Galahad, in August 1955 when he was told that Albert Dimes wanted to see him. He rushed out and caught up with Dimes at the corner of Frith Street and stabbed him in the thigh and stomach. Dimes tried to find refuge in a fruit shop, whose lady owner, a friend of Dimes's, hit Spot over the head with a set of scales. This enabled Dimes to grab the knife, and he stabbed Spot, who staggered to a nearby barber's and collapsed. Both men were taken to hospital.

The account in the *Daily Express*, while not accurate to the last detail, caught the drama of the fight.

The hands of the clock above the Italian Expresso coffee bar pointed to 11.40. Mambo music was blaring from juke boxes. Men in slouched hats and draped suits were taking the air at the corner. Two men were talking under the clock...then as 50-year-old proprietor Mr Harry Hyams was weighing tomatoes the fight started inside his greengrocer's shop.

A stiletto rose and plunged swiftly as the two men fought. Trays of plump melons and plums and peaches toppled down as customers fled, and then 13-stone Mrs Sophie Hyams went into action. She picked up a heavy metal scoop from a weighing machine and began beating the fighting men over the head with it. The men tried to get out of the way. The stiletto kept flashing, but 45-year-old Mrs Hyams kept on banging the scoop at the men as the blood splashed on her white overall... Jack Spot staggered down the street alone as the juke boxes blared. He slumped into the scarlet and cream salon of a hairdressing shop. 'Fix me up,' he whispered. 'Clean me up,' said the man with a six-guinea shirt and £15 pair of shoes.

There were other theories as to why Spot attacked Dimes. One was that Dimes had failed to pay his dues. What is clear is that Spot was the loser, in every way. He had been slashed and stabbed about the head and left arm, and had two wounds in his chest, one of which penetrated a lung. Dimes had been slashed across the forehead and the stomach wound had, a court was told later, 'mercifully just failed to penetrate the abdominal cavity'.

Both men were arrested. Spot said: 'It is between me and Albert Dimes – between us and nothing to do with you.' Dimes was at first more forthcoming. 'You know as well as I do. It was Jackie Spot.' But asked for a formal statement he became vague. 'It was 'a tall man...I don't know his name.'

Spot later told a jury that Dimes had warned him to stay away from racetracks. He had paid £300 for his pitches on the tracks, keeping one for himself and renting the others out. Dimes had told him: 'This is your final warning. I don't want you to go racing any more.' He added that Spot had been making money from the pitches long enough and it was time for someone else to have a go.

Spot now played his trump card, a clergyman named the Reverend Basil Claude Andrews. The 88-year-old cleric claimed he had seen the fight, and that Dimes was the aggressor. He said he had seen accounts of the fight in the newspapers, and decided something was seriously wrong. 'It astonished me', he claimed. 'I thought "Dear me! this is entirely wrong. The darker man was the aggressor. He attacked the fairer man."' The darker man, he said, was Dimes. 'At first I thought I had better keep quiet about it. But it preyed on my mind. Ultimately I decided I had better do something.'

What he did was to swing the case in Spot's favour. After considering their verdict for just over an hour the jury found Spot not guilty. Parson Andrews asked the court if his name could be kept out of the papers because, he said, 'I am pretty well known in London, and have groups of friends, and it is rather a disgraceful affair to be mixed up in.' It soon became clear who these friends were, and why he wanted his name kept secret.

Dimes had not been present in court to hear Andrews' testimony, but when told about it he contacted journalist Duncan Webb. The indefatigable Webb began digging, and that Sunday the *People* carried the front-page headline: 'Parson's Dud Bets Start Hunt by Bookies'.

It emerged that Parson Andrews had a weakness for wine, women and song – well, whisky, women and gambling. He had been curate at Kensal Green cemetery for 39 years, retiring in 1947 on a pension of £250 a year, nothing like enough to cover his gambling debts. He had a reputation among Soho bookies for welshing on those debts.

The following day at Dimes's trial the prosecution admitted that in view of the revelations, and the result of Spot's trial, it would be unsafe to go ahead. Dimes was found not guilty, and the police were left looking foolish.

Parson Andrews told the *Daily Sketch*: 'I wish to deny that I have committed perjury. I wish to deny that I have any hopes of material gain from having come forward as a witness. I did so only in the interests of truth, and I am willing to tell the police that if they come to me.' But under police pressure, he told a very different story.

His landlord, Peter MacDonough, a small-time gambler and friend of Spot, had introduced him to two of Spot's faithful associates, Moisha Blueball (Morris Goldstein) and Sonny the Yank (Bernard Schach). They took him to the Spots' Hyde Park Mansions flat where Rita gave him a cup of tea. He was given £63 to say that he had seen the fight and that it was Dimes who started it.

Moisha, Sonny and MacDonough were arrested, and Rita was brought back from Ireland, where she and Spot had gone to get away from the newspapers.

The trial began on 28 November. The prosecution must have been very nervous about their main witness, an errant clergyman with a colourful past who was also a self-confessed perjurer. They need not have worried.

Parson Andrews excelled himself. With an extraordinary mixture of pathos, contrition, wit and brazen defiance he held the court spellbound. When he was asked why he had lied to the court at the Spot trial he said: 'It was very wicked of me. I was hard up and I was tempted and I fell. It is rather humiliating for me to have to tell you I was desperately hungry. I had had Continental breakfasts and nothing in between. I was very poor and hungry and I should not have yielded but I did. Thank God, I have asked to be forgiven.'

Who could resist his reply when he was asked why he had now decided to tell the truth? 'In the silence of the night, when things come back to you, it was brought to my mind the sin I had committed and the wickedness I had done and the harm I had caused by acting as I had done.'

Certainly the jury couldn't resist and despite the weakness of the rest of the prosecution's case, the four accused were found guilty. Moisha Blueball got two years, Sonny the Yank and MacDonough a year each. Rita, whose striking beauty cannot have failed to make an impression, got a six-month suspended sentence and a £50 fine.

Spot announced that he was quitting the rackets and opting for a quiet life, running a small café. But Spot knew that the other side was planning revenge. He asked for police protection but didn't get it.

In May 1956 Hill heard that Spot was planning to attack him. Days later, as Spot and Rita were returning from inspecting a pub they planned to buy they were attacked on the steps of their Hyde Park Mansions flat by a large gang led by Frankie Fraser, who was wielding a shillelagh.

Rita screamed, then clung to her husband. They were both knocked to the ground and the attackers, who were armed with razors and knives, set about cutting up Jack Spot. Later in hospital, after 78 stitches and a blood transfusion, he agreed to name some of the attackers. A week later, his courage and fighting spirit restored, he changed his mind and told journalists: 'I'm the toughest man in the world. I am staying in London. Nobody will drive me out.'

Although he refused to name his attackers, Rita had no such scruples. She picked out Bobbie Warren, a member of the old White gang whose brother had once been beaten up by Spot, and Frankie Fraser at an identification parade.

The trial at the Old Bailey in June gave the public a rare glimpse of the exotic world of the gangster. Hill set up a kind of headquarters at the Rex café opposite the courts, so that he could keep in touch with proceedings. He wore dark glasses and was surrounded by henchmen. Away from their normal surroundings these denizens of the underworld with their broken noses and scarred faces looked particularly menacing. The judge was given a police escort and broad-shouldered officers ringed the Old Bailey.[23]

The columnist 'Cassandra' protested in the *Daily Mirror*: 'These hoodlums who have never done a day's work, who were brought up in borstals, who have criminal records that leave the ordinary citizens reeling with horror at their callous brutalities, turn up in vast shiny limousines outside the courts of justice to encourage "their boys" when all too occasionally they land in the dock.'

Inside the court things were not going well for 'their boys'. An ill-considered attempt by the defence to blacken Rita Comer's character and suggest that she was lying failed. When defence lawyer Patrick Marrinan asked her: 'Is it not the truth that you are most anxious that your husband should become the king of the underworld again?' she replied with patent sincerity: 'I would be happy if my husband could be left alone and get just a small job. I have had enough of all this.'

Summing up, the judge echoed this when he said: 'If that story was false, what repercussions has she to expect in this world of violence in which she and her children have been living for some time and which she has told us she would give anything to escape?'

The jury decided Warren and Fraser were guilty, and they both got seven years. Speaking later of the attack on the Spots, Fraser said: 'He must have been practising his scream because it was louder than his wife's. Hers was quite loud but his was even better. I just whacked him with the shillelagh a couple of times and someone else cut him and that was that.'

Fraser and Warren were out of the way at a crucial stage, for both Spot and Hill were now ready to call it a day. But not before Hill had some famous last words: 'Billy Hill's the boss – Jack Spot was very cut up about it.'

After the trial Spot said: 'I ain't afraid of anyone, but I want a quiet life now.' That was the last thing that Hill, smarting over the long jail terms his lieutenants were serving, had in mind for Spot. On 20 June 1956 Big Tommy Falco, who worked as a driver for Dimes, was slashed outside the Astor Club near Berkeley Square and had 47 stitches in his arm. He claimed that Spot had attacked him, saying as he did so: 'This is one for Albert.' As he was arrested Spot said: 'You see what they do to me. I should have named the twenty of them' – presumably meaning the men who attacked him and his wife. He also said: 'This is a diabolical liberty. I will get ten years for nothing.'

Spot was saved by a Glasgow gangster named Victor 'Scarface Jock' Russo. When Spot came to trial at the Old Bailey Russo told a strange tale of a plot by Hill to frame Spot. He said he was walking in Soho when Hill, Dimes and some other Hill mobsters drew up alongside him in a big Buick limousine. They asked him to allow himself to be slashed in the face by one of Hill's men, and say it had been done by Spot. The reasoning was that his face was so scarred already it wouldn't make much difference. The payment was £500 before and another £500 after the court case.

Russo took the £500 and left for Glasgow, phoning Hill to say he wouldn't be back for the second instalment. Cassandra in the *Daily Mirror* called Russo 'a hacked up rat' and 'a degenerate with treachery in his heart, compared with whom Judas was a thousandfold saint who had the decency to find a tree and a rope'. Yet Russo had nothing to gain by speaking up for Spot, and much to lose.

The prosecution called Hill as a witness. The judge rebuked him for using underworld jargon. When Spot's counsel asked him if he called himself 'King of Soho' he denied it. Asked how he would style himself he replied: 'The Boss of the Underworld.'

The judge, Mr Justice Streatfield, called Russo's tale, 'one of the strangest that can ever have been told even in the Number One court at the Old Bailey.' The jury took twenty minutes to find Spot not guilty, and although there were calls for Hill and his associates to be prosecuted for perjury, the matter was allowed to drop.

Hill's blatant claim to the title 'Boss of the Underworld' in the witness box at the Old Bailey raised official hackles. There were questions in the Commons, and newspapers speculated about exactly what a boss of the underworld did. The *Daily Herald* attempted to answer the question:

> Crime – even the shady rackets and 'concessions' that do not qualify for that title – does not pay to be disorganised. Gamblers want to run their dens without interference from ambitious 'gatecrashers'. So do the drinking club operators, the bookies and the smaller fry. Remember – they can't go running to the police for protection. Hence the Boss. He must be an organiser, must possess brains which in the respectable world of business would win him a high place. And he must be ruthless enough to dispense a rough justice throughout the underworld. He is the underworld's distorted symbol of the respectable morality it defies. Quiet crime is his motto.

Hill retired to Spain, saying he had had enough. He had become a minor celebrity. The launch of his book, *Boss of Britain's Underworld*, had been attended by publicity-hungry Lord and Lady Docker, and he had organised the return of Lady Docker's jewels when they were stolen. A picture taken at the book launch shows Frankie Fraser draped over the piano. Many of the major 'names' in the underworld of the day were there, with the exception of Spot and his men.

The party, which was held at Gennaro's in Soho – now the Groucho Club – gave the newspapers the chance to be sanctimonious, and as usual they seized it. The *Daily Mail* printed a reproduction of the invitation it had been sent and said: 'A sorry day, I feel, when a gangster's book justifies a gilt-edged invitation.' The *Daily Sketch* called Hill's book 'a primer for gangsters, hold-up men and cosh boys.' There were questions in the House of Commons.

In fact gangsters were providing the papers with good copy. The *News Chronicle* ran a three-day series on the underworld, and the *Sunday Graphic* started a feature called 'Casebook on Crime'. Spot and Dimes appeared on television, and Hill was interviewed by ITN, although the interview was never shown. Some reporters, like Duncan Webb, were partisan and got caught up in the politics of the underworld. Another reporter who strayed from the path of impartiality was Gerald Byrne of the *Sunday Chronicle*, who favoured the Spot camp and repeated comments about Hill being 'a miserable little character'. He wrote about Hill threatening to poison the pigeons in Trafalgar Square and dyeing the fountain water green. His car was smashed up soon afterwards.

The *Daily Sketch* generally took a hard line, but clearly realised its readers were fascinated by the lives of gangsters:

> The jealous rats fighting it out in the streets and the alleys could, in a short time, make Soho a desert where no respectable citizen would risk his reputation or his personal safety...Club owners and others who have managed to live peacefully in the past are now confronted by demands for protection money. The iron vice of crime is tightening on Soho. This is the ugliest challenge that the police have had to meet for many years in London...the only way to meet it is to deal with every single rat, however obscure he may appear at the moment. This is a job of vermin extermination.

Commenting on Hill's decision to retire, one of his associates said: 'Hill's bottle went, he'd lived by violence and now he was afraid of getting it.' Hill's own valedictory message suggests there may have been something in that view: 'So I'm leaving it all to the youngsters. Some young villain will come along to take my place. He will have to fight for it. Several will have to bring the chivs down very hard to get where I am. And the blood will flow through the streets of Soho once again. But by then I'll be sunning myself in the Southern Atlantic or on the Riviera.'[24]

Hill had a villa in Marbella – in the area later to be called the 'Costa del Crime' – and he wanted to spend time there with Gypsy. He did not cut his ties with London completely. He had interests in clubs in London and he wanted his wife Aggie, from whom he was estranged, to continue to run the New Cabinet club in Gerrard Street.

The funeral of the murdered gangster Tommy Smithson in July 1956, which was attended by leading underworld figures, gave Hill the opportunity to make arrangements for his retirement. He met the

Krays and explained that there was no longer any reason for bad feeling between them. The Krays agreed.

Hill became a kind of elder statesman, being visited by travelling gangsters and making occasional trips to London, where he turned up at clubs run by the Krays. The twins were pleased with this apparent endorsement of their plans for universal hegemony, and Hill took the opportunity to hob-nob with Lady Docker and go gambling with property racketeer Peter Rachman and Mandy Rice-Davies, one of the girls in the Profumo scandal. He returned permanently to England in the early seventies and ran a nightclub at Sunningdale. He and Gypsy split up, and Hill lived with a black singer, who committed suicide in 1979. Her death hit him hard, and he retreated into his flat in Moscow Road. When he died in 1984 Jack Spot called him 'the richest man in the graveyard'.

Other names in the Hill–Spot story met equally inauspicious ends or found a less stressful way of life. Little Billy Blythe died after surgery in prison in 1957, aged only 39. Knife-man Teddy Machin was shot dead on his doorstep in 1970. In 1955 Slip Sullivan was stabbed with a two-foot carving knife, apparently by his Irish wife, and was given a lavish gangster's funeral. Moisha Blueball fell in with the Krays, but nevertheless died penniless. Hill's women did better. His wife Aggie was the owner of the New Cabinet club in Gerrard Street when the manager, Selwyn Cooney, was killed in a fight with the Nash brothers in 1960. She moved to Jersey and opened another club, which made her wealthy. Gypsy was accused of stabbing a man in the eye at the Miramar Club in Paddington in 1957. The case was dismissed, and Hill bought her a house at Ilford. When he died, she arranged his funeral and settled his affairs.[25]

Parson Basil Andrews was found by a newspaper reporter living in Oxford on a church pension of £5 a week. 'Meals must be of the most economical sort. Bread and cheese for lunch. A cheap but hot meal at night. Only very occasionally can he afford a drink.'[26]

Spot fell on hard times. He was declared bankrupt and evicted from his flat. The *Daily Worker*, of all papers, reported: 'Some of the more censorious neighbours of Mr and Mrs Comer – Jack Spot of Soho fame – have been appealing to their mutual landlord to tip the Comers the black spot by giving them notice to quit their luxury flat in Bayswater. It is just too painful, it seems, for a Queen of the Bridge Tables to have to meet a King of the Underworld in the lift.'

Rita sold her life story, and with the money she opened the Highball club. Initially successful, it was wrecked by a gang and then burned down. It is not hard to see the hidden hand of Hill in all this. Spot got the message that his days as a kingpin in the underworld were over, and went to Ireland, where he was involved on the fringes of the racing world. He and Rita split up and eventually he returned to London and was to be seen from time to time at boxing matches, full of tales of the old days, living, like superannuated gangsters before and since, on his reputation.

With Spot and Hill off the scene, the only gangster of any stature operating in the West End was Albert Dimes. He had inherited some of the racetrack interests, and acted as an elder statesman in gang disputes. But he was not a hard man, a 'terror' as Harding would have put it, and had the sense to realise that he could never control Soho, let alone the West End.

It is true that Dimes went into business with Frankie Fraser and Eddie Richardson, supplying fruit machines to nightclubs. His name cropped up from time to time in incongruous circumstances, as in 1956 when he was awarded £666 for a back injury he got when a taxi he was travelling in hit a van. He claimed he was earning about £10 a week as a commission agent. That same year the MP Anthony Greenwood, speaking in the House of Commons, called him 'a squalid, cowardly, small-time hoodlum'. Greenwood refused to see Dimes when he called round for an explanation.

Just how influential Dimes was is not clear, although some commentators regarded him as a kind of godfather. He met the American *mafioso* Angelo Bruno when he arrived in Britain in 1966 on a trip organised by a New York gambling club, and later visited him in America to discuss installing gaming machines in clubs. Another major crime figure on the gambling trip was Meyer Lansky, one of the founding fathers of American organised crime. Dimes was certainly the arbiter in disputes between rival gangs.

When he died of cancer in 1972, the actor Stanley Baker, who got to know him when Dimes gave technical advice on Joseph Losey's 1960 film *The Criminal*, attended the funeral, and the Krays sent a £20 wreath with the message 'To a fine gentleman'. This was destroyed by Dimes's friends because it was felt to bring disgrace to the family.[27] At the funeral the priest recalled how proud Dimes was of being able to recite the Creed in Latin.

Like most of the top London crime figures – the Sabinis, Hill, the Krays – Dimes had eschewed the trappings of wealth. *The Times* estimated rather vaguely in 1956 that a gang leader would pull in a five-figure sum annually. The ordinary foot soldier could expect only about £20 a week.

Another Train Robbery

For years before the Great Train Robbery there were underworld rumours of an Irishman who would plan robberies meticulously and sell the plans to criminals. Nipper Read never met the man, known as Mickey, but had telephone conversations with him and even claims the man tipped him off about one raid he had planned.

Read believes Mickey drew up the plans for the Great Train Robbery. The author Piers Paul Read in his book, *The Train Robbers* (1978), says that two of the gang, Gordon Goody and Buster Edwards, met a man with an Irish accent who told them of the large sums of cash carried on the Glasgow to London mail train. Crime writer Peta Fordham, an expert on the robbery and the participants, says that the plans for the raid had been on offer for eight years.[1]

Edwards and Goody were introduced to the Irishman by a go-between in Finsbury Park, London. The Irishman was 'an ordinary, slightly balding, middle-aged man'. In a gentle, lilting voice he gave them details of the mail train.

> The information, this Ulsterman said, concerned the High Value Package (HVP) coach on the overnight mail train from Glasgow to London. It was on this train that the banks sent their surplus money to London – money not only from Scotland but from all the other towns it passed through on its way down. At the same time as this train came from Glasgow, another left London for Glasgow with a fresh supply of money for those banks which were short. On both trains the HVP

coach was the second from the diesel engine. In it were five Post Office workers, sorting the mail...

'Normally,' said the Ulsterman, 'there are sixty or seventy bags on the train when it leaves Rugby, which is the last stop before Euston: but two days after the August Bank Holiday there can be four times as many. Anything up to two hundred and fifty sacks.' He thought the haul could be worth as much as five million pounds.[2]

Buster Edwards and Charlie Wilson were experienced criminals linked to other robbers in a network of informal alliances. Almost all the train robbers had either worked together before or knew each other by reputation. Edwards and Wilson now contacted another member of this group, Bruce Reynolds.

It was Reynolds who took the Irishman's vague outline and turned it into something workable. A fairly successful robber and a glamorous figure who drove an Aston Martin and had contacts throughout the London underworld, Reynolds put together the team for the raid. Most were reliable criminals with special skills. One or two can only be regarded as unfortunate choices.

Reynolds's second-in-command was Gordon Goody, a giant of a man with 'Hello Ireland' and 'Dear Mother' tattooed on his biceps. He shared Reynolds's love of the good life. The others included Wilson, a bookie and former protection racketeer; Edwards, a club-owner and small-time crook; Jimmy White, an ex-paratrooper who had already worked with Reynolds; Tommy Wisbey and Bob Welch, who had been involved in earlier train robberies on the Brighton line with some of the other gang members; Jimmy Hussey, a man with a string of convictions for theft and violence; Roger Cordery, an expert on trains and signals; Roy James, an expert getaway driver who needed money to get into Formula One racing: John Wheater, a solicitor, and his clerk, Brian Field; and Leonard Field (no relation) a florist. Then there was Ronnie Biggs, an incompetent crook whom some of the others were reluctant to work with but who knew a retired driver who agreed to help move the mail train after they had stopped and boarded it. There are also believed to have been others who were never caught. Police believe the hapless Billy Boal was also involved, although the others all denied it. He was to die in prison.

On 8 August 1963 the gang used a false signal to stop the night train from Euston to Glasgow at Bridego Bridge in Buckinghamshire. They coshed the driver, Jack Mills, separated the mail van from the rest of the train, broke in and stole 120 mail bags. Running out of time, they left another six behind them in the train.

The gang drove to their hideout, Leatherslade Farm, about 27 miles away, in a fleet of vehicles. There they counted the cash. They had stolen about £2,600,000. Although it was less than they hoped for they were jubilant. It was the biggest cash robbery in history.

The money was divided up. The gang had planned to clean the farm thoroughly, and in fact they left very little evidence. But there were about fifteen men in the gang, and some prints were left – on a sauce bottle, on a saucer of milk put out for a cat and on a game of Monopoly.

The police chief leading the hunt put out a statement that he believed the gang were still somewhere within thirty miles of the robbery scene. This was based on the robbers' warning to Mills to give them half an hour to get away. Then the robbers saw a small plane circling the area, and panicked. Carrying suitcases filled with money they fled.

By 13 August the police had found the farm and the mail bags. Soon they found the prints of James, Hussey, Edwards and Wilson among others. Tommy Butler, head of the Flying Squad and a veteran of the Hill and Spot campaigns, was put in charge of the investigation.

Butler was relentless and the police had their fair share of luck. Boal and Roger Cordery, who was recruited for his knowledge of railway signals, were arrested in Bournemouth when they tried to rent lodgings from the wife of a police officer. A large sum of money was found in their car. A Dorking couple on a motorcycle who stopped in a wood found a suitcase full of cash. They alerted the police who found another bag. The total amount in the two bags was £100,000. In one of the suitcases was a receipt from a German hotel in the name of Field. This was Brian Field, the solicitor's clerk.

Jimmy White's caravan at Box Hill in Surrey was raided and

£30,000 was found. One after another, the gang were rounded up. The trial began at Aylesbury on 20 January 1964. Biggs, Wilson, Wisbey, Bob Welch, Jim Hussey, James and Goody got thirty years each. Lennie and Brian Field each got 25 years. Cordery, who pleaded guilty, received twenty years and Boal 24. Wheater got three years. Reynolds, who was not arrested until later, got 25 years.

Only £400,000 of the stolen money was recovered. The robbers themselves did not have much time to enjoy it. Some of them escaped and found life on the run expensive. Others were cheated by the people they entrusted the money to while they served their sentences.

Piers Paul Read, in *The Train Robbers*, analysed what happed to the cash. Buster Edwards, he says, lost a fortune of £140,000 through the costs of his escape from prison and living on the run. Hussey made bad investments that cost him £110,000. Goody entrusted his money to someone who stole £40,000. Welch was even less lucky: the person he left his money with stole £100,000. And so on.

Brian Field had his 25 year sentence reduced to five years for receiving. He died in a road accident. Edwards, who had escaped to Mexico with Reynolds, gave himself up in 1966 and got fifteen years. He suffered from depression and hanged himself near the flower stall he kept at Waterloo Station. Wilson, who escaped from Winson Green prison in Birmingham and made his way to Canada, opened his door one day in January 1968 to find Tommy Butler and fifty Royal Canadian Mounted Police officers standing there. After serving his sentence he was murdered in Spain.

Reynolds left Mexico for France and then Torquay. On 8 November 1968 he opened the door to find Butler, who had stayed on at Scotland Yard to track down those train robbers who were still free, standing there. Butler: 'Hello Bruce, it's been a long time.' Reynolds: 'C'est la vie.' After serving his sentence he lived in a flat in Croydon and wrote his memoirs, *Autobiography of a Thief*. Ronnie Biggs, the least of the robbers, escaped from Wandsworth Prison in July 1965 and eventually arrived in Brazil. Old and sick, he returned to Britain in 2001 and was arrested.

The Firm

Nipper Read, the detective who brought the Kray twins to justice, recalled his first sight of Ronnie Kray. It was at the Grave Maurice, a pub in Whitechapel the twins used. Ronnie was dressed in a long cashmere coat, his greased hair was slicked back. 'He looked like Al Capone without his fedora.'[1]

Ronnie Kray had a sense of style and destiny. He was homosexual, more than a little mad, and vicious: he modelled himself on the American gangsters of old, having a barber come daily to his home in Vallance Road in Bethnal Green to shave him and wearing expensive Italian suits: when his cohorts nicknamed him The Colonel the fantasy was complete. He was a rich source of material for the many psychiatrists who examined him.

His twin Reggie had the better business brain, and away from Ronnie he had an easygoing charm. When Ronnie was in jail their businesses flourished. Without Ronnie, Reggie would have become rich: he would not have become famous.

The name Kray is Austrian, and the family had Jewish, Irish and gipsy blood. They grew up in a Dickensian world. Vallance Road, which survived the heavy bombing of the Second World War and the redevelopment that followed, was part of that East End of crushing poverty that Dickens wrote about, the world of Bill Sikes and the thieves' rookeries. One of Jack the Ripper's last victims was murdered nearby in Hanbury Street.

This was an insular world of fierce loyalties and sudden violence and tightly knit and independent families, none more so than the

Krays. Reggie wrote that he came from a family of fighters, including his grandfather John Lee, who was known as the Southpaw Cannonball. His father was a gentler soul, usually on the run from the Army or the police. 'He wasn't a fighting man, like the rest of the men in the family, but he was a hell of a drinker...'[2]

The twins' father, Charles Kray, was a 'wardrobe dealer' like the gangster Arthur Harding, who knew him. He was an unreliable father, a drinker, gambler and absentee husband, according to Pearson, who says he was on drinking terms with most of the famous East End villains of his day. So the task of bringing up the children fell on their formidable mother Violet.

The eldest son, Charles, was born in 1929. The twins followed in October 1933. Violet was a devoted mother and the boys, in particular Ronnie, repaid that devotion in full. Charles was a gentle soul, but the twins were terrors. They learned their street fighting in the hard school of East End street gang battles and outshone all their childhood rivals. Another outlet for their aggression was boxing: they turned professional when they were seventeen and fought with some success, Reggie in particular. But they lacked the self-discipline needed for a successful career in sport.

In 1952 the twins were called up for military service. They were soon in trouble, went absent without leave and then on the run. Sent to military prisons they met other young criminals, including one of the Richardson brothers. In 1954 they returned to Bethnal Green ready for the lives of career criminals.

Their first step was to establish a base in the Regal billiard hall on the Mile End Road. They got a reputation for spectacular violence when Ronnie took a cutlass to a Maltese gang who demanded protection money, and the twins jointly beat up three boxing Poplar dockers.

The dockers were known as the unofficial 'guv'nors' of Poplar and Mile End. They heard of the petty rackets the twins were running from the club, and decided to call them to order. They summoned the twins to a Mile End pub for a drink.

According to Pearson, the twins called at the pub to find the three large dockers alone. The fight took place behind closed doors in the private bar. When the sounds of breaking glass and furniture stopped the landlord went in. Two of the dockers were unconscious, and Ronnie had to be dragged off the third.

By now older criminals had heard of the twins' prowess. Some offered advice, among them Jack Spot and Billy Hill. Under their aegis the twins expanded from their headquarters at the billiards club into protection, collecting from unlicensed gambling clubs and bookies and making local criminals pay a tax on their ill-gotten income. But the twins had larger ambitions: not for them the modest income and status of local crime barons. When Jack Spot invited them to chaperone him at the Epsom spring races in 1955 it seemed their moment had come.

But there was no follow-up. Although the Spot–Hill feud dragged on for another year, the twins were not called on again for their special expertise. For a while they would drop into a club off the Tottenham Court Road where Spot still held court in the evenings, and they were still Spot's nominal allies. Spot, however, was wary of the Krays, and to their intense frustration kept them at arm's length.

The twins visited Spot after Frankie Fraser and his men put him in hospital. They told him they were ready to take over the London underworld if he gave the word. Instead Spot retired.

With Spot and Hill in retirement London seemed wide open, but the twins didn't know where to start. A coalition of gangs, led by the Italians, aspired to fill the vacuum, and were frightening off Spot's old allies by slashing attacks. The twins heard it would be their turn next. Ronnie walked alone into the social club in the Clerkenwell Road the Italians used as a headquarters and after challenging those present to a fight drew a pistol and fired three shots. By luck or judgment he missed, and calmly walked out.

For Ronnie this was a milestone on the road to gangland immortality. This was how in his fantasies real gangsters lived. It confirmed his belief that the other gangs were soft and would collapse if challenged. What he had failed to grasp was that successful gangsters like Hill and Spot used violence only as a means to an end: they really preferred the quiet life. In particular they went out of their way to avoid trouble with the police, and in return the police allowed them to operate as long as they kept their henchmen in order. For Ronnie in particular this was heresy. Success in gangland was a Darwinian struggle. And there would be no truce with the police. 'Coppers is dirt.'[3]

Although the twins had failed to make any impact in the West End, their power was growing. Over a larger area, from Hackney and Mile End down to Walthamstow and the river, the clubs and pubs and many businesses now paid tribute. Reggie had a big American car and a chauffeur. Ronnie too had a car, money, and guns. The twins were becoming rich. Their gang, known as The Firm, was now tougher and more professional. It included financial advisers Leslie Payne and Freddy Gore, hard men such as Connie Whitehead, Albert Donoghue, Ian Barrie, and 'Scotch Jack' Dickson. Freddie 'the Mean Machine' Foreman, a south London gang leader and major-league robber who was to have a long career in crime, was another cohort.

Ronnie's blood lust would sooner or later have to have an outlet. He carried a .32 Beretta with bullets whose tips he had filed off so they would make a bigger hole in his enemies. He made a list of 'those who'd have to go'. But as yet he had never shot anyone.

In the autumn of 1956 a used-car dealer asked Ronnie to sort out a complaining customer. Ronnie thought the customer was backed by south London mobsters. When the customer returned to the car dealer's – in fact he had come to apologise – Ronnie burst in and started blazing away with a Luger pistol. The customer was hit in the leg. Ronnie, every inch the colonel, walked out. He was keeping his pact with destiny.

Not for the first time, Reggie had to save him. The customer, a docker, had spoken to the police. Friends visited him in hospital and suggested that he had been hasty. Police arrested a man and an identity parade was held inside the hospital. The docker identified the arrested man, who had been charged under the name Ronald Kray. The arrested man protested he was Reginald Kray, and produced a driving licence to prove it. The shot docker had an attack of amnesia. Ronnie was safe.

Soon he was in trouble again, and this time Reggie could not save him. Ronnie and a team of his best bruisers descended on a pub where he expected to find a gang of tearaway dockers called the Watney Streeters, with whom he had a quarrel. For once his intelligence – he had a team of young boys who were known as Ronnie's spies – had let him down and the dockers had fled. When Ronnie entered the pub the only person there was a boy called Terry Martin. He was dragged out and Ronnie slashed his head with a bayonet and stabbed him in the shoulder. His gang then kicked the boy unconscious, and according to evidence later given in court, he was lucky to survive. Ronnie was jailed for three years.

Reggie as usual looked after him, seeing Ronnie had the money to bribe his way to a life of ease in prison. With Ronnie away peace descended on their empire and Reggie could get down to making serious money. He looked around for a club he could run, and found what he wanted in the Bow Road. Soon a smoking-jacketed Reggie was greeting minor celebrities, starlets, journalists and playboys. The club, known as the Double R, was a success.

Reggie discovered he had a talent for running clubs, and his older brother Charlie, who was also involved, was a shrewd businessman. They bought another club and opened a car saleroom beside the billiard club. They even opened a successful illicit gambling club next to the car park of Bow Police station.

They were also pulling in hundreds of pounds a week from protection: the vice racketeer Bernie Silver is said to have paid them £60 a week from his clubs. This 'pension' the twins split with their friends, the Nash gang who ran Islington, and Freddie Foreman. In return the Nashes split their pensions from the Olympic club in Camden Town and the Astor and the Bagatelle off Regent Street. There were payoffs from pubs and scrap-metal dealers.

At first Ronnie settled down to do his time in Wandsworth jail, renewing old acquaintances. The hard core of professional criminals paid homage, and he was very much the colonel. He read his favourite book, *Boys' Town*. It was in Wandsworth that he met Frank Mitchell, a young giant of immense strength who could be gentle and childlike or a terrifying psychopath. Ronnie, who had been reading Steinbeck's *Of Mice and Men*, thought Mitchell was like the book's character Lennie. He promised that he and Reggie would look after Mitchell.

Then Ronnie was moved to Camp Hill prison on the Isle of Wight. This was a very different regime from Wandsworth. Camp Hill was progressive: the humane governor believed in the possibility of reform. This was anathema to Ronnie. He didn't like the earnest, strenuous regime of games and self-improvement. There were no old lags with whom he could swop yarns. He turned in on himself and became increasingly paranoid, believing that there was a conspiracy against him. He was moved to the psychiatric wing of Winchester Prison. Finally his mother was told that he had been certified insane.

Ronnie was moved to Long Grove Hospital in Surrey. Soon he was responding to treatment, and the doctors considered sending him back to prison. They decided that he should stay a little longer, and Ronnie was upset. Reggie decided that the old trick of switching places with Ronnie was the answer. Ronnie simply walked out of the hospital dressed in the same clothes as Reggie, and a getaway car took him back to London.

But soon Ronnie was so mad that his family had no choice but to do the unthinkable – turn him in. They went to Scotland Yard and police went round to Vallance Road and picked him up. He was taken to Long Grove and began another recovery with the help of the drug Stematol. In September 1958 the doctors sent him back to Wandsworth Prison to finish his sentence.

Ronnie made a recovery of sorts, but he would never be normal.[4]

Ronnie had been dreaming for years of becoming the overlord of the whole London underworld, the boss of bosses. Now he set out to achieve this by starting a series of small wars. He brought his own brand of mayhem to the streets, starting gang fights in pubs and wrecking Reggie's carefully constructed alliance with the Italians. After a battle with the Watney Streeters at the aptly named Hospital Tavern there were headlines saying the East End had experienced its worst gang fight for years. Reggie's plans for expansion in the gambling clubs of the West End were in ruins. His various enterprises were not prospering: the Double R club was no longer so profitable, and Ronnie's wars were draining away all their money.

As part of his grandiose plan for London-wide domination Ronnie had become interested in the crime scene in the Paddington area of north London. Like a shark sensing blood in the water, he had been attracted by the smell of fire-bombed clubs and the whiff of gunsmoke as gangsters fought it out on the streets. It was there he heard about Peter Rachman, the vicious rack-renter and ponce, who was ripe for a shake-down. When Rachman refused to pay up Ronnie sent his boys to beat up Rachman's rent collectors. As Reggie put it: 'He had to pay up – it was either that or his rent collectors were set upon. They were big, but our boys were bigger.'

In 1960, to get the Krays off his back Rachman told them about a gambling club, Esmeralda's Barn in Wilton Place off Knightsbridge, and its owner, a businessman named Stefan De Fay. Rachman believed, rightly, that De Fay would cave in if threatened by gangsters. The Krays duly threatened, and De Fay signed his controlling interest over to them for £1,000.

This was one of the biggest coups of the Krays' career: at its most prosperous the club netted them £40,000 a year. A key figure in the acquisition and running of Esmeralda's Barn was the twins' main financial adviser Leslie Payne. He was, says Pearson, a most unlikely man to have been mixed up with the Krays. Called 'Payne the Brain', he was an accomplished long-firm fraudster and fixer who lived a cosy suburban existence with his pretty wife and family in Dulwich in south London. But he saw the potential of the twins, particularly in business fraud.

Payne introduced the twins to the long-firm fraud. This was a simple but effective way of making a lot of money quickly, and despite a long history it always seemed to to work. A bogus company would be set up, and premises acquired. Goods would be ordered, sold and the suppliers paid. This would go on for months. Then, when the suppliers' confidence had been gained, a much larger order would be placed and the firm and the goods would vanish. Nobody was hurt except the insurers. In 1962 the twins cleared more than £100,000 from long-firm frauds. A legitimate company, Carston Trading, was set up with offices in Portland Street. It had a receptionist and secretaries, a warehouse and an account with the Bank of Valletta.

They also expanded outside London, forming an alliance with the leading gang in Glasgow and taking over clubs in Birmingham and Leicester.

The twins needed all the money they could get to pay their growing band of followers. They now had a payroll of about £600 a week. In his memoirs, Payne reckoned that in the mid-sixties between a third and a half of all the illegal gaming clubs in London were paying them protection money. They were also running long-firm frauds and four clubs. Payne described their 'board meetings' at which the club managers would hand over the profits.

One of the clubs was the Kentucky in Stepney, whose customers included theatre director Joan Littlewood, actor Roger Moore and *Carry On* actress Barbara Windsor. During his final trial at the Old Bailey Ronnie told the judge that if he had not been in court he would probably have been taking tea with Judy Garland.

At Esmeralda's Barn all was well until Reggie was jailed for six months over a botched attempt at extortion by another man. Ronnie was left to enjoy long nights at the club on his own. As Pearson says, he soon got lonely and bored. He could not just sit back and watch the punters parting with their money. He started to take an active interest in how the club was run, granting credit and when the punters could not pay, threatening them. The punters drifted away, and the club collapsed in 1963.

Still, the Krays were at the height of their fame and power in the early 1960s. They had friends in showbiz, and, as we shall see, at the heart of politics. Nipper Read, their nemesis, said that if someone had a drink with them it was like having tea with Princess Margaret. Although for years the police had turned a blind eye to the twins' rackets, by the early sixties they were becoming curious. But there now occurred a scandal which set back police efforts to nail the Krays for years and allowed them to carry on unscathed.

In 1964 Ronnie met the Tory grandee Lord Boothby at the latter's Belgravia home, ostensibly to discuss a business deal. Photographs were taken of the event. On 12 July the *Sunday Mirror* splashed on the story. 'Peer and a Gangster: Yard Inquiry' was the headline. The following day the *Daily Mirror* ran an editorial saying: 'This gang is so rich, powerful and ruthless that the police are unable to crack down on it. Victims are too terrified to go to the police. Witnesses are too scared to tell their story in court. The police, who know what is happening but cannot pin any evidence on the villains, are powerless.'

The *Sunday Mirror* story claimed that the Metropolitan Police Commissioner, Sir Joseph Simpson, had ordered a top-level investigation into the alleged homosexual relationship between a peer who was a 'household name' and a leading thug in the London underworld involved in West End protection rackets. Among the things the police were said to be looking into were Mayfair parties the thug and the peer had been to, the peer's visits to Brighton along with a number of 'prominent public men', his relationships with East End gangsters and a number of clergymen. There were also allegations of blackmail.

Boothby had been sailing close to the wind for years. He had been having a long-term relationship with Lady Dorothy Macmillan, the wife of the former Conservative Prime Minister, Sir Harold Macmillan. He was also a homosexual who shared Ronnie Kray's appetite for good-looking young men, and had been having an affair with an associate of the Krays, a young burglar named Lesley Holt.

On 16 July the *Daily Mirror* returned to the attack with the headline, 'The picture we dare not print'. The accompanying story described the picture as being of a 'well-known member of the House of Lords seated on a sofa with a gangster who leads the biggest protection racket London has ever known'.

Boothby decided to brazen it out, and the full story did not come out until years later, after Boothby had died. He issued a statement which in effect defied the papers to name him. 'I am not a homosexual. I have not been to a Mayfair party of any kind for more than twenty years. I have met the man alleged to be the King of the Underworld only three times, on business matters; and then by appointment at my flat, at his request, and in the company of other people.'

Boothby was taking an enormous risk; the pictures, one of which showed him with his boyfriend and the Krays, would have condemned him, and homosexual acts were still a crime at the time. He was saved by the timidity of Cecil King, boss of the Mirror

Group. King was a member of the establishment, and in the climate of deference which then pervaded journalism he was not going to implicate the top echelons of the Tory party in a major scandal.

Even the Labour Prime Minister, Harold Wilson, is said to have wanted the matter hushed up. The reason: the well-known Labour politician, Tom Driberg, a notorious and voracious homosexual, had been introduced to the twins by Joan Littlewood. Driberg's biographer, Francis Wheen, says that the politician was invited to Ronnie's parties where 'rough but compliant East End lads were served like so many canapés'. Wilson feared that the Labour party too would be embroiled in the scandal, so King, whose papers supported Labour, had an even stronger motive for discretion.

In the face of Boothby's blank denial King caved in. The *Daily Mirror* printed 'an unqualified apology' and Boothby was paid damages of £40,000 – around £500,000 in today's money. (In 1967 he married a Sardinian woman named Wanda. The message to the underworld was clear – he was cutting his ties with them.) Ronnie Kray also got an unqualified apology, but no money. The twins later appeared on television to say how hurt they felt at the slur on their good name, Ronnie looking particularly lugubrious as he said the affair had cost them 'eight grand'.

Although the affair had cost the twins £8,000, the benefits to them were great. The police had in fact been investigating them when the scandal broke, and Nipper Read was deeply disturbed by what he found. With their contacts in high places they would soon be too powerful to prosecute successfully. However, Read's team had enough evidence to make a powerful case. Then the scandal broke, and the Met Commissioner, Sir Joseph Simpson, claimed that no investigation was taking place into 'a peer and a man with a criminal record'. This made the evidence gathered so far more or less useless.

Another consequence of the *Mirror* apology was a reluctance on the part of the press to dig any deeper into the Krays' rackets. So the twins, who had been attracting more and more media attention, could be sure that there would be no more hostile publicity for the moment.

And the police now made a disastrous error in their campaign against the Firm. There had been a fourth man in one of the Boothby photographs, a friend of the Krays named 'Mad' Teddy Smith. In January 1965 he went to the Hideaway club in Soho and wrecked it, giving the impression that he was there to collect protection money for the twins. The owner of the club, Hew McCowan, the son of a wealthy baronet, had already told Read that the twins were pressuring him to hand over half his profits. Read saw an opportunity to undo all the damage the *Mirror* affair had done. On 10 January the twins were arrested and accused with Smith of demanding money with menaces.

The twins, who were refused bail, now mounted a brilliant campaign. They hired the best legal team available, they hired private detectives to look into the background of witnesses in the trial and members of the Firm were set to work to fix the jury. At that time it took just one dissenting member of a jury to force a retrial.

In the first trial the jury failed to reach a verdict. The second was stopped when the Krays' defence counsel introduced evidence dug up by a private detective that McCowan had appeared in cases involving homosexuals and was a police informer. The three defendants were freed.

They returned in triumph to the East End. Nipper Read later recalled that there were street parties to welcome them back. To their fellow criminals and to many other Eastenders it looked as if they really could walk on water, he said. With a delicate sense of irony that was not usually their strong suit, they bought McCowan's club, renamed it El Morocco and held a wild celebration party. The police were left licking their wounds, and the Krays seemed invulnerable. It was to be four years before their grip was broken, and their reign of terror, fraud and murder brought to an end.

The Krays had modelled themselves on the gangsters in American movies, and to some extent on the real thing. They enjoyed the company of George Raft, who was both movie gangster and associate of the Mafia, when he came to London to pursue gambling-club interests. He was eventually barred from Britain because of his Mafia connections. Ronnie met the American *mafioso* Angelo Bruno, who also knew Albert Dimes, when he was in London. The twins dealt in stolen American securities in association with Mafia-linked American criminals. This was to be one of their bigger money-spinners.

Reggie had meanwhile married, to the disgust of his brother. His bride was Frances Shea, a Hoxton girl. She was a 16-year-old schoolgirl when she caught his eye, not a gangster's moll at all but pretty and sweet. They married in 1965 when she was 21. Although Frances wanted a quiet wedding Reggie turned it into an East End extravaganza, with a cavalcade of Rolls-Royces and a guest-list that included all the famous local characters.

On 9 March 1966 George Cornell, a member of the south London Richardson gang, was drinking in the Blind Beggar pub on the Mile End Road, in the Krays' heartland. With him was Albie Woods, a bookmaker, who later described what happened. Two men entered the pub and, recalled Woods, 'All of a sudden George said, "Look who's here."' They were his last words. Woods saw a man aiming a gun at Cornell and there was a shot. Cornell slipped to the floor and died later in hospital. His killer was Ronnie Kray.

Cornell had famously called Ronnie a 'fat poof' but there were other reasons for his execution. For one thing, Ronnie was once again spiralling down into insanity, compiling his little lists of those who would have to go. Cornell's name was on the list: once one of the Watney Street tearaways, he had switched his allegiance to the Richardsons at the same time as Frankie Fraser. So the south Londoners were beginning to look more formidable.

Musing on those times, Ronnie Kray later said the Richardsons were 'a mightily powerful and feared organisation'. Feared because if anyone crossed them the Richardsons were ruthless in their retribution.[5]

There were other reasons. The twins wanted a slice of Cornell's interests in West End pornography and the Richardsons countered with demands of their own. At a tense meeting in the Astor club between the two gangs, both armed, tempers were so frayed it seemed shooting would break out at any moment. This led Ronnie to believe that the Richardsons would try to disrupt their arrangements with the American Mafia, now poised to become much more profitable. The Americans wanted a greater stake in

London's burgeoning gambling scene, and were investing heavily in gaming clubs in the capital. What they wanted from the twins was a guarantee of peace, and Ronnie was in no mood for peace until he had settled scores with the Richardsons.

The Firm was put on a war footing. Ronnie mobilised his allies in the north London gangs and organised the stockpiling of weapons, including machine guns. His spies brought in a constant stream of information about his enemies. The twins wore bullet-proof vests as they waited for their opportunity. After the 'fat poof' remark Ronnie put his spies on Cornell's tail.

The widely expected war with the Richardsons never happened. In the early hours of 8 March 1966 there was a shoot-out at a club named Mr Smith's at Catford in south London. The Richardsons had been asked to deal with a gang of local heavies, the Hawards, who were preying on the club. Eddie Richardson went there with some cohorts including Mad Frankie Fraser and Jimmy Moody. In the fight that followed one of the local heavies, Dickie Hart, regarded as an ally of the Krays, was shot dead and Richardson and Fraser badly wounded.

Soon most of the Richardson gang leaders were under arrest. That left Cornell, and on the night after the Mr Smith's club shoot-out Ronnie Kray slipped a Mauser pistol into his pocket and headed for the Blind Beggar. Perhaps he saw a chance to move in on the Richardson's territory. Certainly he wanted revenge for Cornell's taunts. He did not hide the fact that he was a homosexual, but any reference to it had to be on his own terms. He had once cut a friend up badly for simply saying he was putting on weight.

Twenty years later Ronnie Kray vividly remembered Cornell's last moments.

> I took out my gun and held it towards his face ... I shot him in the forehead. He fell forward onto the bar ... That's all that happened ...
>
> I felt fucking marvellous. I have never felt so good, so bloody alive, before or since. Twenty years on and I can recall every second of the killing of George Cornell. I have replayed it in my mind millions of times.[6]

It was an open secret in the East End that Ronnie had killed Cornell. On the night of the murder a journalist strode into the newsroom of the *Daily Mirror* and proclaimed; 'Ronnie Kray has shot a man dead in the Blind Beggar.' But the witnesses as usual had a collective attack of amnesia. Superintendent Tommy Butler, who was in charge of the case, organised an identity parade, which included Ronnie Kray, at Commercial Road police station. The barmaid from the Blind Beggar, on whom he had been pinning his hopes, looked up and down the line but failed to pick out anyone. Her memory, she said, was weak.

The message to the underworld was clear: once again the Krays had shown they could act with impunity. Anyone stepping out of line would be dealt with. There was now no gang left in London capable of challenging the twins. Ronnie recalled that everyone was frightened of them – 'people were actually ringing up begging to pay protection money'.

It had been, Ronnie said later, a 'wearying' time, so he and Reggie took a holiday. They went to Morocco and stayed with retired gangster Billy Hill and his girlfriend Gypsy. 'We had a bloody marvellous time,' said Ronnie.

As if there was not enough drama in their lives already, on 12 December 1966 the twins had Frank Mitchell sprung from Dartmoor. Quite why they sprang Mitchell, known as the Mad Axeman, is not clear. Ronnie had befriended the simple-minded giant in Wandsworth, and promised him that the Firm would look after him. According to one account, they intended to use Mitchell, whose name was a by-word for violence, as a counter-terror to Mad Frankie Fraser. But by the time Mitchell was free Fraser was not, and anyway the Firm was not exactly short of muscle. Another theory is that Mitchell, unhappy that the authorities would not give him a release date, put pressure on the Krays to fulfil their promise to help him. The twins' biographer, John Pearson, wrote that it was simply an exercise in public relations at a time when their allies were becoming alarmed at their increasing tendency to violence.

Mitchell had spent eighteen of his 32 years in custody. He was on the run from a hospital for the criminally insane when he threatened an elderly couple with an axe, hence his nickname. He was now detained in Dartmoor 'at Her Majesty's pleasure', in effect an indefinite sentence. After earlier clashes with the authorities, when he was birched for attacking warders, he had settled down, although he was unhappy that he hadn't been given a release date. Treated sympathetically, he could be a model prisoner. Soon he was a trustee, and was allowed out with working parties. The warders were too frightened to discipline him and he would simply wander off, riding ponies or visiting pubs. He even had an affair with a schoolteacher. Some of the time he spent in the gymnasium, toning up his impressive physique.

December 1966 was a bad time for the twins to be embarking on new adventures. They had just been deported from Morocco, where they had fled because of Ronnie's fears that people were talking to the police about the Cornell murder. Reggie's unhappy wife Frances had tried to kill herself, and Ronnie had gone to ground in a Finchley flat, turning it into a fortress and refusing to come out. Reggie was left to run the rackets, look after Frances and plan the escape.

In fact, after some initial problems, the escape couldn't have been simpler. On 12 December Mitchell was picked up by car from a Dartmoor pub where he was allowed to spend lunch time. He was taken to London, where the twins had persuaded a man called Lennie Dunn, who kept a bookstall in the East End, to hide him in his flat. An attractive West End club hostess, Lisa, was provided for him, and with the help of Mad Teddy Smith and Dunn he settled down to write letters to *The Times* and the *Daily Mirror* saying he would return to prison if he was given a release date.

> Sir, the reason for my absence from Dartmoor was to bring to the Notice of my unhappy plight to be truthful, I am asking for a possible Date of release. From the age of nine I have not been completely free, always under some act or other. Sir, I ask you, where is the fairness in this. I am not a murderer or a sex maniac, nor do I think I am a danger to the public. I think that I have been more than punished for the wrongs that I have done.

To Mitchell the flat became another prison. Lisa later wrote that 'his virility was greater than any man I have ever known', and they spent the first two days in bed together, with intervals when Mitchell got out to do press-ups. But the Mad Axeman was becoming moody. The twins had said he could see his family, and his idol Ronnie had not been to see him as promised. When Lisa and the minders that the twins had left in charge of him tried to persuade him to give himself up to the police, he shouted that he would kill anyone who tried to make him go back. Then he forced one of the minders to give him a gun, and wrote a letter to Reggie saying that unless he was taken to another haven he would contact his parents. He told Reggie he had a gun, and was prepared to kill anyone who tried to stop him.

The twins held a crisis meeting at the Finchley flat. Ronnie's attitude to Mitchell had changed completely. The gentle giant was now a threat who could destroy the Firm. He had to go.

When Reggie visited Mitchell's hideout next day and told him he was being taken to a place in the country, Mitchell, who was smitten by Lisa, said she must go too. Of course, said Reggie. Behind Mitchell's back, Lisa told one of the Firm that she wasn't going. She was told on no account to tell this to Mitchell.

On Christmas Eve, Mitchell, now happy that he was to be taken to a house in the country with servants and animals and his beloved Lisa, was told a car was coming for him. At 8.30 a.m., Firm member 'Big Albert' Donoghue, who had helped Mitchell get away from Dartmoor, arrived and said a van was waiting. Mitchell was told he was being taken to a farm in Kent and the girl would follow later. He was escorted to the van by Donoghue and other members of the Firm. As the Old Bailey was told later, he was shot almost as soon as he got into the back of the van. Donoghue described how two gunmen, south London gang leader Freddie Foreman and Alfie Gerrard, emptied their pistols into him. No trace of his body was ever found.

Although there were the usual rumours about how the body was disposed of, including one that it formed part of the foundations of a prestigious City building – commonly assumed to be the fate of almost all gangland victims – Freddie Foreman later said the body had been disposed of at sea.

Giving evidence against Foreman and the three Krays, Donoghue told how Foreman had described hacking up Mitchell's body, and found that there were three bullets in his heart. 'He had a tiny brain,' Foreman told Donoghue, cupping his hands to show how small it was. The judge ruled that since Donoghue was also involved in Mitchell's escape, his evidence could not be accepted without corroboration. Foreman and the Krays were acquitted.

After the murder Donoghue went back to the flat and removed all traces of Mitchell's stay. Then he went to a Christmas Eve party with Reggie Kray. Lisa was told to forget she had ever met Mitchell, or else. She spent the night in bed with Donoghue.

On 7 June 1967 Reggie's wife Frances committed suicide by taking an overdose of drugs. The Firm laid on a gangster's funeral for her. There were ten limousines, and the Firm and their allies littered the graveyard in Chingford with expensive wreaths. Reggie wrote a poem which was printed on a gold-and-white memorial card.

> If I could climb upon a passing cloud that would drift your way
> I would not ask for a more beautiful day
> Perhaps I would pass a rainbow
> With Nature's Colours so beautifully aglow
> If you were there at the Journey's End, I would know
> It was the beginning and not the End
>
>   Reg

Describing this time, Reggie said later that grief drove him to drink. Gin and the support of his mother made it possible for him to carry on. 'I will never forget little Frances. I loved her and she loved me. I had lost one of the two women I had loved in my life. The other was my mother, who was a great support to me at this time. She knew the agony I went through, the torture.[7]

To make matters worse, Ronnie was mentally ill again. There were times when it seemed that both the twins were now mad. Grief and drink drove Reggie to extremes that must have reminded members of the Firm of the worst times with Ronnie. He burst into the home of a friend named Frederick after hearing that he had made remarks about Frances, and shot him in the leg in front of his wife and children. He shot another man in the leg over a debt. Ronnie walked up to a former friend, George Dixon, at the Green Dragon

Club, drew a pistol and pulled the trigger. The gun failed to fire. Ronnie gave Dixon the faulty bullet. 'It's just saved your life,' he told him. 'Wear it on your watch chain as a souvenir.'

Members of the Firm were not safe. Mad Teddy Smith disappeared after an argument with Ronnie about some boys: he was never seen again. Ronnie's driver, a man named Frost, also vanished. One theory was that he had tried to blackmail Ronnie. Fear was beginning to undermine the apparently sound foundations of the Firm.

One of the many people Ronnie had decided would have to go was Leslie Payne, the accomplished fraudster who had taught the twins about long-firm frauds and other swindles which made them a lot of money in the early sixties. Ronnie's increasingly erratic behaviour had frightened Payne off, and Ronnie feared that his estranged friend would talk to the police. In September 1967 Ronnie gave a thug named Jack 'the Hat' McVitie a contract to kill Payne.

McVitie was either a hard man or a drunken loudmouth, according to which account you accept. He accepted £100 from Ronnie for the contract and then bungled it. Having failed to kill Payne he also failed to return the £100. It is said he also, in his cups, boasted of ripping off the twins. Drunk, he staggered into the Regency Club with a sawn-off shotgun and made threats against them. Any one of these affronts would be reason enough for Ronnie to want Jack the Hat dead.

McVitie was murdered at a party in a flat in Evering Road owned by 'Blonde' Carol Skinner, a friend of Reggie's. She was told to take her guests to another party across the road. Then the Lambrianou brothers, new associates of the Firm, were sent to search for McVitie. As he entered the flat Reggie tried to shoot him in the head but the gun jammed. He struggled and tried to escape. Ronnie, his face contorted with rage, screamed at him: 'Be a man, Jack.' McVitie replied: 'I'll be a man, but I don't want to die like one.'

Reggie then stabbed him in the face, stomach and throat. Reggie later claimed it was his cousin, young Ronnie Hart, who was the murderer. But the killing had been seen by several members of the Firm.

McVitie's body was wrapped in a bedspread, taken away and

disposed of. Theories abound about its fate, as usual. The consensus seems to be that it was taken to south London, where the Krays' ally, gang leader Freddie Foreman, arranged to get rid of it – perhaps on a farm in Kent or Essex. Tony Lambrianou says the car used to transport the body was taken to a scrap yard and crushed. Blonde Carol got new carpets and furniture: the flat was scoured to get rid of the blood. Reggie wrote later: 'I did not regret it at the time and I don't regret it now. I have never had a moment's remorse.'

Time was running out for the twins. The members of The Firm were becoming increasingly apprehensive, wondering whose turn it would be next to disappear. Nipper Read, promoted and appointed to the Murder Squad at Scotland Yard, began picking up members of The Firm and trying to persuade them to talk. He found Lesley Payne, the target of the bungled murder attempt by McVitie, a willing talker. Payne had a good memory and he gave Read a meticulously detailed account of the long-firm frauds, the contacts with the Mafia, and the sale of bonds. He was also able to give some account of the shootings and knifings, and perhaps most valuable of all, the names of the victims. Read saw these as the key to the investigation.

Payne had been granted immunity from prosecution, and Read used him to persuade frightened victims of the Krays that it would be safe to give evidence against them. It was an uphill struggle. 'A few days later Nipper found himself asking a man the twins had maimed and ruined why he would not help him put them safely away. "I hate the sight of blood," the man replied, "particularly my own."'[8]

As the evidence against the twins began to pile up, they planned their own counteroffensive. Ronnie was for killing Read, but Reggie dissuaded him. (Read heard a rumour that a contract had been taken out for his murder, and used to check under his car for explosives every morning.)

Reggie realised the key to their strategy must be to ensure that nobody talked. Members of the Firm were each given two or three potential witnesses to look after, by pointing out where their best interests lay. Ronnie bought a snake which he called Read. Then he went to America with an American named Alan Cooper, a man who could appear at one moment to be wrapped in a cloud of fantasies and the next to be an international criminal of stature, with contacts among continental gangsters and the Mafia. Cooper persuaded him that to gain the confidence of the Mafia leadership he should discreetly dispose of a man who was causing them problems. Ronnie's hitman tried to shoot the would-be victim as he took his morning constitutional in Hyde Park, but somehow the man eluded him and after several failures Ronnie changed tack. He decided that a spectacular murder, which would be noticed even in American Mafia circles, would be better.

The chosen victim was George Caruana, the club owner who had employed Tommy Smithson in the 1950s. Caruana had fallen out with another club owner and there was a £1,000 price on his head. This time Ronnie decided to use explosives. Caruana would be blown up in his red Mini.

None of the Firm knew anything about explosives, so Cooper provided a hitman of his own, a young man named Paul Elvey, who had already apparently tried unsuccessfully to carry out a murder for the twins in the Old Bailey by injecting a witness with cyanide using a hypodermic triggered from inside a briefcase. Elvey flew to Glasgow to collect explosives. The police were waiting. Nipper Read, after eight anxious months of waiting for the twins to make a mistake, pounced.

Elvey talked. At first Read was inclined to regard him as a fantasist. Then he found the hypodermic and the cyanide. Cooper was taken in, and he had a strange tale to tell. Cooper claimed that not only was he working for the US Treasury Department, but also that Read's superior, John Du Rose, knew all about it. Read and Cooper tried to set the twins up but by now they were wary of Cooper. Nevertheless the police decided they now had enough to charge the whole Firm and have them remanded in custody. With the Firm off the streets, they were convinced they could persuade witnesses, including the barmaid who had been in the Blind Beggar when George Cornell was shot, to overcome their fears and give evidence. At dawn on 9 May 1968 most of the Firm were arrested, including the three Kray brothers.

At pre-trial court hearings it was clear that the wall of silence the twins relied on had fallen at the first push from Nipper Read and his team. Among others who had been persuaded to talk was the barmaid from the Blind Beggar, who now said she saw Ronnie Kray kill George Cornell.

There were even greater shocks at the Old Bailey trial, which began on 7 January 1969. Billy Exley, who had helped run the twins' long-firm frauds, their cousin Ronnie Hart and hard man Scotch Jack Dickson gave evidence for the prosecution. They were among more than twenty criminals and former associates of the Krays who, seeing the twins were no longer a threat, helped bring them down. Among them was Albert Donoghue, who had been ordered by the twins to take the blame for the murder of Frank Mitchell. Ronnie went into the witness box to make a defiant last stand, but he and Reggie had already steeled themselves for a guilty verdict.[9]

They were found guilty of the murders of Cornell and McVitie but not guilty, along with Foreman, of the murder of Frank Mitchell. The judge recommended that they should serve at least thirty years. They were 35. Charles Kray and Foreman each got ten years for their part in cleaning up after McVitie's death.

In March 1995 Ronnie Kray died in hospital. His funeral in Bethnal Green was a fitting tribute. The four pallbearers were said in the order of service to be 'a symbol of peace'. They represented four of the capital's criminal power blocs – Johnny Nash of the Nash family, 'Ginger' Dennis, who had been jailed with Mad Frankie Fraser for the 1955 attack on Jack Spot, Freddie Foreman and Charlie Kray. Reggie was there, handcuffed to a policewoman. In his epitaph for his twin he said: 'Ron had great humour, a vicious temper, was kind and generous. He did it all his way but above all he was a man.'

In April 2000 Reggie attended another family funeral – that of his brother Charlie, who had died aged 73. After leaving prison in 1973 having served his sentence for helping get rid of McVitie's body, he claimed he was unemployable because he was a Kray. And his golden touch as a businessman had deserted him. The Kray nostalgia industry should have been a goldmine. T-shirts, books, videos, Kray waistcoats and belt buckles and photographs brought in a good income. But Charlie's lavish lifestyle used it all up and more.

When the twins agreed to sell the film rights to their life story they got not the £2 million Reggie hoped for, but the £255,000 Charlie negotiated. The twins were furious, and did not speak to their older brother for almost a year.

He was paid £100,000 as a consultant for the film, but was said to have spent it in two years. When his son Gary died of cancer in 1996 he was unable to pay for the funeral. Reggie paid the bill.

With money and drink problems piling up in 1997 he became involved in a £39 million cocaine-smuggling plot. Charlie was jailed for twelve years. This would have been a very stiff sentence for anyone whose name was not Kray: the two dealers who actually supplied the drugs got nine and five years.

It is unlikely that any gang in the future will have such a hold over the London underworld as the Krays. Others will kill more people and make more money: the growth in drug trafficking alone will ensure that. What undid the Krays was Ronnie's crazy unpredictability. All gangs rule by fear, but towards the end the members of the Firm felt that any one of them could be next. As the police were closing in they began to think the unthinkable – that they might have to kill the twins. There were jokes about Reggicide and Ronniecide. As Albert Donoghue said: 'We knew it couldn't last. The Colonel was going crazy.'

Reggie summed it all up years later in prison, in valedictory mood: 'What the hell. At least we reached the top of the pile. We've seen and done things most ordinary guys could only dream about, met people and felt excitement most people never get the chance to feel.'[10]

He died in October 2000, having been released on compassionate grounds because of bladder cancer. The East End wound itself up for one last big gangland funeral. Eighteen black limousines carrying superannuated former gangsters and some very minor celebrities followed a Victorian hearse drawn by six black horses to St Matthew's Church. Freddie Foreman, who was not asked to be a pallbearer and missed the funeral, sent flowers with a note saying 'Always with respect'. The evangelist minister who read the address claimed that Kray became a Christian in the months before his death. The coffin was carried from the church to the strains of 'My Way' sung by Frank Sinatra. Reggie was buried in the family plot at Chingford Mount in Essex.

The Torture Gang

There seems on the face of it no reason why the Krays and the Richardson brothers, Charlie and Eddie, should have clashed so disastrously. The Richardsons operated mostly in south London, and although they had a wide-flung illegal business empire, they were mostly fraudsters. They were recognised as being better business brains than the Krays. Mad Frankie Fraser, who joined the Richardsons after working with Billy Hill, said: 'Using racing terms, there would be no race, comparing the Richardsons with the Krays. The Richardsons were miles in front, brain power, everything.'

Charlie Richardson was born in Twickenham in 1934, the son of a former prizefighter. The family later moved to Camberwell in south London. Eddie Richardson was born in 1936. Much has been made of their 'middle-class' origins but they were in trouble with the law from an early age. Petty crime landed Charlie in a remand home, then an approved school. Freed, he tried various money-making schemes, including selling ice cream. It was scrap metal which was the foundation of his fortune.

Charlie and his uncle Jim bought two old planes as scrap, and soon he had a scrapyard which prospered, partly through hard work and partly through the judicious buying of stolen scrap.

His career was interrupted by the call-up for National Service. Like other underworld characters the young man who was already forming his own gang was not prepared to take orders. After a court martial he was sent to the military prison at Shepton Mallet where he met the Krays. Other criminal alumni of Shepton Mallet included Johnny Nash and Frank Mitchell.

Free once more, Charlie Richardson set about expanding his business interests. He opened the first of his drinking clubs, the Addington in Addington Square. By now he understood that the police could be as much a help as a hindrance. He wrote later: 'The most lucrative, powerful and extensive protection racket ever to exist was administered by the Metropolitan Police. As I got older and became involved in more and more dealings, legal or otherwise, I made regular payments to the police. It was a sort of taxation on crime.'

Inevitably their kind of business involved a certain level of violence, but Charlie Richardson seems to have tried to limit it: not for him the hit lists and the mad rages of Ronnie Kray. He describes how he and his men carried out a revenge attack on a local gangster named Jack Rosa and members of his gang in the Reform Club at the Elephant and Castle in south London. After they had finished 'they lay unconscious at our feet in pools of blood and teeth'.[1]

The Krays, however, were a very different matter from local small fry like the Rosas. There was a fight in an East End pub and members of the Kray Firm crossed the river and turned up at a Richardson scrapyard in New Church Road to seek redress. It took considerable powers of persuasion to get them to go away.

Charlie Richardson liked to think of himself as a businessman first, a criminal second. He wrote of 'heading the biggest firm on the manor... To outsiders it might have looked like a gang, but gangs are what kids have – or big kids in American films. I was a businessman who had to protect his interests.'[2]

There are those who say that while the Krays reigned in the East End the streets were safe for old ladies to walk at night, and that there was little petty crime. Charlie Richardson makes the same claim for his manor. Thieves who stole from local people would get a 'smack' and be told to 'fuck off to the West End to steal from rich people'.[3]

After serving six months for receiving a wholesale shipment of bacon in 1959, Charlie was charged with receiving stolen metal. He fled to Canada with his girlfriend, Jean Goodman, leaving behind his wife Margaret and their five children. While he was away Eddie looked after the business.

In 1961 he returned, beat the receiving charge and began a new phase of his business. He added a new twist to the long-firm fraud. A warehouse in Mitre Street, Aldgate, had been stocked with silk stockings. These were sold off, and the building was torched. This was the gang's first venture into arson, and their excessive zeal led to much of the street being wrecked by an explosion.

The manufacturers of the stockings were told that unfortunately the stock was not insured. In fact the stock had been insured, so the Richardsons' profit was doubled. They made £250,000 from the swindle.

A group of clever fraudsters now gathered around the Richardsons. One was Brian Mottram, an old friend, who was also involved in the Mitre Street business. Another was Jack Duval, who was eventually to prove the Richardsons' undoing. Duval was a Russian-born Jew, a former Foreign Legionnaire who had served in the RAF during the war. He was a club owner and also an accomplished fraudster. Charlie Richardson would later call him ' a turd that floated down the Thames to my part of London'.

Duval ran a ticket fraud that swindled airlines out of £500,000, and he even managed to become owner of the Bank of Valletta. In March 1963 Duval's past began to catch up with him and he fled to Milan. At some stage he took some money from a firm in which he and the Richardsons had a joint interest. After he returned to Britain Charlie summoned him. Duval was given a beating and went into hiding. It was then that Charlie discovered that Duval had given him dud cheques. He went looking for the fraudster, and when he failed to find him decided to punish instead an associate of Duval's, Lucien Harris.

Harris seems an unlikely associate of this cast of villains. An educated man, he was also a crossword puzzle compiler. Richardson witheringly described him as having 'an accent and manner to go with his shop-window-dummy appearance and his fancy name.'

Harris's testimony about his ordeal at the hands of Richardson's torturers was the main plank in the prosecution's case against the south London gang. First Richardson asked him where Duval was. Harris replied that he did not know. Richardson, who had sent out for a takeaway meal, shoved a piece of hot scampi into Harris's eye.

His brother Eddie asked: 'Is this going to take long? There's something I want to watch on the telly.'

Then, according to Harris, the infamous black box, which was to figure so prominently in the Richardson torture trials, made its appearance. The box was a generator, a piece of old scrap. Harris said wires were attached to his toes and Roy Hall, one of the Richardson gang, turned the handle of the generator. Harris said the electric current flung him to the floor. He was then stripped and orange juice poured over him to make the shocks more effective. 'The leads were attached to my legs, my penis, the anus, the chest the nostrils and the temples.' Each time the leads were reattached the handle of the generator would be turned. Another of the gang, John Bradbury, stabbed him in the foot. Then, as casually as it began, the torture session was over. According to Harris, Charlie said he had stood up bravely to the torture. A bottle of Scotch was produced, Harris had a couple of drinks, Charlie gave him £150 and a clean shirt and allowed him to leave.

Another of Duval's friends, Bunny Bridges, also suffered this rough interrogation. He was attacked by Cornell and then the black box was used. But he didn't know where Duval was. He was sent to Manchester to see if Duval was there with his ex-wife.

Eddie Richardson, a much less ambitious man than his brother, had teamed up with Frankie Fraser to install fruit machines in clubs. Through his old connection with Albert Dimes, Fraser had contacts in Soho, then the most profitable area for fruit machines. While they built up a business which provided them with a comfortable living, Charlie Richardson was extending his empire overseas. He had heard of the possibility of obtaining the mining rights on four million acres in Namaqualand in South Africa. The group which owned the rights needed finance, and Charlie went to Africa to investigate the possibilities, including the possibility of smuggling out diamonds in frozen fish. Thomas Waldeck, the geologist involved in the mining scheme, persuaded Charlie that the real money was to be made in mining. He offered to sell Richardson half his stake. Charlie, who had fallen for Jean La Grange, wife of a South African journalist, agreed.

Then Waldeck and Richardson fell out, and Waldeck was shot

dead on the porch of his home in June 1965. Richardson's associate John Bradbury was picked up by the police but released for lack of evidence.

Meanwhile the torture went on. One man who was given a gratuitous beating was involved in a swindle run by car park attendants at Heathrow Airport. After they had collected customers' parking charges the attendants would alter time clocks to show the customers had stayed for a shorter time. They were making £1,000 a week, and Charlie Richardson wanted half. Their leader had already agreed to pay up, but Charlie had him beaten just to show him who was boss.

Back in Africa, Bradbury was picked up again by the police after drunkenly boasting that he had shot Waldeck. This time he confessed to being involved and named Charlie Richardson. There were troubles too on the home front. A man named James Taggart who had been tortured by the gang went to see Gerald McArthur, the Chief Constable of Hertfordshire. Other victims of the gang now began to talk to the police.

On the night of 7 March 1966 the Richardson gang were beaten and humiliated in the fight at Mr Smith's club in Catford, south London. Their clash with a local gang, the Hawards, left Kray associate Richard Hart dead and Eddie Richardson and Frankie Fraser badly wounded.

The Haward brothers, Billy and Flash Harry, had been acting as unofficial minders at Mr Smith's club in exchange for free drinks. When they looked like trying to turn the club into their headquarters the management asked Eddie Richardson if he could get rid of them. Seeing an opportunity to install his gaming machines at the club, Eddie agreed.

On 7 March Eddie and Frankie Fraser were drinking in the club when the Hawards arrived. Jimmy Moody, a friend of Eddie's, and more Richardson henchmen turned up later. The two groups drank together affably enough until about 3 a.m. when Eddie told the Hawards: 'Right, drink up. I'm running the club.'

A fight started between Richardson and one of the Haward gang, Peter Hennessey. Then Hart pulled out a pistol and opened fire, according to Frankie Fraser. Harry Rawlins was shot in the shoulder.

The fight continued outside, where Fraser's thighbone was broken by a bullet, and Hart was shot dead. Another man was shot in the groin, and Billy Haward had serious head injuries. Eddie Richardson was shot in the thigh.

Fraser was later acquitted of Hart's murder but convicted of affray. He was sentenced to five years' prison. Billy Haward got eight years and a Haward ally, Henry Botton, five. The jury failed to agree on the cases of Eddie Richardson and Jimmy Moody. On retrial Eddie was jailed for five years, and Moody was found not guilty.

Two days after the battle at Mr Smith's, Ronnie Kray walked into the Blind Beggar and shot George Cornell dead. Roy Hall, a member of the Richardson gang, went to the Krays' home in Vallance Road and fired shots at the windows. Violet Kray told him to come back at a civilized hour, and he went away.

The gang war that Ronnie Kray had gleefully anticipated never happened: early on the morning of 30 July 1966, the day of England's soccer World Cup Final against West Germany, a team of police led by Gerald McArthur arrested eleven of the Richardson gang, including Charlie Richardson. When their trial opened at the Old Bailey on 4 April 1967, prosecuting counsel Sebag Shaw told the jury: 'This case is not about dishonesty and fraud, it is about violence and threats of violence, not, let me say at once, casual acts of violence committed in sudden anger or alarm but vicious and brutal violence systematically inflicted deliberately and cold-bloodedly and with utter and callous ruthlessness.'

Charlie Richardson was jailed for 25 years – the longest punishment ever handed out for grievous bodily harm. Eddie got ten, as did Roy Hall and Frankie Fraser. The Richardsons were finished as a major force in London crime.

Mr Smith's club lost its licence. It had changed its name but a police raid found there were 300 people present and the guest book was full of scribbles and blanks. The directors blamed the gang fight between the Richardsons and the Hawards for its downfall. Jimmy Moody, who had helped to ferry the wounded to hospital, was shot dead years later in an East End pub. He had been in the headlines earlier when he escaped from Brixton Prison with IRA man Gerard Tuite.

In July 1983 Henry Botton was shot dead on the doorstep of his home in Greenwich.

Eddie Richardson was released from prison in 1976. In October 1990 at Winchester Crown Court he was jailed again for 25 years for importing cocaine from South America.

Frankie Fraser got another five years for leading the 1969 Parkhurst jail riots. He also got what he called a 'thorough beating' from prison officers, and needed sixty stitches in his head. In 1991, free once more, he was gunned down outside the Turnmills nightclub in Clerkenwell. He lived to tell the tale. 'The bullet was a .22, it came in by my right eye, went all round my face under my nose and lodged by my left eye. But it was good fun, good action, it makes a good night's drink, after all.'[4] The powerful north London Adams family were rumoured to be involved.

The Enforcer

In January 2000 south London gang leader Freddie Foreman confessed in an ITV programme to the murders of Frank Mitchell and a small-time crook namer Ginger Marks, whose disappearance had long fed the rumour machine of the underworld. He also hinted that he had other chilling tales to tell of the disappeared, if only he would.

Nipper Read, interviewed on the same programme, said that at the time of the Kray trial he had no idea that Foreman was such an important figure in gangland, and suggested that he too should have been serving thirty-plus years with Reggie Kray.

Foreman, a moon-faced soft-voiced man, apologised to the families of his victims and said he wished none of it had happened. He told how he had used a small boat, which was part of a smuggling operation he ran from Newhaven in Sussex, to dump the bodies, weighted and trussed in chicken wire, in the busy shipping lanes of the English Channel. Had there been more? He sighed and seemed to suggest there had indeed been more.

Foreman also filled in gaps in the chronicle of the Krays, showing how it was partly the muscle he and his team provided that made them so formidable. The killing of Ginger Marks in January 1965 – before the Krays had killed Cornell and McVitie – did his reputation no harm at all.

Marks was long assumed to have been shot down in the street after being mistaken for another man on whom a contract had been taken out. It was also suggested that he had been given the job of burning down Leatherslade Farm where the Great Train Robbers hid out, but had failed to do so. There were several theories about how the body was disposed of: it had been set in concrete and dumped in the Thames, it had been buried in someone else's grave. The *News of the World* offered a reward of £5,000 for information leading to the recovery of the body. 'It is accepted that he was the unintended victim of a 'crime of passion' feud between two south London gangs,' the paper said. This was close to the truth.

Ten years later in December 1964 a man named George Evans was arrested for the attempted murder of Freddie Foreman's brother George, whom he suspected of having an affair with his wife. He was acquitted, and later claimed that he was with Marks when he was attacked by Freddie Foreman and Alfie Gerrard, the killers of Frank Mitchell, and two other men.

On TV Foreman said he wanted revenge after his brother was shot: 'It was payback time. The sooner I got it over with...I just couldn't live with it.' Marks was gunned down in the street and his body later dumped at sea. Foreman said 'everyone' knew he had done it. Asked if people had stayed silent out of fear, he said: 'No, it was respect.'

The murder made a powerful impression on the Krays, Foreman said. 'The twins I suppose looked on it as an achievement in a way.' It also impressed other gangsters who might have thought of challenging the hegemony of the Krays. 'I was back-up for the Krays. Other people thought twice when they knew I was behind them.' Foreman also admitted that he intimidated witnesses who saw Ronnie Kray kill George Cornell.

Foreman began his life of crime as a petty thief just after the war. There was a ready market for electrical goods such as refrigerators and radios. He met Charlie Kray whom he described as 'a good fence'. From petty crime he moved on to payroll robbery. He described a payroll van robbery in which one of his team was shot through the head by a guard in the back of the van. The man was taken to a compliant doctor, but it was too late to save him. He too ended up in the sea.

Foreman was sentenced to ten years in prison for being an accessory in the McVitie case. In 1989 he was jailed for six years for his part in Britain's biggest cash robbery, the £7 million Security

Express raid in 1983. He had been hiding out on Spain's Costa del Sol, but the Spanish police drugged him and put him on a plane back to Britain.

When his autobiography, *Respect – the Managing Director of British Crime*, was published there was a champagne launch at London's Café Royal. Barbara Windsor was there.

Foreman's revelations could help bring about a change in the law. Police chiefs have been pressing for new rules which would allow criminals wrongly acquitted of serious crimes to be tried again. Ronnie Knight's admission that he 'got away with murder' after being cleared of involvement in the killing of Tony Zomparelli gave impetus to calls for reform. Because of the ancient law of 'double jeopardy' Knight could not be tried for the murder again. The Law Commission has recommended that second prosecutions might be ordered by the High Court where there was strong new evidence that could not have been discovered before the first trial if the prosecution had acted with 'due diligence'.

Alf Gerrard was found dead in a friend's flat in Brighton in 1981. An inquest showed that he died of cirrhosis of the liver. The former Bermondsey restaurant owner is believed to have carried out at least half a dozen contract killings.

The Lesser Breeds

Police fears that other gangs were waiting in the wings to take over the mantle of the Krays and Richardsons were not justified. Foreman was more of a robber than a major gangster, and the remaining important gangs either lacked the ambition or the imagination. The most important of these second-division gangs were the Nashes.

The six Nash brothers – Billy, Johnny, Jimmy, Ronnie, George and Roy – came from Islington. They achieved notoriety in 1960 after the Pen club killing. At the time the *Sunday Pictorial* called them 'the wickedest brothers in England.'

The Nashes had worked their way up the ladder of crime, starting out by extorting protection money from small businesses and then moving into clubs. In the early 1960s it was estimated that Johnny Nash, the second oldest after Billy, had twenty clubs under his protection. The family were friends of both the Krays and the Richardsons.

On 7 February 1960 Jimmy Nash was in the Pen club in Spitalfields with his girlfriend and two male friends. The club was believed to have been financed with money stolen from the Parker Pen company, and the clientele were the kind of people who would know about such matters. A fight broke out and the club's owner, Billy Ambrose, who was on leave from a prison sentence, was shot in the stomach when he tried to intervene. Selwyn Cooney, who ran the Cabinet club in the West End for Billy Hill, was shot twice in the head. His body was carried out and laid on the pavement outside. Ambrose drove himself to hospital.

James Morton in *Gangland* says the whole thing sprang from a trivial traffic accident. A car driven by prostitute Vicky James, known as Blonde Vicky, hit Cooney's car, and Cooney sent her the bill for the damage. Blonde Vicky was a friend of Ronnie Nash and when Nash met Cooney in a Notting Hill drinking club there was a fight. So when Jimmy Nash saw Cooney in the Pen club he attacked him, breaking his nose. 'That will teach you to give little girls a spanking,' he said. Ambrose fought back and there were gunshots.

There were the usual problems with prosecution. More than thirty people had been drinking in the club at the time of the shooting, but only four could remember seeing anything. Nash, who admitted punching Cooney but denied murder, was jailed for eighteen months for grievous bodily harm. The *Sunday Pictorial* commented: 'As far as the law is concerned, all that happened to Cooney is that he leaned on a bullet that happened to be passing.'

The Nashes never aspired to ultimate power. Indeed Billy, writing in the *Sunday Pictorial*, said he and his brothers would quit the rackets if they could. 'We have the toughest reputation in London. That means there are fools all over London who would like to take us and make their names.' So they quietly cultivated their clubs, avoiding the limelight.

A gang with a higher profile were the Dixons, former associates of the Krays. Bert Wickstead said he went after the brothers, George and Alan, 'for the simple reason that they were marching around the East End, boasting that they had taken the place of the Krays'.

The Dixons had worked as enforcers for the Krays, and attended their Monday strategy meetings. It was George Dixon that Ronnie tried to murder by putting a gun in his mouth and pulling the trigger. The gun jammed, and later the two gangs were reconciled.

In July 1972 after a long trial the Dixons and Phillip 'Little Caesar' Jacobs, a successful pub owner, were jailed for assault, extortion and conspiracy. George Dixon and Jacobs each got twelve years, and Alan Dixon nine. After his release George Dixon went into the motor trade and Alan into entertainment.

At the end of the trial someone shouted from the dock: 'Wickstead's reign is now going to be at an end.' The Tibbs family must have wished that were true.

The family patriarch, Big Jim Tibbs, had long had a fearsome reputation. Robert Murphy wrote in *Smash and Grab*: 'On the outer edges of east London, Big Jim Tibbs had taken over from the Upton Park mob and acknowledged allegiance to nobody. To cross the iron bridge into Canning Town, the westward edge of Big Jim's fiefdom, was something even the boldest, fiercest and most ambitious of the new generation of gangsters – the Kray brothers – feared to do.'

Whether the Tibbses had ambitions to become major crime figures is open to doubt. They were involved in a long simmering feud with a family called Nicholls which occasionally burst into violence.

After Albert Nicholls, who was in his twenties, attacked George Tibbs, who was in his sixties, in a pub in 1968 Nicholls was badly beaten outside his Poplar minicab office. His attackers were Jimmy Tibbs, his brother Johnny and George's son, young George. Nicholls tried to protect himself with a shotgun but it was taken from him and he was shot with it. Bert Wickstead described his injuries: 'A shotgun blast inflicted terrible injuries to his legs and the lower part of his abdomen. There were three large lacerations in the scalp and cuts to the face. The tip of his nose was partially severed and he lost the tip of a finger.'[1]

At the subsequent trial Mr Justice Lyell directed that the trio be acquitted of murder and gave them suspended sentences for wounding. He told them: 'You have been guilty apart from anything else of the most appalling folly. I sympathise with your feelings but at the same time, living in the part of London where you live, there is a great deal too much violence.'

The tit-for-tat violence went on, with the Nicholls faction generally getting the worst of it. In November 1970 Robert Tibbs survived having his throat cut outside the Rose of Denmark pub. Lenny Kersey, who was said to have called the Tibbses 'pikeys' [gipsies] was slashed with knives and an axe as he left his flat in Mile End. He had 180 stitches in the wounds.

His wife, who saw what happened, said: 'I saw the men hacking at somebody on the ground and tried to stop the horrible thing. Then I saw it was my husband. His face was falling apart. I screamed the place down. My friend also screamed and dropped her baby.'[2]

The violence rumbled on. On 22 April 1971 a bomb went off in Jimmy Tibbs's car outside a school. His four-year-old son was with him. They both survived. Bert Wickstead went after the Tibbses. He wrote in his autobiography, *Gangbuster*: 'They were a highly organised gang. They were becoming steadily more powerful, more ruthless, more ambitious. They were also more wicked and crueller than their opponents.'

In October 1972 seven members of the Tibbs family and their friends were jailed. James Tibbs senior got fifteen years, Stanley Naylor twelve, Michael Machin eleven and Jimmy Tibbs ten.

A defence lawyer told the court of the tradition of family loyalty in east London. 'It is something the East End might teach the rest of the country about. But if it goes wrong and leads to vengeance and violence, then it goes badly wrong.'

Vengeance and violence were things some members of the formidable Arif family from Stockwell specialised in. The family, of Turkish-Cypriot origin, have been described as the kings of the Old Kent Road. They owned pubs, restaurants and clubs, rumoured to have been bought with cash from a series of major armed robberies.[3]

The Arifs almost singlehandedly revived the fashion for armed robbery at a time when the police were themselves better armed. In a shoot-out at Reigate in November 1990 one of the Arif gang, Kenny Baker, was shot dead after he and three of the family ambushed a Securicor van. Police rammed the van and won the shoot-out. Dennis Arif was jailed for twenty-two years: his brother-in-law, Anthony Downer, got eighteen years, as did Dennis's brother Mehmet, who was wounded.

The Arifs have accumulated a formidable total of years in jail. Dogan, who is in his fifties and is regarded as the head of the family, got fourteen years for an £8.5 million cannabis-smuggling plot. Police believe the Arifs had been successful armed robbers for about twenty years. It is possible that the £800,000 the Securicor van was carrying would have been used to bankroll a permanent move into drugs.

Not that the family is short of cash. 'We reckon they have made millions,' a detective told the *Sun* newspaper. Earlier in 1990 there was a £30,000 family wedding party at the Savoy in London. The Securicor robbery trial was told that many other families had attended including 'the Colemans, Frasers, Whites, Adams and Hiscocks.'

Supercrooks and Supergrasses

The gang leader Billy Hill organised the first big post-war robbery in London, a raid on a mail van which netted £287,000 in May 1952. In his memoirs Hill wrote that the night before the robbery the nine men involved were taken to a flat in the West End and locked in before the briefing on the operation began. Hill's men had been following the van for months and its route was known. Hours before the raid one of the robbers disconnected the van's alarm while the staff were on a tea break. When the van set out from Paddington Station the robbers followed in stolen cars. In Eastcastle Street near Oxford Street the robbers used their cars to stop the van, attacked the crew and stole the van.

They had been expecting to find only between £40,000 and £50,000 and there wasn't enough room in the fruiterer's lorry they had brought to hide all the mailbags. Hill told them to leave thirteen mailbags behind in the mail van. The lorry was driven to Spitalfields market. After keeping it under observation for 24 hours to make sure the police had not found it the gang drove it to Dagenham marshes and unloaded it.

Soon the police officer leading the investigation, Chief Superintendent Bob Lee, who had led the ambush of the 1948 airport robbers and also 'warned Hill off from attempting a £7 million postage-stamp heist during the war' knew the names of those involved but he never found any proof. There were rumours of police collusion – the robbers always said they had left more bags in the van than the police said they found.[1]

The sixties and seventies were the heydays of the bank robbers. Banks were virtually unprotected: there were no alarm systems linked to police stations, no video cameras, no counter-to-ceiling security screens. The robbers would simply burst in, jump on to the counter, fire a shotgun into the ceiling to intimidate the staff and make off with large amounts of cash. By the summer of 1972 armed robberies were taking place at the rate of about one a week, and police believed major criminals could call on 3,000 men in London to take part in such crimes.

Bank robbers felt themselves to be an underworld elite, living glamorous lives with fast cars, pretty girls, designer clothes and racing weekends at Longchamps. 'They saw the Krays as old-fashioned and mocked them with the nicknames "Gert and Daisy", chumps who had been caught because they stuck their necks out, dinosaurs who liked Matt Monro while the new boys played The Doors and T. Rex on their newly discovered car tape-decks as they slung their "happy-bags" stuffed with sawn-off shotguns, masks and gloves into the back seat.'[2]

Duncan Campbell writes in *The Underworld* that many of these robbers were from Hornsey Rise – 'Hungry Hill as the young hoodlums liked to call it' – and the area that spanned Holloway and Finsbury Park, the Angel and Hoxton. How the last-named has persisted as a stronghold of gangland down the years.

Bertie Smalls, the first of the 'supergrasses', was a noted bank robber. He was one of the six raiders who stole £138,000 in the Wembley bank job of August 1972. It took them less than two minutes to get in and out again weighed down with bags of cash as they ran to their getaway vehicles.

The former armed robber turned pundit John McVicar gives us an insight into the mindset of these bandits: 'The professional criminal wants respect, prestige and the recognition of those who subscribe to his own need of machismo. The field in which he tries to achieve this is one in which profit, crime and gangsterism overlap.' He confessed in his autobiography: 'As a criminal I have been a lamentable failure. Whatever money I earned by crime I could have earned as a labourer in half the time I have spent in prison...Money has been a secondary goal: crime has always been directed to more powerful objectives.'[3]

Smalls, described by Duncan Campbell in *The Underworld* as 'a short, squat man who looked like the film actor Bob Hoskins and held ferociously right-wing views', led a team of robbers who pulled off a series of raids in the late 1960s and early 1970s. One of the colleagues on whom he later informed said, 'he loved violence. He couldn't handle straight company, he liked to be with one of his own...' Smalls also had a pungent sense of humour. As he rushed past a woman witness carrying the proceeds of a bank raid he said: 'What a way to earn a fucking living, eh girl?'

By late 1972 the police felt they had enough evidence to arrest Smalls. He had been identified from a photograph by a witness as being one of the raiders on a National Westminster branch at Palmers Green in May of that year. A Jaguar car used in another raid was traced to a garage at Tower Bridge in which he had an interest. After an earlier £296,000 robbery at Ralli Brothers in Hatton Garden in March 1969 another witness identified him from a photograph. In December 1972 the Smalls' au pair took the police to the house near Northampton where the robber planned to spend Christmas. Smalls heard a noise at the door and, believing it was the cat, opened it . His wife Diane said: 'You let the rats in, not the cat.'[4]

Smalls offered to do a deal: in return for a *written* guarantee that he would be given immunity from prosecution, he would talk. The agreement, much criticised later, was drawn up with the Director of Public Prosecutions, Sir Norman Skelhorn. Smalls helped to jail 21 men for a total of 308 years. Some got small reductions on appeal.

In the Court of Appeal Lord Justice Lawton was scathing about the immunity deal. 'Above all else the spectacle of the Director recording in writing at the behest of a criminal like Smalls his undertaking to give immunity from further prosecution is one which we find distasteful. Nothing of a similar kind must happen again.' Supergrasses would never again buy their freedom at the expense of former partners.

There were rumours that a contract for the murder of Smalls had been taken out, but some months after the trial his armed guard was withdrawn and the family lived under another name without molestation. Smalls said that if he went into a pub and saw a friend or relative of someone he had 'grassed' he would simply leave.

*

The wages of sin were getting ever greater, as far as robbers were concerned. In April 1983 about fifteen men dressed in black broke into the headquarters of Security Express in Shoreditch, east London. They forced the supervisor, Greg Counsel, to admit other members of the staff as they arrived for work, and then tied them up. Then they obtained the combination of the safe by pouring petrol over one of the guards and threatening to turn him into a human torch unless he revealed it. In a five-hour operation the gang stole nearly £6 million.

One of the men involved, Allen Opiola, was already under police observation and when they questioned him about another big robbery he revealed that he had allowed his home to be used for storing the loot from the Security Express robbery.

Opiola agreed to give evidence against the gang in return for a light sentence. He was given three years and three months, with a recommendation that he should serve it in police custody.

In January 1985 Johnny Knight, brother of the well-known Ronnie, was arrested. He and Terry Perkins, said to be the ringleaders, were each jailed for 22 years at the Old Bailey. Mr Justice Richard Lowry called them ruthless and evil men, and added: 'Your aim was to live in luxury.'

Other major crime figures also faced the court. Knight's brother James got eight years for handling stolen money, John Horsely and Billy Hickson six for the same crime. Only £2 million of the loot was found, and the judge said: 'Other guilty men have not been caught.'

Nearly five years later south London gang boss Freddie Foreman was extradited from Spain and jailed for nine years for handling money from the raid. It was pointed out in court that before the raid he and his wife had £75 in their bank accounts but within seven months had deposited £360,000. His barrister told the court: 'There has been a suggestion that he was leading the life not only of Riley but of a very rich Riley. He was not. He was certainly not living a nine-to-five life in Spain but it was not a life of luxury or ostentation.'

The Brink's-Mat warehouse robbery of 26 November 1983 was a classic inside job. Tony Black, a security guard at the warehouse on the Heathrow Airport trading estate, tipped off robber Brian 'The Colonel' Robinson, who was living with his sister, about large cash deposits regularly made on Friday nights. Robinson put together a team and gave Black some Plasticine to make impressions of the warehouse keys. Black, who had been promised that cash would be deposited in a Swiss bank account for him if the raid was successful, made the impressions and passed them over.

So began one of the biggest robberies in British criminal history, one that would lead to the tragic death of a police officer and gradually draw in many of London's criminal elite. In various trials associated with it over the years crooks large and small clocked up sentences of more than 200 years.

At a signal from Black the gang used their keys to get into the warehouse. One guard was punched and coshed, others had petrol poured over them, another was threatened with castration.

One of the robbers, Micky McAvoy, whispered to Black as he lay on the floor: 'It's all right, we got the lot.' Instead of the £1 million to £2 million the gang had expected they got away with 6,400 gold ingots, worth about £26 million.

Under interrogation Black crumbled and gave police the names of Robinson, Micky McAvoy and Tony White, who were arrested. Black pleaded guilty and got six years. Robinson and McAvoy were given 25 years and White was acquitted.

Meanwhile the search for the gold went on. Because of its high degree of purity the bullion could not be disposed of through the trade. A Bristol bullion company, Scadlynn Ltd, was found to be smelting large amounts of gold. Garth Chappell, managing director of Scadlynn, and six others were charged with, among other things, disposing of the stolen gold. Chappell got ten years, another of the defendants, Brian Reader, got nine. Kenneth Noye, who had already been acquitted of murdering a police officer who was helping in the investigation, got the maximum sentence of fourteen years.

Criminals are by definition flawed. Noye, one of the most successful criminals of the eighties and nineties, a virtuoso at corruption and fraud, was brought down by a fit of temper.

In May 1996 Noye was involved in a 'road rage' incident on the

M25 in Kent. During it he stabbed to death Stephen Cameron, a 25-year-old electrician. Although he went on the run and evaded justice for four years, it was effectively the end of a spectacular criminal career.

Noye had already rebuilt that career after being found not guilty of murdering a police officer whom he stabbed to death, and then serving a long jail sentence for laundering gold from the £26 million Brink's-Mat robbery. Shrugging off these setbacks he built a series of alliances across the underworld, corrupted police officers and prison guards, used his position of influence inside the Freemasons to advantage and added to his enormous wealth.

Noye came from the ranks of the lower middle class, unlike most of the south London villains who were his first accomplices. Kathy McAvoy, wife of the Brink's-Mat robber 'Mad' Micky McAvoy, said: 'Noye wasn't from south London, he was from the suburbs and that's just not the same. Noye wasn't the real thing and he knew the rest of us thought that.'[5]

Noye was born in Bexleyheath, Kent, in May 1947. His father James was a post office engineer and his mother Edith, a devout Christian, worked three days a week at a nearby dog-track. At the age of three Kenneth broke his nose when he fell out of a tree while stealing apples. This gave his handsome features a suitably battered look that may have helped his first criminal venture – running a protection racket at Bexleyheath Secondary Modern school where he went at the age of eleven. One of his fellow pupils, Mick Marshall, recalled: 'He was vile, he didn't give a damn who he hurt. But everybody knew Kenny had a knack of getting away with blue murder.'[6]

After school he became involved in petty crime, receiving and smuggling, and spent time in Borstal. He met his future wife, Brenda Tremain, a legal secretary, at the lawyer's chambers where he had gone for advice after a brush with the police.

He began to mix with the aristocracy of crime, the Krays, Richardsons, Frankie Fraser and others. Ostensibly he was a respectable businessman, living with Brenda and their two sons in a mansion in Kent and dealing in cars, property and timeshares. Behind this front he had moved into a higher league of crime, becoming a fence and armourer to the underworld and providing services like money-laundering that the major robbers were not capable of organising for themselves.

His first fortune was made in gold smuggling. He would import gold illegally and make huge profits by evading the VAT due when it was sold. The gold was coming in from Africa, Kuwait and Brazil. It has been estimated that between 1982 and 1984 he made more than £4 million.

'He was in his element. Opening the front door of his house, Hollywood Cottage in West Kingsdown, Kent, triggered a stereo blasting out Shirley Bassey singing the theme song to the James Bond film *Goldfinger*. There were expensive clothes, jewellery and limousines. Noye bought his wife a squash club. For himself he acquired a succession of blonde and brassy mistresses, some of whom were partners of his friends and associates.'[7]

Noye's interest in gold and the ways it could be moved around the world and illegally traded were invaluable to the underworld after the Brink's-Mat robbery at Heathrow Airport in November 1983.

The gang included some of the major figures from London's underworld, among them John 'Little Legs' Lloyd, who was a friend of Noye, McAvoy and Robinson, major-league robbers from south London. They turned to Noye with his proven record as a fence to launder the three tons of gold ingots.

On a dark night in January 1985 Noye confronted a man in a balaclava in the garden of his home at West Kingsdown. There was a struggle and Noye stabbed the masked man ten times. Noye says he asked the dying man who he was and he gasped out: 'SAS...on manoeuvres.'

In fact the masked man was a policeman, Constable John Fordham, who had been taking part in a stake-out of the Noye home. Police suspected Noye and another man in the house at the time, Brian Reader, of being involved in the gold robbery.

Noye and Reader were charged with murder. Noye said of the moment he confronted PC Fordham: 'I just froze with horror. All I saw when I flashed my torch on this masked man was the two eye-holes and the mask. I thought that was my lot. I thought I was going to be a dead man. As far as I was concerned I was fighting for my life.'

In 1986 when he faced a jury at the Old Bailey he pleaded self-defence and they believed him: although the prosecution had told the jury how Noye had plunged his knife up to the hilt in the unarmed officer's body ten times, he and Reader were acquitted of murder.

Another policeman, Neil Murphy, who was Detective Constable Fordham's partner on the night he was killed, said he tried to distract Noye by shouting. Murphy said: 'Noye also had a gun. I could hear him shouting, "We will blow your head off." I could see figures standing over John's body.

'Afterwards in the ambulance I could see John's chest going up and down. I said, "Look, he is breathing," but the ambulanceman said it was just the oxygen he was using.'

Noye's house was searched and police found eleven bars of gold and copper coins which could be used in melting down the precious metal. He was tried with six others on charges including disposing of the gold. Found guilty, he was given the maximum sentence of fourteen years for handling stolen goods. After the verdict he shouted to the jury: 'I hope you all die of cancer.'

With years in prison ahead of him, Noye made the best of things by corrupting the system. At Albany prison on the Isle of Wight he gave one officer a £600 watch on his wife's birthday. After he was released from prison two officers who were escorting a prisoner to a weight-lifting competition called on Noye. The prisoner was Derek Kandler, a friend of Noye, and he took them all to a Thai restaurant.

Prison provided Noye with new opportunities. He had handed back nearly £3 million of the Brink's-Mat loot to avoid having his home seized, and with new contacts he decided drugs were the quickest way of recouping his losses. At Swaleside prison he met Pat Tate, a drug dealer from Essex. Tate persuaded him to invest £30,000 in an ecstasy shipment, and he made a quick profit. Police believe that it was ecstasy from that shipment that killed the teenager Leah Betts.

In December 1995 Tate was shot dead with two other men in a

Range Rover parked in a country lane near Chelmsford, Essex. Another of Noye's associates, car dealer Nick Whiting, was abducted from his showrooms in West Kingsdown by an armed gang in 1990. His body was found on Rainham Marshes in Essex. He had been stabbed nine times and then shot twice with a 9mm pistol.

Thanks to his expertise in corrupting officials Noye escaped arrest for another drug plot. While he was finishing his sentence at Latchmere he had become involved in a cocaine deal with the Miami Mafia. He was tipped off that he was under surveillance by the US Drugs Enforcement Agency. The tip came from John Donald, a detective with the National Criminal Intelligence Service, who was jailed for eleven years in 1996 for corruption.

Commander Roy Clark, one of his senior officers, said: "Donald was more than corrupt, he committed acts of treachery beyond belief. He sold operational secrets to those involved in organised crime and put the lives of police officers at risk.'

There are misgivings among senior officers about Noye's links to the Freemasons. In the late 1970s he joined the Hammersmith Freemasons' Lodge in west London, having been sponsored by two police officers. He eventually became master of the lodge.

'In the early Eighties, a police contact approached a customs officer and told him to "lay off" Noye. The Customs man, at first surprised and then angry, warned that if the conversation went any further, he would have to report it officially.'[8]

Police pursuing Noye after the road-rage murder were astonished by his range of contacts. After he had served his Brink's-Mat sentence he went to northern Cyprus, where he met fugitive tycoon Asil Nadir, the former Polly Peck boss who is wanted in Britain on fraud charges. Noye invested in a time-share development on the island, and discussed other business deals with Nadir.

Then he got involved in a plot to swindle £1 billion from cash-dispensing machines. His partners included 'Little Legs' Lloyd. 'According to one former member of the gang, Martin Grant, Noye put money into the venture and then threw a pre-operation party in a Kent hotel at which six expensive prostitutes were present. Noye boasted later that he had gone to bed with each of them.'[9]

The plot collapsed and Noye's partners were arrested and sent to prison. Frustrated police could not arrest Noye because they lacked the evidence. There was speculation that, once again, he had been tipped off just in time.

Other criminals Noye has been linked with include Tommy Adams of the north London crime family. They were filmed by police investigating the handling of the Brink's-Mat gold. His close friend Micky Lawson was cleared of handling that gold, but during the trial of Detective Sergeant Donald, the corrupt National Criminal Intelligence Service officer, the court was told that Noye and Lawson were behind 150-kilo cocaine shipments from the US.

Armed robber Tony White, jailed in 1997 for drug smuggling, has also been linked to Noye, as have money-launderer Keith Hedley, shot dead on his yacht in Corfu in 1996, and club owner and veteran gangster Joey Wilkins, with whom Noye stayed while on the run in Spain.

In April 1996 Noye was back in Cyprus, this time accompanied by his mistress Sue McNichol-Outch. He visited Asil Nadir before returning to Britain. A month later Noye's Land Rover Discovery pulled in front of Stephen Cameron's van. Stephen's fiancée Danielle Cable saw Noye pull a knife and stab Stephen to death before driving off in his Land Rover.

Noye now moved fast. He arranged to have the Land Rover scrapped and another very similar one, paid for with £20,000 in cash, parked in the drive of his new £400,000 home in Sevenoaks, Kent. He contacted a friend, John Palmer, who had also been involved in the Brink's-Mat gold disposals. Palmer, a time-share fraudster, arranged his escape.

Noye drove to Bristol, flew by helicopter to France, then by private jet to Spain and on to the Canaries. Later he returned to Spain, and using a passport in the name of Alan Edward Green he settled in Atlanterra, between Cadiz and Gibraltar.

By 1998 Noye had settled into a £330,000 villa. He had acquired a new girlfriend, Mina al-Taifa, who has Lebanese-French blood, but Sue McNicholl-Outch also came to stay from time to time.

Despite his great wealth Noye needed money, because it was too dangerous to take cash from his various accounts as police were monitoring them. He linked up with a marijuana smuggler in Gibraltar and reportedly made £1 million.

According to Paul Lashmar and Kim Sengupta in the *Independent*, the crucial tip-off to police came from former club-owner and veteran gangland figure Joey Wilkins, with whom Noye stayed after fleeing to Spain.

They claimed that Wilkins, who is also on the run after absconding from an open prison, is believed by underworld sources in Spain to be a British police informer, which explains why he has not been extradited. 'According to underworld sources, Wilkins waited a few weeks and then quietly passed Noye's mobile phone number to the police. Detectives then used the option, available in exceptional circumstances through the National Criminal Intelligence Service, to request the aid of GCHQ. It was able to locate the user of the number down to Noye's new villa.'

Police have always insisted that they were tipped off about Noye by a holidaymaker who recognised him. But there were other leads. Noye's wife Brenda also visited him, and it was one of her visits in 1998 which helped police to pinpoint where he was staying. Two Kent police officers travelled to the Atlanterra area and spotted Noye riding his 600cc Yamaha trail bike along a coast road.

Danielle Cable was then taken to the town and identified Noye as he sat in a restaurant with Mina. He was arrested by Spanish police.

Brenda Noye is living in Cornwall under her maiden name and has a new man in her life, a fisherman. Mina al-Taifa is living in Marbella with her teenage son. She told reporters that she did not remember a Kenneth Noye.

Noye is believed to have millions of pounds in an Irish bank. For a man so obsessed by money that he illegally connected his house to the electricity supply of a local school and stole a piece of garden furniture from a 94-year-old neighbour, it must be tantalising almost beyond endurance.

Noye's last victim is Danielle Cable. After police found that a contract had been put out on her life she was taken into a witness protection programme and given a new identity and a new life. She has had to move away from her parents and friends and the area where she grew up.

In May 2001 John 'Goldfinger' Palmer, cleared fourteen years earlier of melting down gold from the Brink's-Mat raid at his West Country mansion before selling it back to the owners, bankers Johnson Matthey, was jailed for eight years. The Old Bailey heard how he cheated British tourists out of about £30 million in the world's biggest timeshare swindle. Police believe he used the cash from the bullion smelting to found a £300 million timeshare and money-laundering empire. Palmer, fifty, was said to be near to tears as he appealed to the judge for leniency. It was Palmer who spirited Noye out of the country after the murder of Stephen Cameron.

In October 2001 Noye lost his appeal against the murder conviction. The court was told that one of the witnesses at the murder trial, Alan Decabral, who had told the jury that he witnessed the killing and that Noye had a look on his face that appeared to say 'that sorted him out. You have got yours, mate,' was a liar. The Lord Chief Justice said the jury would have reached the guilty verdict even without Mr Decabral's evidence.

After the murder trial Mr Decabral was shot dead in a car park in Kent. Noye claims he had nothing to do with this murder.

The attractions of Spain to British criminals on the run were obvious from the late seventies onward. There was no extradition treaty with Britain after 1978, and there were opportunities to develop the drugs and smuggling rackets. The credit for spotting the potential of the Marbella area has been given to Ronnie Knight, who bought a plot of land near Fuengirola with his brother Johnny and built a house there.

Soon other British criminals arrived. There were the Famous Five – Knight, Freddie Foreman, Ronald Everett, once a close friend of the Kray twins, John James Mason, who had been cleared of the £8 million Bank of America robbery in Mayfair in 1976, and Clifford Saxe, at one time the landlord of the Fox pub in Kingsland Road, Hackney, where the robbery is said to have been planned.

Another criminal who set up home near Marbella was Charlie Wilson, the Great Train Robber. On 23 April 1990 a young man arrived at the house on a mountain bike and told Patricia Wilson that he wanted to speak to her husband. Wilson took him out to the patio, where he had earlier been celebrating his wedding anniversary with some guests.

Moments later there was the sound of an argument and two loud bangs. Patricia found Wilson dying by the pool, shot in the neck. His dog had been injured so badly it had to be put down.

An inquest was held in London in November 1991 and Mrs Wilson told it: 'I heard the man say, "I am a friend of Eamonn." I had a feeling there were two people there, although I couldn't say why. I heard two loud bangs, and at first I thought it was from the building site next door, but then I heard the dog screaming. Charlie was lying at the side of the pool face down. The man had gone and the gate was open. I saw blood coming from his mouth and Charlie did a sort of press-up and gestured in the direction the man had gone.'

Police believed Wilson was involved in drug trafficking, although this was strongly denied by the Wilson family. Detective Superintendent Alec Edwards told the inquest: 'As far as the Spanish police and the British police are concerned, there is circumstantial evidence that this is a drug-related incident.'

Wilson got a gangland funeral. Train robbers Bruce Reynolds, Buster Edwards, Roy James and Robert Welch were among the mourners, and the Kray twins sent wreaths. Wilson's favourite song, 'My Way', which had become a kind of underworld standard on these occasions, was played.

Ronnie Knight once said that the Costa del Crime, as the tabloids called it, was 'paradise found'. After the Wilson killing the mood darkened. In 1985 the Spanish and British governments patched up their differences and signed an extradition treaty, although it was not retroactive. In 1989 Freddie Foreman was flown back to Britain and tried for his part in the 1983 Shoreditch Security Express robbery – a crime for which Knight was also wanted. Foreman was jailed for nine years. Knight, the very image of the playboy criminal cocking a snook at the law, gave himself up and in January 1995 at the Old Bailey he admitted handling £314,813 from the Security Express robbery. He was jailed for seven years.

Knight served four years of the Security Express sentence. In July 2000 he was fined £200 for shoplifting at a Waitrose supermarket in Brent Cross, north London. Knight, 66, admitted stealing groceries worth £39.74, although he had £270 in cash. He told magistrates at Hendon, north London: 'I am so sorry that I have done this. I hope the children still want me.'

On 18 April 2000 Italian police saw a stolen Lancia on a dirt track near Ascoli, about 100 miles east of Rome. When they asked two men standing nearby for their documents one pulled a gun. In a struggle he was shot dead. The dead man was Valerio Viccei, the mastermind of Britain's biggest robbery, the Knightsbridge safe-deposit raid of 1987 in which between £40 million and £80 million was stolen. The true figure will never be known, because much of the loot had been hidden in the safe deposit by gangsters, who are not likely to make a claim.

Viccei, 45, was still serving a 22-year jail sentence for the crime, having controversially been moved to a top-security prison in Italy after serving only five years in a British jail. The authorities at Pescara in southern Italy allowed him out on day release, and police believe he was using his free time to plan another robbery.

In a newspaper interview not long before his death Viccei, who was nicknamed the Italian Stallion because of his success with beautiful women, claimed he was going straight and was a 'successful businessman'.

Viccei pulled off a string of bank robberies in London, including Coutts in Cavendish Square, and kept the proceeds in the Knightsbridge Safe Deposit Box Centre, opposite Harrods. He met the managing director of the deposit, 31-year-old Parvez Latif, and wooed him over champagne and expensive meals. He was also sleeping with Latif's glamorous girlfriend, Pamela Seamarks. Latif, who was heavily in debt, was dazzled by Viccei's playboy lifestyle, his Ferrari Testarossa and taste for pure Colombian cocaine. Gradually Latif was drawn into the plot to loot the deposit centre. Viccei promised him vast wealth as his cut if the robbery was successful.

On Sunday 12 July 1987 Latif stuck a notice to the door of the deposit centre. "We apologise to all our customers for any inconvenience caused to them during the improvements to our security system. Business as usual from tomorrow. Thank you.'

Viccei, who had put together an international team of robbers, rang the bell, which was answered by Latif. Because the deposit's guards were not part of the plot both Viccei and Latif had to keep up an elaborate charade. Viccei and his team pretended they were customers, and once inside Viccei pulled out a gun. Other members of the team then arrived and together they attacked the steel deposit boxes with power drills and sledgehammers.

Viccei wrote in his autobiography, *Knightsbridge, the Robbery of the Century*: 'The atmosphere was one of pure ecstasy. We had just pulled off the boldest, largest and most spectacular robbery in recent times.' This was no exaggeration: Viccei filled the bathtub of their hideout with cash and jewels, and the floor of the room was also covered in jewels. There were also drugs and antiques.

But Viccei had cut his hand during the robbery and left bloody fingerprints, which were identified. Instead of leaving the country he lingered and was trapped in a traffic jam at Marble Arch in his Ferrari.

At his trial Judge Robert Lymbery told him: 'The stakes were colossal. Having lost you have to pay the price accordingly. In this court I have seen a man of charm and courtesy, a man of substantial abilities. But these qualities, combined with others, serve to make you a very dangerous man.'

His former girlfriend, Pamela Seamarks, now a Home Counties wife, was unmoved by his death. 'I detest everything about him and the life he led me into,' she said. 'I'd hate the same thing to happen to any other girl searching for success and excitement.' At the time she was 'led into' a life of luxury by Viccei, she was thirty.

Sin City

Vice was one of Victorian Britain's biggest industries. One estimate put the number of prostitutes in London in the 1830s at 80,000, many of them children. (By contrast, in the 1950s there were believed to about 5,000.) This vast illicit enterprise was surprisingly public. Whores paraded in the most fashionable parts of the city, particularly inside and outside the main theatres. Covent Garden, the Haymarket, Regent Street, Cremorne Gardens and St James were bazaars of sexual opportunity. Although Victorian moralists called it the road to ruin, prostitution brought relative affluence to many young women and riches to some. At the same time, a warning to the carefree young women promenading in the same streets were the diseased losers in this highly competitive market, 'alcoholics, semi-imbeciles, female flotsam of all kinds, soliciting an almost inconceivable interest in their dishevelled bodies or offering to cooperate in the squalidest perversions for a few coppers.'[1]

London had teemed with prostitutes since the Middle Ages. In 1483 the city authorities issued a proclamation against 'the Stynkynge and Horrible Synne of Lecherie ... which dayly groweth and is used more than in days past by the means of Strumpettes, mysguded and idyll women dayly vagraunt'. There were whores in Smithfield, St Giles (of course), Shoreditch, Southwark, Ave Maria Alley by St Paul's Cathedral, at the Bell in Gracechurch Street, the Harry in Cheapside. There were brothels in Aldersgate, Billingsgate, Bridge, Broad Street, Aldgate, and Farringdon, among other wards.[2]

Burford says that one prostitute in the ward of Bridge was known

216

as Clarice la Claterballock. Our vocabulary of nicknames for whores is impoverished: then they were known as, among many others, punks, fireships, jilts, doxies, cracks, mawkes, trulls, trugmoldies, molls, blowzabellas and punchable nuns.

Procuresses or bawds sometimes showed a gift for advertising. Mother Cresswell of Clerkenwell had 'Beauties of all Complexions, from the cole-black clyng-fast to the golden lock'd insatiate, from the sleepy ey'd Slug to the lewd Fricatrix'. *The Whore's Rhetorick* satirised her instructions to young whores: 'You must not forget to use the natural accents of dying persons... You must add to these ejaculations, aspirations, sighs, intermissions of words, and such like gallantries, whereby you may give your Mate to believe that you are melted, dissolved and wholly consumed in pleasure, though Ladies of large business are generally no more moved by an embrace, than if they were made of Wood or stone.'[3]

Mother Cresswell kept a stable of young girls who could be despatched anywhere on request, and many of the requests came from the Court. Among her many establishments was a house in Lincoln's Inn Fields where she sold 'Strong Waters and fresh-fac'd Wenches to all who had Guineas to buy them with', although this was not her principal place of business. That was in Back Alley off Moor Lane in Cripplegate – Moorgate Underground Station stands on the site. This substantial building was described by the conman and wencher Richard Head in 1663. He and a companion went to Mother Cresswell's, 'famous for the good Citizens' Wives that frequented her house... she still rode Admiral over all the other Bawds in Town'. They were led into a handsome room, and a servant brought them French wine and meats. Presently Mother Cresswell, described by Head as the 'old matron', came in, greeting them by chucking them under the chin. She asked to see their money and then sent in a 'nice young girl'. They could not agree a price, so she sent in 'a raving beauty'. Mother Cresswell claimed she was of 'superior birth serving only Persons of Quality'. The girl asked for a guinea, [£1.05 pence], Head offered half a crown [12.5p] and they agreed on half a guinea.[4]

Mother Cresswell was among the most successful of all the bawds. Her lover Sir Thomas Player backed the Duke of Monmouth for the Protestant succession, and she lent him large sums to further his cause. When he came to grief a £300 bond she had guaranteed for him was called in, and she seems to have been unable or unwilling to pay, although her will showed her to be still wealthy. She was sent to Newgate, where she died in 1685. She left £10 in her will for a sermon at her funeral, stipulating that it must speak well of her. The preacher, taking liberties with the facts, said: 'By the will of the deceased it is expected that I say nothing but well of her. All that I shall say therefore is this: She was born well, she lived well and she died well, for she was born with the name Cresswell, she lived in Clerkenwell and she died in Bridewell.' She was long remembered for her bawdy cry of 'No money, no cunny.'[5]

In the sixteenth century many of the brothels were in Southwark, on land owned by the Bishop of Winchester – the women were known as Winchester geese. The stews or brothels had to be painted white and carry a distinctive mark: one of the best-known was the Cardinal's Hat. In the middle of the sixteenth century a particularly severe wave of syphilis caused Henry VIII (himself a sufferer) to close the Southwark brothels. They reopened under Edward VI, closed again under Mary Tudor and then reopened under Elizabeth. The association between acting and whoring was strong. Philip Henslowe, the theatre impresario, and his son-in-law, the actor Edward Alleyn, owned brothels, and Southwark became London's theatreland.[6]

Bawds and whores were often prosecuted, and the punishment was humiliating: they were 'carted', that is taken by cart to the pillory, preceded by minstrels and a crowd beating on barbers' basins to drum up a jeering crowd. When they reached the pillory a document called a Cause detailing their offences was read out, and then stuck on their heads. They were then carted to the red-light district of Cocks Lane and ritually expelled from the city.

In the eighteenth century Covent Garden and the Strand were plagued by hordes of streetwalkers. Boswell's journals recount his many encounters with lusty young girls in the 1760s. One evening in 1762 he picked up such a girl in the Strand and went into a court 'with intention to enjoy her in armour [a condom]. But she had none ... she wondered at my size, and said that if ever I took a girl's maidenhead, I would make her squeak.' This may have been one of the seventeen sexual encounters which ended in the torments of venereal disease for the great diarist and biographer.[7]

For men of the town and sex tourists there were guides to the charms on offer. Archenholz writes: 'A tavern-keeper in Drury Lane prints every year an account of the women of the town entitled *Harris's List of Covent Garden Cyprians*. In it the most exact description is given of their names, their lodgings, their faces, their manners, their talents and even their tricks. It must of course happen that there will be sometimes a little degree of partiality in these details; however, notwithstanding this, 8,000 copies are sold annually...' Harris had a way with double entendres, as his appeal to the susceptibilities of seafarers over the charms of a Miss Devonshire of Queen Anne Street shows: 'Many a man of war has been her willing prisoner, and paid a proper ransom; her port is said to be well-guarded by a light brown *chevaux-de-frieze* ... the entry is rather straight; but when once in there is very good riding ... she is ever ready for an engagement, cares not how soon she comes to close quarters, and loves to fight yard arm and yard arm, and be briskly boarded.' Or he could be more frankly pornographic. This is Miss Wilkinson of 10 Bull and Mouth Street:

> ... a pair of sweet lips that demand the burning kiss and never receive it without paying interest... Descend a little lower and behold the semi snowballs ... that want not the support of stays; whose truly elastic state never suffers the pressure, however severe, to remain but boldly recovers its tempting smoothness. Next take a view of nature *centrally*; no *folding lapel*; no *gaping orifice*; no *horrid gulph* is here, but the *loving lips* tenderly kiss each other, and shelter from the cold a small but easily stretched passage, whose *depth* none but the *blind boy* has liberty to fathom ... [8]

Harris also tells us that Lord Chesterfield liked to have his 'eyelids licked by two naked whores'.

There were other guidebooks besides Harris's for the sexually adventurous. In 1691 appeared among others *A Catalogue of Jilts, Cracks & Prostitutes, Nightwalkers, Whores, She-friends, Kind*

Women and other of the Linnen-lifting Tribe. It was a list of 21 women who could be found in the cloisters of St Bartholomew's Church during Bartholomew Fair in Smithfield. Like Harris's guide it listed the women's physical attributes: 'Mary Holland, tall graceful and comely, shy of her favours but may be mollified at a cost of £20. Elizabeth Holland [her sister] indifferent to Money but a Supper and Two Guineas will tempt her.' Dorothy Roberts could be had for a bottle of wine; Posture Moll, a flagellant, wanted only half a crown; Mrs Whitby, who had obviously come down in the world, had previously charged more than five guineas but would now accept ten shillings from 'any ordinary fellow'. There are two black women in the list: 'Bridget Williams, a pretty little Negress... not yet mistress of her profession so can be offered half-a-crown... and bullied out of her money again', and Mrs Sarah Heath, 'a Negress... her fee is higher... will make no concession about fee'.

Covent Garden had many attractions besides its 'posture molls', and the 'mollie houses' for homosexuals. Coffee houses, for long bastions of male exclusivity, had gradually been invaded by whores looking for pick-ups. Tom and Moll King's coffee house, located in the wooden shacks which ran the length of one side of the Piazza, attracted fashionable whores 'all dressed up fine and pritty and elegantly as if going to a box at the Opera'.

After midnight the scene became even more gaudy, with actress-whores and their followers, 'the All-Night Lads, otherwise the Peep-o-Day Boys', arriving. Nickie Roberts says that whole colourful crowd spoke in underworld cant to keep police informers guessing.[9]

Some women used prostitution to climb the social ladder. Sally Salisbury, a dazzling beauty and wit, was the most famous whore of her day. Born Sarah Pridden in 1692, the daughter of a bricklayer, she grew up poor in the slums of St Giles. Her biographer wrote: 'At different seasons of the year she shelled beans and peas, cried nose-gays and newspapers, peeled walnuts, made matches, turned bunter [prostitute] &c., well knowing that a wagging hand always gets a penny.'[10]

Her first rich lover was the notorious rake Colonel Charteris, who abandoned her when she was fourteen. She then went to work for Mother Wisebourne, proprietor of a whorehouse in Covent Garden

Heart of darkness: Wentworth Street, Whitechapel. In 1836 six consecutive houses, 102–107, were all brothels. Mayhew said it ranked with St Giles as one of the worst places, 'both as regards filth and immorality'.

A gleam of hope: police enter a dangerous slum looking for criminals. Dickens told how the police quickly won an ascendancy over the criminal ghettoes and their denizens.

Prisoners exercising at Newgate Prison in the middle of the nineteenth century.
Every aspect of prison life, including the food, was deliberately made as unpleasant
as possible.

Boss of Britain's Underworld: Billy Hill (*second right*) with members of his first gang. His rivalry with fellow mobster Jack Spot had a comic-opera quality.

Boss of bosses: Darby Sabini (*below*), who dominated the London underworld for two decades. His gang fought legendary battles for control of the racecourses in the interwar years.

Above: The retired Billy Hill at the funeral of Tommy Smithson in 1957. Hill took the opportunity to make a peace pact with the Krays. It was said he had lost the stomach for violence.

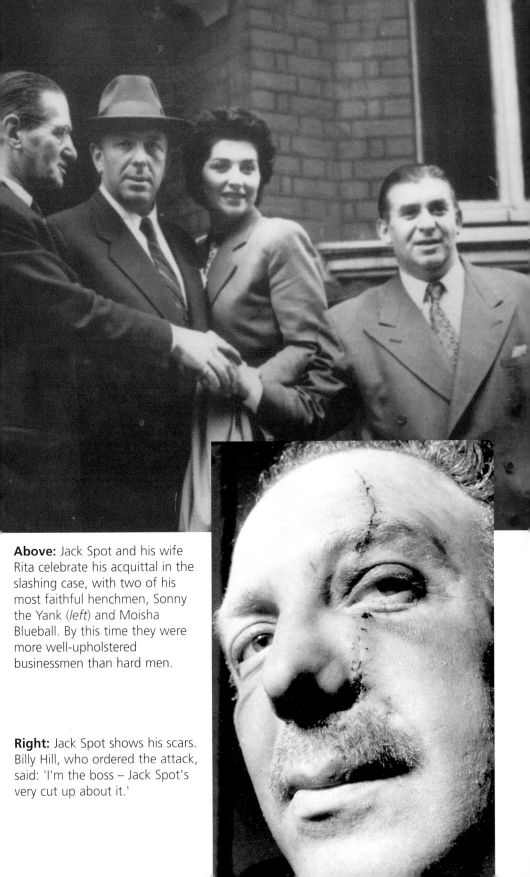

Above: Jack Spot and his wife Rita celebrate his acquittal in the slashing case, with two of his most faithful henchmen, Sonny the Yank (*left*) and Moisha Blueball. By this time they were more well-upholstered businessmen than hard men.

Right: Jack Spot shows his scars. Billy Hill, who ordered the attack, said: 'I'm the boss – Jack Spot's very cut up about it.'

Right: Frankie Fraser joins the Richardson team. Someone remarked that it was like China acquiring the atom bomb.

Below: The Kray twins at the zenith of their power. Ronnie (*left*) dreamed of total control over London's underworld.

The histrionic funeral of Reggie Kray, perhaps the last of its kind. This type of display is dying out as gangland becomes less cinematic.

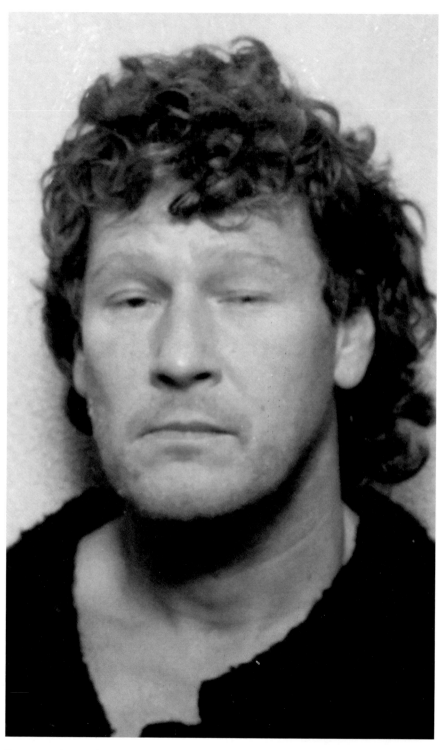

Tommy Adams, the only member of the family to pay for his crimes. He was trapped by electronic listening devices hidden in a black taxi he used to do his drugs deals. His brothers regularly check for such bugs.

that was reputed to be the most expensive in London. Mother Wisebourne – the keepers of brothels were usually called Mother – used to visit prisons, clutching her Bible, to buy the freedom of likely girls, and also looked for recruits among children whose parents rented them out to beggars for the day. She examined the children who were offered for sale outside the church of St Martin in the Fields. Those she chose would be 'drest with Paint and Patches...and let out at extravagant Prices...she was always calling them young milliners or Parsons' daughters'.[11]

Sally was a catch indeed. She could be waspish, and was unabashed in high society. Among her clients was Viscount Bolingbroke, Secretary of State in Walpole's corrupt administration, who paid 'the highest price for the greatest pleasure'. Other conquests included the Duke of Richmond, the Duke of St Albans, who was Nell Gwyn's son, the poet Matthew Prior and the Prince of Wales, later to become King George II. After a riot at Mother Wisebourne's in 1713 the quick-tempered Sally was sent to Newgate. She was released on the order of Judge Blagney, who had fallen for her, and 'then crowned his infatuation by becoming her personal slave'.[12] At a grand society ball the hostess, outshone by Sally, commented on the whore's jewels.

'They had need be finer than yours, my Lady,' said Sally. 'You have but one Lord to keep you, and to buy you jewels, but I have at least half a score, of which number, Madam, your Ladyship's husband is not the most inconsiderable.'

'Nay, my Lady' cried another guest. 'You had better let Mrs Salisbury alone, for she'll lay claim to all our husbands else, by and by.'

'Not much to yours, indeed, Madam,' replied Sally tartly. 'I tried him once and am resolved I'll never try him again; for I was forced to kick him out of bed, because his — is good for nothing at all.'[13]

Her end was sad. Here is how César de Saussure described it:

Some time ago a courtesan, of the name of Sally Salisbury, famed for her rare and wonderful beauty, her wit and fun,

became the fashion in London, and was favoured by
distinguished personages. One night, at a wine supper, one of
her admirers having displeased her by some uncomplimentary
speech, she seized a knife and plunged it into his body. Next
morning she was conveyed a prisoner to Newgate. You will
suppose her lovers abandoned her in her distress. They did no
such thing, but crowded into the prison, presenting her with
every comfort and luxury possible. As soon as the wounded
man – who, by the way, belongs to one of the best-known
English families – was sufficiently recovered, he asked for her
discharge, but Sally Salisbury died of brain fever, brought on
by debauch, before she was able to leave the prison.

The brain fever was probably the fatal Newgate jail fever. Sally,
who was about 34 when she died, was the model for Hogarth's print
series *A Harlot's Progress* and John Cleland's novel *Fanny Hill*.[14]

Sally's first seducer, Colonel Francis Charteris, is shown in Plate 1
of *A Harlot's Progress*. He lurks in a doorway, with a cringing
servant, watching a sweet young country girl newly arrived in town
being propositioned by a bawd. The Colonel was lucky to be alive to
contemplate fresh sexual adventures. In February 1730 he was tried
for the rape of his servant Anne Bond, having frightened her 'into
Compliance with his filthy Desires' by holding his pistol to her head.

The court was told that Anne, who was out of work, was sitting
by the door of her lodgings one day when a woman offered her a job
as servant to Charteris. As soon as she took up her post he laid siege
to her. At seven one morning 'the Colonel rang a Bell and bid the
Clerk of the Kitchen call the Lancashire Bitch into the Dining
Room'. Charteris locked the door, threw her on to the couch, gagged
her with his nightcap and raped her. When she threatened to tell her
friends he horsewhipped her and took away her clothes and money.

Charteris's rich and aristocratic friends packed into the court to
hear him sentenced to death. He was in Newgate less than a month,
and received a royal pardon, negotiated by an aristocratic friend. He
had been seen giving generous gifts to the Prime Minister, Robert
Walpole. 'It was a bitter rebuff to popular notions of justice.'[15]

Charteris, who a made a fortune from South Sea stock and had great estates in Lancashire, was a hate figure for the poor. Known as the Rape-Master of Great Britain, he boasted of seducing more than a hundred women, and sent out servants to find 'none but such as were strong, lusty and fresh Country Wenches, of the first size, their B–tt–cks as hard as Cheshire Cheeses, that could make a Dint in a Wooden Chair, and work like a parish Engine at a Conflagration'.[16]

Charteris's crimes were mind-boggling, and made entertaining reading in a flood of pamphlets. He was accused of rape, using loaded dice, fraud, bearing false witness, denying his bastard children and, not least, being an associate of Robert Walpole. He owned brothels, financed by cheating at cards. 'He once nearly cheated the Duchess of Queensberry of £3,000 by placing her in front of a mirror in which he could see her cards.'

After a girl had been rescued by her sister, neighbours stormed Charteris's house with 'Stones, Brickbats, and other such vulgar Ammunition'. When he was released from Newgate after the Anne Bond case, he was set upon by a London crowd.[17] He died in 1731, probably from venereal disease, and, the mob threw 'dead dogs &c. into the grave' with him.

Charteris got brothel keepers to procure women for him. Among them was Mother Needham, whose brothel was considered a cut above those in Covent Garden, Soho and Bloomsbury because it was in Park Place, St James's. Her clients were considered particularly high class. It was there that Sally Salisbury, who had moved on after Mother Wisebourne's death, stabbed her lover. Despite her friends in high places Mother Needham was arrested in 1731 by the magistrate Sir John Gonson, a scourge of prostitutes, and placed in the pillory. The *Daily Courant* reported that 'at first she received little Resentment from the Populace, by reason of the great Guard of Constables that surrounded her; but near the latter End of her Time she was pelted in an unmerciful manner.' She had been allowed the unprecedented concession of lying face down in the pillory, which may be why she survived.

Around 1750 London got its first brothels modelled on the sumptuous French establishments. A madam named Mrs Goadby, who was a frequent visitor to Paris, opened a house in Berwick

Street, Soho, and 'catered to all tastes, at the most exclusive prices'. Others followed her lead, and 'soon the French-style *maison* became a widespread phenomenon in London'[18]. A Miss Fawkland kept three adjoining houses in St James Street, Westminster, patronised among others by Lords Cornwallis, Buckingham, Bolingbroke and Hamilton, and the writers Sheridan and Smollett. She put her girls through a training course before they took up their duties. The houses were called temples, the first being the Temple of Aurora, which specialised in girls aged between eleven and sixteen. Here elderly customers were allowed to fondle the girls but not to have sex with them. From here the girls could graduate to the next-door Temple of Flora, which was a luxury brothel. Finally there was the Temple of Mysteries, which 'catered to a whole gamut of outlandish tastes, notably the sado-masochistic practices so beloved of the upper classes'.[19]

The penalties for keeping a disorderly house under a law of 1752 were not severe: a small fine, a spell in the pillory and a brief period in prison. 'An exception was Mary Bunce. who was fined £20 and given six months' imprisonment for running a disorderly house near the Hay Market.'[20] The fact that she had another 21 such houses may have accounted for the relatively harsh punishment.

The great scandal of Victorian times was child prostitution. A German traveller wrote: 'Every ten yards one is beset, even by children of twelve years old, who by the manner of their address save one the trouble of asking whether they know what they want. They attach themselves to you like limpets... Often they seize hold of you after a fashion of which I can give you the best notion by the fact that I say nothing about it.'

Perhaps the most heart-rending description of an exploited child was given by the Russian author Dostoevsky in *Vremya*; he noticed in the Haymarket how 'mothers brought their little daughters to make them ply the same trade.' One little girl was 'not older than six, all in rags, dirty, barefoot and hollow cheeked; she had been severely beaten and her body, which showed through the rags, was covered with bruises... Nobody was paying any attention to her... the look of such distress, such hopeless despair on her face... She kept on shaking her tousled head as if arguing about something, gesticulated and spread her little hands and then suddenly clasped them together and pressed them to her little bare breast.' We can only hope that she had been taken there by a prostitute to give her a dubious air of respectability, rather than for sex.

There were many brothels, but most prostitutes were street-walkers. The Haymarket was known as 'Hell Corner'. The French historian and statesman Hyppolite Taine recorded a stroll down the Haymarket and the Strand in the 1860s in *Notes sur L'Angleterre*: 'Every hundred steps one jostles twenty harlots; some of them ask for a glass of gin; others say, "Sir, it is to pay my lodging." This is not debauchery which flaunts itself, but destitution – and such destitution! The deplorable procession in the shades of the monumental streets is sickening; it seems to me a march of the dead. That is a plague-spot – the real plague-spot of English society.'

The Victorians were obsessed with prostitution. A series of studies and surveys examined every aspect of the problem, particularly health. William Acton, in *Prostitution Considered in its Moral, Social and Sanitary Aspects*... (1857), wrote of 'rouged and whitewashed creatures, with painted lips and eyebrows, and false hair, accustomed to haunt Langham Place, portions of the New Road, the Quadrant [Regent Street]...the City Road, and the purlieus of the Lyceum' who were 'a mass of syphilis'.

Infection with syphilis and gonorrhoea was widespread, but guilt and secrecy made it difficult to gauge the true scale. The toll was terrible: in the 1830s, it was reckoned that 8,000 people died of the disease each year, and in the capital's hospitals 2,700 children aged between eleven and sixteen were treated for syphilis each year. In 1856 three hospitals – Guys, St Bartholomew's and King's College – treated 30,000 cases of VD between them. The children of infected parents were among the victims. In 1855, 269 babies under a year old died of syphilis in England and Wales.

A prostitute told Mayhew's collaborator Bracebridge Hemyng of her daily routine. She rose and dined about four in the afternoon and went on the streets for an hour or two, 'if I want money'. Afterwards she would go to the Holborn Casino, 'and if anyone likes me I take him home with me'. If she was unsuccessful she would go to various cafés in the Haymarket, and try her luck there. If she was again unsuccessful she would go to the 'cigar divans', but that was almost the last resort: 'You don't as a rule find any good men at the divans.' These divans were places men went late at night to buy and smoke cigars, drink and pick up whores.

The Holborn Casino was an enormous dance hall, 'glittering with a myriad prisms', where young middle-class men could pick up working-class whores who 'dressed up flash'. The men were 'medical students, apprentice lawyers, young ships' officers, clerks, well-off tradesmen'.[21]

The most luxurious of the dance halls was the Portland Rooms, where the most expensive courtesans sought customers between midnight and four or five in the morning. 'The CanCan was danced there, in every unrestrained form, the women behaving in a more bacchantic fashion than in other places, but the police did not interfere.'[22]

The most celebrated of the cafés, or night houses, in the 1850s and 1860s was the Café Royal in Princess Street, Leicester Square, known after the woman who ran it as Kate Hamilton's. Kate weighed twenty stone 'with a countenance that had weathered countless convivial nights'. There is an engraving showing Mrs Hamilton in her low-cut evening dress holding court among the swells and the gaudily dressed tarts, easily keeping order with her foghorn voice and sipping champagne from dusk to dawn. Chesney describes her as 'shaking with laughter like a giant blancmange'. High-class night houses such as Kate's made their money by selling food and drink at outrageous prices – champagne and moselle at twelve shillings a bottle.[23]

The Argyll Rooms in Great Windmill Street sold less champagne – its status can be guessed from the fact that it sold mostly beer and soda water. It had a dance floor and gallery, and was regarded as a pick-up place for prostitutes. Although for a long time the authorities tolerated it because they felt it was better to have its prostitutes in one place rather than dispersed in the streets, it fell victim to the rising tide of Victorian morality and closed in 1878.

Cremorne Gardens, on a riverside site in Chelsea, opened in

1830. It was a typical pleasure garden used by families for picnics, fireworks, concerts and so on. At night the atmosphere changed. The *Saturday Review* commented that 'none but an idiot' could fail to notice that at dusk the women there were augmented by 'a large accession of fallen [women] characters'. The garden also fell victim to Victorian values: it lost its licence in 1871, and closed six years later.

Bracebridge Hemyng interviewed many prostitutes. One of them, who called herself 'Swindling Sal', was a powerfully built working-class woman of about 27 who associated with criminals, particularly a burglar called Joe the Magsman, who was clearly one of her lovers. Hemyng interviewed her in a bar, and recorded her vigorous turn of phrase: 'She changed places, she never stuck to one long; she never had no things to be sold up, and as she was handy with her mauleys [fists], she got on pretty well. It took a considerable big man, she could tell me, to kick her out of a house, and then when he done it she always give him something for himself, by way of remembering her. Oh! they had a sweet recollection of her, some on 'em.'

This impression of truculence is strengthened by her reference to 'rows' she had been involved in. 'Been quodded [imprisoned] no end of times. She knew every beak as sat on the cheer as well as she knew Joe the Magsman, who, she *might* say, wor a very perticaler friend of her'n.'

She generally made about £4 a week. 'Sometimes I gets three shillings, half a crown, five shillings, or ten occasionally, according to the sort of man.'

Like many prostitutes, Sal had been a servant but hated the life. She chose to work in the sex trade instead:

> I was a servant gal away down in Birmingham. I got tired of workin' and slavin' to make a living, and getting a — bad one at that; what o' five pun' a year and yer grub, I'd sooner starve, I would. After a bit I went to Coventry...and took up with soldiers as was quartered there. I soon got tired of them. Soldiers is good...to walk with and that, but they don't pay;

cos why they ain't got no money; so I says to myself, I'll go to Lunnon and I did. I soon found my level there.

Another prostitute Hemyng interviewed, a friend of Swindling Sal, was called 'Lushing Loo'. She had a more genteel appearance than Swindling Sal, and was neatly if cheaply dressed. At first she seemed too depressed to speak, and Hemyng gave her half a crown which she spent on brandy. After she had drunk it she began to answer his questions. 'My heart's broken...I wish I was dead; I wish I was laid in my coffin. It won't be long...I've just driven another nail in. Lushing Loo, as they call me, will be no loss to society...'

Her story was similar to that of some other 'fallen women'. She had been seduced by a cousin when very young and this had been her 'ruin'. When Hemyng asked why she did not enter a refuge she replied: 'I don't want to live. I shall soon get DT [delerium tremens – a form of madness brought on by alcoholism], and then I'll kill myself in a fit of madness.'

Many women were condemned to prostitution by wages that were below subsistence level. In the 1880s the pioneer sexologist Havelock Ellis met a widow of 32 with two children:

She was earning eighteen shillings a week in an umbrella factory in the East End: she occasionally took to the street near one of the big railway stations. A comfortable and matronly person, who looked quite ordinary except that her skirts were shorter than normally worn. If talked to she would remark that she was 'waiting for a lady friend', talk in an affected way about the weather and parenthetically introduce her offer. She will either lead a man into one of the silent neighbouring lanes filled with warehouses, or will take him home with her. She will take what she can get...sometimes £1, more often only 6d; on an average she earns only a few shillings an evening. Though not speaking well of the police, says they don't interfere as much with the regulars; never gave them money, but sometimes gratified their desires to keep on good terms.

Accommodation and introduction houses were used by women who wanted to keep their working and home lives separate. The rooms could be hired for short periods. There was a belt of luxurious houses stretching across the heart of central London from Bond Street through the Strand to Covent Garden. Poorer areas had cheaper versions. Men could also take street girls to coffee houses and restaurants which let rooms by the hour, as did some de luxe ladies' dress shops in Mayfair. Sometimes the pretty shop assistants were also for hire.[24] Some accommodation house owners also ran an introduction service, and advertised the whores' attractions in directories such as *The Man of Pleasure's Pocket Book* of the 1850s.

JAN FOWLER. Tall, slender, of graceful form and carriage; light hair, with a surprisingly fair and transparent complexion, a full blue eye fringed with beautiful silken lashes, through which her luscious orbs dart a thousand killing shafts.

Hemyng divided prostitutes into groups according to their habits and relative prosperity. At the top were what he called the 'seclusives', women who were mistresses kept by one man, who lived alone in a 'superior style'. Next were the 'board lodgers', who stayed in brothels and gave the madams a portion of their earnings. And finally there was the group to which Swindling Sal and Lushing Loo belonged, who lived in 'low lodging houses'. The 'seclusives' might earn £30 a week and the Swindling Sals £4 – still a good income.

Several rungs down the ladder were the sailors' tarts in the East End, in the slums and docks of Whitechapel and Wapping, the public houses and brothels of the Ratcliffe Highway, and the soldiers' tarts who gathered round the major barracks. The streets round Wellington Barracks and the parks were places where the soldiers could also meet dollymops – amateurs who had jobs as maids or shop-girls and milliners.

The parks were also used for promenading in carriages or on horseback by the women at the top of the profession. These courtesans, resplendent in silks and satins, would saucily acknowledge their admirers and lovers in public with a wink or a gesture of their whips. They were, says Chesney, a standing scandal of the London season in the 1860s. At night they were replaced by the 'park women', among the most degraded of the capital's prostitutes, broken down and diseased and a danger to the soldiers who patronised them. Hemyng said they would 'consent to any species of humiliation for the sake of acquiring a few shillings'. He added: 'These women are well-known to give themselves up to disgusting practices, that are alone gratifying to men of morbid and diseased imaginations. They are old, unsound and by their appearance utterly incapacitated from practising their profession where the gas lamps would expose the defects in their personal appearance, and the shabbiness of their ancient and dilapidated attire.'

Syphilis was an ever-present threat to their customers, and by 1864 the War Office and the Board of Admiralty acted to stop the spread of the disease. The Contagious Diseases Acts of 1864–9 authorised the detention and medical examination of suspected prostitutes near barracks and dockyards. If they were found to be diseased they could be detained for a cure. After protests from women's rights campaigners these Acts were repealed in 1886, although to judge by some of Hemyng's observations the danger was great. A woman was pointed out to him as she solicited in the Knightsbridge Music Hall, 'who my informant told me he was positively assured had only yesterday had two buboes lanced ... she was so well-known that she obtained the soubriquet of "the Hospital" as she was so frequently an inmate of one, and she had so often sent others to a similar involuntary confinement.'

Occasionally a whore or courtesan would find a wealthy husband. Agnes Willoughby was bought from her keeper, 'Bawdyhouse Bob' Roberts, by William Frederick Windham, a wealthy young Norfolk landowner, who then married her. Windham, known as 'Mad' Windham since his days at Eton, had inherited Felbrigg Hall and the family estate, and he gave Roberts the timber on the estate in exchange for Agnes, although he allowed him to keep her until the wedding day.

In 1862 three of Windham's uncles tried to have him committed to an asylum as insane. They were Lord Bristol, Lord Alfred Hervey and General Windham. To prove that he had not been sane at the time of the marriage the family spoke of 'his gluttony, masturbation, lack of personal hygiene, a broad Norfolk accent despite years at Eton'. He had other eccentric or alarming habits which included 'taking over the engines of passenger express trains without authority, as well as his propensity for patrolling the West End in police uniform as a means of "arresting" those street-girls who took his fancy.'[25]

General Windham was apparently known himself for certain 'foul practices'. He had been accused of indecent exposure in Hyde Park and got off when his counsel put in a plea of insanity. Because of this he could not give evidence for fear of being cross-examined, and the jurors found his nephew to be sane.

Mad Windham died four years later at the age of 26, leaving his bride and infant son in possession of his estate with an income of £5,000 a year.

Some actress-whores also made fortunes, and several married into the aristocracy. Kitty Fisher was one of the most successful of these 'demi-reps'. According to the German Archenholz, Kitty was 'indebted to nature for an uncommon portion of beauty, judgment, and wit, joined in a most agreeable and captivating vivacity.'

This lady knew her own merit; she demanded a hundred guineas a night for the use of her charms, and she was never without votaries, to whom the offering did not seem too exorbitant. Among these was the Duke of York, brother to the King; who one morning left fifty pounds on her toilet [dressing table]. This present so offended Miss Fisher that she declared that her doors should ever be shut against him in future; and to show by this most convincing proof how much she despised his present, she clapt the banknote between two slices of bread and butter, and ate it for breakfast.

Perhaps Kitty was given to exaggerating this episode. Casanova wrote: 'We went to see the well-known procuress Mrs Wells, and saw the celebrated courtesan Kitty Fisher who was waiting for the Duke of — to take her to a ball... she had on diamonds worth 5,000 francs... she had eaten a banknote for 1,000 guineas on a slice of bread and butter that very day...'

Other women turned to prostitution briefly to raise themselves out of poverty. Arthur Munby, poet, civil servant and indefatigable investigator of the lives of working-class women, tells the story of one of them in his diaries. Her name was Sarah Tanner, and he first knew her in about 1854 when she was 'a maid of all work' to a tradesman in Oxford Street. This was before she became a prostitute. He described her as 'a lively honest rosy-faced girl, virtuous and self-possessed'. When he met her a year or so later in Regent Street she was dressed in finery that could mean only one thing. '"How is this?" said I. Why, she had become tired of service, wanted to see life and be independent; and so she had become a prostitute, of her own accord and without being seduced. She saw no harm in it; enjoyed it very much, thought it might raise her and perhaps be profitable.' Sarah took it seriously as a profession, learning to read and write 'in order to fit herself to be the companion of gentlemen'.

Over the next few years Munby saw Sarah from time to time as she solicited on the streets, and usually stopped for a chat. 'She was always well but not gaudily dressed, always frank and rosy and pleasant; and never importunate; nor did I ever hear her say a vicious word...'

He did not see her again until 1859, and another transformation had taken place. She was now dressed 'quietly and well, like a respectable upper servant'. Sarah had saved enough over three years of prostitution to open a coffeehouse, the 'Hampshire Coffeehouse over Waterloo Bridge'.

There were also male brothels. In May 1726 the *London Journal* wrote of twenty 'Sodomitical Clubs' where 'they make their execrable Bargains, and then withdraw into some dark Corners to perpetrate their odious Wickedness'. They included Mother Clap's in Holborn, the Talbot Inn in the Strand, and even the 'Bog-Houses' of Lincoln's Inn.

As far back as 1559 there was a Mollies' House opposite the Old Bailey, and in 1661 there was the Three Potters in Cripplegate Without. The Fountain in the Strand was a known haunt of homosexuals throughout the eighteenth century. There was a male brothel in Camomile Street, Bishopsgate – the manager was known as the Countess of Camomile.

There was 'a tremendous upsurge in sodomy' around the beginning of the eighteenth century, and in 1707 a raid on a 'Sodomites' Club' in the City caused a great scandal. About forty men were arrested, including the respected Cheapside mercer Jacob Ecclestone, who later committed suicide in Newgate. Another respected City figure, the Cheapside draper William Grant, hanged himself there, and the curate of St Dunstan's-in-the-East, a Mr Jermain, cut his throat with his razor, as did another merchant, a Mr Bearden. Several others also committed suicide before the case came to trial. All these men frequented the alleys around the Royal Exchange. The favourite meeting place was Pope's Head Alley. In nearby Sweetings Alley the 'breeches-clad bawds' congregated.

In October 1764 *The Public Advertiser* reported that: 'A bugger aged sixty was put in the Cheapside Pillory...the Mob tore off his clothes, pelted him with Filth, whipt him almost to Death...he was naked and covered with Dung...when the Hour was up he was carried almost unconscious back to Newgate.'

Some used the reaction against the upsurge in sodomy to blackmail innocents. In September 1724 a young man walking in the streets was accosted by a man who seized him and cried out, 'A sodomite! A sodomite!' The terrified young man was advised by a passing gentleman to give the blackmailer five or six guineas, but he protested that he did not have the money. The two older men then followed him to the place where he worked, hoping to get money, but were driven off by one of the young man's colleagues, who drew his sword. The blackmailers ran off, 'leaving the boy prostrate with shock'. In January 1725 two men were found guilty of a similar attempt at blackmail, and were sentenced to 'two hours on Tower Hill Pillory, two hours on the Cheapside Pillory, a fine of Twenty pounds and six months in Newgate'.

Women whores were annoyed at all this unwanted competition:

> How Happy were the good old English Faces
> 'til Mounsieur from France taught PEGO a Dance
> to the tune of Old Sodom's Embraces.

But now WE are quite out of Fashion.
Poor whores may be NUNS, since MEN turn their GUNS
And vent on each other their Passion.
But now, we find to our Sorrow we are over-run
By the Parks of the BUM
and Peers of the Land of Gomorrah!

After the Restoration the Societies for the Reform of Manners began to campaign against whores and brothels. In 1726 they succeeded in closing down more than twenty mollies' houses, including the famous Mother Clap's. She was found guilty of keeping a 'sodomitical house' and put in the pillory at Smithfield, dying afterwards of her injuries. Three of her prostitutes were hanged.

The trial record shows that Mother Clap's house in Holborn was a meeting place for homosexuals. One of the witnesses for the prosecution was Samuel Stephens.

Stephens: On Sunday night, the 14th November last, I went to the prisoner's house in Field Lane, in Holborn, where I found between 40 and 50 men making love to one another, as they called it. Sometimes they would sit in one another's laps, kissing in a lewd manner and using their hands indecently. Then they would get up, dance and make curtsies, and mimic the voices of women. 'O,Fie, Sir! — Pray, Sir — Dear, Sir, — Lord, how can you serve me so? — I swear I'll cry out. — You're a wicked devil, — and you've a bold face. — Eh, you dear little toad! Come, buss!' Then they'd hug, and play, and toy, and go out by couples into another room on the same floor, to be married, as they called it. The door of that room was kept by — Eccleston, who used to stand pimp for 'em, to prevent anybody from disturbing them in their diversions. When they came out they used to brag, in plain terms, of what they had been doing. As for the prisoner, she was present all the time, except when she went out to fetch liquors. There was among them William Griffin, who has since been hanged for sodomy; and — Derwin, who had been carried before Sir George Mertins, for sodomitical practices with a link-boy...I went to the same house on two or three Sunday nights following, and found much the same practices as before. The company talked all manner of gross and vile obscenity in the prisoner's hearing, and she appeared to be wonderfully pleased with it.

In 1814 Robert Holloway published *The Phoenix of Sodom: or, the Vere Street Coterie*, about the notorious male homosexual brothel at the White Swan in the street running north from Oxford Street.

Holloway's book gives a description of the interior of the brothel:

The fatal house in question was furnished in a style most appropriate to the purposes it was intended. Four beds were provided in one room: — another was fitted up for the ladies' dressing-room, with a toilette and every appendage of rouge, &c. &c.: a third room was called the Chapel, where marriages took place, some times between a female grenadier, six feet high, and a petit maitre not more than half the altitude of his beloved wife! These marriages were solemnised with all the mockery of bride maids and bride men; and the nuptials were frequently consummated by two, three or four couples, in the same room, and in the sight of each other! ... Men of rank and respectable situations in life might be seen wallowing either in or on the beds with wretches of the lowest description... Sunday was the general, and grand day of rendezvous! and to render their excuse the more entangled and doubtful, some of the parties came from a great distance ... to join the festivity and elegant amusements of grenadiers, footmen, waiters ... and all the Catamite Brood ...

In July 1810 officers from Bow Street, supported by troops, raided the premises and 23 people were arrested. Seven of them were sentenced to prison terms ranging from one to three years' imprisonment. They also had to endure a brief spell in the pillory. Here is a contemporary newspaper report of their ordeal, both in the pillory and travelling to and from it.

About 12 o'clock the City Marshalls arrived with more than a hundred constables mounted, armed with pistols, and a hundred on foot. This force was ordered to rendezvous in Old Bailey Yard where a caravan used occasionally for carrying prisoners from the jails of London to the hulks [prison ships] waited to receive the culprits. The caravan was drawn by two shaft horses led by two men armed with a brace of pistols. The gates of the Old Bailey were shut and all strangers were turned out. The miscreants were then brought out and placed in the caravan; Amos began a laugh, which induced his vile companions to reprove him, and they all sat upright apparently in a composed state, but having cast their eyes upwards, the sight of the spectators on the tops of the houses operated strongly on their fears, and they soon appeared to feel terror and dismay. At the instant the Church clock went half past twelve, the gates were thrown open. The mob at the same time attempted to force their way in but they were repulsed. A grand sortie of the police was then made. About 60 officers armed and mounted as before described went forward with the City Marshalls. The caravan went next followed by about 40 officers and the Sheriffs. The first salute received by the offenders was a volley of mud and a serenade of hisses, shouting and execration, which compelled them to fall flat on their faces in the caravan.

The mob, and particularly the women, had piled up balls of mud to afford the objects of their indignation a warm reception. The depots in many places appeared like pyramids of shot in a gun-wharf. These were soon exhausted and when the prisoners passed the old house which once belonged to the notorious Jonathan Wild they resembled beasts dipped in a stagnant pool. The shower of mud continued during their passage to the Haymarket. Before they reached half-way to the scene of their exposure they were not discernible as human beings. If they had had much further to go the cart would have been absolutely filled over them.

The one who sat rather aloof from the rest was the landlord of the house, a fellow of stout bulky figure who could not stow himself away as easily as the others who were slighter; he was therefore as well as on account of his being known attacked with double fury. Dead cats and dogs, offal, potatoes, turnips etc. rebounded from him on every side, while his apparently manly appearance drew down peculiar execrations on him, and nothing but the motions of the cart prevented his being killed on the spot.

At 1 o'clock four of them were exalted on the new pillory made purposely for their accommodation. The remaining two, Cook and Amos, were honoured by being allowed to enjoy a triumph in the pillory alone... Before any of them reached the place of punishment their faces were completely disfigured by blows and mud; and before they mounted their persons appeared one heap of filth.

Upwards of fifty women were permitted to stand in a ring who assailed them incessantly with mud, dead cats, rotten eggs, potatoes and buckets of grub, offal and dung which were brought by a number of butchers' men from St James's Market. These criminals were very roughly handled; but as there were four of them they did not suffer so much as a less number might. When the hour was expired they were again put in the cart and conveyed to Coldbath Fields Prison... and in their journey received similar salutes to what they had met with on their way from Newgate.

When they were taken from the pillory the butchers' men and the women who had been so active were plentifully regaled with gin and beer procured from a subscription made on the spot. In a few minutes the remaining two, Cook... and Amos... were desired to mount. Cook held his hands to his head and complained of the blows he had already received; and Amos made much the same complaint and showed a large brickbat which had struck him in the face. The under-Sheriff told them that the sentence must be executed and they reluctantly mounted.

Cook said nothing but Amos, seeing the preparations that were making, declared in the most solemn manner that he was innocent; but it was vouchsafed from all quarters that he had been convicted before and in one minute they appeared a complete heap of mud and their faces were much more battered than those of the former four. Cook received several hits in his face and had a lump raised upon his eyebrow as large as an egg. Amos's two eyes were completely closed up; and when they were untied Cook appeared almost insensible, and it was necessary to help them both down and into the cart when they were conveyed to Newgate by the same road they had come and in their passage they continued to receive the same salutations the spectators had given them on their way out. Cook continued to lie upon the seat of the cart but Amos lay down among the filth until their entrance into Newgate sheltered the wretches from the further indignation of the most enraged populace you ever saw. As they passed the end of Panton Street, Strand, on their return a coachman stood up in his box and gave Cook five or six cuts with his whip. (*Morning Herald*, 28 September 1810)

The ferocity of the crowd is difficult to explain. The women who took such a prominent part – as women were to do when Oscar Wilde was tried later in the century – may have included many streetwalkers who resented the competition. Henriques (*Prostitution and Society*, Vol III) suggests that 'highly placed male homosexuals may possibly have fomented the feelings of the mob' to conceal their own complicity.

In 1833 two Members of Parliament were found not guilty in separate trials. One of them, W J Bankes, had been accused of attempting to commit an unnatural crime in the grounds of Westminster Abbey. Charles Greville, clerk to the Privy Council, wrote in his diary: 'Nobody can read the trial without being satisfied of his guilt...The foreman said he left the court without a stain.' To which a wit added: 'On his shirt'.

For whatever reason, male homosexuality was less obtrusive in the middle years of the nineteenth century. Whether this was because it had become more furtive or whether social conditions led to a drop in the number of practising homosexuals is unclear. There were certainly strong and even passionate friendships among men, as Tennyson's *In Memoriam* bears witness.

When the tide of Victorian morality was at the full, homosexuality was the crime that dared not speak its name. In 1871 two young men, Ernest Boulton and William Park, were arrested for dressing as women and mixing with prostitutes in the Burlington Arcade, at the Alhambra in Leicester Square and the Surrey Theatre south of the river. They were charged with inciting persons to commit an unnatural offence. From descriptions of their behaviour it seems clear to us today they were soliciting, but the judge suggested that they might have done it for a 'frolic' and the jury agreed, finding them not guilty.

For society, this state of innocence was not to last much longer. The trial of Oscar Wilde in 1895 forced the Victorians to confront the evidence for male homosexuality. There were revelations about a homosexual brothel in Little College Street, Westminster. The prosecutor spoke of 'these rooms, with their heavily draped windows, their candles burning on through the day, and their languorous atmosphere heavy with perfume'.

The Criminal Law Amendment Act of 1885 made almost any sexual contact between males a serious criminal offence, and also opened the way to blackmail. It was called a 'blackmailer's charter' at the time, and men who could now face prison if convicted of what had hitherto been overlooked were now open to extortion.

There had been no executions for this felony in London between 1731 and 1756. When the new Crimes Against the Persons Act abolished the death penalty for more crimes buggery was excepted. The last two men to be hanged were John Smith and James Pratt in 1835, and it was not until 1861 that the death penalty for buggery was abolished.

Other tastes were catered for. Flagellation had its own special brothels. Mother Burgess's in Covent Garden was well enough known to be named in a satire of 1738, *The Paphian Grove*:

> With Breeches down, there let some lusty Ladd,
> (To desp'rate *Sickness* desperate *Cures* are had!)
> With honest Birch excoriate your Hide
> And flog the *Cupid* from your scourged *Backside*!

So popular were flagellation houses that one madam, Mrs
Berkley, was reputed to have made £10,000 in eight years. Another
madam, Mary Wilson, published the two-volume *Exhibition of
Female Flagellants* in 1777. George IV is said to have patronised
the Covent Garden establishment of Mrs Colet.[26]

The Criminal Law Amendment Act of 1885 in effect made brothels
illegal, bringing an end to the good times for bawds and pimps.
After that date they had to operate clandestinely, or face fines or
prison. The penalties for procuring young women or enticing them
to become inmates of brothels were harsher. Britain never went as
far in the direction of direct regulation of brothels as her continental
neighbours, but turning the exploiters into criminals was an
important step.

The First World War saw the introduction of officially sanctioned
'morals police'. Patrols of uniformed women enforced curfews for
girls, and had powers to search women's houses for enlisted men
and put a stop to private drinks parties. Their duties were to lurk
about army camps and and keep an eye on the young women who
were drawn to the neighbourhood as 'the result of unnatural
excitement produced by the abnormal conditions now prevailing'.[27]

There were chains of brothels, but this vast criminal industry
consisted mostly of small-scale enterprises, pimps controlling a few
women. From Arthur Harding we get the impression of criminals
attempting to control sections of the East End vice trade, for
instance the Jewish prostitutes, in the early years of the twentieth
century, but it is not really until the 1920s that the business threw up
some major criminals.

Darby Sabini's attitude to women has been mentioned. On one
occasion he was asked for help by the Italian father of a young
woman, Anna Monti, who had been lured into prostitution by a vice
king named Juan Antonio Castanar. Anna lived in Little Italy and
her parents, like many other Italians in the area, regarded Sabini as
someone who could redress wrongs that were beyond the law.
Castanar, a Spaniard who drove a Rolls-Royce, was a famous tango
dancer and had a dancing school in Archer Street, Soho. He used
this to lure pretty young women into white slavery abroad. He and

a rival, a Frenchman named Casimir Micheletti, dominated the vice scene in the West End.

Sabini paid Castanar a visit and Anna, who had been sent to the Middle East, was restored to her family. But Sabini was not finished with Castanar. Within weeks his dance studio had been destroyed by fire, and shortly afterwards his headquarters were also firebombed. The Sabinis were not suspected: instead rumours deliberately spread on the underworld grapevine put the Castanar and Micheletti gangs at each others' throats. There were stabbings and shootings, and questions in the House of Commons. Finally the two gangs' leaders were arrested and deported. Castanar tracked Micheletti to Montmartre and shot him dead. Castanar was sent to Devil's Island.

In the thirties women could make a good living working on the streets. Inspector Fred 'Nutty' Sharpe, who in the mid-thirties was head of the Flying Squad, estimated that in a four-hour day or night they could earn between fifteen and twenty pounds: at the time, a girl working in a shop would earn about £2 a week. And these women were by no means at the top of their profession. A woman police officer remarked on the friendliness of the prostitutes to their rivals on the streets. 'They are a friendly lot, ready to help one another, exchanging clothes with each other and even loaning small sums to a rival down on her luck and out of business for the time being.'

French prostitute Marthe Watts, who became part of the Messina vice empire, came to England in 1937 and at first found the climate and the long hours spent streetwalking difficult. But after she got a regular 'beat' on Bond Street she made a good living. Some of the Englishman's sexual preferences surprised her. She wrote that she was 'astonished' at the number of men who wanted her to tie them up and beat them.

Edward Smithies in *Crime in Wartime* says that the women were divided into three main groups. At the top were women who did not solicit on the streets, but like present-day call-girls relied upon introductions and arrangements by telephone. Next were the street women who did solicit outside but took their clients either to their own flats or to houses of assignation. And finally there were women who both solicited and had sexual intercourse outside. As women grew older and lost their looks they found themselves moving down through the categories.[28]

At the upper levels of the profession the girls might live in style, with flats in Mayfair or another fashionable district, maids and motor cars. The flats would be luxuriously furnished and the clients would expect and be prepared to pay a high price for their pleasure.

There were also expensive private hotels which were really brothels. London had a number of these in the late 1930s. Inwood tells of one in Marylebone Road which apart from catering for prostitutes and their clients had another peculiarity: genuine travellers who turned up with luggage were turned away.[29]

Further down the scale there were blocks of flatlets let wholly to prostitutes. Some streets in the fashionable West End contained a number of these houses, one of them in Upper Berkeley Street. Some prostitutes preferred self-contained flats which they could share with a friend, partly to save on the rent and partly as a form of protection against dangerous clients. This left them open to the accusation that they were keeping a brothel. A magistrate warned a prostitute who shared a flat in Baker Street in order to halve the 'very substantial' rent of £3 15s that she ran this risk. Foreign visitors were intrigued by the friendly and informal relationship between magistrates and prostitutes. When the American broadcaster and critic Alexander Woolcott visited Bow Street he was asked what was the difference between British and US courts. He replied: 'The old-world courtesy with which your magistrates treat your whores'.[30]

Other accommodation was provided for prostitutes by shopkeepers, caretakers and private householders. A dress designer who rented an expensive apartment near Grosvenor Square allowed it to be used for prostitution. Men would phone her and ask her to find them a girl. She would call one of the 52 women whose numbers she kept in a book, and the man and the woman would meet at the flat.

Some prostitutes preferred to solicit and have sex in the open air. It saved renting an expensive flat, and it meant they could refuse some of the clients' demands – such as insisting that they took their clothes off.

Wartime brought a boom in the vice industry. At the time, the business of prostitution was much as it had been in Victorian times, with cheap whores in the East End and around docks and railway stations. In the west, Hyde Park was used for selling sex. Others solicited for trade on the streets of the West End, many around Marble Arch and the Bayswater Road. Theatres and cinemas, dance halls, nightclubs and hotel lounges were also used for pick-ups. The more expensive women might have apartments in Soho, Shaftesbury Avenue or Russell Square. Both men and women used cars to solicit.[31]

War and the blackout and the arrival of vast numbers of British and foreign troops in London brought a flood of women into the West End to service them. Some were married women whose husbands were away from home in the forces. Some were young women who saw a chance to make easy money, but had no intention of making a career in prostitution. Doorways, parks and any dark open space were used. 'In the blackout, the whole of London served as Hyde Park, with couples copulating undisturbed in the darkness.'[32] The Messinas' veteran prostitute Marthe Watts whose contribution to the war effort was to have 49 clients on VE Day, said in her autobiography there was a 'vast seller's market for the commodity we had to offer'.

The Second World War brought what prostitutes later recalled as the 'years of plenty'. The rise in wages meant that more men could afford their services, and as demand began to outstrip supply prices rose. Prostitutes would also allow their clients less time – the beginning of the notorious 'short time'.

War changed the economics of the industry in other ways. Before the Blitz, the exodus from the city and particularly from the West End meant that prostitutes could rent apartments in 'respectable' blocks that were previously closed to them. After that rents rose, and the prices the women charged rose with them. The arrival of the American Army in southern England affected rates: US Army sergeants were paid four times as much as their British equivalents, and by 1945 US soldiers were being charged £5 for 'short time', which was more than British servicemen could afford.

These rates drew more and more women on to the streets, although it is impossible now to know just how many. It has been very conservatively estimated that there were 3,000 prostitutes in London in 1931, and 6,700 by 1946.[33] Among them were a number of fourteen and fifteen-year-olds. With peace many of the women went back home to the suburbs to become respectable housewives again and greet their husbands returning from overseas service.

By 1944 there were fears that the fortunes being made by brothel-keepers would lead to corruption of the police, and magistrates began to crack down. Then attention turned to women soliciting on the streets, and arrests rose from 1,983 in 1945 to 4,289 in 1946 and 5,363 in 1948.[34] This was partly due to the ending of the blackout: with the lights back on, it was obvious that there were far more women on the streets. But the war had caused a rise in demand for prostitutes' services, and with the departure of the Americans, prices fell and more men could afford to pay for sex. And there seems to have been a permanent increase in the demand for illicit sex, a result of the war. At the same time the flagrant display of sex for sale seemed to cause offence in a way it had not before the war.[35] The solution was the 1959 Street Offences Act, which forced the women to find less public ways of selling sex.

Vice Empires

Like his successors, Darby Sabini despised but tolerated organised vice, and the Messina brothers could not have dominated West End vice as they did from the early 1930s on if he had not allowed them to operate. There were five brothers – Carmelo, Alfredo, Salvatore, Attilio and Eugenio. Their father Giuseppe, a Sicilian, had first been involved in keeping brothels in Malta, where Salvatore and Alfredo were born. The family moved to Egypt and Giuseppe ran a chain of brothels in several cities. His success alerted the authorities and the family were expelled in 1932. They looked around for other markets for their talents and in 1934 Eugenio arrived in London, followed later by his brothers.

Duncan Webb, who launched a crusade against the Messinas in the pages of the *People*, wrote: 'By bribery and corruption they organised marriages of convenience both in Britain and abroad to enable their harlots to assume British nationality. They ruled their women by persuasion, threat or blackmail and the use of the knife and the razor. They ruled the streets of the West End by similar methods. Indeed, so terror-stricken did the underworld become at the mention of the word "Messina" that in the end they found little difficulty in building up their vast empire of vice.'

The Messinas' prostitutes were given their own maids who enforced the 'ten-minute rule'. That was how long a man could stay with one of the girls before her maid knocked on the door to announce it was time for him to go. The Messinas' girls were regimented: they had to start work at four o'clock in the afternoon

245

and carry on until six the following morning. Marthe Watts, who became the mistress of Gino Messina, said that during the war 'London became filled with British and Allied troops and with war workers away from home. Time was short, money was loose, morals were out.'

Watts says in her memoirs[1] that Gino introduced the ten-minute rule because he was afraid that if allowed longer customers would demonstrate to the girls greater sexual prowess than he was capable of. But prostitutes throughout London were introducing ten or fifteen-minute rules at this time for the precise reason that Marthe Watts herself notes – the 'vast seller's market in the commodity we had to offer'. They sought to get rid of each client as quickly as possible. Every minute spent off the street meant that customers were lost. Marthe Watts' most heroic effort was, appropriately enough, on VE Day, when she succeeded in taking home 49 clients, working through the night until six o'clock the following morning. Watts said that she earned £150,000 for Gino Messina between 1940 and 1955.

By 1945 the girls were bringing in thousands of pounds a week for the Messina family. Such wealth attracted the attention of rival pimps and also of the indefatigable Duncan Webb, the man who helped Billy Hill write *Boss of Britain's Underworld*. Webb was already on the trail of the Messinas when a gang led by the Maltese Carmelo Vassallo started demanding protection money from the girls. Their demands were modest enough: £1 per girl per day. The girls were earning £100 a night each for the Messinas, who paid them £50 a week.

The Messinas hit back, Eugenio cutting off two of Vassallo's fingertips in one encounter. Eugenio was jailed for three years for this assault. Not satisfied, the girls went to the police and four of the Vassallo mob were given up to four years' penal servitude. Police had been watching when the Vassallos drove up to some of the girls near Piccadilly and one of them shouted: 'It's better for you to give us the money, otherwise I will cut your face.' In the car the police found a hammer wrapped in newspaper, a knife and a cosh.[2]

Questions were asked in Parliament, and the Home Secretary, Chuter Ede, was told that the Messinas were said to be making half a million pounds a year from prostitution and to have twenty girls working for them. Ede, refusing to order a special inquiry into vice in London, said: 'Any inquiry would not help the police because their difficulties arise from the fact that, although they may have good reason to suspect such activities, they are sometimes unable to obtain evidence upon which criminal proceedings could be based.'

So the remaining Messinas were free to prosper – until Duncan Webb struck. Webb was an outstanding example of the type of investigative journalist who flourished at the time. He wrote curiously stilted prose with a high moral tone, and had a tendency to place himself at the centre of events. 'The reason the underworld chaps talk to me is because they trust me,' he wrote. 'They know I cannot be bought or sold, nor is there a lot of which I am afraid.' When he heard a thug was threatening to cut his throat, he confronted him with the words: 'I am Duncan Webb. The last I heard of you was that you were going to cut my throat. Here is my throat. Cut it.'

Clearly so vainglorious a man would not be easily put off, and now he was determined to expose the Messinas. He later wrote that a car tried to run him down in Old Compton Street in Soho. 'A streetwalker came up to me. With a sneer on her lips, she said: "That was meant for you, dearie."'

Reckoning day for the Messinas came on 3 September 1950, when Webb named the 'four debased men with an empire of crime which is a disgrace to London'. At that stage the brothers owned properties that operated as brothels in Shepherd Market, Stafford Street, Bruton Place and New Bond Street, all in the West End. Webb catalogued their connections with prostitutes and exposed their cover addresses before passing his dossier on to a grateful Scotland Yard.

The following week Webb reported that he was attacked in the street and that his assailant had informed him: 'The Messinas are pals of mine. It's about time you journalists were done proper.'

Webb's exposé included photographs of the Messina women and their flats. Scotland Yard set up a special task force to break the brothers, and London became too hot for them.

Webb later wrote: 'After I had cleaned up the notorious Messina vice gang and driven them from the country...'[3] And for once the journalistic hyperbole was justified. Three of the Messinas, Eugenio, Carmelo and Salvatore, bolted to France. For a while Attilio remained, helping to tidy up their affairs, then he too left. Alfredo was now the sole remaining brother in England, living with a prostitute named Hermione Hindin in Wembley. In March 1951 he was arrested there by detectives led by Detective Superintendent Guy Mahon. Alfredo offered him a £200 bribe, a fact made much of by the judge at his Old Bailey trial in May 1951, Mr Justice Cassels.

Messina told the court that Mahon saw the money in his safe and called another officer into the room and announced that he was going to charge Alfredo with bribery. Judge Cassels told the jury: 'It would be unlikely that a police officer, who could have no other interest in this case than discharging his duty, would stoop so low – as well as stooping to get the money out of the safe – as to pull £200 out of the safe and then turn round and say to this man, "I am now going to charge you with bribery".' He told Alfredo: 'You thought that as far as the police of this country were concerned, you could do anything. You are an evil man.' He then gave him what now seems the very light sentence of two years, and fined him £500.

The author Rhoda Lee Finmore wrote of Alfredo in the introduction to her book on the trial: 'He dresses in a semi-flashy style, and oozes a lubricious self-satisfaction.' Some substance was given to the rumours of the Messinas' vast wealth by the details of Alfredo's bank accounts that emerged at the trial. He had accounts in Casablanca, Tangier, Brussels, Gibraltar and Paris, and cash in a safety-deposit box in Selfridges department store in London. In 1945 he had bought Mrs Hindin a £987 mink coat.

Years of wandering now began for the Messina brothers. Their London empire was managed for them by Marthe Watts, who had the words *'Gino le Maltais, homme de ma vie'* tattooed on her left breast. Watts' autobiography is refreshingly free of the moralising which afflicts other prostitutes' memoirs, but fails to explain why she was so faithful to Eugenio or Gino, whom she portrays as a brutal, jealous, greedy pervert. After he was sent to prison, she wrote, she was 'looking forward to a great celebration when he came out'. During the months that Gino spent in prison she earned him £22,000. 'I was very pleased with myself when I told him that.'

Attilio slipped back into the country and lived at Chalfont St Giles in Buckinghamshire with another of their prostitutes, Robena Torrance. He was arrested for living off her immoral earnings and jailed for six months. The recorder, Gerald Dibson, told him: 'You made a sumptuous but revolting living from the suffering bodies of the women you trapped, seduced and reduced to a form of slavery. You caused great suffering and it is only right that you should suffer.'

His brothers Eugenio, Carmelo and Alfredo ran the vice empire from Paris until November 1953 when Eugenio was kidnapped and they had to pay a ransom of £2,000 to get him released. Eugenio and Carmelo moved to Brussels but were soon in trouble. They had been sending Belgian girls to Britain to staff their brothels, and they were arrested there in 1955 in possession of loaded revolvers.

Eugenio was jailed for seven years. Carmelo, who was now in poor health and had not long to live, was deported. He moved first to Ireland and then entered England using a false passport. In October 1958 he was arrested as an illegal immigrant, jailed for six months and then deported to Italy, where he died six months later at the age of 43.

As the Messinas faded from the scene, part of the business passed to relatives. There was a challenge too from the East End, where the alliance of the Jew Bernie Silver and the Maltese 'Big Frank' Mifsud had been running brothels and gaming clubs. Silver, from Stoke Newington in north London, had been in the Parachute Regiment during the war. He was discharged on medical grounds in 1943. He went into vice in the East End and kept a brothel in Brick Lane. He became one of the Messinas' satellites.

As he grew wealthier he acquired expensive tastes – he was buying a £27,000 yacht when he was arrested on vice charges in 1973. By then the partnership, known as the Syndicate, was making £100,000 a week, according to the police. Mifsud, a former traffic policeman from Malta, was described as aggressive, generous, forever buying drinks, always loaded with money but dressed 'like a bum'.

They had watched the breakdown of the Messina empire and the internecine warfare of the Maltese factions which tried to replace the brothers. From a strip club they owned in Brewer Street Silver and Mifsud expanded until they owned most of Soho's strip clubs. With Silver providing the brains and Mifsud the muscle, the Syndicate imposed a kind of peace in the area for two decades.

One of the threats to that peace was Tommy Smithson, the thug who had been cut up by the Hill gang at the behest of Hill's lover Gypsy. After that attack Smithson returned to terrorise the Maltese and his takings could be £500 a night from protecting clubs. This would be spent on high living and, as he was a generous man, on hand-outs to people who were down on their luck.

In June 1956 Smithson was found dying from gunshot wounds outside Caruana's house in Carlton Vale in west London. The *Daily Mirror* said he had been 'murdered Chicago Style in broad daylight...the crepe-soled killers walked in Indian file. In the upstairs room at Number 88 there were two dull "plops"' – presumably indicating the sound of a silenced pistol.

At the time, there were two theories about the reason for Smithson's death. One was that the Maltese had grown tired of his demands. The other, favoured by the police, was that he had fallen foul of Silver and Mifsud. The senior Scotland Yard detective Bert Wickstead called the killing 'a landmark inasmuch as it let every other contender for the vice position in the West End know that the Syndicate were in pole position and would brook no interference to thwart their powers'.

Years later it became clear that he was right, although the killer, Phillip Ellul, confused the issue by claiming that the murder followed a fight he had with Smithson. He later heard that Smithson was looking for him, and was carrying a gun. 'So I thought to myself – mmm – and went and got me a gun.' He went to the house in Carlton Vale, looking for someone else, and found Smithson there. 'I said listen, Tom, you carry a gun, you use it. I'm carrying one and I'm going to use it. And I just – BANG – shot him in the shoulder. He said, "Phillip!" So I cocked it and it jammed. So I hit him and he went right over the bed.' Ellul went out to try to unjam his gun. Smithson locked the door and shouted, 'That man's crazy.'

Some other Maltese tried to calm Ellul but he kicked the door open. 'One kick, you get the strength. I just walked in, put the gun to his neck and BANG. I said let's go. Smithson's behind me, he's bleeding. I said, "Now you're satisfied. It had to come to this." I never had any qualms about what happened there.'

Ellul told Smithson to 'say your last prayers' before killing him. He was arrested, convicted and sentenced to death, then reprieved 48 hours before the sentence was due to be carried out. He served eleven years in jail.

Smithson was given what was becoming the customary gangland send-off, with a half-mile cortege through Leytonstone in east London, limousines filled with men in dark glasses and wreaths with messages such as 'To a gentleman'. His mother had a statue of an angel erected over his grave.

Bert Wickstead had been investigating the Syndicate and its methods. He found that Silver had added an ingenious twist to the selling of sex by letting flats to prostitutes at exorbitant rents – flat farming, as it was called. The girls had rent books showing they paid between £3 and £5. In fact they were paying far more – £25 to £30.

Silver was acquitted and he and Mifsud waxed rich with their various rackets. Wickstead's first attempt to close in on the Syndicate, in October 1973, was frustrated when the pair fled abroad after being tipped off by a detective in his squad that they were about to be raided. Wickstead later wrote: 'I enlisted the aid of the press' by persuading them to print stories with headlines like 'The Raid That Never Was.' The idea was to make the Syndicate think that he had given up the hunt. Silver appears to have fallen for this line, and the following month he was back in London when Wickstead struck again.

Silver was arrested at the Park Tower Hotel in London, where he was having dinner with a girlfriend. He was taken to Limehouse police station in the East End, where Wickstead felt he could trust the police better than he could those at West End Central. Then Wickstead raided the Scheherazade club in Soho, where some of Silver's henchmen were drinking and dancing. Wickstead stepped up on to the stage to announce that everyone was under arrest. Buses took the guests, staff and even the band to Limehouse police station, where the party continued. Wickstead said: 'I put them all in the charge room and they were thoroughly enjoying themselves, the band was playing and everybody was singing.'

Silver and Mifsud went on trial at the Old Bailey in September 1974. The Syndicate was accused of running what prosecutor Michael Corkery called 'a vicious empire... an unsavoury world of prostitutes, ponces and pimps'. The court heard of tiny rooms above strip clubs let to prostitutes for £100 a week.

After a trial that lasted 63 days, Silver was found guilty of living on immoral earnings and given six years in jail. He was also fined £30,000. Six Maltese men were also jailed. The judge, Lord Justice Geoffrey Lane, told them: 'The profits you reaped were enormous.' There had been reports that the Syndicate had salted away £50 million in Swiss bank accounts. Mifsud got five years, a sentence later quashed on appeal.

Wickstead now returned to the murder of Tommy Smithson. Silver and Mifsud were both charged with the crime. One witness, Victor Spampinato, who had been present when Phillip Ellul killed Smithson, was traced to Malta and agreed to give evidence. At a dramatic preliminary hearing at Old Street court he told how he had been given the message that 'this punk has got to be eliminated'. Then he described how Ellul had shot Smithson. Neither man was paid for his part in the killing. There is a story that when Ellul went to collect his money after serving his sentence a sixpence was thrown on the floor. He was given a passport and told to leave the country.

This treatment should have made both men keen to give evidence against the Syndicate, but neither did. Spampinato did not turn up at the trial, and was traced to Malta. He now mysteriously owned a villa, drove a new car and was said to have a bankroll of £30,000.

Ellul at first agreed to give evidence, but instead went to the United States and did not return. The word in the underworld was that he had been paid £60,000 for his silence. Both Silver and Mifsud were cleared of conspiracy to murder Smithson. Now in bad health, Mifsud moved to Malta, where he died in 1999. Silver eventually returned to the West End, but the Syndicate was now a spent force, and others moved in. However, the great days were over for both the gangsters and the old-style vice business.

In 1969 Joseph Wilkins, a former used-car salesman who had interests in one-armed bandits and nightclubs, took over Winston's, fashionable with middle-aged businessmen looking for 'hostesses'. He also had interests in the 800 club in Leicester Square, once a haunt of Princess Margaret, the Islet Town club in Curzon Street and the Crazy Horse Saloon in Marylebone, run by former Rolls Razor washing-machine tycoon John Bloom.

When Wilkins applied for a licence for Winston's its former owner, Bruce Brace, claimed Wilkins had used strong-arm tactics to take over the club. Wilkins admitted that he paid no money for the 27,000-member club, but claimed he had settled debts of £6,000. He got the licence, but the club soon closed.

Wilkins and some of his staff soon found themselves in trouble with the law. There were allegations that drunken punters were being robbed after visiting his clubs, and he was charged with conspiracy to pervert justice over licences. He was acquitted, but while waiting trial on another conspiracy charge he and an accomplice were shot and wounded in Beak Street. His wife claimed the Krays, who were serving life sentences, were behind the shooting.

Soho was changing. The Street Offences Act of 1959 had driven many prostitutes off the streets. Under the Act women could be convicted of soliciting on the uncorroborated word of a policeman. The term soliciting now meant 'not only spoken words but also various movements of the face, body and limbs such as a smile, a wink, making a gesture and beckoning or wriggling the body in a way that indicates an invitation to prostitution.'[5] The 5,000 women needed somewhere else to ply their trade. One outlet was the escort agency, and Wilkins had the foresight to get in early. He was behind the Eve International, Playboy Escort, Glamour International and La Femme escort agencies. Eve International was said to have 200 girls on its books, charging from £14 a night upwards and bringing in £100,000 for the agency. These figures were inflated considerably when Wilkins was charged, with his wife and henchmen, with living off immoral earnings. The girls were said to be charging £40 for a 'quickie' and £100 for 'longer', and making £400 a week each for themselves. Wilkins was jailed for three and a half years, reduced to two years by the Court of Appeal.

Another outlet for the girls were the near-beer joints, which did not have a licence to sell alcohol. The prostitutes used them as places to pick up clients. They also began to advertise in phone booths all over London, which were soon wallpapered with explicit cards complete with photos. Vigilante groups would go round the booths ripping these up, and men employed by the girls would follow, pasting up replacements.

The Soho vice industry is not what it was. In the eighties the police clamped down on what was left of the peep-show and porn clubs, and even the miserable sex and porn shops seem to be on the retreat. Westminster Council imposed a limit of sixteen sex shops for the whole of Soho. However, the escort agencies are flourishing, as are the prostitutes, and there are still some strip clubs where customers are charged up to £10 for a bottle of alcohol-free lager. In the 1980s and 1990s Old Compton Street got a sprinkling of gay pubs and clubs. According to the *Independent* in February 1991, presiding over the strip clubs was Jean Agius, another Maltese – 'short and thin with sparse hair, pale and very unhealthy-looking. Over a track-suit he wore a showy but moth-eaten fur coat. It was all slightly sad.' However, the *Independent* pointed out that he owned a Rolls-Royce Corniche and a Bentley.

After a series of concerted police raids on Soho brothels in February 2001 the Home Office said the Albanian mafia had taken over much of the Soho sex industry. Inspector Paul Holmes, of the Metropolitan Police clubs and vice unit, said the Albanians had reached an accommodation with the Maltese and East End gangsters who have traditionally dominated Soho, and the transition had not been accompanied by the extreme violence seen when Albanians had taken over vice empires in Italy and Germany. 'The people that run these places want a set level of money and don't care whether the girls are from Albania or Mars. But we are concerned at what will happen when the turf is full and the Albanians start setting up their own places.'[6]

Bent Coppers

The Trial of the Detectives which began in 1877 shook the capital's various police forces to their foundations. Criminals had been systematically corrupting police officers – including nearly all the most senior officers at Scotland Yard – in order to get evidence against themselves destroyed.

Police corruption had been a problem ever since the force was set up. After the Fieldings died the Bow Street Runners were reputed to have become very corrupt. One officer, Townsend, was believed to have left a fortune of £20,000, and another, Sayer, £30,000. Sir John Moylan, in his book *Scotland Yard and the Metropolitan Police* (London, 1929) wrote that 'the Runners were hand in glove with the thieves'. But there was no proof.[1]

Finally a House of Commons committee in 1828 seems to have got at the truth. The Runners were acting as go-betweens for thieves and banks. Banknotes and bonds stolen from the banks would be restored for a price, and no questions asked, with the Runners getting a cut. The Runners did not even know that this was the very crime, a capital offence for a hundred years, for which Jonathan Wild had been arraigned.

'Your committee,' the MPs said in their report, 'have assiduously directed their attention to these compromises for the restitution of stolen property, which general rumour and belief have represented so often to have taken place. They regret to say their enquiries have proved such compromises to have been negotiated with an unchecked frequency, and under an organised system far beyond what had been supposed to exist... Although it is evident that they have not been informed of anything like all the transactions that must have occurred under so general a system, they have proof of more than sixteen banks having sought, by these means, to indemnify themselves for their losses; and that property of various sorts, to a value of above £200,000, has, within a few years, been the subject of negotiation and compromise.'

To the thieves and receivers the off-loading of banknotes and bonds which were not easily negotiable was vastly preferable to the risks of trying to cash them. The report says they often demanded payment in cash, 'for fear of the clue to the discovery of those concerned the notes might give'. More damningly the committee recorded it had proof 'of nearly £12,000 having been paid to them by bankers only, accompanied with a clearance from every risk and perfect impunity to their crimes'. This colluding with criminals did not trouble the bankers who gave evidence. One of them, described by the committee as 'highly respectable' said: 'I have no hesitation in mentioning that at a meeting in our trade I have heard it said over and over again, by different individuals, that if they experienced a loss to a serious amount they should compound' – in other words, do a deal with the thieves.

The corruption revealed at the Trial of the Detectives in 1877 was far more serious. At the trial, the mastermind of the scheme to corrupt the police, Harry Benson, and his chief accomplice, a young criminal named William Kurr, appeared as the main witnesses for the Crown. Benson, an ingenious and successful crook who had at one stage been making £4,000 a week from crime, had been sentenced six months before to fifteen years' penal servitude for a series of outrageous frauds. Kurr got ten years. Benson decided that since he had not got the immunity from prosecution he had paid for, the corrupt officers must pay the price.

It emerged that Benson had bribed police at Scotland Yard and in America, warders at various prisons including Newgate, Post Office inspectors, Superintendent Bailey of the City of London Police and others. He had paid the Scotland Yard officers for tip-offs when police were on his trail and about to arrest him.

Chief Inspector Nathaniel Druscovich, Chief Inspector George

Palmer, Inspector John Meiklejohn and a solicitor named Edward Froggatt were all sentenced to hard labour for two years.

The laws against street betting brought a rich harvest of bribes for the police. The bookies would find some hard-up man willing to face prosecution in return for a small hand-out.

The tidal wave of money that swept through Soho with the growth of the porn and vice industries washed away any inhibitions the criminals had about offering bribes, and the police about accepting them. Quite simply, the criminals regarded these pay-offs as a form of insurance, and they were happy to pay. When the clamour of rumour and scandal grew so loud in 1955 that something had to be done, Superintendent Bert Hannam produced a report that slated West End Central police station in particular. The Metropolitan Commissioner, Sir John Nott-Bower, went to the station, stood on a chair and told the assembled officers that he did not believe a word of it.

In November 1969 *The Times* published a story that the authorities could not ignore. It claimed three officers – Sergeant John Symonds, Detective Sergeant Gordon Harris and Detective Inspector Bernard Robson – were 'taking large sums of money in exchange for dropping charges, for being lenient with evidence offered in court, for allowing a criminal to work unhindered'.

The Times team had tape-recorded meetings between the police officers and a minor criminal named Michael Perry. Some choice quotes from Symonds included: 'We've got more villains in our game than you've got in yours, you know... Always let me know straight away if you need anything because I know people everywhere. Because I'm in a little firm in a firm. Don't matter where, anywhere in London, I can get on the phone to someone I know I can trust, that talks the same as me. And if he's not the right person that can do it, he'll know the person that can.'

Here was a strong hint of something rotten right at the heart of the London police service. Some years later, in 1974, one of the witnesses at the trial of the Syndicate of Silver and the Maltese at the Old Bailey told the court that when police raids became a problem, 'a man at the Home Office was fixed to have it stopped'.

But long before that police and public alike stared into the abyss of corruption.

The Times trial was a minor affair. Robson was jailed for seven years, and Harris for six. Symonds, who went on the run, gave himself up seven years later and got eighteen months.

The bribes in *The Times* trial were a pitiful £275, nothing to the rewards the police could expect when the underworld opened its cornucopia of gifts, bribes, sweeteners, free holidays and sex. Pornography was now a big money-spinner and some members of the Yard's Obscene Publications Squad – known as the Porn Squad – including officers up to the rank of commander saw to it that free market economics applied to the flood of blue films and girlie magazines.

Behind the porn revolution – and the downfall of the Porn Squad – was one of the most colourful couples in the history of the Soho underworld, Jimmy Humphreys and his feisty wife Rusty. Humphreys was born in Southwark in 1930, and early in his career numbered such well-known local names among his friends as Mad Frankie Fraser, Jimmy Brindle and the Great Train Robbers Bruce Reynolds and Buster Edwards. After a routine career of minor crime, in 1962 he opened a club in Old Compton Street in Soho. There he met and married June Packard, a dancer who reinvented herself as Rusty Gaynor, queen of the Soho strippers.

Rusty, whose father was a respectable master builder, had started out as a chorus girl, but soon had bigger ideas. She hired the best choreographers and arrangers and even went to Paris to see what the *Folies Bergère* had to offer.

Soon the Humphreys had several clubs, where strippers danced to taped music. As their empire grew, they naturally came into contact with members of the Porn Squad who wanted to share in the good fortune of the couple who now, apart from their clubs, had a large manor house in Kent as well as a flat in Soho. In no time at all the Humphreys had acquired a retinue of Porn Squad hangers-on with large appetites for cash and gifts.

A good time was being had by all, and everything, every bribe and gift and dirty weekend with Porn Squad members and girls from his clubs at his holiday home in Ibiza, was secretly recorded by

Humphreys in a series of diaries which he kept in safety-deposit boxes. They had a terrific story to tell: among the senior officers now rolling merrily along on the gravy train were Commander Wally Virgo of the CID, Bill Moody, head of the Obscene Publications Squad and Commander Ken Drury, head of the Flying Squad.

Drury was one of the most corrupt officers in London. By a delicious irony he had been one of the chief investigating officers in *The Times* corruption case. How he got away with his lavish lifestyle and addiction to the good life for so long – he drove a Lancia bought from a porn dealer – is hard to understand without knowing the culture of the police at the time. The man who had the overall control of *The Times* case, Frank Williamson, an inspector of constabulary, said there were three types of officers at the Yard: those who were corrupt, those who were honest but turned a blind eye to the corruption, and those who were too stupid to realise some of their colleagues were corrupt. Drury's appetite for the Humphreys' hospitality was so gross that his colleagues worried about how much weight he was putting on. So Humphreys bought him an exercise bicycle and a rowing machine.

Humphreys now wanted to sell obscene books from his Soho premises, but was meeting resistance from the Porn Squad. At a dinner in the Criterion restaurant in 1969, when he and Rusty were guests of senior detectives including Wally Virgo, Humphreys complained that Moody would not give him the all-clear to start trading. Bernie Silver, who was also present, offered to introduce him to Moody, and eventually the deal was done. As Humphreys recorded in his diary, the price was high: £14,000 to get the ball rolling, £2,000 a month to keep the police off his back. And Silver was to become his partner, at the insistence of Moody.

It was to be a bumpy ride for all concerned. While Silver was out of town Humphreys had an affair with his mistress, Dominique Ferguson. Silver threatened reprisals, and Drury charged £1,050 to straighten matters out. Rusty was jailed for three months for possessing a gun.

Investigators for the *Sunday People*, as the *People* was now called, were again on the case, and in 1971 the paper named Silver and Humphreys, among others, as pornographers. The *Sunday*

People also claimed there was police corruption. There was a police investigation but it came to nothing.

In February 1972 the paper returned to the charge. Under the headline 'Corruption, the charges against the police', it said:

Police officers in London, particularly some of those attached to Scotland Yard's Obscene Publications Department, are being systematically bribed by dealers in pornography. It is this that largely explains why their businesses flourish; why immense stocks of 'dirty' books, magazines and films are not confiscated. That is the unanimous opinion of the *Sunday People* reporters who have been investigating pornography in Britain.

The paper had amassed a formidable weight of evidence. One porn dealer estimated that he paid some officers in the Obscene Publications Squad an average of £1,500 a year. The money would be handed over in a pub or a restaurant. A blue-film maker said he had paid a detective sergeant £30 to get a prosecution dropped, and was told that a licence to operate would cost him £200 a month plus a percentage of the profits. The manager of a film club said he had paid off thirteen officers over the years. Others had borrowed blue films from him.

The paper's front-page was even more sensational. There was a photograph of Drury on holiday in Cyprus with the Humphreys. Drury and his wife had been their guests during the two-week stay in Famagusta, and Humphreys had paid most of the costs, which came to more than £500. Rusty was said to have liked the commander – she drank him under the table in a champagne-drinking competition.

Drury, who had signed the hotel register with his police rank, tried to brazen it out, claiming that far from being on holiday, he had been on the trail of escaped Great Train Robber Ronnie Biggs. Humphreys backed him up.

In March Drury was suspended from duty and in May he resigned. Piling one indiscretion on another, Drury sold his story to the *News of the World* for £10,000. In it he claimed Humphreys was a police informer, a 'grass'. This was madness: Humphreys, in danger now of underworld revenge, was bound to retaliate.

Humphreys had other problems. Peter Garforth, a thief who had an affair with Rusty before she knew Humphreys, was attacked and badly cut up. He named Humphreys as one of his attackers. The pornographer fled to Amsterdam, was arrested and sent back to Britain, where he was jailed for eight years.

A detective named Gilbert Kelland, later an assistant commissioner, was appointed to head the investigation into police corruption. He visited Humphreys in Wandsworth Prison and for three months listened in astonishment as the pornographer spilled the beans. Humphreys didn't need total recall – he had his diaries.[2]

In February 1976 Drury, Virgo and Moody were arrested in a series of dawn raids. At the same time dozens of officers were taken in. It was the biggest police scandal since 1877. Drury got eight years, reduced to five on appeal: of the 74 officers investigated, twelve resigned, 28 retired, eight were dismissed and thirteen were jailed. It was clear that the Yard had been the biggest criminal organisation in London. Kelland wrote: 'We strongly believed that, for the eventual benefit of the force, the crow of corruption had to be nailed to the barn door to convince and remind everyone of the need for positive action and eternal vigilance.'[3]

Humphreys was given a royal pardon in 1978 for his part in this coup, and released. He and Rusty left the country and he became a bookmaker in Mexico and Florida. By the nineties they were back in England, renting flats to prostitutes. It is said that Rusty occasionally acted as a 'maid' for the women. In summer 1994 they were both jailed for eight months.

Further attempts to clean up the Metropolitan police took place under Sir Robert Mark, appointed Commissioner in 1972, and his successors. Mark, a former Chief Constable of Leicester, got a less than enthusiastic welcome from the capital's cynical detectives. In his autobiography *Sir Robert Mark – In the Office of Constable* he quoted *Hamlet*:

> The time is out of joint: O cursèd spite
> That ever I was born to set it right

Marks set out to reform the force from top to bottom. He told a meeting of the CID 'that they represented what had long been the most routinely corrupt organisation in London, that nothing and no one would prevent me from putting an end to it and that if necessary, I would put the whole of the CID back into uniform and make a fresh start.' In 1978 officers from outside London were brought in to investigate allegations of corruption against London detectives. At first Operation Countryman promised much. The team compiled a list of 78 Met officers and eighteen from the City of London against whom there were allegations of various kinds of corruption. But obstruction within the force stopped any real progress, and in 1982 the operation was wound up. Eight Met officers were prosecuted as a result of the investigation. None was convicted. Another Met chief, Sir Paul Condon, said in the late 1990s that there were 250 corrupt officers in the CID. *The Times* commented in May 1998:

Some of the Yard's leading detectives are alleged to have pocketed up to £100,000 a time to recycle drugs or to lose evidence against major underworld figures. Officers are accused of investigating an armed robbery using an informant and then taking up to £400,000 from the robbers. Others stole drugs ranging from cannabis to heroin from dealers and then sold those drugs to other dealers.

Race and Riots

The First World War bequeathed to the modern age and the criminal alike new technology. Firearms became more plentiful and combined with the use of the motorcar presented a challenge to which the police were slow to respond. 'Motor bandits' such as Ruby Sparks and his driver, the 'Bob-Haired Bandit' Lillian Goldstein, carried out a series of smash-and-grab raids that the police found difficulty responding to until they had their own fast cars. After the war cars were themselves stolen in large numbers by organised gangs. They would be provided with new number plates and registrations, a process known as 'ringing the changes'.

After a series of shootings of police officers Scotland Yard set up the Flying Squad in 1919. To start with it had two old army vans with holes cut in the sides for observation. One of their first successes was against a gang which operated from both Camden Town and the Elephant and Castle. The vans were deployed to watch both.

Superintendent Walter Hambrook described what happened: 'On the second evening out we saw a man we all knew to be a desperate gangster jump into a half-ton covered van which was standing in the Old Kent Road.' As the van headed for the Elephant and Castle it picked up six more men, three of them known criminals. The Flying Squad followed them to their base in a garage and kept watch. 'We were now hot on their scent,' wrote Hambrook.

Eventually the gang returned to the garage, carrying jemmies which they threw into the van, and drove off towards Pimlico Road.

Superintendent Hambrook, who had begun to weigh up the odds of his men's truncheons 'against desperadoes who I knew would use lethal weapons as soon as we challenged them', saw their van stop in Pimlico Road, and three men get out, one with a jemmy.

When the officers challenged them the gang piled back into their van and drove off, with the police in pursuit. Eventually, says Hambrook, they 'got athwart the van' and forced it to stop. A pitched battle followed, with the gang using 'knuckle-dusters, loaded life preservers [coshes] and daggers'.

Hambrook used his [walking] stick 'to great advantage' but was laid low by a life preserver. Nevertheless the police won the battle, the van was found to be laden with 'burglarious implements' and the suspects were charged with being in possession of these by night, with intent to break and enter premises. They were identified as men who had struck down a PC with a jemmy a few nights before. 'These were the first arrests made by the new mobile force.' Hambrook's injuries, although not serious, prevented him from attending court that day, '. . . but it was a merry experience, and one that I am proud to have had.' (He comes across as a bit of a gung-ho character, but his heart was in the right place. For example, he deplored the way some French and German police treated extradited prisoners when he handed them over, showing scant regard for their dignity or comfort.[1])

Transport was changing the city in other ways. The capital's population had continued to grow relentlessly, from around a million in 1800 to 4.5 million in 1881. Between 1890 and 1940 it grew by another 3 million, from 5,638,000 to 8,700,000. The digging of the London Underground and the expansion of surface railways and the electric tram system encouraged the trend. Vast new suburbs sprang up – Becontree in Essex grew from 9,127 inhabitants in 1921 to 89, 362 ten years later. A three-bedroom semi could be bought for about £400. The replacement of horse-drawn buses by motor buses in the decade before the First World War was another spur to urban sprawl.

The result was a thinning out of the populations of the historic heartlands. This was particularly true of the City, where pompous banks and offices replaced residential buildings. Other central districts affected included the Strand and Holborn. As the middle classes migrated – mostly westwards – central areas lost about 135,000 inhabitants between 1851 and 1881.[2]

The rich and then the middle classes moved out, the poor moved in and the areas became slums. Some newer developments became slums simply because they were unfashionable or too expensive. Somers Town in the Euston and St Pancras area of north London is an example. Built for the working classes, it proved too expensive. The houses were let out as single rooms and the area rapidly sank down the social scale. And there were shocking slums which survived from another age. Shoreditch and Stepney in the east were bywords for overcrowding and squalor. The London County Council had laid down a standard of twelve houses per acre, but in 1931 Drysdale Street, Shoreditch, with its 120 houses had eighty per acre. 'In 1933 it was noted of Stepney that the "amount of property which is hopelessly defective and altogether deplorable is very large. Damp, dilapidation of every kind, obsolete design and construction, vermin...abound throughout the whole borough, and impart to much of it a character of unrelieved defectiveness."'[3]

The contrast with the West End was stark. Around Piccadilly Circus and Leicester Square, not far from the exclusive upper-class male clubland of Pall Mall, a new middle-class and middle-brow entertainment and pleasure district was developing. The restaurants of nearby Soho became popular, and the mood of sexual liberation that followed the First World War gave the area a vibrant nightlife, with clubs where gangsters and aristocrats mingled with the respectable middle class. The *Daily Mail* reported that there was a new kind of women which it called 'Dining Out Girls':

> The war-time business girl is to be seen any night dining out alone or with a friend in the moderate-price restaurants in London. Formerly she would never have had her evening meal in town unless in the company of a man friend. But now, with money and without men, she is more and more beginning to dine out.

Despite the depression or because of it, the entertainment industry flourished, taking its lead to some extent from the US. Most towns had at least one stylish cinema and a dance hall. In London the firm of J Lyons and Co. with their modest Lyons Corner House restaurants were making eating out a pleasurable experience for ordinary people for the first time.

A revolution in taste and eating habits was taking place, although the vast increase of ethnic restaurants came towards the end of the century. London restaurants had long had a reputation for unimaginative and stodgy food – meat and three veg, thick brown gravy, glutinous puddings. In 1933 the first sandwich bar, Sandy's, opened in Oxendon Street, Soho, and soon there were many more, as well as snack bars, all over London. The first coffee bar, the Mika, opened in Frith Street in the fifties. Nowadays there are whole streets given up to eateries of one kind and another, with the occasional pub in between. This trend is more pronounced in London than elsewhere in the country. A survey has shown that Londoners spend a third more on eating out and buying snacks and take-aways than people elsewhere. 'The world of quick eating and quick drinking, a phenomenon previously noted in the pie-shops of the fourteenth century no less than in the baked-potato vans of the nineteenth, thus re-established itself. Sandwiches are now the staple ingredient of the London lunch ... '[4]

However, in many parts of London the steamed-up caff has shown a remarkable resilience. Somehow they seem the ideal setting for the Cockney diet, which in the years before the Second World War included saveloys and pease pudding, sausages and black pudding, fried fish and various shellfish, pickles, faggots, jellied eels and of course fish and chips. At the beginning of the twentieth century Walter Besant described in *East London* what Cockneys were eating then: salt fish for Sunday breakfast, slabs of pastry known as Nelson, the evening trade in faggots, saveloys and pease pudding, the pie-houses or 'eel-pie saloons' with the traditional Cockney fare of jellied eels, saveloys and hot meat pies with mashed potatoes. Generations of Londoners were raised on such fare, and, inevitably, London gangsters too. However, when the Kray twins entertained the author John Pearson at a country mansion they provided cold tongue and coleslaw salad, with brown ale and Yugoslav Riesling.

The gangster Jack Spot was just one of the London Jews who made a stand against Oswald Mosley's British Union of Fascists. By 1934 the BUF had become openly anti-Semitic, and was getting support in parts of London which had large or growing Jewish populations, among them Hackney and Stoke Newington. As support elsewhere waned Mosley organised a series of rallies in Jewish areas in east London in 1936. There was fighting at Victoria Park in 1936 between the BUF and anti-Fascists, and a proposed march through the East End on 4 October united a coalition of left-wing organisations, including the Communist Party, with the Jews.

The BUF mustered 3,000 Blackshirts, but the route they planned through Stepney was lined by up to 100,000 anti-Fascists and the BUF took police advice and marched away to the west. The Battle of Cable Street was largely between the police and the anti-Fascists.

As marches and demonstrations continued, the authorities acted. The Public Order Act of December 1936 outlawed the wearing of uniforms for political ends and banned paramilitary organisations. The BUF nevertheless held its biggest indoor meeting just two months before the outbreak of the Second World War when an estimated 20,000 people gathered at Earl's Court. In 1940 the leaders of the BUF were arrested.

Crime rose in the interwar years – by the late 1930s it was increasing by about 5 per cent a year. But it was mostly minor crime. Murders, at about a dozen a year (not including infanticide) were fairly rare, and there were on average only about a hundred robberies with violence. Londoners could feel safe from crime, but not from motorists. During the 1920s deaths on London's roads averaged about 1,000 a year. The figure reached almost 1,400 a year from 1929 to 1934 before falling to a little over 1,000 a year for the rest of the decade.[5]

The Second World War left a legacy of ruined houses, and open spaces which seemed to promise much. 'Greater London lost 116,000 houses...and had another 288,000 in need of major repairs. Another million, over half the remaining stock, needed smaller repairs of some sort.'[6] School life was disrupted, and this was believed to be one of the reasons for the post-war crime wave. Old working-class districts were broken up and their bombed-out inhabitants went, many reluctantly, to new towns beyond the suburbs. Even so there was still a serious shortage of houses, and the answer seemed to lie in high-rise blocks of flats. They were not cheap to build, but the Tory government in 1956 introduced subsidies so that tall flats attracted three times as much government support as houses. The results are still with us.

Other housing policies brought other ills. Peter Rachman built up a property empire in the Notting Hill, Shepherd's Bush, Paddington and Earl's Court areas during the late 1950s and early 1960s. While working as a clerk in an estate agency he realised the opportunities the 1957 Rent Act gave to unscrupulous landlords. They could now charge new tenants much higher rents than existing tenants, whose low rents were legally protected. All the landlord had to do was persuade or force the existing tenants to leave and he could replace them with prostitutes, who could pay far more. 'Rachmanism' was the process of getting them out.[7] The techniques he used included assaults with savage dogs, illegal eviction, threats, introducing intolerable neighbours and cutting off essential services. Rachman, a Pole who came to London in 1946, was a friend of the gangster Billy Hill. Mandy Rice-Davies, one of the girls at the centre of the Profumo Affair, was his mistress.

The first group of five West African slaves was brought to London in 1555. By the end of the century, in 1596 and 1601 numbers had grown to the extent that Queen Elizabeth I unsuccessfully ordered the expulsion of 'the great numbers of negars and Blackamoores which...are crept into this realm'.[8] In the eighteenth century there was a fashion for black slaves in the city, as is plain from Hogarth's engravings. Others arrived as sailors. Stephen Inwood in *A History of London* suggests that before 1800 there were never more than 5,000 in the city.

In August 1958 there were serious race riots in Notting Hill. There had been minor riots against blacks in Stepney in 1919, Deptford

Broadway in 1949 and Camden Town in August 1954, but the attacks which began after the pubs closed on Saturday, 23 August 1958 were on a much larger scale. Black people and their homes were attacked and there were attempts by drivers to run down black people in the streets. A gang of nine youths from Shepherd's Bush went 'nigger hunting', wounding at least five solitary black men.

On the following weekend trouble broke out again and continued for days. Houses occupied by black families were attacked by large crowds of whites, who chased individual blacks through the streets. Agitators from Mosley's Union Movement tried to fan the flames. After the police had brought the riots under control the nine 'nigger hunters' were each jailed for four years.

Soon the police found themselves in direct conflict with black Londoners. Since the 1950s there had been complaints of racism against the Met, as the Metropolitan Police was known. This led to some of the worst social unrest the capital has seen. At the Notting Hill Carnival in 1976 400 officers and 200 civilians were hurt in riots. The 1981 Brixton riots, the worst on the mainland during the twentieth century, were largely about policing methods. In 1985 after further trouble over police raids and arrests, the terrible Broadwater Farm Estate riot broke out in Tottenham. PC Blakelock, a local community policeman who was helping to guard firefighters, was surrounded and attacked. His body was recovered by a group of his colleagues who fought their way into a large armed crowd. He had forty wounds.

The Stephen Lawrence murder inquiry showed the depth of racial prejudice in the Met. The Macpherson inquiry spoke of 'institutional racism'. This great institution, already accused of systemic corruption, seemed to have lost its way.

'Teddy boys' were involved in instigating the Notting Hill riots by attacking black-owned cafés and houses. They were one of the first signs of that cult of youth that led to 'Swinging London' in the sixties. They first appeared in the early 1950s in Southwark and Lambeth, where youngsters began wearing 'Edwardian' clothes based on styles which had been promoted by West End tailors after the war. This look was refined into a uniform consisting of long velvet-collared jacket, tapered trousers, 'brothel creeper' shoes with thick crepe soles and bootlace ties. The 'duck's arse' quiff of swept-back Brylcreemed hair was *de rigueur.*[9]

Most of the teddy boys came from the more lawless of London's slum areas, reviving atavistic fears of rookeries. A youth was stabbed to death on Clapham Common in 1954 by a gang of teddy boys wielding flick knives. They were involved in riots in cinemas: one of them, in the Elephant and Castle Trocadero during a showing of the Bill Haley film *Rock Around the Clock* in 1956, was particularly destructive. In 1958 there were dance-hall brawls in which a young man and a police officer were stabbed to death.

By 1960 it was clear that the city was in the grip of a crime wave. Before the war indictable crimes were running at about 95,000 a year. In the immediate post-war years (1945–8) they rose to nearly 130,000 a year before dropping back to 95,000 in 1953–5. After that there was a relentless rise. Between 1955 and 1967, 'the number of reported indictable offences in Greater London tripled to 295,000'.[10]

Criminologists were at a loss for an explanation. The disruption of war was blamed, but the crime figures continued to rise into the 1970s, when most of the culprits had been born after the war. One explanation may be that there were simply a lot more portable goods to steal, as full employment brought relative affluence.

Killers and Hit Men

Alfie Gerrard, murderer of Frank Mitchell, Ginger Marks and others, (see page 179) was the archetypal hired killer, cold, friendless, disliked even by his associates. He was unusual in surviving so long, and in dying an almost natural death. Even more unusual in having a son who was also a hit man, hired by Ronnie Knight to dispose of the man who killed his brother.

In 1999 there was a distant echo of that era, a time when gangsters favoured camel-hair coats and Jaguar Mark II cars. On Sunday 5 December gunmen shot Tommy Hole and his companion Joey 'The Crow' Evans as they sat in a pub in Canning Town, watching football on a giant TV screen. Both men were criminals, and as one woman neighbour interviewed on television suggested, 'It's just villains killing other villains.'

But according to Ross Benson in the *Evening Standard*, it was far more complicated than that. Hole, who was 57 when he died, was an associate of Ronnie Knight, the gangster and former husband of actress Barbara Windsor. According to Benson, Knight graduated from robbery to protection rackets in the early 1970s and tried to move into Soho. 'That was a bad move. The restaurant he targeted was in the patch controlled by "Italian Albert" Dimes, a crook with butcher-boy good looks who the FBI named as the Mafia's London liaison.'

Dimes, says Benson, sent an enforcer named 'Eyetie Tony' Zomparelli to deal with Knight and his team. In the ensuing fight Zomparelli stabbed Knight's 23-year-old brother David to

271

death. Zomparelli was jailed for four years for manslaughter. Ronnie Knight vowed to kill him.

When Zomparelli was released from prison Alfie Gerrard's son, Nicky 'Snakehips' Gerrard, was waiting. Benson says, 'Snakehips had followed his father into the family business. According to a police officer involved in the case, it was Snakehips who in 1970 shot dead Andre Mizelas, 48, the Mile End-born owner of the Andre Bernard hairdressing chain, whose celebrity clients included the actress Julie Christie and the Queen's great-aunt, Princess Alice, Countess of Athlone.'

Mizelas, says Benson, had defaulted on a £100,000 loan from a south London moneylender 'who is still alive and owns a large block of flats near the site of the killing'. Snakehips was paid £5,000 for the murder, which took place as Mizelas was driving his red sports car through Hyde Park.

It was Snakehips who settled accounts with Zomparelli, firing four bullets into the back of his head as he played a pinball machine in a Soho amusement arcade on 4 September 1974. Unfortunately he had paid a petty criminal named George Bradshaw £325 to act as his lookout while he disposed of Zomparelli. Bradshaw turned informer, and Snakehips and Knight were arrested. They were later acquitted because of lack of evidence.

Knight, ever the cheeky Cockney, declared: 'I knew I was innocent. Gawd love me, I was being set up. Framed. As large as life.'

Knight, who cannot be tried a second time for the killing, later told how Snakehips had phoned him after murdering Zomparelli. 'Ronnie, it's done. Are you covered?' Knight says he replied: 'Don't worry, I've got so many witnesses here there ain't a court big enough to hold them.'

Knight opened a bottle of champagne and toasted his dead brother. He paid Snakehips £1,000 for disposing of Zomparelli. It later emerged that Snakehips may have had an extra incentive: he was said to be seeing Zomparelli's wife, a former stripper named Rozanna.

Snakehips called round at Knight's Soho nightclub to collect his money. He told Knight the killing had been a piece of cake. That evening Knight called at the theatre where his wife Barbara Windsor was appearing with her fellow *Carry On* star Sid James. Barbara had heard of the murder. Knight says in his autobiography that as she got into his car she asked him where he had been at the time. 'I assured her that I had been in the club as usual and that it had been a full house.'

It was Snakehips' turn in 1982. He was leaving his daughter's eleventh birthday party when two men in balaclavas approached his car and blasted him with shotguns. He staggered fifty yards down the road with his killers in pursuit. They battered him with the butts of the guns and then killed him with a shot to the head.

One theory is that Snakehips had become too violent even for the gangland bosses who used him to dispose of at least ten – some reports say thirteen – other criminals. His wife Linda described him as a real family man who doted on his three children. Yet he had threatened to kill his mother's butcher for selling her a piece of substandard meat. A criminal who knew him said: 'When you've got a mad dog in the family, it's sad but you've got to put him down.'

Hole, who knew Snakehips and was living with a woman relative of his, was charged with the murder. At the last moment the main police witness changed his mind about identifying Hole as the man he saw waiting to ambush Snakehips. So Hole had another seventeen years, much of which he spent in prison for drugs offences. Police believe that he returned to crime when he was released in 1999.

Hole will be remembered for a particularly gruesome murder attempt. While an accomplice held a man down Hole drove over him three times.

Hit men were used by both sides in a gang war that broke out in south London in the early nineties. Ahmet Abdullahi, a member of the Arif crime family was shot dead in a betting shop in Walworth in March 1991. Patrick and Tony Brindle were cleared of the murder. They were the brothers of David Brindle, who was shot dead in August 1991 in The Bell pub in Walworth. A bystander was also killed. As they opened fire one of the two gunmen had shouted, 'This is for Abbi' – the nickname of Ahmet Abdullahi.

On 1 June 1993 Jimmy Moody was drinking a pint of bitter in the

Royal Hotel in Hackney, east London. Moody, a veteran gangster, former member of the Richardson gang and survivor of the Mr Smith's club shoot-out in 1966, had been on the run for thirteen years since escaping from Brixton prison with IRA man Gerard Tuite.

Another man entered the pub and ordered a drink. When it arrived he pulled out a revolver and shot Moody dead, cursing as he did so. He escaped in a stolen Ford Fiesta which had been parked outside. There was speculation that Moody was himself a hit-man, and that he had been involved in the killing of David Brindle.

In September 1995 Tony Brindle survived being shot three times by a gunman outside his flat in Docklands. As the gunman opened fire he was himself shot by undercover officers disguised as gasmen. He was Michael Boyle, said to be an Irish terrorist gunman, whom police had been tracking. They had been tipped off by Irish police about Boyle, believed to be a member of the Irish National Liberation Army. As they tracked him they saw him leave a 'safe house' wearing a wig and drive to Brindle's luxury home in Rotherhithe. Tony Brindle was walking to his car when Boyle, who was armed with a Magnum revolver and a Browning pistol, opened fire. Horrified police who were videoing the scene saw Boyle leap from his car and run towards Brindle. The officers cut him down with rifle fire, hitting him in the arm, elbow, chest, heel and between the shoulder blades.

Boyle was later given three life sentences at the Old Bailey after the court was told that the shooting was the latest incident in an eleven-year feud. Boyle, 50, had also planned to kill Brindle's brothers Patrick and George. After the trial Tony Brindle launched a lawsuit against the police, claiming they failed to ensure his safety. Brindle got legal aid to pursue his claim.

Boyle, who was said to have been paid £25,000 to kill Brindle, was one of several nationalist and Loyalist Irish gunmen specially imported for gangland hits in London.

In April 2001 David Roads, who was convicted at the Old Bailey in 1997 of being the armourer in the Boyle shooting, was shot dead in an alley in Kingston-upon-Thames. A newspaper reckoned that 55-year-old Roads was the ninth person to be killed in the feud.

With the new century just months old concern at the growing

number of contract killings in Britain – estimated at about thirty a year – led police to compile a register of convicted and suspected contract killers, and their techniques. They listed four main reasons for such killings: disputes over debts, drug deals that go wrong, vengeful lovers and gangland feuds.

Police estimate that up to twenty hit men are operating out of the south-east, charging between £1,000 and £20,000 for a murder. Jason Bennetto wrote in the *Independent* on 31 May 2000: 'One infamous London hitman, known as Mad Georgie, is said to be behind 23 murders. He is credited with thinking up the motorbike hit in which two men, whose crash helmets cover their faces, use a powerful off-road scrambler motorcycle. The killers will speed up to their target, and the pillion rider will jump off, shooting his victim with a handgun or sawn-off shotgun. The two men then flee on the motorcycle, taking a predetermined route.'

Robbing the Bank of England

Convicted forgers got short shrift in the eighteenth century, as the Newgate Calendar bears witness. Coining was treason, and the punishment was an agonising death. Traditionally minor offences had been punished by fines. In more serious cases offenders were sent to the pillory or lost both their ears and had their noses slit.[1] But as the state began to weigh the scales ever more heavily in favour of the rich and against the poor, statute after statute was passed to cover every conceivable kind of forgery.

The death sentence for coining and forgery was dropped in the 1830s and a maximum sentence of life imprisonment was substituted. Mayhew's research suggested that this sentence had little deterrent effect. Inspector James Brennan, mentioned in court reports of the 1850s and 1860s as an assiduous pursuer of coiners, fought battles with gangs of these forgers. In one of them he and his men arrested five out of a gang of seven after a fight which raged over three floors of a building in Southwark the coiners were using to make their fakes.[2]

Brennan was confronted on the top landing by three toughs, one of whom he recognised as an underworld bodyguard. Brennan tackled two of them: the third jumped over his head and ran down the stairs. At this point a fourth man came from a room at the top of the stairs, hit Brennan over the head with an iron saucepan and forced him against a window. He was saved by two other officers, one of them his son, and the fight went on.

Brennan's son struck his father's attacker with a crowbar, and the man fell through the window into the courtyard below. Another of the gang jumped from a window and tried to escape across the roof of a shed, which gave way under him.

The leader of the gang, a man named Green, was trapped with another man and two women in the third-floor room. He tried to destroy the plaster moulds used to make the coins, but enough were saved to secure convictions at the Old Bailey trial that followed in 1855. The judge awarded Brennan £10 for his 'manly and efficient part' in the affair.

Bank of England notes were also forged. In the eighteenth century the most basic form of forgery involved using chemicals to change the value written on the note. The forger would buy a banknote, often with a face value of £11, and chemically erase all but the initial 'e' of eleven. Then he would write in 'ighty' to make the face value £80.[3]

The Victorian counterfeiter was generally less ambitious: the favourite denominations were £5 and £10. After the notes had been crumpled and soiled to make them look old, they would be passed at horse fairs, markets, hotels and public houses.[4]

The ambition and daring of the gang of forgers who swindled the Bank of England out of £100,000 in 1873 were of quite a different order. They were all Americans: the brothers George and Austin Bidwell, George Macdonnell and Edwin Noyes. George Bidwell, who was in his thirties, had arrived in Britain in 1872 via France, where he had swindled various banks out of £6,000. He was joined by the others, who were all in their late twenties.

Austin Bidwell, posing as a businessman who had exclusive rights to build Pullman railway cars in England, opened an account at the Bank of England. This account was soon busy as he deposited genuine bills of exchange. These bills, which were issued by banks to their customers, were more secure than banknotes. When they were presented at a bank for payment, they would be scrutinised carefully, and unlike banknotes, they could not be readily transferred from one person to another.

In December 1872 George Bidwell sent ten genuine bills of exchange with a face value of £4,307 into the account. They were posted from Birmingham, where his brother was supposedly building the Pullman railway cars, and they were accepted by the bank.

His brother Austin now travelled to Paris and bought another bill of exchange with a face value of £4,500 from Rothschilds Bank. The accomplices had already bought blank forms for bills of exchange in various languages, and while in Paris Austin Bidwell also bought forms identical to those used by the Rothschilds.

First the Bidwell gang passed the genuine Rothschild bill, on 17 January 1873. They then changed three more, for £4,250. These were the gang's first forgeries on the bank.

The Bank of England was now hit with a blizzard of forgeries, but the gang had been so patient and so painstaking in building up the confidence of the bank's officials that none was queried. On 25 January eight bills with a face value of £9,350 were passed. They were followed by bills for £11,072.

The only limit on the gang's greed was time. The bills were due to be redeemed by the issuing banks after three months – at the end of March. The forgeries would then be discovered. So the forgers went into overdrive. On 21 January the gang swindled the bank of £4,250. After that the amounts usually increased sharply, and on 27 February they got away with £26,265. Their haul amounted to £100,405. 7s. 3d.

George Bidwell said later: 'It appears as if the bank managers had heaped a mountain of gold out in the street, and put up a notice, "Please do not touch this", and then left it unguarded with the guileless confidingness of an Arcadian.'[5]

The gang were using their haul to buy gold coins and negotiable bonds, both untraceable. These were then moved into accounts abroad. They were preparing to depart.

But on 28 February when the last of their forged bills of exchange were presented to the Bank of England a clerk noticed that two £1,000 bills lacked an essential date. The bills had been forged in the name of a London bank, B W Blydenstein and Co. Thinking it a mere oversight, an official of the Bank of England sent the bills back to have the date written in. Blydensteins replied: 'We have no record of these bills and can only assume they are forgeries.'

Noyes was arrested as he called at a bank to collect foreign currency. George Bidwell, who had been waiting for him, saw Noyes taken into custody and managed to get away. Austin Bidwell was arrested in Cuba on 20 March. Macdonnell managed to board a ship for America but was arrested as he arrived in New York. George Bidwell was arrested in Edinburgh on 2 April.

The trial was sensational in several ways. Rumours that guns had been smuggled to the prisoners led to the courtroom being searched, and the judge, Mr Justice Archibald, carried a gun under his robes. Three Newgate warders accepted bribes to help the gang escape.

The four were sentenced to penal servitude for life. George Bidwell was released in 1887 because of ill-health, his brother in 1890, and the others in 1891. George Bidwell, who left prison a broken man, wrote about his release: 'Though I began those years a black-haired, robust young man, at the end I found myself a gray-haired cripple; yet, on this first opening of the world anew before my ravished eyes, how beautiful everything appeared! Even dull-looking old London appeared glorious. And the throngs of people in the streets! I could not tire of looking at them.'[6]

In Durance Vile

The prison regime the Bank of England swindlers experienced was very different from the eighteenth century system. The old laxity had gone, replaced by a brutal routine of close confinement and deprivation.

In the seventeenth and eighteenth centuries prison sentences were short, and society meted out retribution by transportation, branding, whipping, the pillory or the gallows. Only a minority of offenders were imprisoned as a form of punishment, and sentences were short.

As we have seen in 'Sin City' the pillory was no soft option.

As the number of criminals rose in the eighteenth century alternatives were sought, and in 1718 transportation to the American colonies was resumed and judged a success – thirty thousand people were transported between 1718 and 1775. Plantations in America and the West Indies were hungry for labour.[1]

The end of the American War of Independence in 1783 brought a sharp rise in crime, and the government brought old warships, known as hulks, anchored on the Thames into use as temporary prisons. In 1787 the growing clamour for a return to transportation saw the first convict fleet leave for Australia.

In the 1930s the reform-minded Prison Commissioner Alexander Paterson said: 'Men are sent to prison as a punishment, not for punishment.' This was far from being the attitude of his Victorian predecessors, who insisted that prison was a place of active punishment.

A Parliamentary report in 1836 suggested that the lax regime in prisons was turning first-time offenders into hardened criminals, and a wave of reforms followed. The report said of the experience of the young criminal:

Instead of seclusion and meditation, his time is passed in the midst of a body of criminals of every class and degree, in riot, debauchery and gaming, vaunting his own adventures or listening to those of others; communicating his own skill and aptitude in crime, or acquiring the lessons of greater adepts...
He is allowed intercourse with prostitutes who, in nine cases out of ten, have originally conduced to his ruin; and his connection with them is confirmed by that devotion and generosity towards their paramours in adversity for which these otherwise degraded women are remarkable. Having thus passed his time, he returns a greater adept in crime, with a wider acquaintance among criminals and, what perhaps is even more injurious to him, is generally known to all the worst men in the country; not only without the inclination, but almost without the ability of returning to an honest life.

New prisons were built: Pentonville was started in 1840, Tothill Fields at Westminster in 1836, the Surrey House of Correction at Wandsworth in 1849, the same year as the City House of Correction at Holloway, and Brixton, for women, in 1853. Older prisons were modernised and improved.

Henry Mayhew had written that it was 'unwise of a wise and great nation to make a moral dustbin of its colonies' and in 1853 transportation was abolished for convicts serving less than fourteen years. Transportation ceased altogether during the 1860s. Those of the capital's convicts who would formerly have been dumped in Australia were now confined in hulks at Woolwich or in the many prisons.[2]

The first aim of the new prisons was to inflict 'a just measure of pain' in order to bring about a change for the better in the morals of the prisoners. The first step was to end fraternisation. Prisoners were masked with 'scotch caps' and it was an offence to 'reveal the features' punishable by solitary confinement on bread and water.

Under this 'separate system' convicts were confined one to a cell, with their work brought in to them. The aim, as the Surveyor-General of Prisons, Sir Joshua Jebb, said, was to ensure that prisoners would be 'effectually prevented from holding communication with, or even being seen sufficiently to be recognised by other prisoners'.[3] The belief was that this isolation would cause the convict to reflect on his wickedness and to repent, and that it would also stop experienced criminals from corrupting the young. The capital's criminals were already recognised as the most hardened and expert in the country, and those the new system didn't break became even more fiercely committed to their code and their caste.

The system was abandoned in the 1860s. It didn't work, as the statistics for re-offenders showed. Crime rose by a fifth in the forty years or so it was in force, and the figures for re-offenders showed little improvement. The effects on mental and physical health were obvious: following the introduction of the system at Pentonville in 1842, mental breakdowns there were four times the level of other prisons.

There were other ways of breaking the spirit of recalcitrant convicts, of which solitary confinement was just the most severe. In solitary, men were kept in total darkness on a diet of bread and water. The ordinary prison diet was hardly adequate, and certainly not appetising.[4]

Detailed instructions were given to the prison cooks to make the food as unpalatable as possible. This made 'its taste and consistency so repulsive that it made some prisoners nauseous and even diarrheic. These experiences ran through the prisoners' memoirs, from the persistent driving hunger of imprisoned labour leader John Burns in the 1880s to Oscar Wilde's gastrointestinal troubles in the 1890s (and neither was on the lowest diet').[5]

Burns later went into politics, and movingly told his fellow MPs in the House of Commons: 'I am not ashamed to say that at one or two o'clock in the morning I have wetted my hands with my spittle, and gone down on my hands and knees on the asphalted floor in the hope of picking up a stray crumb from the meal I had ten hours before.'

The Irish revolutionary Michael Davitt, who also sat in the Commons, stunned the House and the nation with his description of the privations he experienced in prison. He had seen men eat candle ends, the marrow of putrid bones they were meant to grind up, even a used poultice found in a garbage heap by the prison cesspool. Davitt wrote, in *The Prison Life of Michael Davitt*: 'To find black beetles in soup, "skilly", bread, and tea, was quite a common occurrence, and some idea of how hunger will reconcile a man to look without disgust upon the most filthy objects in nature, when I state as a fact that I have often discovered beetles in my food, and have eaten it after throwing them aside, without experiencing much revulsion of feeling at the sight of such loathsome animals in my victuals.'

Pointless work was another device for crushing the spirit. Shot drill was one example. Men would stand around three sides of a square, three yards apart, with a warder at the centre. At the end of each line was a pile of cannon balls, or shot. On command the first man would take a ball from the pile, walk to his neighbour and place the ball on the ground in front of him. The second man would pick it up and place it in front of the next man, and so on. When the whole pile had been transferred to the other end of the line the process was reversed. The work continued for an hour and a quarter every afternoon, and the men showed obvious signs of distress.

Henry Mayhew witnessed shot drill in action at the House of Correction in Coldbath Fields and described its effect on the prisoners.

One, a boy of seventeen, became more and more pink in the face, while his ears grew red. The warder was constantly shouting out, 'Move a little quicker, you boy, there.' The shot is about as heavy as a pail of water, and it struck us that so young a boy was no more fitted for such excessive labour than prisoners above the age of forty-five, who are excused.

The men grew hot, and breathed hard. Some who at the beginning had been yellow as goose-skin had bright spots appear, almost like dabs of rouge, on their prominent cheek-bones. When all were evidently very tired, a rest of a few seconds was allowed. Then the men pulled out their handkerchiefs and wiped their faces, others who had kept their waistcoats on took them off, and passed their fingers round their shirt-collars, as if the linen were clinging to the flesh, while the youth of seventeen rubbed his shirt-sleeve over his wet hair as a cat uses a paw in cleaning itself.

A warder near us, with whom we conversed, said: 'It tries them worse taking up, because there's nothing to take hold of, and the hands get hot and slippery with the perspiration, so that the ball is greasy like. The work makes the shoulders very stiff too.

This exercise continues for an hour and a quarter. We counted the distance that each man walked over in the course of a minute, and found that he traversed the three yards' space fourteen times. According to this, he would have to walk about one mile and three quarters, picking up and putting down, at every alternate three yards, a weight of twenty-four pounds. It is not difficult to understand how exhausting and depressing such useless work must be.[6]

The treadwheel, a series of steps on a giant wheel turned by prisoners endlessly climbing on it for up to six hours a day in compartments two feet wide, was simply a form of torture, which could make men cry with pain and despair.

Mayhew says the prisoners called it 'grinding the wind', and adds: 'That is really the only denomination applicable to it.' It was justified on the basis that the hard labour the men had been sentenced to must be just that – hard. The fact that it was entirely useless added to its effectiveness in the eyes of those who opposed reform.

The prints and photographs that remain of prisoners on the treadwheel fail to capture its full penal properties. They do not convey the motion, the noise, the palpable strain and smell of intense physical effort. To go on the wheel was to be cast into a machine. A slip could bring injury or even death to the novice, and at the very least the experience was gruelling.[7]

A prison warder said of the treadwheel: 'You see the men could get no firm tread like, from the steps always sinking away from under their feet, and *that* makes it very tiring. Again, the compartments are small, and the air becomes very hot, so that the heat at the end of the quarter of an hour renders it difficult to breathe.'

Mayhew pointed out that prisoners would wound themselves severely in an attempt to avoid the treadwheel, and he suggested that it might put young offenders off manual labour for life. He quoted a prison inspectors' report of 1838: 'The prison either leaves him to all the baneful effects of utter idleness, or else its discipline consists in teaching him to tread the wheel, an employment which is enough to make him avoid all labour to the end of his days.'

Another particularly pointless form of labour was the crank. Prisoners who were thought to be malingering by the medical officers would have this drum-like machine installed in their cells, and would be required to turn the crank handle ten thousand times a day. As the handle turned, sand was scooped from the bottom of the drum and tipped out again. The turns of the handle were recorded on a meter. It was reckoned that this lonely torture took the average prisoner eight hours and twenty minutes of continuous labour.

Mayhew records: 'It was said that after a couple of days at this employment, the most stubborn usually ask to go back to their previous occupation.'

Hulks – dilapidated warships – were introduced as temporary prisons in 1776, although they continued to be used well into the nineteenth century. The regime was even tougher than prison. The convicts were given a restricted diet and put to public work at the arsenal at Woolwich, the quarries at Portland or the dockyard at Portsmouth. Mayhew described seeing a group of them leave Pentonville for the hulks before dawn, manacled and chained. 'Each cheek was puckered with smiles at the sense that they were bidding adieu to the place of their long isolation from the world.'

What awaited them was different, but not better, than prison. There could of course be no separate system. After they had returned from their labour ashore the men were confined on the lower decks in unspeakable conditions almost without supervision. Mayhew wrote of the early days of the hulks, when 700 men were crowded together on the *Justitia*: 'The state of morality under such circumstances may be easily conceived, crimes impossible to mention being commonly perpetrated.'

Although the decks of the hulks were washed with chloride of lime to ward off illness the ships were pest holes, especially in the beginning. One warder told Mayhew that he

> well remembers seeing the shirts of the prisoners, when hung out upon the rigging, so black with vermin that the linen positively appeared to have been sprinkled over with pepper; and that when the cholera broke out on board the convict vessels for the first time, the chaplain refused to bury the dead until there were several corpses on board, so that the coffins were taken to the marshes by half a dozen at a time, and interred at a given signal from the clergyman; his reverence remaining behind on the poop of the vessel, afraid to accompany the bodies, reading the burial service at the distance of a mile from the grave, and letting fall a handkerchief when he came to 'ashes to ashes and dust to dust', as a sign that they were to lower the bodies.[8]

Also moored at Woolwich was the hospital ship *Unité*. Mayhew quoted an earlier report of the conditions on board:

> Even so late as 1849, we find the *Unité* hospital ship at Woolwich described in the following terms; – The great majority of the patients were infested with vermin; and their persons, in many instances, particularly their feet, begrimed with dirt. No regular supply of body-linen had been issued; so much so, that many men had been five weeks without a change, and all record had been lost of the time when the blankets had been washed; and the number of sheets was so insufficient, that the expedient had been resorted to of only a single sheet at a time, to save appearances. Neither towels or combs were provided for the prisoners' use, and the unwholesome odour from the imperfect and neglected state of the water-closets was almost insupportable. On the admission of new cases into hospital patients were directed to leave their beds and go into

hammocks, and the new cases were turned into the vacated beds, without changing the sheets.

The diet on the hulks, for men doing hard manual labour for long hours, was woefully inadequate. The day started at 5.30 a.m. with a pint of cocoa and a 12-ounce piece of dry bread. Then the men would be ferried ashore to work in the arsenal, breaking granite, clearing drains, building roads, scraping the rust off shells and generally labouring to build the great weapons storehouse. They were ferried back to the hulks for the main meal of the day at 11.30 a.m. This consisted of a pound of potatoes and some boiled meat, which was often rotten, and six ounces of bread.

Then it was back to the arsenal to work until 5 p.m., when they would return to the hulks for supper, which was a pint of gruel and bread. The diet for those on a punishment regime was a pound of bread per day, and water.

The meat was usually ox-cheek, either boiled or made into soup. On two days each week the meat would be replaced by oatmeal and cheese. Each man was allowed a quart of small beer four days a week, and river water that had been imperfectly filtered on the others.

During the first years of the hulks' existence the meat was rotten, the ox-cheeks having been 'kept too long and stinking'. The prison reformer John Howard watched as the men were served biscuits mouldy and green on both sides., Mayhew describes breakfast on board the *Defence* hulk, the men eating silently, with 'the munching of the dry bread by the hundreds of jaws being the only sound heard'.

Some men managed to escape with the help of free labourers who would hide clothes for them somewhere in the arsenal. 'The convict slipped for a moment from his gang, put the clothes on, and passed out of the arsenal gates with the crowds of free men. Or else he made a dash for it, bolted past the sentinels, swam the canal, reached the marshes and made off to the wood at hand.'

Others escaped from the hulks. In 1776 five prisoners on the *Justitia* seized the officers' weapons and locked up the warders. They then escaped in a boat brought alongside by friends. Two of them were killed in the ensuing pursuit, and another two recaptured. Among other escapes around the same time, 22 men forced their way into the captain's cabin and took pistols and swords. They then rowed to the north bank of the river and freed themselves from their chains with tools they took from a blacksmith's.

A unit of sailors caught up with them at East Ham and in the firefight which followed one of the prisoners was killed and three recaptured. The others fled into Epping Forest, and a few managed to remain free. The rest were recaptured over the following months, and hanged.

A far more serious attempt at a break-out happened in 1778. The *Morning Chronicle* wrote that the captain of the hulks, Stewart Erskine, received an anonymous letter warning him that there was going to be trouble, and that his life and those of his officers were in danger.

> The Captain, upon this warning, immediately went to the shore. where about 250 convicts were then at work, and cautioned his people, who were placed to guard them, to be prepared. Shortly after 4 o'clock in the afternoon, about 150 of them assembled in a body, having first armed themselves with pikes, taken from the *chevaux de frize*, with axes and spades, and proceeded to the only pass where they could make their escape, which was firmly guarded by about 20 well-armed men.
>
> The Captain remonstrated strongly, and repeatedly endeavoured by gentle means to dissuade them from such an attempt which, if persisted in, must cost some of them their lives. This had no effect on their desperate leaders, one of them instantly attacked and wounded the Captain, still pressing forward to the pass, throwing showers of heavy stones, and threatening to murder all who opposed them.
>
> At last the ship's people were obliged to make use of their firearms, which, with the assistance of those of a party of artillery, obliged the convicts to retire. Two of their leaders were killed on the spot, and seven or eight more were much wounded.

The following day 36 convicts rushed the warders on one of the hulks and when the crew opened fire one of them was killed and eighteen wounded. The hopelessness of such attempts was no deterrent. The prisoners probably felt that if they stayed they would soon die anyway. During one two-year period 176 prisoners out of a total of 632 on the hulks died – more than a quarter. During a Parliamentary inquiry the director of the project, Duncan Campbell, had to admit that when men were being transported to America 'upon an average of seven years, the loss of convicts in jail and on board will be one seventh'.

For too many of the men on the hulks the only escape was the grave. Mayhew describes the featureless graveyard. 'We thought it was one of the dreariest spots we had ever seen... We could just trace the rough outline of disturbed ground at our feet... There was not even a number over the graves; the last, and it was only a month old, was disappearing. In a few months the rank grass will have closed over it, as over the story of its inmate. And it is, perhaps, as well to leave the names of the unfortunate men, whose bones lie in the clay of this dreary marsh, unregistered and unknown. But the feeling with which we look upon its desolation is irrepressible.'

One man's story sums up the horror of the hulks. George Barrington was born in Ireland about 1755, and studied medicine in London. His health was poor and he turned pickpocket, for a while successfully. Among his victims was said to be Count Gregory Orloff, the discarded lover of Catherine the Great of Russia. Barrington relieved him of a jewelled gold snuffbox of great value.[9]

Earlier he had been sent to the hulks for three years for another offence. At the Old Bailey he had appeared, 'a very genteel man, about 21, and very far from athletic: his hair dressed *à la mode*; clothes quite in the taste; a fine gold-headed taper cane with suitable tassels, and elegant Artois buckles. In short he is the *genteelest* thief ever remembered to have been seen at the Old Bailey, and it is a *great pity* he should be condemned to so *vulgar* an employment as ballast-heaving.'

A writer in the *Scots Magazine* told of the impression Barrington made when he arrived on board the *Justitia*. 'From an appearance the most genteel [he] is become an object of commiseration. His behaviour is mild, humble, patient. He entertains a just sense of his dishonest course of life, and performs his lot with all possible industry in a state of true contrition.'

Barrington had an 'associate and friend', a Miss West, who sent him two guineas every week, and visited him when she could. On one of these visits she picked the pocket of another prisoner who was flush with cash, and was indignant when Barrington made her give the money back.

Because of his good conduct Barrington was surprisingly freed after serving only a third of his sentence. But his period of freedom was brief. The Committee on Transportation which sat in 1785 had pointed out that men who had served in the hulks were treated as pariahs: 'No parish will receive them and no person set them to work; being shunned by their former acquaintances, and baffled in every attempt to gain their bread, the danger of starving almost irresistibly leads them to a renewal of their former crimes.'

Within months Barrington was back on the *Justitia*, this time serving five years. In an attempt to commit suicide he stabbed himself in the chest.'The wound, tho' deep and dangerous, did not prove fatal; and medical assistance being called in, and seasonably applied, a cure was effected. It was, however, effected very slowly; and the wound having been given in the breast, seemed in its effects, after nearly two years' continuance, to bring a consumption on the unhappy patient.'

In this plight, a rare act of kindness saved him. Barrington said that 'colds that I had repeatedly caught had ulcerated my lungs, and labour often exceeding my strength by day, and putrefied air by night, had greatly reduced and wasted my frame. The surgeon finding that the usual medicaments were not sufficient, applied to the superintendent, and obtained a milk and vegetable diet for me. This was a regimen never allowed there, but like extreme unction to those that were at the point of death.'

Barrington survived to be released again. He was given a pardon after four years on condition that he left the country and never returned. He went first to Ireland, and then Edinburgh, but the pull of the capital was too strong. He returned to London and in 1783 was again at the Old Bailey, this time for breaching the conditions of his pardon. When he heard the court planned to send him back to the hulks at Woolwich to serve out his sentence he cried out: 'My Lord, my disease is of such a nature, it is not in the power of medicine to relieve me if I go down to that place, and certain death must be the result.'

Surprisingly, once again he found mercy, of a kind, and he was allowed to serve out the remaining eleven months of his sentence at Newgate. Released, he went back to the only way of making a living that he knew, and he was transported to New South Wales.

In 1792 he was freed for good conduct and, 'in spite of a predilection for the rum bottle, he won such success that when he died in 1804, he held the responsible appointments of Superintendent of Convicts and High Constable.'[10]

Patrick Colquhoun, founder of the Thames River Police, was one of many who spoke out against the hulks, calling them 'seminaries of profligacy and vice' which 'vomit forth at stated times upon the public a certain number of convicts, who having no asylum, no home, no character, and no means of subsistence, seem to have only the alternative of joining their companions in iniquity and of adding strength to the criminal phalanx.' Yet the hulks, intended originally as a temporary measure, continued in use until July 1857 when the last of them, the *Defence*, was destroyed by fire at Woolwich.

Reformers campaigned for improvements in the prisons. Some of them, like Elizabeth Fry, risked death from jail fever to see the conditions for themselves. Henry Grey Bennett, chairman of the 1816 Select Committee on the Police, who himself wanted to fight crime by reforming the prisons, paid tribute to her:

I visited Newgate in the beginning of the month of May 1817, and went round, first, the female side of the prison: I had been there a few weeks before, and found it, as usual, in the most degraded and afflicting state; the women were then mixed all together, young and old; the young beginner with the old offender; the girl, for the first offence, with the hardened and drunken prostitute; the tried and the untried; the accused with the condemned; the transports with those under sentence of death; all were crowded together, in one promiscuous assemblage; noisy, idle and profligate; clamorous at the grating, soliciting money and begging at the bars of the prison, with spoons attached to the ends of sticks. In little more than one fortnight the whole scene was changed, through the humane and philanthropic exertion of Mrs Fry, the wife of a banker in the city, assisted by others of the Society of Friends; and it is but justice to add, seconded by the Lord Mayor, Aldermen and Sheriffs of London. In the first yard I visited were seventy- eight women, fines and transports together; the fines being persons under sentence of imprisonment for short terms; sixty-five of these were employed in needle-work which had been procured for them: there were also with these women seventeen children. Of the seventy-eight, sixty-four were under sentence of transportation, and fourteen for short terms of imprisonment; twenty-two of them slept in one room, which was only twenty-four feet by eighteen. In one fortnight the work done was three hundred and forty-two shirts, and sixty-four shifts, fifty-nine aprons, and two hundred and fifty pinbefores.

Large though the contribution of the reformers was, what was needed was official action. A start was made with Peel's Prison Act of 1823, which attempted to classify convicts according to their crimes and to standardise penal practice.[11]

The ban on prisoners speaking to each other continued, at least informally, but many learned how to speak without moving their lips, like ventriloquists. Jim Whelan, an IRA gunman sentenced for a raid on a Liverpool post office in 1923, described hearing a working party returning to Maidstone jail: 'There was a strange susurration which I could not locate or identify. It was rather like the murmuring sound made by the wings of a thousand starlings when they are ganging up in the autumn. I was hearing the "silent system" of the English convict prisons for the first time.'

This was the sound of prisoners speaking without moving their lips, what Whelan called 'the lip-still murmur', and even the most malevolent warder was powerless to discipline the culprits. 'No man was punished for talking in all my time in English jails: it was illegal to punish people for such acts. What happened was that when a man spoke, a warder told him to stop, he spoke again, and was reported:

not for talking, but for disobeying an order. It was all perfectly legal and very simple.'[12]

Discipline was still harsh in the interwar years. Flogging was a common punishment. The prisoner would be strapped to a flogging triangle, his head held so that he could not turn and see who was inflicting the punishment.

There were also punishment diets. The bread-and-water diet was still used, although it could be imposed for only fifteen days. The other punishment diet, bread, porridge and potatoes, could be imposed for as long as 42 days. The burglar Ruby Sparks was so hungry he ate the table in his Dartmoor cell:

At Dartmoor I chewed away nearly all my wooden table in the punishment cell. Ate it, mouthful by mouthful, swallowing the chewed pulp of splinters to fill my empty stomach. The table wasn't anything particularly tasty. It was just a scrubbed wooden ledge, soggy from years of Dartmoor's eternal dampness. It's flavour was soap and firewood. But I'd eaten it. The lot![13]

He was given another fourteen days' punishment and put in a cell with a metal table.

The regular food was bad enough. Wilfred Macartney, a Communist who served a sentence in Parkhurst in 1927 for an act of subversion, recalled:

The next thing the prison authorities do is to publish a false prospectus in the shape of a menu given to every convict; and how pleasant it is to read the various dinners! – 'treacle pudding' (it's like a dirty old rubber sponge); 'beef-steak pudding' 'savoury bacon'; 'sea pie' ; 'beef stew'; 'pork soup' etc. The vile concoctions masquerading under these honest names would make a hungry pig vomit with disgust. 'Sea pie' is a mess in a filthy tin, defying analysis. The top is a livid scum, patterned with a pallid tracery of cooling grey grease, and just below this fearsome surface rests a lump of grey matter like an incised tumour, the dirty dices of pale pink, half-cooked carrots heightening the diseased anatomical resemblance. The stuff looks as if its real home were a white pail in an operating theatre.[14]

The food, the beatings by warders and the generally harsh regime led to a riot at Dartmoor on Sunday 24 January 1932. It followed a period of unrest, and a morning when the prisoners were 'incensed by the sobs and shrieks of "Silly Arthur", a weak-minded prisoner being bludgeoned by the warders for his "innzlence".'[15]

When the prisoners were let out into the exercise yards they refused to obey orders. The burglar Ruby Sparks described how the mutiny began:

> It wasn't until next day, when those of us who were left had come out into the exercise yard and were trudging around, that they started to sort us out. So I hit the screw nearest to me, knocking him cold, and then it occurred to me to put on his cap. I had just pulled it on to my head when I heard an uproar from the other yard, and about a dozen lags came running through to me, shouting: 'Ruby – we've started it!'
>
>   That was how the Dartmoor mutiny actually started – both exercise yards just blew up at the same time, and all the screws went running to the gate and out of the prison. All that could get out. They left Dartmoor in charge of us lags.

The mutiny was mostly good-natured, and none of the warders was seriously hurt. One of the prisoners, Billy Mitchell, was shot in the throat as he shouted abuse from the rooftops.

In the aftermath a group of warders, led by the prison's governor wielding a pick-shaft, laid into the prisoners. The medical staff had to treat at least seventy of the convicts for head wounds.

An inquiry found that the riot was caused not by the bad food and the brutality of the regime, but was incited by ringleaders of the 'motor bandit' type. This was a reference to Sparks, who had carried out a series of daring robberies in a car driven by his partner Lillian Goldstein, an expert driver known as the 'Bob-Haired Bandit'. Sentences totalling almost a hundred years were handed out, including four for Sparks. He escaped that extra term on a technicality. Billy Mitchell, the prisoner who had been shot, was permanently paralysed, but was still made to serve out the remainder of his sentence.

From Reefers to Crack

There was a little pub in Air Street, where Swan and Edgars now stands, where the bright young things of the gay twenties splashed vintage champagne. A part of the shop that is now Austin Reeds used to be the Chinese restaurant presided over by the prince of London's dope smugglers and white slave traders, the infamous Brilliant Chang... The first place in Britain where reefer cigarettes – marijuana – were smoked was in the Nest Club in Kingly Street...
Robert Fabian, London After Dark, Naldrett Press, 1954

In no other area of personal freedom has the state intervened so drastically as drugs: with predictable and disastrous results. Yet for a long time drugs such as laudanum and opium were freely available, free enough for the writer De Quincy to experience and describe the torments of addiction, which he does so eloquently in *Confessions of an Opium Eater*.

In 1854 James Balfour, a research worker for various temperance bodies and the Statistical Society, gave this evidence to the Select Committee on Public Houses about the village of Pavenham in Bedfordshire:

...and another thing they were much addicted to was, that 16 out of every 20 women were opium eaters... The majority of females at Pavenham are consumers of opium; I discovered it by close investigation at first, of a young female, the mistress of the lace school; I was very much astonished at her different appearance towards the latter part of the day to what it was in the morning, when I first went in. I said to the lady at whose house I was staying, the proprietor of the village inn, that it struck me that opium was consumed. She said, 'No'. I said, 'My strong impression is that it is, and I must investigate it.' I did so, and I found that it was, and had for a considerable number of years been consumed in that village. It was sold in as small quantities as a halfpenny worth, at the hucksters' shops.

Morphia, a chemical form of opium, was first produced in the 1820s. The hypodermic syringe followed in the 1850s, and Bayer, the German pharmaceutical company, launched heroin in 1898 with the claim that it had the 'ability of morphine to relieve pain, but safer'.

In the nineteenth century British exports of opium from India to China led to the Opium Wars. Worried about the effect of the drug on public health in their country, the Chinese seized the British cargoes and burned them. The British retaliated and the Second Opium War (1857–60) forced the Chinese to accept the trade.[1]

Ironic then that a Chinese was at the centre of a notorious drugs scandal that dented official complacency in Britain itself about the dangers. On 27 November 1918 a popular young actress named Billie Carleton attended the Victory Ball at the Albert Hall. The following morning her maid found her dead in bed, with a gold box containing cocaine on the dressing table. She got the drug from her boyfriend, a costume designer named Reggie de Veuille, whose suppliers were a Chinese named Lau Ping You and his Scottish wife Ada.

In the wave of moral indignation and panic which followed Ada was sentenced to five months' hard labour: the Marlborough Street magistrate Frederick Mead called her the 'high priestess of unholy rites'. Her husband was fined £10. Reggie de Veuille admitted conspiracy to supply cocaine at the Old Bailey and was given eight months' hard labour.

There were calls in Parliament for the deportation of all Chinese and attention soon focussed on another Chinese, a man known as 'the Brilliant Chang'. He was a close friend of Billie Carleton, and the *World Pictorial News* said he 'dispensed Chinese delicacies and the drugs and vices of the Orient' at his restaurant in Regent Street. The paper wrote of his 'obsession' with white women and claimed that when women gave in to his demands for sex in exchange for drugs, 'the flame of evil passion burned more brightly within and he hugged himself with unholy glee'.

In March 1922 Freda Kempton, a young dancing teacher, was found dead from a cocaine overdose. Chang had been with her the night before. He told the coroner at her inquest: 'She was a friend of mine but I know nothing about the cocaine. It is all a mystery to me.' The coroner ruled that the evidence was not strong enough to link Chang with the death, but commented that it was 'disgraceful that such a dangerous drug as cocaine should be handed about London to ruin the bodies and souls of inexperienced girls'. Good-looking young women were waiting outside the court to congratulate Chang.

Chang moved from Regent Street and opened the Shanghai restaurant in Limehouse, which was then London's Chinatown. In 1924 the premises were raided by the police and a large quantity of cocaine discovered. Chang was jailed for eighteen months and then deported. The Recorder of London said at his trial: 'It is you and men like you who are corrupting the womanhood of this country.'

The cases were grist to the mill of the burgeoning popular press. The *Daily Express* wrote: 'You will find the woman dope fiend in Chelsea, in Mayfair and Maida Vale. An obscure traffic is pursued in certain doubtful teashops.' The *Daily Mail* said: 'Men do not as a rule take to drugs, unless there is a hereditary influence, but women are more temperamentally attracted.' The *Empire News* was more direct.'Mothers would be well advised to keep their daughters as far away as they can from Chinese laundries and other places where the yellow men congregate.'

After his deportation there were rumours that Chang was living in Europe and directing the London drug scene from afar. In 1927 he was arrested for drug dealing in Paris, and absconded while on bail with a young woman. There were also rumours – perhaps put about by his own men – that he was a penniless derelict. The *Daily Telegraph*'s crime reporter, Stanley Firmin, wrote: 'A strange

Nemesis overtook him. He went blind and ended his days not in luxury and rich silks but as a sightless worker in a little kitchen garden.' Since it was estimated that he made more than a million pounds from drug trafficking this seems unlikely.

Chang seems to have been something of a charmer. When he saw a woman in his restaurant who caught his fancy he would send her a note;

Dear Unknown,

Please don't regard this as a liberty that I wrote to you. I am really unable to resist the temptation after having see you so many times. I should extremely like to know you better and should be glad if you would do me the honour of meeting me one evening when we could have a little dinner or supper together. I do hope you will consent to this as it will give me great pleasure indeed, and in any case do not be cross with me for having written to you,

Yours hopefully, Chang.[2]

Superintendent Robert Fabian, 'Fabian of the Yard', told in *London After Dark* how in his first week on the beat in Soho an older officer pointed out a man called Eddie Manning and warned him to beware of him. 'He's the worst man in London.'

Manning, a Jamaican, had been jailed for sixteen months in 1920 for shooting three men in the legs in Cambridge Circus. One of them had punched and insulted an actress friend of Manning's. In 1922 a drug addict named Eric Goodwin died from a heroin overdose at Manning's house. Fabian wrote: 'We strongly suspected Eddie was giving dope parties in various parts of London, and injections of cocaine at 10s. a time... He had his own team of strong-arm villains – both white and coloured boys who were usually full of drugs – and kept a profitable sideline in protecting prostitutes.'

Manning was arrested carrying cocaine and opium in Primrose Hill in north London. He also had a silver-topped cane which had a secret compartment for drugs. He got six months. In 1923 he was arrested again for similar offences and got three years' penal servitude. When he got out he opened a club, and in 1929 Fabian arrested him for receiving property stolen from Lady Diana Cooper's car. Jailed for another three years, he died in prison.

The link in the popular mind between drugs, Limehouse and the Chinese was strong. As long ago as 1868 a magazine wrote about opium smoking in a Chinese 'opium den' in Bluegate Fields, an alley in neighbouring Shadwell, and two years later Dickens made such a den the centrepiece of his account of the East End in the unfinished *The Mystery of Edwin Drood*. In 1870 Gustave Doré published an engraving of the same opium den in *London: A Pilgrimage*. This 'reinforced the belief that the East End was a place of racial, sexual and social danger.'³ In 1930 a burglar named George Ingram told a journalist: 'Dope-taking, prostitution, associations between white women and Chinese and Negroes – all these things may be found in Limehouse...'

Sydney Horlor, author of popular novels, was asked by the *Star* newspaper to write a series of articles about the underworld. The results were reprinted in his *London's Underworld* in 1934. He described how with a guide he watched a woman addict in an expensive car stop in Hyde Park on a Sunday to buy drugs from a supplier. His companion said of the woman: 'She's hopelessly neurotic – her nerves are shot to the devil through travelling at too fast a pace – and she's simply got to have dope to keep going. By this time she isn't too particular how or where she gets it.'

Horlor described meeting a 'trafficker' in a Soho café.

He was willing to talk. The first revelation was that there were periodic invasions of London by dope addicts from all over the country. The present supplies of these poor wretches have run out, they are forced to replenish. It was the job of such men as himself to meet the demand.

'Do you find any difficulty?'

'Yes, it's becoming harder every day to get adequate supplies. The nations are uniting, as you know, in fighting this "evil drug", and things... have become very difficult. If I had the dope now which I handled a couple of years ago I could make a great fortune. The thing is that the number of addicts is increasing with the supply diminishing.

'Why you'd scarcely believe me perhaps when I tell you that famous men and women in Society have fallen on their knees when I've told them that I had not any that I could let them have through my supplies not coming through. Some have even threatened to kill themselves.'

Horlor summed up: 'The drug traffic affects all classes of society from famous hostesses and men of brilliant intellect down to the poor drabs of street walkers whose needs are supplied by men of colour.

'Opium smoking is dying out; cocaine is – and promises to be – the chief evil. The reasons are that this drug is so easy to pass, so valuable to possess and so vital to the needs of those who are addicted to its use. 'It is deadly in its effects. It kills in time.'[4]

In *Line-up for Crime* in 1956 Duncan Webb of the *People* told how he set out to trace the supply line for drugs from the docks to the East End and on to the West End.

If you want to see the drug trade operating with flourishing abandon, go down to the East End and get into some of the clubs which operate there from eleven o'clock at night until the early hours. There you will find Greeks, Cypriots, Maltese, Turks, Negroes, the cosmopolia of Stepney and Poplar indulging in their night life just as do their counterparts in the wealthier West End. White girls with Negroes, black girls with white men, Maltese pimps with prostitutes of all nationalities, all drinking, drugging, dancing, gambling, singing, jiving, gesticulating in a nocturnal madness that defies convention, outrages morals, ignores society, mocks the law.

Awareness of the addictive properties of drugs grew slowly, although Samuel Crump had written in the eighteenth century that users deprived of opium even for a single day 'became languid, dejected and uneasy'. The invention of the hypodermic syringe encouraged the use of morphia, which led to a greater awareness of the symptoms of dependency and withdrawal. Soon medical experts were investigating the abuse of cocaine, opium and other drugs.[5]

As recently as 1893 a body set up by the British government, the Indian Hemp Drugs Commission, produced a 3,000-page report stating that moderate use of cannabis and opium produced no ill effects. It was World War One that reversed official complacency. British soldiers on leave in London sought out supplies of drugs that might make life in the trenches bearable. At the time morphine and cocaine were sold openly. Harrods sold kits labelled 'A Useful Present for Friends at the Front' which included morphine, cocaine, syringes and spare needles. Military chiefs used the Defence of the Realm Act in 1916 to forbid the supply of cocaine and opium to troops on active service. This became the first Dangerous Drugs Act in 1920.

The fact that addiction was largely a middle-class problem probably led to a humane approach by the authorities. In 1926 the government-sponsored Rolleston Committee was asked to consider whether addicts should be punished. The committee recommended that addiction should be regarded as an illness, and that addicts should be allowed drugs on prescription. This was the basis of British drugs policy until the 1960s.

An explosion of drug-taking in the sixties led to a rethink. Doctors had to inform the Home Office of addicts, and drug dependency centres were set up. Recreational use of cannabis had been outlawed in 1928 when the goverment signed the 1925 Geneva Convention on the manufacture, sale and movement of dangerous drugs. It continued to be used for psychiatric purposes until absolutely banned by the Misuse of Drugs Act in 1971.[6]

In *London After Dark*, Superintendent Robert Fabian wrote about the 'coloured fellows' who were believed to be the only serious users: 'Simple folk, believe me, but they often get bad names through the young trollops who become their camp followers.' He added: 'They have the brains of children, can only dimly know the cruel harm they do to these teenage girls who dance with them and try thrilled puffs at those harmless-looking marijuana cigarettes.'

The Times, which had earlier told its readers that 'most cocainomaniacs carry revolvers to protect themselves from imaginary enemies', warned in 1957: 'White girls who become friendly with West Indians are from time to time enticed into hemp smoking. This is an aspect of the hemp problem – the possibility of its spreading among irresponsible white people – that causes greatest concern to the authorities. The potential moral danger is significant, since a principal motive of the coloured man in smoking hemp is to stimulate his sexual desire.'

Despite such warnings the authorities did not yet see drugs as a serious threat. The Drugs Squad had only one car, and in 1961 Sir Ronald Howe, head of Scotland Yard's CID branch, wrote: 'In this country drug trafficking presents a very small problem. Englishmen don't take drugs, they prefer Scotch whisky.'

It was the pop-and-pot culture of the 1960s that raised public awareness of drugs, and it was fitting that the most notorious drug smuggler of the time had a kind of rock superstar allure. Howard Marks was a charming Oxford physics graduate who was recruited by MI6, the government security service, while he was a major importer of cannabis.

Marks, who was born in 1945 in Wales, was a clever grammar school boy who graduated from Balliol College Oxford and became a drug dealer, employing dozens of his friends. With an Irishman named Jim McCann he took over a warehouse on an industrial estate near Shannon Airport to store the drugs and paid couriers £2,000 to £3,000 a time to drive consignments of cannabis to England.

It was at this time that MI6 recruited him, basically for his charm. They hoped he would penetrate east European security by seducing women who worked at the Czechoslovakian embassy.

Soon Marks was smuggling cannabis into the US. In 1973 he was arrested after drugs were found in rock music equipment his team had exported to that country. He told customs officers that he had been recruited by MI6 to infiltrate IRA drug-smuggling operations.

Marks was extradited to Britain where he was granted £20,000 bail. In April 1974 a man who claimed to be from the Customs and Excise called at his rented house in Oxford and took Marks away, and he vanished.

While the newspapers speculated about how a man said to have links to MI6, the IRA and drug rings could just disappear on the eve of an Old Bailey drugs trial, Marks went on the run. From a hide-out on the Isle of Dogs in east London he went to Denmark and then to a resort near Genoa in Italy.

He began to travel the world setting up drug deals. For years he lived a frenetic life of travel, smuggling, smoking drugs and accumulating and losing several fortunes. He was variously involved with the CIA, the Mafia and major drug smugglers across the world. He also set up legitimate businesses, including a massage parlour and a travel agency.

New Year's Eve 1979 saw him in the Western Isles of Scotland, organising the shipping of a huge consignment of cannabis from Colombia. Fifteen tons of cannabis were brought ashore and stored in warehouses in Scotland and England, enough, he wrote later, for every inhabitant of the British Isles to get simultaneously stoned. Unfortunately for Marks, his Colombian and American partners became anxious that the drugs were not being sold fast enough and began to make inquiries. Marks said: 'This was simply mad. In the end they approached a man who turned out to be a customs informant, and that is how it all got discovered. Just impatience really.'

Ten tons of the cannabis were found and some of the gang arrested. Marks was trapped in the unlikely surrounding of the Swan at Lavenham in Suffolk where he had booked in with his girlfriend, Judy Lane. As Marks ordered a drink a young man standing at the bar spoke to him. A rueful Marks recalled: 'He said, "Can I have a look at your watch", and he was putting the handcuffs on me at the same time.' The young man was Higher Executive Officer of Customs and Excise, Nicholas Baker.

The trial was notable for Marks's charm under pressure and the appearance of a *deus ex machina* in the form of a Latin American who claimed to be a member of the Mexican security police. His testimony changed the course of the trial. The mysterious 'agent', Jorge del Rio, was called by the defence. He claimed he was involved in antiterrorism operations of such importance that he could not give details in open court. Press and public were cleared from the court, and del Rio told the jury that he had paid Marks $150,000 for his help in a drugs deal. He claimed that somehow this deal would help Mexico's fight against terrorists.

Crown Counsel John Rogers appealed to the jury to treat the story with the contempt it deserved, and Marks himself believes it gave them an excuse to find him not guilty. 'I don't think for one minute they believed the defences presented to them. They just didn't want us nice guys to spend countless years in prison for transporting beneficial herbs from one part of the world to another.'

Marks was given a three-year sentence for the charge he was facing when he first disappeared. Because of the time he had spent in prison this meant he was soon free. By the 1980s he was Europe's biggest marijuana smuggler, bringing up to fifty tons of the drug into Britain each year.

In July 1988 an international hunt for him, led by the American Drugs Enforcement Agency, ended with him being arrested at Palma, Majorca. Things looked bleak for him. The prosecution had tapes of conversations between Marks and Lord Moynihan, the half-brother of former Tory government minister Colin Moynihan, in which they discussed setting up a cannabis plantation on an island off the Philippines.

At Palm Beach Federal Court in Florida Marks pleaded guilty to cannabis importation charges, and was sentenced to 25 years, reduced on appeal to twenty. He was sent to the penitentiary at Terre Haute, Indiana, where he taught some of the world's toughest criminals English grammar and philosophy. True to the image he projects in his autobiography *Mr Nice*, he was released in 1995 after seven years on grounds of good behaviour.

Marks went back to Spain and began work on his memoirs. Despite the huge deals he was involved in and the enormous amounts of money involved, he said he made only two to three million dollars, and that he had spent it all. He invited anyone who could find the millions he was said to have hidden to keep it.

'For a long time I conned myself into thinking I was only breaking the law because the law was foolish,' he said. 'I do sincerely believe the law is foolish, but I do think I would have gone that way anyway. If I was living in Saudi Arabia I would have opened a bar.'

Today he is a campaigner for the legalisation of cannabis, and has made a pop record, 'Let Me Grow More Weed'. 'It is a serious message that cannabis, which is less harmful than cigarettes, should be legalised,' the married father of four was reported as saying in the *Independent* in 1999. The previous year, in a readers' quiz in the *Independent*, he admitted smoking 'between 20 and 30 joints' a day.

The first 'crack factory' in Britain was discovered in Peckham, south London, in August 1988. Crack, a smokable form of cocaine, was already notorious in America for causing almost instant addiction, and drug squad officers had been anxiously anticipating its arrival here. It was known that the drug gave an intense 'high' that lasted only about fifteen minutes, leaving the addict with a craving for more.

Crack was introduced to Britain by Yardies, Jamaican gangsters with a deserved reputation for violence. Described by one police officer as 'disorganised organised crime', Yardies certainly pushed up the body count after they began to arrive in the eighties. But mostly they seemed to be killing each other.

The Yardie gangs, known as 'Posses', were spawned by murderous political campaigns on the Caribbean island in the 1970s and early 1980s. Six hundred people died in the 1981 election campaign, and in the police crackdown that followed many of the killers and gangsters emigrated, mostly to the US and Canada. A few came to Britain. They quickly became involved in drug racketeering, and others soon followed them.

Yardie gangs in the USA and Jamaica have memberships numbered in the hundreds. In the UK a typical gang might have about several dozen foot soldiers. Most of those killed were involved in turf wars between drugs gangs, with Brixton at the epicentre. Other areas most affected are Harlesden in the north-west of the capital and Dalston to the north of the City.

When the Peckham 'crack factory' flat was raided there were three Jamaicans inside, two of whom had just arrived from Jamaica. The other was from the Bronx in New York. A police officer involved in the raid said: 'Our view was that this estate, and others with a large black community, had been specially targeted by foreign dealers as places where they could sell crack.'[7]

Another flat, this time on the Milton Court Estate in Deptford, south-east London, was so well protected by a cast-steel door and steel-cased inner door that police needed oxyacetylene cutters and hydraulic rams to get in. Clients would be handed their drugs through a slit in the outer door, and never saw the supplier. When the police finally got in and arrested the dealer they found 43 rocks of crack and some cocaine powder.[8]

Fears of a crack crimewave were intensified when Special Agent Robert M Stutman, head of the New York City office of the Drug Enforcement Agency (DEA) was invited by senior police officers here to address them on the problem. Stutman's apocalyptic description of the situation in the US ended with this warning: 'I will personally guarantee that two years from now you will have a serious crack problem because ... we are so saturated in the United States with cocaine, there ain't enough noses left to use the cocaine that's coming in.'

His address galvanised the government. Home Secretary Douglas Hurd called a meeting of European ministers and warned of the 'spectre hanging over Europe'. British police officers went to America to seek advice. As a result, a combined police and customs team of 24 officers was set up, led by Commander Roy Penrose.

At first, predictions of a 'crack explosion' seemed alarmist. Seizures of the new drug remained small, and it was estimated that the proportion of cocaine used in the crack form was probably only 20 to 30 per cent. But then the wars between Yardie gangs in London and Moss Side in Manchester began.

The following anecdotes of the Yardie wars have been chosen at random: Yardie activities have after all been called 'disorganised organised crime'.

In September 1988 Rohan 'Yardie Ron' Barrington Barnet was shot dead in a gunfight in Harley Road, Harlesden. On Christmas Day Steven Mendez, who was sitting in the back seat of a car, was shot and killed during a street battle between gangs in Camden.

In November 1991 links with American Yardies were revealed when Leroy, a member of a New York gang, was arrested while selling crack in White City, London. He and the man with him, Victor Francis, were both wanted for murder in the US.

In February 2000 four Yardie gangsters who shot another Yardie dead in a bizarre dispute over a car parking space were jailed for life at the Old Bailey. The four, members of the Lock City Crew based at a sports complex in Brent, north London, had attacked men from the Cartel Crew from Brixton. They were armed with handguns and a sawn-off shotgun, and one of the Cartel gang, Dion Holmes, was shot through the heart.

The dispute began after the wife of a Cartel Crew member was ticked off for parking in the wrong place at the sports centre. She threatened a security man with a broken bottle, and was escorted away by police.

Twenty minutes later she returned with her husband. The Lock City Crew, who had turned the £50 million centre into their headquarters and kept firearms and drugs in a private room there, took this as a sign of disrespect. They went to a betting shop and beat up a man they took to be a member of the rival gang. Then they picked up a bag of firearms and confronted the Cartel Crew outside the centre.

Holmes died in the ensuing shoot-out. Two other gangsters were wounded. People visiting the centre tried to flee, but found all the doors locked.

Prosecutor Richard Horwell told the court the Lock City Crew's 'hackles had risen, and no doubt they wanted to defend their territory and teach this other impudent group a lesson they would never forget'.

In December 1998 armed police stormed a fortified drug den in the heart of the West End which showed how far the Yardies had come since the raid on the Peckham crack factory ten years earlier. The doors of the building, old EMI recording studios which had been turned into a club called Backbeat, were backed by steel shutters. Closed-circuit TV cameras watched at strategic points, and lookouts in the surrounding streets used mobile phones to keep in touch with those inside. Yardie gangsters, said to be armed with guns, machetes and electric cattle prods, stood guard.

The mastermind of the operation was Maryann Quinn, a woman with Jamaican roots. The muscle was organised by her former lover Floyd Alexander, known in Yardie circles as Tank. The club was a front for a drug-dealing operation of amazing audacity, given its location.

The club was advertised in student magazines and inside it there were signs in four languages. Clients were said to have come from all over Europe. Upstairs, between 5.30 p.m. and 3 a.m., there would be between 300 and 400 clubbers dancing. In a special 'smoking' room up to 100 more would sit on the floor, passing joints.

In the basement, drugs were being sold. Punters could pass £10 or £20 through a hole in the wall and in return be handed a packet of drugs. All they saw was a hand in a surgical glove which took the money and handed over the packet.

Police took the threat of the Yardie guards seriously. They arrived outside the club concealed in two articulated lorries. Men of the Yard's SO 19 specialist firearms squad abseiled down from the roof and kicked their way into the building through the upper-floor windows. They threw stun grenades into rooms believed to be guarded by armed Yardies. With 120 armed policemen taking part, it was the biggest operation of its kind in British police history.

More than 90,000 bags of drugs were seized, along with 21 kilos of cannabis. Samurai swords, machetes and £125,000 in cash were also found.

Quinn and Alexander were each jailed for five years for conspiracy to supply cannabis. Quinn, who was 39 at the time she was sentenced and had a young baby by one of the Yardies, claimed she was forced to allow drug dealing at the club by Yardie gangsters, but police believe she was the ringleader. 'She wanted to make a million and get out,' said Detective Inspector Lewis Benjamin, who also described her as 'a very strong character and very devious'.

Quinn was well on the way to achieving her ambition when she was caught. When police raided her house they found £78,000 hidden there. There was also £7,500 in coins from the club's pool tables, money she described as 'loose change.'

A senior police officer said: 'She had a BMW, several bank accounts, and had paid off her mortgage. She had leases on numerous houses, flats and business property.'

As the new century loomed the tempo of the Yardie wars became frenetic. From the beginning of 1999 to August 2000 there were 29 drug-related murders in what are called 'black-on-black' attacks in

London. In the first seven months of 2000 there were another 23 non-fatal shootings, many of them failed murder attempts.

The killing of Menaliek Robinson in Hackney in June 2000 had all the hallmarks of a Yardie gangland hit. Four men on two motorbikes blocked his BMW front and back, then one of the pillion passengers dismounted and fired two shots through the window of the car. Robinson, 20, staggered from the car and collapsed on the pavement. One gunman stepped towards him and shot him dead.

The local paper, the *Hackney Gazette*, suggested it was revenge for his involvement in a previous killing in which a young man died in the neighbouring borough of Haringey. Robinson, who was 16 at the time, was jailed for grievous bodily harm.

Robinson's murder happened in a hot-spot of violent crime. Three months earlier staff at a nearby petrol station in Upper Clapton Road refused to return a credit card to a customer after they discovered that it had been stolen. The man left and returned with a handgun. He opened fire and the staff were saved by the bullet-proof glass in their booth.

Two months later about a hundred yards away in Upper Clapton Road a man was shot six times as he waited in traffic in his car. Mehmet Adiguzel, 37, was reputed to have connections with Turkish organised crime. The killing took place in daylight and the street was busy. A shopkeeper, who asked not to be named, told the *Independent* that he heard the shots: 'When I looked out of the window a woman was screaming hysterically and a man holding a gun was running past my window. He got in a waiting car and was driven off.

'I went to the man's car to help, but it was too late. I don't know about the rest of the country, or even the rest of the capital, but round here it's like the Bronx.'

Three weeks later in nearby Chatsworth Road a man was shot several times by a gunman wearing an Afro wig. The victim survived. Asked if anyone had seen anything a Turkish shop worker said: 'Don't be ridiculous. Round here? Would you see anything? Of course you wouldn't.'

On the evening of Monday 31 July 2000 people queuing outside the Chicago nightclub in Peckham, south-east London, were sprayed with automatic pistol fire by two men standing across the street. Eight people were hit, among them a girl aged fifteen. Police believe the gunmen had spotted a rival drugs dealer among innocent bystanders and opened fire.

It was this level of terrifying violence that spurred the police to augment its Operation Trident investigation of what is termed black-on-black crime with the formation of a 160-strong squad of detectives. Officers in the squad say they have been able to intercept Yardie killers who are sent to this country 'every two or three months' to carry out killings, often for as little as £500 or £2,000. They have also discovered links between crack dealers in London and others in Liverpool, Manchester, Bristol, Birmingham, Nottingham and Aberdeen.

Modern Times

Solly Nahome was reaching for the lock of his front door when he heard the Honda motorcycle drive up. It was the last thing he heard. The rider of the machine fired four bullets into his head and drove away.

The killing, in December 1998, brought a sudden flurry of press interest in the Adams family, a north London crime clan who had quietly been growing in strength and reputation for years. Solly Nahome was a Hatton Garden diamond merchant and the papers said he was the family's financial adviser, the man who laundered their illegal drugs millions. Solly, 41, funnelled the money into diamonds or off-shore accounts, or used it to finance property deals.

The killing brought one of the family, 43-year-old Patrick 'Patsy' Adams, back from Spain. The papers speculated that he was going to 'sort out' the killers. The *Daily Mail*'s Geoffrey Levy wrote that 'nobody kills people who work for the Adamses – or arranges for them to be killed – except the Adams family.'

Patsy is one of eleven children of a Catholic family brought up on a tough north London estate. His parents, the redoubtable Florence and ex-lorry driver George, still live there. Like the Krays, the boys are said to venerate their mother. The parents are described as 'the salt of the earth' but three of their sons took early to crime, taking the traditional route of offering 'protection' to street traders and eventually establishing a drugs syndicate.

There was a rival family of toughs, the Reillys, operating in the same area. According to local folklore, Patsy set up an ambush.

312

First one of his lieutenants insulted one of the Reillys, George, in front of his wife in a pub. The Reillys left to get guns. As they were driving back, they ran into an ambush. Their car was raked with gunfire, and although nobody was killed they did not trouble the Adams family again.

After that the brothers went about their business, quietly building up their clubs and drugs empire. So quietly that the police seem to have become frustrated and information about the family was leaked. A series of stories in the newspapers during the 1990s, particularly in the *Independent*, named them as a new and fearsome combination that had become the most powerful gang in the capital. One story claimed they had a tame Tory MP on their payroll.

The Brink's-Mat bullion robbery is believed to have funded the Adams family's move into drugs. If Patsy provides the menace, older brother Terry is said to be the brains behind their success. A quiet family man who has an antique collection worth an estimated £1 million, Terry operates like the managing director of a public company. He used to hold meetings with Solly Nahome four times a week to discuss business projects. These are said to have included a plan to take over the famous Tottenham Hotspur football club before entrepreneur Alan Sugar bought it, and a possible £30 million revamp of the London Arena in Docklands.

Terry's stature was highlighted in a torture trial at the Old Bailey in May 1999. The victim was David McKenzie, a successful financier with an office in Mayfair. He had invested money for the Adams family, but when investments failed lost £1.5 million of their cash.

Christopher McCormack, 44, Patsy Adams's golf partner and a close friend of the other brothers, was accused of a savage attack on McKenzie, who said he had been summoned to a meeting at Terry Adams's mansion in Finchley, north London.

McKenzie told the court of this meeting with Terry Adams: 'Everyone stood up when he walked in. He looked like a star ... a cross between Liberace and Peter Stringfellow. He was immaculately dressed in a long black coat and white frilly shirt. He was totally in command.'

McKenzie said that at another house in Islington he was attacked by McCormack, who is over six feet tall and heavily built. The attack lasted more than twenty minutes: he was kicked and beaten, three of his ribs were broken. He was slashed with what is believed to have been a Stanley knife, two tendons in his wrist being severed and his nose and left ear left 'flapping off'.

When McKenzie took the stand at the Old Bailey, the gasps of shock were audible. 'They'd made an unbelievable mess of him,' said one observer. 'His face was in a terrible state.' Christopher McCormack appeared in the dock with Terry Adams's brother-in-law, John Potter, at whose home the savage attack took place. However, although Potter admitted that McKenzie had been attacked in his house, he maintained that the aggressor was a complete stranger.

How a total stranger got into Mr Potter's home and beat his guest so savagely is a question worth pondering. John Potter's story did, however, impress the jury. He was cleared of committing acts intended to pervert the course of justice.

But what of the man police really wanted to nail – Christopher McCormack? He admitted to meeting David McKenzie three times as he tried to recover the debt as 'a favour for my old mate Patsy'.[1]

The jury heard that DNA tests showed that blood spots on McCormack's motorcycle jacket were McKenzie's: McCormack said that they must have come from an earlier meeting when he broke up a fight between McKenzie and another man. This was yet another thing for the jury to ponder. After a day and a half considering their verdict they decided McCormack was innocent. When he heard the verdict McCormack thanked them and said: 'Come and have a drink over the pub.'

Geoffrey Levy in the *Daily Mail* recounted blood-curdling stories of the family's violence. 'The Adams family are known to be "worse than the Krays" when there is "work" to be done. And no one likes doing his work more than Patsy. "When he is after someone his eyes light up," says one underworld figure. "He's a very frightening man."'

Levy then recounts a tale of the murder of an accountant. This man is said to have stolen £40,000 from the family while working for them. He was found cowering in a car with his girlfriend. He pleaded to be allowed to live because she was with him. According to the story, one man shot her through the head, said 'You're not with her now,' and shot the accountant dead.

Geoffrey Levy wrote that a drugs dealer known as 'Manchester John' borrowed £100,000 for a drugs deal but could not pay the money back on time. He was beaten up and made to sign over the deeds to his flat instead. When it was found that the flat was worth £20,000 less than the debt, he was 'believed to have [been] taken... "up north", killed... and buried... '

Gilbert Wynter, an associate of the Adams family, stabbed the former British high jump champion Claude Moseley through the back with a Japanese samurai sword. The brothers had found that the athlete, who was working for them, was also ripping them off in drugs deals. Wynter was charged with murder but the Old Bailey trial collapsed when the prosecution's key witness was said to be too terrified to give evidence. Wynter disappeared in 1998. Geoffrey Levy said there were rumours that he had been strangled and his body dumped in the foundations of the Millennium Dome.

A series of setbacks in 1998 dented the family's reputation for invincibility. Three days before Solly Nahome was murdered one of the family's henchmen, Paul Anthony, was jailed for eighteen years for the 'cold-blooded shooting' of a businessman in a London nightclub. Two months earlier the third Adams brother, Tommy, 40, got seven-and-a-half years for drugs offences. Tommy, who ran the family's clubs, had set up a drugs network independently of the family and the suggestion was that it brought him £4 million in six months before he was caught. He was trapped by electronic listening devices hidden in a black taxi he used to do his drugs deals. Since then his brothers regularly sweep their homes and cars electronically for bugs.

Because of their suspected criminal activities both at home and abroad – they are rumoured to distribute drugs including cocaine and ecstasy to clubs throughout Europe – they are being subjected to the most intensive police surveillance in British criminal history. Scotland Yard, Interpol, the customs, and MI5 have all at one time or another tried to find a weak spot in a criminal empire that now encompasses money laundering, drugs, money lending and counterfeiting. They have interests in property development, antiques and horse racing. The surveillance may have shaken them – they are now believed to have sold off at least some of their clubs and moved the centre of their operations abroad.

Whether the Adams family could possibly be responsible for all the crimes attributed to them by the press is doubtful. Any spectacular crime – in one instance masterminding a counterfeiting operation – is likely to be laid at their door. Other crimes are more securely linked to them: in March 2000 a Crown Prosecution Service clerk was found guilty at the Old Bailey of passing the names of 33 police informers to an Adams family intermediary. He got £1,000 for his treachery. Police intercepted the list before it reached the Adamses.

Organised crime is one of this country's biggest industries, and it is enjoying an unprecedented boom. The National Criminal Intelligence Service announced in August 2000 that it was costing the country an estimated £50 billion a year, and its director general, John Abbott, said: 'The activities of organised crime threaten the economic fabric of this country, its tentacles reaching into the deepest and most remote crevices of our way of life.'

Not surprisingly gangsters are getting richer. Government agencies believe there are 39 criminal 'Mr Bigs' in the country with collective wealth of £220 million. None of these men has ever been convicted. They are the wealthiest in a list of 400 major criminals thought by the NCIS and Customs and Excise to be worth £440 million.[2]

Faster communications and a degree of electronic sophistication have given foreign criminals – Colombian drug suppliers, Chinese triads, Turkish heroin traffickers, West Indian Yardies – a foothold in the UK underworld. But the majority of the country's 938 leading gangs are made up of 'British Causasian' criminals – white, working-class men.

Today guns are widely available and used. In 1999 there were 33 murders in London linked to organised crime, and in the same year a sub-machine-gun could be bought in the city for £200. Contract killings, rare until the nineties, are now almost commonplace. Kidnappings are also much more common: there were 72 in 1999, most of them of criminals by other criminals.

It is unlikely that any gang will ever again dominate the capital to the extent that Jonathan Wild, or even the Kray twins, managed. But today the potential pickings are far greater, and there is room for many more criminals to grow rich without having to fight each other tooth and nail. While some gangs show the old loyalty to their 'manor' – the Arifs in south London, and to some extent the Adams family in north London – others form loose alliances which are dissolved after a successful crime, and the various participants are free to form other alliances.

Characters

Nightclubs have long been the focus of much underworld activity, and have attracted their share of official opprobrium. Kate Meyrick, queen of the nightclubs in twenties London, was a victim of this attitude. Nowadays she would be regarded as a successful businesswoman, courted by gossip columnists and City bankers.

Mrs Meyrick was born in County Clare and was famous as the first woman in Ireland to ride a bicycle. She married a doctor who abandoned her, leaving her at the end of the First World War with eight children to support, including two sons at Harrow and four daughters at Roedean.

Her first venture into clubs was as co-manager of Dalton's in Leicester Square, a frequent target for the police because of its reputation as a pick-up point for prostitutes. Although already in her forties, she went on to open dozens of clubs.

Fabian of the Yard described her as a neat, stern little woman 'who might easily have run a first-class seminary for well-brought-up young ladies.' If she was dowdy, the gangsters who frequented her clubs provided colour. She said: 'An evening-dress constituted no guarantee at all of its wearer's credentials: a party of apparently quite decent men might easily – only too often did – turn out to be one of the numerous gangs of bullies or racecourse terrorists who held sway.'[1] Or they might be police: Fred 'Nutty' Sharpe, who was to become head of the Flying Squad, describes raids on some of Mrs Meyrick's clubs, which were suspected of minor infringements of the licensing laws:

I went to the Manchester Club in evening dress and opera hat with a friend who was a man about town. We gained admittance without difficulty and at the same time a colleague similarly attired found his way in the '43' where the licensing laws were being flouted... The music stopped as the cry went up 'It's a raid'... I think the majority of them regarded it as a lark, for it gave them a thrill, but they changed their views when they appeared before the beak [magistrate].[2]

The 43 club was in Gerrard Street and was one of the clubs she opened after Dalton's was raided and she was fined. Others included the *Folies-Bergère* in Newman Street, the Little club in Golden Square, the Manhattan in Denman Street and the Silver Slipper in Regent Street. The 43 club, where a box of chocolates worth 3s 6d cost an exorbitant 2 guineas, was the most famous and successful, attracting bohemians like the artists Augustus John and Jacob Epstein and the writers Joseph Conrad and J B Priestley as well as gangsters and aristocrats. Kate's adopted daughter, Renée Meyrick, recalled: 'We would see the cream of Britain's aristocracy sitting at their tables while practically rubbing shoulders with them would be the roughest and toughest of the underworld, including the Sabini gang, who at that time were up to all sorts of tricks on the racecourses all over England.'

The gangsters were rowdy and demanded free drinks, but the real trouble came from the police. Kate got her first spell in Holloway prison in 1924 when she was fifty. Her reputation won the respect of the shoplifters who ran the place, and she made the best of things. While she was away her expensively educated daughters, who later married into the aristocracy, kept the clubs going.[3]

Further jail terms followed. On 22 May 1928 Kate got another six months in Holloway. Shortly after being released she was arrested again and charged with bribing a police officer. She got fifteen months' hard labour. She returned to the West End and opened more clubs, but in 1932 after two more six-month sentences she promised that she would retire. Her health was broken and she had lost her fortune in the Wall Street crash. When she died a year later, dance bands in the West End fell silent for two minutes as a tribute.

In her last months Kate wrote her memoirs, which end with the words: 'What does the future hold in store? It may hold disappointment, perhaps. But one thing I know it can never, never take away from me, and that is the love of Life, *real* Life, brilliant and pulsating.'

The smash-and-grab maestro and burglar Ruby Sparks was a regular at Mrs Meyrick's 43 club. Sparks was the most famous of the 'motor bandits' with his partner Lillian Goldstein. She was his getaway driver and her skill was legendary.

Sparks was born into a family of criminals in Tiger Yard, Bermondsey, in south-east London. His mother was a receiver, his father a bare-knuckle fighter who used to pickle his knuckles in brine. Ruby started his own criminal career by stealing registered letters from mail trains. His accomplices would pack him into a hamper and then send it on the train. Once aboard Ruby would emerge from hiding and rifle the mailbags.

He graduated to burglary, and it was after a robbery at the home of an Indian maharajah that he got his nickname Ruby. He found a box of red stones in a desk and after being told by a fence that they were fakes, he gave them away to any friend who wanted one. Later he discovered that he had given away £40,000 worth of real rubies.[4]

Goldstein came from a respectable Wembley Jewish family. She worked as a dressmaker until an unhappy love affair with a married criminal sent her off the rails.

Nutty Sharpe of the Flying Squad said of her: 'She usually drove a big Mercedes car. Sitting at the wheel with her man's raincoat collar turned up around her close-fitting little black hat, there wasn't much of her to see.' Of her legendary skill as a driver he said: 'She could whiz that great long tourer about with the skill of an artist'.

Newspapers described her as 'a girl bandit with dark bobbed hair, a small innocent-looking face and an active and intelligent brain'.[5]

Their career together lasted about five years. In 1927 Sparks was jailed for three years after being caught burgling a country house. The Bob-Haired Bandit was acquitted. For Sparks a series of jail sentences followed. He was a leader in the 1932 Dartmoor Prison mutiny, and in 1940 he escaped from the prison after being sent there for five years in 1939. He hid out in Goldstein's home in Wembley Park. He described their reunion.

> I was a bit taken aback how shocked her face was. I'd tried to spruce up before I saw her, and had got a lot of the muck off, but my fingers and mouth were burst open with frostbite and from so much punishment diet. I'd got sores all over me like sailors used to get before they found out about lime juice.
>
> She looked at me and I looked at her. The King and Queen of smash and grab. She looked older and tired and there was grey in her hair and the beginnings of lines down the side of her mouth. I saw she was screwing up her eyes to see me, and I asked her, 'Lil, do you wear spectacles now?' She looked a bit uncomfortable and said, 'Yes, sometimes, but only for reading.'[6]

Sparks teamed up with Billy Hill but Hill was caught during a raid in Bond Street. For a time Sparks worked with younger, more violent criminals but felt uncomfortable. After five months he was caught and sent back to Dartmoor. Lillian was convicted of harbouring him and sentenced to six months' imprisonment but served only three weeks. The judge then released her, saying she had 'followed a natural womanly instinct in trying to succour and protect this man, with whom you had intimate relations over a period of years.'

Lillian Goldstein told Sparks she had 'had enough of this bandit queen lark' and went back to Wembley Park for good. Sparks became an ice-cream salesman, then opened a newsagent's in the Chalk Farm area, and finally at the end of the war a club, the Penguin in Regent Street.[7]

The role of the investigative crime reporter is sadly diminished. I worked at the *People* when Sam Campbell was trying to build it up, and remember him, green eyeshade in place like the best Hollywood editors, writing the leading articles, reading proofs and rewriting headlines. One of the main weapons in his campaign was the reporter Duncan Webb.

Webb had great success as a crusading journalist exposing

criminals, particularly the vice kings of Soho. Yet he married a woman who had been a nightclub hostess and was the former wife of a murderer, and he ghosted the partisan life of gangster Billy Hill, whom he regarded, with reservations, as a 'genius and a kind and tolerant man'.

There is a consistency to Webb's short life. He was determined to expose wrongdoing, and not to count the cost, which included having his arm broken by Jack Spot and being attacked by hoodlums in the pay of the vice kings. When his editor at the *Evening Standard* didn't share his obsession with the shadier side of life in London, he left, later writing: 'One of the reasons I left... was that my superiors claimed that it was not the business of a newspaper to go prying into the affairs of corpses with no arms. Lady So-and-So, the wife of the proprietor, would not like it, I was told. They pooh-poohed the idea. "We are a respectable newspaper," they said. "After all, murders are so vulgar." '[8]

In 1949, by now working for the People, Webb got a little too close to his subject for objectivity. The body of car dealer Stanley Setty was found on the Tillingham marshes in Essex. He was typical of a kind of shady post-war businessman, involved in currency and coupon frauds. He was also said to be a gunrunner.

The man who was eventually arrested, Donald Hume, swam in the same pool of corrupt deals involving stolen cars and forged petrol coupons.[9] Webb met and courted his ex-wife Cynthia and married her shortly before his death in September 1958 at the age of 41.

Webb's greatest journalistic triumph was the exposure of the Messina brothers, the Soho vice kings. While he didn't invent the phrase, 'I made an excuse and left', he found himself in many tricky situations. He described how, as he tried to interview the Messinas' girls by pretending to be a client, he was picked up by a Frenchwoman in Shepherd's Market. 'She was tall and extremely fat. Over her shoulders fox furs were draped. Her jet-black hair, parted in the centre, was swept back. Her lips were thick. She took me into a flat at 49a Hertford Street.' When Webb decided to leave he offered the woman ten shillings. 'She literally roared. She spat at me through clenched teeth. Even on the lower deck in the Navy I never heard such a torrent of obscene blasphemy.'[10]

On another occasion he picked up a Swiss woman called Jean in Bond Street. She took him to a room in Stafford Street and after he had learned what he could he told her that he had changed his mind about having sex. 'She spat at me, aimed several blows at me and pushed me towards the door. As I was about to descend the stairs she gave me a violent kick in the back.'[11]

When his exposé of the Messinas was printed his friendship with Billy Hill protected him from their revenge. Hill, who had the traditional English gangster's dislike of ponces and foreigners, summoned some of his heavies. The five angry brothers went to the Brunswick Arms in Bloomsbury, Webb's local, for a showdown. They found Webb with Billy Hill and some tough-looking men, and discreetly retreated.[12]

Marthe Watts, the Messina prostitute and madam who retired after more than 400 convictions for prostitution, and might have been expected to harbour a grudge against the man who did so much to destroy their empire, wrote in her memoir *The Men in My Life* of 'my poor friend Duncan, whom I came to know so well'. It was as good a tribute as any to a puzzling man.

Bibliography

Ackroyd, Peter. *Dickens' London*. London, Headline, 1987.

Ackroyd, Peter. *London: A Biography*. London, Chatto and Windus, 2000.

Acton, William. *Prostitution Considered in its Moral, Social and Sanitary Aspects...* 1857.

Anon. *An Authentic History of the Parentage, Birth, Education, Marriages, Issue and Practices of the Famous Jonathan Wild*. 1725.

Archenholz, J W Von. *A Picture of England*. 1789.

Archer, Thomas. *The Pauper, the Thief and the Convict*. 1865.

Beames, T. *The Rookeries of London, Past, Present and Prospective*. 1850.

Beveridge, Peter. *Inside the CID*. Evan Brothers, 1957.

Bidwell, George. *Forging His Chains*. Connecticut, Hartford, 1888.

Biron, Sir Chartres. *Without Prejudice*. London, Faber and Faber, 1936.

Bloch, Ivan. *Sexual Life in England Past and Present*. London, 1958.

Booth, Charles. *Life and Labour of the People in London*. London, Macmillan, 1902.

Burford, E J. *Wits, Wenchers and Wantons, London's Low Life: Covent Garden in the 18th Century*. London, 1986.

Burford, E J. *The Orrible Synne*. London, Calder and Boyars, 1973.

Burnett, John. *Liquid Pleasures, a Social History of Drink in Modern Britain*. Routledge, 1999.

Burrington. *An answer to Dr William Bracknridge's Letter...* 1775.

Campbell, Duncan. *The Underworld*. London, Penguin, 1996.

Chesney, Kellow. *The Victorian Underworld*. London, Penguin, 1991.

Clutterbuck. *Drugs, Crime and Corruption.*
The Complete Newgate Calendar. Privately printed for the Navarre Society, London, 1926.

Cox, Barry; Shirley, John; and Short, Martin, *The Fall of Scotland Yard*. London, Penguin, 1997.

Day, S P. *Juvenile Crime, its Causes, Character and Cure*. 1858.

Defoe, Daniel. *The...Account of the Life...of the Late Jonathan Wilde*. 1725.

Defoe, Daniel. *The History of the Remarkable Life of John Sheppard*. 1724.

Dickens, Charles. 'On Duty with Inspector Field', in *Reprinted Pieces*.

Dilnot, George, Bles, Geoffrey, (ed). *The Bank of England Forgery*, London, 1929.

Ehrman, John. *Pitt the Younger*. London, Constable, 1969.

Fabian, Robert. *London After Dark*. Naldrett Press, 1954.

Fabian, Robert. *Fabian of the Yard*. Cedar Books, 1956.

Fordham, Peta. *The Robbers' Tale*. London, Hodder and Stoughton, 1965.

Fraser, Antonia. *The Weaker Vessel*. London, Mandarin Paperbacks, 1993.

George, M Dorothy. *London Life in the Eighteenth Century*. London, reprinted Penguin, 1992.

Gilmour, Ian. *Riot, Risings and Revolution*. London, Pimlico, 1992.

Gosling, John. *Ghost Squad*. London, W H Allen, 1959.

Hart, Edward T. *Britain's Godfather*. True Crime Library, 1993.

Henriques, Fernando. *Prostitution and Society*. London, 3 vols, 1962–8.

Hibbert, Christopher. *The Roots of Evil*. 1963.

Hill, Billy. *Boss of Britain's Underworld*. Naldrett Press, 1955.

Hollingshead, J. *Ragged London in 1861*. 1861.

Holloway, Robert. *The Phoenix of Sodom: or, the Vere Street Coterie*. 1813.

Horlor, Sydney. *London's Underworld*. London, Hutchinson, 1934.

Hughes, David. *The Age of Austerity*. London, Penguin, 1964.

Inwood, Stephen. *A History of London*. London, Macmillan, 1998.

Janson, Hank. *Jack Spot: Man of a Thousand Cuts*. Alexander Moring, 1959.

Johnson, W Branch. *The English Prison Hulks*. Phillimore and Company Ltd, Shopwyke Hall, Chichester, Sussex, 1970.

Kray, Reggie and Ronnie with Fred Dinenage, *Our Story*. Pan Books, London, 1988.

Lambrianou, Tony. *Inside the Firm*. Smith Gryphon, 1991.

Leeson, Ex-Detective Sergeant B. *Lost London*. Stanley Paul and Co, no date.

Linebaugh, Peter. *The London Hanged*. Allen Lane, 1991.

Lock, Joan. *Scotland Yard Casebook*. London, Robert Hale, 1993.

Low, Donald A. *The Regency Underworld*. Sutton, 1999.

Macartney, Wilfred. *Walls Have Mouths*. London, Gollancz, 1936.

Martin, Frank. *Rogues' River, Crime on the River Thames in the Eighteenth Century*. Ian Henry Publications, Hornchurch Essex, 1983.

Mayhew, Hemyng, Binney and Halliday. *London Labour and the London Poor*, 1861–2.

Mayhew and Binney. *The Criminal Prisons of London and Scenes of Prison Life*. London, Griffin Bohn and Company, 1862.

McLynn, Frank. *Crime and Punishment in Eighteenth-century England*. London, Routledge, 1989.

McVicar, John. *McVicar By Himself*. London, Arrow, 1979.

Misson, H. *Memoirs and Observations of his Travels over England*. 1719.

Moore, Lucy. *The Thieves' Opera*. London, Viking, 1997.

Morris Norval and Rothman David J, (ed) *Oxford History of the Prison*. Oxford University Press, 1995.

Morton, James. *Gangland*. Warner Books 1993.

Murphy, Robert. *Smash and Grab: Gangsters in the London Underworld 1920–60*. London, Faber and Faber, 1993.

Murray, Venetia. *High Society in the Regency Period*. London, Penguin, 1998.

Narborough, F. *Murder on my Mind*. Allen Windgate, 1959.

Nokes, David. Introduction to Henry Fielding's *Jonathan Wild the Great*. London, Penguin, 1982.

Pearson, John. *The Profession of Violence*. Panther, 1973.

Picard, Lisa. *Dr Johnson's London*. London, Weidenfeld and Nicholson, 2000.

Pike, L O. *A History of Crime in England...* 1876.

Plumb, J H. *Men and Places*. The Cresset Press, 1963.

Porter, Roy. *London: A Social History*. Hamish Hamilton, 1994.

Porter, Roy. *English Society in the Eighteenth Century*. London, Viking, 1982.

Porter, Roy. *The Greatest Benefit to Mankind: A Medical History of Humanity from Antiquity to the Present*. London, Fontana Press, 1997.

Pringle, Patrick. *The Thief Takers*. London, Museum Press Ltd, 1958.

Read, Leonard and Morton, James. *Nipper*. London, Macdonald, 1991.

Read, Piers Paul, *The Train Robbers*. London, W H Allen and Co, 1978.

Richardson, Charles. *My Manor*. London, Sidgwick & Jackson, 1991.

Richmond, Dr Guy. *Prison Doctor*. Nunaga, 1975.

Roberts, Nickie. *Whores in History*. London, HarperCollins, 1992.

Rogers, Pat. *The Augustan Vision*. London, Weidenfeld and Nicholson, 1974.

Rose, Andrew. *Stinie, Murder on the Common*. The Bodley Head, 1985.

Salgado, Gamini. *The Elizabethan Underworld*. London, 1992.

Samuel, Raphael. *East End Underworld. Chapters in the life of Arthur Harding*. Routledge and Kegan Paul, 1981.

Sharpe, F D. *Sharpe of the Flying Squad*. John Long, 1938.

Silverman, Jon. *Crack of Doom*. London, Headline, 1988.

Smithies, Edward. *Crime in Wartime*. London, George Allen, 1982.

Thomas, Donald. *The Victorian Underworld*. John Murray, 1998.

Tietjen, A. *Soho*. London, Allan Wingate, 1956.

Tobias, J J. *Crime and Industrial Society in the Nineteenth Century*. Pelican, 1972.

Tristan, Flora. *Promenades dans Londres*. 1840.

Uglow, Jenny. *Hogarth: A Life and a World*. London, Faber and Faber, 1997.

Viccei, Valerio. *Knightsbridge, the Robbery of the Century*. London, Blake Hardbacks, 1992,

Wakefield, E G. *Facts Relating to the Punishment of Death in the Metropolis*. 1832.

Walker, Captain C. *Authentic Memoirs of the Life, Intrigues and Adventures of the Celebrated Sally Salisbury*. 1723.

Waller, Maureen. *1700: Scenes from London Life*. London, Hodder and Stoughton, 2000.

Walpole Correspondence. Yale, Newhaven, 1934–7.

Watts, Marthe. *The Men in My Life*. Christopher Johnson, 1960.

Webb, Duncan. *Line-up for Crime*. Frederick Muller, 1956.

Weinreb, Ben and Hibbert, Christopher. *The London Encyclopaedia*. Papermac, 1993.

Whelan, Jim. *Jail Journey*. London, Secker and Warburg, 1940.

White, Jerry, *London in the Twentieth Century*. London, Viking, 2001.

Wilson, A N. *The Faber Book of London*. London, Faber and Faber, 1993.

Wilson, Mary. *Exhibition of Female Flagellants*. 1777.

Notes

PREFACE

1. Peter Ackroyd. *London: A Biography*, Chatto and Windus, 2000.
2. Crime statistics from early in the last century are unreliable because of serious underreporting of offences. Nevertheless, the contrast between the 88 robberies known to the police in 1906 and the total of almost 27,000 recorded in 1997–8 is startling. (Jerry White. *London in the Twentieth Century*, Viking 2001.)

INTRODUCTION

1. The canting vocabulary of the underworld had ancient origins. In the eighteenth century thieves might *bite the bill from the cull* – steal a sword from a man's side. They would take *lobs* from behind *rattlers* – remove luggage from a moving coach. Some would *nim the nab* – steal a man's hat from his head and make off with it. *Clouters* took handkerchiefs from pockets, *files* took watches or cash. Burglars would *mill a ken* – rob a house. *Milling the gig with a betty* was breaking down the door with an iron crowbar, *milling the glaze* was smashing a window before a robbery. *Faggot and stall* was gagging all the people in a house before the thieves escaped with the loot. (Maureen Waller, *1700: Scenes from London Life*, Hodder and Stoughton, 2000.) To *snitch* or *babble* was to make a confession or inform, *make* and *nime* was to steal, *mill* was to rob, *rapp* to commit perjury, *run*

329

rusty to betray, *bone* to take. In the nineteenth century we get *chiv* for knife, *bug hunting* for robbing drunks, *broadsman* for cardsharp, *cracksman* for safebreaker, *crow* for look-out man, *family* for members of the criminal class, *flying the blue pidgeon* for stealing roof lead, *finny* for a five pound note, *glim* for venereal disease, *haybag* for a woman, *hoisting* for shoplifting, *judy* for a woman or prostitute, *jerryshop* for pawnbroker, *kidsman* for organiser of child thieves, *macer* for cheat or sharper, *miltonian* for policeman, *nibbed* for arrested, *pig* for policeman or detective . . . and many, many others.

2. Pat Rogers. *The Augustan Vision*. Weidenfeld and Nicholson, 1974.
3. Ian Gilmour. *Riot, Risings and Revolution*. Pimlico, 1992.
4. Christopher Hibbert. *Highwaymen*. London, 1967.
5. *The Gentlemen's Magazine*, 1661.
6. James Uglow. *Hogarth, A Life and a World*. London, Faber and Faber, 1997.
7. J W Von Archenholz. *A Picture of England*. 1789.
8. Roy Porter, *London: A Social History*, Hamish Hamilton, 1994.
9. Mare M L and Quarrell W H. *Lichtenberg's Visits to England*. Oxford, 1938.
10. L O Pike. *A History of Crime in England* . . . 1876
11. Christopher Hibbert. *The Roots of Evil*. 1963.

THE ORIGINAL GODFATHER

1. Daniel Defoe. *The History of the Remarkable Life of John Sheppard*. 1724.
2. Defoe, *ibid*.
3. Defoe, *ibid*.
4. Defoe, *ibid*.
5. When he parted from Milliner later Wild cut off her ear with his silver sword 'to mark her for a bitch'. Yet he seems to have paid her a pension for life. She had been known as his wife, although he was apparently already married. He had five 'wives' in all. Defoe writes about one of them: 'In this the time of his prosperity he married a third wife (his two former, *if they were*

wives, being still living). Her name was Elizabeth Man, who though she was a woman of the town, was yet a very sensible and agreeable person; and her short history is this. He loved her above all the other women he had taken for wives, and lived publicly with her, which he did not with any of the rest. He had no children by her, but she was, as he himself confessed, a true penitent for all her former life, and she made him an excellent wife. She expiated her former bad life by a formal full confession and penance, having on that occasion been persuaded to turn Roman Catholic, and having received absolution from her confessor, lived a very sober life for some years, after which she died and was buried at St Pancras in the Fields. And Jonathan retained such an impression of the sanctity and goodness of this wife, that he never forgot it as long as he lived; and ordered himself to be buried close to her when he died, which his friends took care to see performed, about two of the clock in the morning.'

6. In 1718 Hitchen published an anonymous pamphlet exposing Wild. 'The thief-taker is a thief-maker,' it said. Wild replied in another pamphlet, accusing Hitchen of 'plundering the purses, abusing the persons, and the highest impositions, as well upon the guilty as the innocent.' He also accused Hitchen of homosexuality. 'I'll take care ... that no sodomitish assembly be held without your Excellency's presence and making choice for your own use, in order to which I'll engage to a female dress for your Excellency much further than what your Excellency has been accustomed to wear.'

    Nine years later Hitchens was found guilty of 'sodomitical practices' and sentenced to stand in a pillory near the Strand. He wore a suit of armour while he was in the stocks, but nevertheless was so badly battered he was released before his hour was up, and never recovered. He died less than six months later from his injuries.

7. Frank McLynn. *Crime and Punishment in Eighteenth-century England*. London, Routledge, 1989.

8. Lucy Moore. *The Thieves' Opera*. Viking, 1997.

9. Moore, *ibid*.

10. McLynn, *ibid.*
11. McLynn, *ibid.*
12. One of Wild's victims, John Meffs, who was hanged in London in 1721 at the age of forty, had a remarkable life. The son of French Huguenot parents, he was apprenticed to a weaver but became a thief. He had been sentenced to hang in 1717, but bailiffs served a writ for debt on the hangman before he could carry out the sentence. The mob waiting to see the execution pounced on the hangman, and 'beat him to death'. Meffs was reprieved, and transported to America. On the voyage out his ship was captured by pirates, who included the legendary women Anne Bonny and Mary Read. Most of the felons agreed to throw in their lot with the pirates but Meffs refused, and was marooned on a desert island. He found a canoe, and made his way to the American mainland. He later returned to England, became a thief again and was captured and imprisoned in Newgate. He escaped with the aid of a bricklayer and fled to Hatfield, where he fell into the hands of Wild, who turned him in to the authorities in return for 'a very handsome sum'. (Peter Linebaugh, *The London Hanged*, Allen Lane, 1991)
13. Defoe, *ibid.*
14. Defoe, *ibid.*
15. Defoe, *ibid.*
16. Patrick Pringle. *The Thief Takers*. London, Museum Press Ltd, 1958.
17. Quoted Ben Weinreb and Christopher Hibbert. *The London Encyclopaedia*. Papermac, 1993.
18. Linebaugh, *ibid.*
19. Linebaugh, *ibid.*
20. Linebaugh, *ibid.*
21. Linebaugh, *ibid.*
22. David Nokes, introduction to Henry Fielding's *Jonathan Wild the Great*, Penguin, 1982.
23. Moore, *ibid.*
24. Daniel Defoe, *The ... Account of the Life ... of the Late Jonathan Wild*. 1725.
25. Linebaugh, *ibid.*

THE GREAT WEN

1. 'The Great Wen' is a traditional derogatory reference to London.
2. Dorothy M George. *London Life in the Eighteenth Century.* Penguin, 1965.
3. Burrington. *An answer to Dr William Bracknridge's Letter...* 1775.
4. 'London' by Samuel Johnson.
5. Nickie Roberts. *Whores in History.* London, HarperCollins, 1992.
6. H Misson. *Memoirs and Observations of his Travels over England.* 1719.
7. Ned Ward. *The London Spy.* 1709.
8. The play didn't just make the fortunes of Gay and Rich: the Duke of Bolton was so captivated by the actress Lavinia Fenton, who played Polly Peachum, that he attended the play every night and at the end of the season made her his mistress. Gay wrote to a friend: 'The D of B I hear hath run away with Polly Peachum, having settled £400 a year on her during pleasure, and upon disagreement £200 a year.' When the Duke's wife died 22 years later he married Lavinia, who had borne him three sons.

FOOTPADS AND PICKPOCKETS

1. Frank McLynn. *Crime and Punishment in Eighteenth-century England.* London, Routledge, 1989.

LIGHT AND HEAVY HORSEMEN

1. Patrick Colquhoun. *A Treatise on the Commerce and Police of the River Thames.* 1800.

HIGHWAYMEN AND SMUGGLERS: GENTLEMEN AND RUFFIANS

1. Peter Linebaugh. *The London Hanged.*
2. Walpole Correspondence, No. 20 page 199, Yale, Newhaven, 1934–7.

3. Anon. *An Authentic History of the Parentage, Birth, Education, Marriages, Issue and Practices of the Famous Jonathan Wild.* 1725.
4. 'Sir Robert Walpole's Wine'. J H Plumb. *Men and places*. The Cresset Press, 1963.
5. *Ibid.*
6. John Ehrman. *Pitt the Younger*. Constable, 1969.

CITADELS OF VICE AND CRIME

1. J J Tobias. *Crime and Industrial Society in the Nineteenth Century*. Pelican, 1972.
2. J Hollingshead. *Ragged London in 1861*. 1861.
3. T Beames. T*he Rookeries of London, Past, Present and Prospective*. 1850.
4. Charles Dickens. 'On Duty with Inspector Field', in *Reprinted Pieces*.
5. In 1851 the St Giles area had 69 common lodging houses, fifteen slaughter-houses, a workhouse, a police-station and 'upwards of seventy streets, courts and alleys, in which there is no thoroughfare, or which are approached by passages under houses'. Its population density, birth, illegitimacy and death rates, were well above the London average.
6. Tobias, *ibid.*
7. Charles Booth. *Life and Labour of the People in London*. Macmillan, 1902.
8. Dr Tobias wrote the biography of Isaac 'Ikey' Solomons, who some see as the model for Fagin in *Oliver Twist*. Property worth £20,000 was said to have been seized when his house was raided. The writer of programme notes for a performance of *Oliver Twist* at the Royal Surrey Theatre in 1838 cited Solomons to demonstrate the authenticity of Dickens's portrait of Fagin, and he added: 'The City Officers, in pursuing that great receiver of stolen goods, Ikey Solomons, discovered cellars and trap doors, and all sorts of places of concealment, which they found full of stolen goods.'

   Solomons was said to have paid the highest prices for stolen banknotes. He was arrested in 1827 and was found to have a fortune in cash, watches and jewellery on him. The police went to a house where Solomons had been staying and found property worth about £350.

Solomons escaped from the Black Maria on his way to Newgate – the police found out, too late, that it was driven by his father-in-law – and made his way to Australia where he joined his wife Ann, who had been transported with other members of his family. After a long legal battle he was sent back to England to face trial. He was found guilty, sentenced to fourteen years' transportation, and on 31 May 1831 he left Newgate for the last time, bound for Van Diemen's Land. He and Ann were reunited but discovered that by now they loathed each other. When Ann was pardoned in 1840 they split up, and Ikey died ten years later. He left only £70.

9. Henry Mayhew and John Binney. *The Criminal Prisons of London and Scenes of Prison Life*. London, Griffin Behn and Company, 1862.

SCHOOLS OF VICE

1. S P Day. *Juvenile Crime, its Causes, Character and Cure*. 1858.
2. Henry Mayhew, Bracebridge Hemyng, John Binney and Andrew Halliday. *London Labour and the London Poor*. 1861–2.
3. J J Tobias. *Crime and Industrial Society in the Nineteenth Century*. Pelican, 1972.
4. E G Wakefield, *Facts Relating to the Punishment of Death in the Metropolis*, 1832.
5. Mayhew, Hemyng, Binney and Halliday. *London Labour and the London Poor*. 1861–2.

THE GREATEST TRAIN ROBBERY

1. The story of the Great Bullion Robbery and Jim the Penman was told in *The Trial of Jim the Penman*, ed. George Dilnot, Geoffrey Bles, 1929. There are recent retellings of it by Donald Thomas in *The Victorian Underworld* and Kellow Chesney, whose book is also called *The Victorian Underworld*.

CHARLIES, PEELERS AND THE MET

1. Frank McLynn. *Crime and Punishment in Eighteenth-century England*. London, Routledge, 1989.
2. The Runners could not live on their pay of a guinea a week, later raised to 25 shillings, or on their share of rewards, which brought in only a further twenty to thirty pounds a year, as a House of Commons committee was told in 1816. But they could make a good living from private detective work, which they seem to have been remarkably free to undertake.

    A Runner named Henry Goddard, who was born in 1800 and enlisted in the Foot Patrol in 1824, left an invaluable record, *Memoirs of a Bow Street Runner*, (London, Museum Press Limited, 1956) which sheds much light on the service. One case he was involved in will give a flavour of the times and police methods.

    On the evening of 30 October 1836 the Defiance mail coach left Dover for London, carrying among other things bags of gold. When the coach arrived in London the gold was checked and one bag was missing.

    Goddard questioned the guard and coachman, and the porter who loaded the gold into the coach, a man called Matthews. He also visited all the stations between Dover and London where the coach had changed horses, questioning all the ostlers, stable-keepers and passengers involved, and searched stables and lofts. He finally came to the conclusion that the porter Matthews was the thief, although the owners of the hotel where the man was employed told him he was mistaken, as Matthews had worked for them for many years and was thoroughly honest.

    Goddard had Matthews's garden dug over, without finding any gold. A month later he searched Matthews's house again, finding that he had bought new furniture, and then discovered twenty gold sovereigns hidden in one of the rooms. Matthews was arrested but acquitted at his trial.

    Three months later, as Goddard was standing on the steps of Bow Street police station, Matthews approached him and asked him if he would meet him that afternoon. Goddard agreed, but at the last moment was sent off on Home Office business. When he failed to turn up Matthews went to Dover and 'told the inspector of police there that he was a wretched man and had never been happy since his trial. He admitted to the inspector that he stole the bag of gold, and had buried it in his next-door neighbour's garden.'

THE EAST END

1. F D Sharpe. *Sharpe of the Flying squad*. John Long, 1938.
2. Ex-Detective Sergeant B Leeson, *Lost London*. Stanley Paul and Co, no date.
3. Leeson, *ibid*.
4. Andrew Rose. *Stinie, Murder on the Common*, The Bodley Head, 1985.

GUNS AND GANGSTERS

1. Raphael Samuel, *East End Underworld. Chapters in the life of Arthur Harding*. Routledge and Kegan Paul, 1981.
2. Sir Chartres Biron. *Without Prejudice*. London, Faber and Faber, 1936.
3. *Illustrated Police News*, 23 December 1911.

CAREER GANGSTERS

1. Raphael Samuel. *East End Underworld*. London, Routledge, 1981.
2. Samuel, *idid*.
3. Robert Murphy. *Smash and Grab: Gangsters in the London Underworld 1920–60*. London, Faber and Faber, 1993.
4. Murphy, *ibid*.
5. F Narborough. *Murder on my Mind*. Allan Windgate, 1959.
6. Edward T Hart. *Britain's Godfather*. True Crime Library, 1997.
7. Billy Hill. *Boss of Britain's Underworld*. Naldrett Press, 1955.
8. James Morton. *Gangland*. Warner Books, 1993.
9. Murphy, *ibid*.

10. Hart, *ibid.*
11. Ronnie and Reggie Kray. *Our Story*. London, Pan Books, 1988

CHANGING THE MAP OF THE UNDERWORLD

1. Donald Thomas. *The Victorian Underworld*. John Murray, 1998.
2. Robert Murphy. *Smash and Grab, Gangsters in the London Underworld 1920–60*. London, Faber and Faber, 1993.
3. Stephen Inwood. *A History of London*. London, Macmillan, 1998.
4. Inwood, *ibid.*
5. Billy Hill, *Boss of Britain's Underworld*. Naldrett Press, 1955.
6. Edward Smithies. *Crime in Wartime*. London, George Allen, 1982.
7. Quoted in Murphy, *ibid.*
8. John Gosling. *Ghost Squad*. WH Allen, 1959.

THE BATTLE FOR THE WEST END

1. Robert Murphy. *Smash and Grab, Gangsters in the London Underworld 1920–60*. London, Faber and Faber, 1993.
2. *Daily Sketch*, 29 September 1958.
3. *London Evening Standard*, 6 January 1986
4. Murphy, *ibid.*
5. Murphy, *ibid.*
6. Leonard Read and James Morton. *Nipper*. Macdonald, London, 1991.
7. Billy Hill. *Boss of London's Underworld*. Naldrett Press, 1955.
8. Hill, *ibid.*
9. Murphy, *ibid.*
10. David Hughes on *Spivs in The Age of Austerity*. Penguin, London, 1964.
11. Hill, *ibid.*
12. Hill, *ibid.*
13. Hill, *ibid.*
14. Murphy, *ibid.*
15. Hill, *ibid.*
16. *Daily Sketch*, 3 October 1955.

17. Peter Beveridge. *Inside the CID*. Evan Brothers, 1957.
18. Murphy, *ibid*.
19. Murphy, *ibid*.
20. Duncan Campbell. *The Underworld*. London, Penguin, 1996.
21. John Pearson. *The Profession of Violence*. Panther, 1973.
22. Pearson, *ibid*.
23. Murphy, *ibid*.
24. Murphy, *ibid*.
25. Murphy, *ibid*.
26. Murphy, *ibid*.
27. James Morton. *Gangland*. Warner Books, 1993.

ANOTHER TRAIN ROBBERY

1. Peta Fordham. *The Robbers' Tale*. London, Hodder and Stoughton, 1965.
2. Piers Paul Read. *The Train Robbers*. WH Allen and Co, London, 1978.

THE FIRM

1. Leonard Read and James Morton. *Nipper*. London, Macdonald, 1991.
2. John Pearson. *The Profession of Violence*. Panther, 1973.
3. Pearson, *ibid*.
4. Pearson, *ibid*.
5. Reggie and Ronnie Kray. *Our Story*. London, Pan Books, 1988.
6. Reggie and Ronnie Kray, *ibid*.
7. Pearson, *ibid*.
8. Pearson, *ibid*.
9. Reggie and Ronnie Kray, *ibid*.
10. Duncan Campbell. *The Underworld*. London, Penguin, 1996.

THE TORTURE GANG

1. Charles Richardson. *My Manor*. London, Sidgwick & Jackson, 1991.

2. Richardson, *ibid.*
3. Richardson, *ibid.*
4. Duncan Campbell. *The Underworld*. London, Penguin, 1996.

THE LESSER BREEDS

1. James Morton, *Gangland*. Warner Books, 1993.
2. Morton, *ibid.*
3. Morton, *ibid.*

SUPERCROOKS AND SUPERGRASSES

1. Robert Murphy, *Smash and Grab, Gangsters in the London Underworld 1920–60*. Faber and Faber, 1993.
2. Duncan Campbell, *The Underworld*. Penguin, 1996.
3. John McVicar, *McVicar By Himself*. London, Arrow, 1979.
4. James Morton. *Gangland*. Warner Books, 1993.
5. The *Independent*, 13 April 2000.
6. The *Independent*, 15 April 2000.
7. Kim Sengupta and Paul Lashmar, the *Independent*, 15 April 2000.
8. The *Independent*, 15 April 2000.
9. The *Independent*, *ibid.*

SIN CITY

1. Kellow Chesney, *The Victorian Underworld*. Penguin, 1991.
2. E J Burford, *The Orrible Synne*. London, Calder and Boyars, 1973.
3. Antonia Fraser, *The Weaker Vessel*. London, 1993.
4. Burford, *ibid.*
5. Burford, *ibid.*
6. Roy Porter, *London: A Social History*. Hamish Hamilton, 1994.
7. Boswell's tastes were catholic. Between the ages of twenty and 29 he slept with three married gentlewomen, four actresses and Rousseau's mistress Thérese Le Vasseur; kept three lower-class women as regular mistresses, and had sex with sixty

streetwalkers. He caught gonorrhoea seventeen times. Some of his friends thought his sexual appetites abnormal. He resented having to pay the surgeons five guineas a time for treatment. Condoms had been known since the seventeenth century. They were usually made from sheep's intestines and were used to avoid infection rather than pregnancy.

8. Jack Harris, *List of Covent Garden Ladies or the New Atlantis*, 1764.
9. Nickie Roberts, *Whores in History*. London, HarperCollins, 1992.
10. Captain C Walker, *Authentic Memoirs of the Life, Intrigues and Adventures of the Celebrated Sally Salisbury*, 1723.
11. E J Burford, *Wits, Wenchers and Wantons, London's Low Life: Covent Garden in the 18th Century*. London, 1986.
12. Roberts, *ibid*.
13. Captain Walker, *ibid*.
14. Lucy Moore, *The Thieves' Opera*. Viking, 1997.
15. Jenny Uglow, *Hogarth, A Life and a World*. London, Faber and Faber, 1997.
16. *Some Authentic Memoirs of the Life of Colonel C—s, Rape-Master of Great Britain*, 1730.
17. Uglow, *ibid*.
18. Roberts, *ibid*.
19. Some idea of the tastes catered for by London brothels in the second half of the eighteenth century is given in a price list for Mrs Hayes' 'cloister', a house in the fashionable West End. Although the style is facetious, the prices are believed to be accurate.

Sunday the 9th January

A young girl for Alderman Drybones. Nelly Blossom, about 19 years old, who has had no one for four days, and who is a virgin ....20 guineas
A girl of 19 years, not older, for Baron Harry Flagellum. Nell Hardy from Bow Street, Bat Flourish from Berners Street or Miss Birch from Chapel Street .... 10 guineas
A beautiful girl for Lord Spaan. Black Moll from Hedge Lane, who is very strong.. 5 guineas

For Colonel Tearall, a gentle woman. Mrs Mitchell's servant, who has just come from the country and has not been out in the world .... 10 guineas
For Dr Frettext, after consultation hours, a young agreeable person, sociable, with a white skin and a soft hand. Polly Nimblewrist from Oxford, or Jenny Speedyhand from Mayfair .... 2 guineas
Lady Loveit, who has come from the baths at Bath, and who is disappointed in her affair with Lord Alto, wants to have something better, and to be well served this evening. Capt. O'Thunder or Sawney Rawbone .... 50 guineas
For his Excellency Count Alto, a fashionable woman for an hour only. Mrs Smirk who comes from Dunkirk, or Miss Graceful from Paddington ....10 guineas
For Lord Pyebald, to play a game of piquet, for *titillatione mammarum* and so on, with no other object. Mrs Tredrille from Chelsea .... 5 guineas

20. Lisa Picard, *Dr Johnson's London*. London, Weidenfeld and Nicholson, 2000.
21. Chesney, *ibid*.
22. Dr Fernando Henriques, *Prostitution and Society*, Volume III, London, 1968.
23. Roberts, *ibid*.
24. Roberts, *ibid*.
25. Donald Thomas, *The Victorian Underworld*. London, John Murray, 1998.
26. Roberts, *ibid*.
27. Roberts, *ibid*.
28. Edward Smithies, *Crime in Wartime*. London, George Allen, 1982.
29. Stephen Inwood, *A History of London*. London, Macmillan, 1996.
30. Smithies, *ibid*.
31. Inwood, *ibid*.
32. Smithies, *ibid*.
33. Edward Smithies, *Crime in Wartime*. London, George Allen, 1982.

34. Smithies, *ibid.*
35. Smithies, *ibid.*

VICE EMPIRES

1. Marthe Watts, *The Men in My Life*. Christopher Johnson, 1960.
2. James Martin, *Gangland*. Warner Books, 1993.
3. Duncan Webb, *Line-up for Crime*. London, Frederick Muller, 1956.
4. Duncan Campbell, *The Underworld*. London, Penguin, 1996.
5. Nickie Roberts, *Whores in History*. London, HarperCollins, 1992.
6. The *Independent*, 18 June 2001

BENT COPPERS

1. The Regency diarist and commentator Captain Rees Howell Gronow has left us a description of Townsend at the coronation of George IV at Westminster Abbey in July 1821:

> At this gorgeous solemnity it fell to my lot to be on guard on the platform along which the royal procession had to pass, in order to reach the Abbey. The crowd that had congregated in this locality exceeded anything I had ever before seen; struggling, fighting, shrieking and laughing were the order of the day among this motley assemblage. Little Townsend, the chief police officer of Bow Street, with his flaxen wig and broad-brimmed hat, was to be seen hurrying from one end of the platform to the other, assuming immense importance. On the approach of the cortege you heard this officious person, 'dressed with a little brief authority', hallooing with all his might, 'Gentlemen and ladies, take care of your pockets, for you are surrounded by thieves;' and hearty laughter responded to Mr Townsend's advice.
>
> When the procession was seen to approach, and the royal canopy came in sight, those below the platform were

straining with all their might to get a peep at the Sovereign, and the confusion at this moment can be better imagined than described. The pickpockets, of course, availed themselves of the confusion, and in the twinkling of an eye there were more watches and purses snatched from the pockets of his Majesty's loyal subjects than perhaps on any previous occasion.

Amidst the crowd a respectable gentleman from the Principality [Wales] hallooed out in his provincial tongue, 'Mr Townsend, Mr Townsend, I have been robbed of my gold watch and purse, containing all my money. What am I to do? What am I to do to get home? I have come two hundred miles to see this sight, and instead of receiving satisfaction or hospitality, I am robbed by those cut-throats called "the swell mob".' This eloquent speech had a very different effect upon the mob than the poor Welshman had reason to expect: for all of a sudden the refrain of the song of 'Sweet Home' was shouted by a thousand voices; and the mob bawled out, 'Go back to your goats, my good fellow.' The indignities that were heaped upon this unfortunate gentleman during the royal procession, and his appearance after the King had passed, created pity in the minds of all honest persons who witnessed this disgusting scene: his hat was beaten over his eyes, and his coat, neckcloth &c. were torn off his body. For there were no police in those days, and with the exception of a few constables and some soldiers, there was no force to prevent the metropolis from being burnt to the ground, if it had pleased the mob to have set it on fire.

2. The diaries ended up in the hands of the police. The first was found in a wall safe by police who arrested Mrs Humphreys at the beginning of 1972. She handed the second into Scotland Yard four months later. They gave a day-to-day account of his activities in 1971 and 1972. The diaries were supplemented by other documents written by Humphreys. They showed that Virgo and Moody were paid £53,000 over a period of sixteen months.
3. Gilbert Kelland, *Crime in London*. Grafton, 1987.

RACE AND RIOTS

1. Joan Lock, *Scotland Yard Casebook*. London, Robert Hale, 1993.
2. Roy Porter, *London: A Social History*. Hamish Hamilton, 1994.
3. Porter, *ibid*.
4. Peter Ackroyd, *London: A Biography*. Chatto and Windus, 2000.
5. Stephen Inwood, *A History of London*. Macmillan, 1998.
6. Inwood, *ibid*.
7. Inwood, *ibid*.
8. Inwood, *ibid*.
9. Inwood, *ibid*.
10. Inwood, *ibid*.

ROBBING THE BANK OF ENGLAND

1. Frank McLynn, *Crime and Punishment in Eighteenth-century England*. London, Routledge, 1989.
2. Donald Thomas, *The Victorian Underworld*. John Murray, 1998.
3. McLynn, *ibid*.
4. Thomas, *ibid*.
5. *The Bank of England Forgery*, edited George Dilnot, Geoffrey Bles, London, 1929.
6. George Bidwell, *Forging His Chains*. Hartford, Connecticut, 1888.

IN DURANCE VILE

1. Donald Thomas, *The Victorian Underworld*. John Murray, 1998.
2. Thomas, *ibid*.
3. Thomas, *ibid*.
4. Thomas, *ibid*.
5. *Oxford History of the Prison*, edited by Norval Morris and David J Rothman, Oxford University Press 1995.
6. Henry Mayhew and John Binney. *The Criminal Prisons of London and Scenes of Prison Life*. London, Griffin Bohn and Company, 1862.

7. Morris and Rothman (ed), *ibid*.
8. Mayhew and Binney, *ibid*.
9. W Branch Johnson, *The English Prison Hulks*. Phillimore and Company Ltd, Shopwyke Hall, Chichester, Sussex, 1970.
10. *Ibid*.
11. Donald A Low, *The Regency Underworld*. Sutton, 1999.
12. Jim Whelan, *Jail Journey*. London, Secker and Warburg, 1940.
13. Ruby Sparks, *Burglar to the Nobility*. London, Arthur Barker, 1961.
14. Wilfred Macartney, *Walls Have Mouths*. London, Gollancz, 1936.
15. Sparks, *ibid*.

FROM REEFERS TO CRACK

1. Did Queen Victoria smoke cannabis? She is said to have used cannabis cigarettes to ease the pain of menstrual cramps. A young Irish doctor working in Calcutta in the 1830s had seen that cannabis was used there to treat a wide range of illnesses. His observations were published in England and by mid-century the drug was being widely used.
    'We do not know whether she took hashish, the most powerful form of cannabis, produced from the resin of *Cannabis indica*; Dr O'Shaughnessy's preference was for using the ganja which is made from the flowering heads of female plants. The queen was not a lonely enthusiast: cannabis was one of three top drugs prescribed during the last forty years of her reign. The discovery of the hypodermic syringe in the 1850s mildly impaired its progress, however, since hemp products are not water soluble and could not be injected.'(Miranda Seymour, the *Independent*, 13 May 2000)
2. Quoted in A Tietjen. *Soho*. London, Allan Wingate, 1956.
3. Stephen Inwood. *A History of London*. London, Macmillan, 1996.
4. Sydney Horlor. *London's Underworld*. London, Hutchinson 1934.
5. Roy Porter. *The Greatest Benefit to Mankind: A Medical History*

of Humanity from Antiquity to the Present. London, Fontana Press, 1997

6. Philip Robson. *Forbidden Drugs.* Oxford University Press, 1999.
7. Clutterbuck. *Drugs, Crime and Corruption.*
8. Jon Silverman. *Crack of Doom.* London, Headline, 1988.

MODERN TIMES

1. Jo-Ann Goodwin, *Daily Mail*, 19 August 2000.
2. The *Independent*, August 2000.

CHARACTERS

1. Kate Meyrick, *Secrets of the 43*. John Long, 1933.
2. F D Sharpe, *Sharpe of the Flying Squad*. John Long, 1938.
3. Robert Murphy, S*mash and Grab, Gangsters in the London Underworld 1920–60*. London, Faber and Faber, 1993.
4. Murphy, *ibid*.
5. Sharpe, *ibid*.
6. Quoted Murphy, *ibid*.
7. Sparks's intelligence and drive were clearly impressive. During the Second World War the Home Secretary, Herbert Morrison, visited him in the punishment cells at Dartmoor and offered him the chance of a new life in the army. Sparks agreed, thinking it would be like 'the companionship of a good thieving team in the old days, the risks and jokes, the careful planning of a job, then going in there with your heart pounding.' But as with Jack Spot, who found anti-Semitism rife in the army and made so much trouble he was discharged, Sparks found army life distasteful. A bullying corporal picked on him, and within weeks Sparks had deserted.
8. Robert Murphy, *Smash and Grab*. London, Faber and Faber, 1993.
9. Hume murdered the notorious car dealer, gunrunner and super-spiv Stanley Setty in 1949. They had been partners, Hume supplying Setty with stolen cars and finding customers for his forged petrol coupons. He visited Setty in his flat and stabbed

him to death with a German SS knife. He cut up the body, carrying the head in a baked-beans carton, and dumped it in the sea off the Essex marshes from a small aircraft.

On 22 October an Essex wildfowler found Setty's torso, washed up on Tillingham marshes. Hume was tried for murder and acquitted, but jailed for twelve years as an accessory after the fact. He was released in 1958 and told a newspaper that he really had murdered Setty.

In 1959 he murdered a taxi driver in Switzerland during a bungled robbery. He was jailed for life, and after sixteen years in a Swiss prison he was transferred to Broadmoor.

10. Murphy, *ibid*.
11. Murphy, *ibid*.
12. Murphy, *ibid*.

Index